P9-CRB-193

ALSO BY LIANA FINCK

A BINTEL BRIEF: LOVE AND LONGING IN OLD NEW YORK

passing for human.

PASSING FOR HUMAN

A GRAPHIC MEMOIR

LIANA FINCK

RANDOM
HOUSE
NEW YORK

PASSING FOR HUMAN IS A WORK OF NONFICTION. SOME NAMES AND
IDENTIFYING DETAILS HAVE BEEN CHANGED.

COPYRIGHT © 2018 BY LIANA FINCK

ALL RIGHTS RESERVED.

PUBLISHED IN THE UNITED STATES BY RANDOM HOUSE, AN IMPRINT AND DIVISION OF
PENGUIN RANDOM HOUSE LLC, NEW YORK.

RANDOM HOUSE AND THE **HOUSE** COLOPHON ARE REGISTERED TRADEMARKS OF
PENGUIN RANDOM HOUSE LLC.

HARDCOVER ISBN 978-0-525-50892-2
EBOOK ISBN 978-0-525-50893-9

PRINTED IN THE UNITED STATES OF AMERICA ON ACID-FREE PAPER

RANDOMHOUSEBOOKS.COM

9 8 7 6 5 4 3 2 1

FIRST EDITION

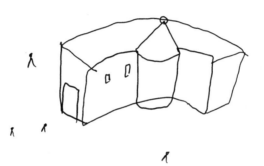

FOR GIDEON, WHO TELLS THE BEST STORIES

"THE DAY WAS GREEN.
THEY SAID, 'YOU HAVE A BLUE GUITAR,
YOU DO NOT PLAY THINGS AS THEY ARE.'"

—WALLACE STEVENS,
"THE MAN WITH THE BLUE GUITAR"

A NOTE: SOME NAMES (INCLUDING MINE) HAVE BEEN CHANGED. SOME FACTS HAVE BEEN TAMPERED WITH. ALL CHARACTERS, ESPECIALLY MY PARENTS, ARE SEEN THROUGH MY EYES, WHEN I WAS YOUNGER.

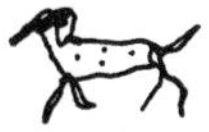

PASSING FOR HUMAN

ONCE UPON A TIME, I LOST SOMETHING.

LET'S CALL IT "MY SHADOW."

prologue

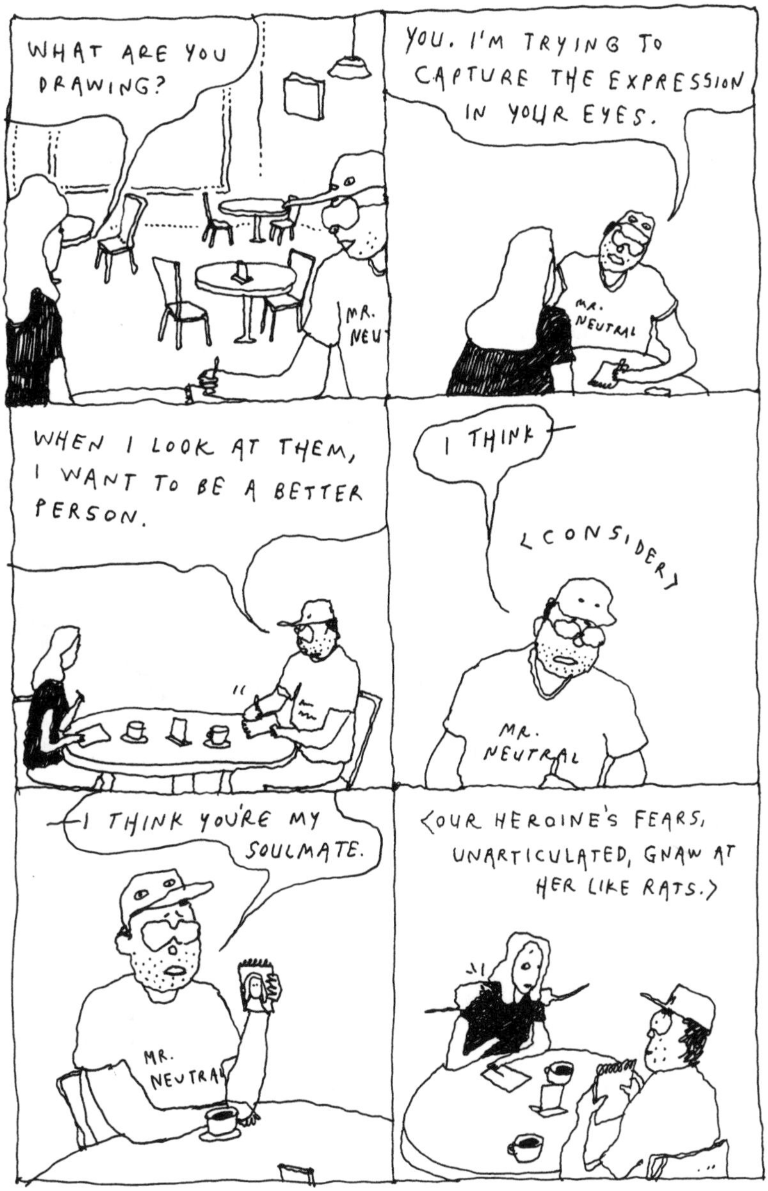

WHAT ARE YOU DRAWING?
YOU. I'M TRYING TO CAPTURE THE EXPRESSION IN YOUR EYES.
MR. NEUTRAL
WHEN I LOOK AT THEM, I WANT TO BE A BETTER PERSON.
I THINK
<CONSIDER>
MR. NEUTRAL
I THINK YOU'RE MY SOULMATE.
MR. NEUTRAL
<OUR HEROINE'S FEARS, UNARTICULATED, GNAW AT HER LIKE RATS.>

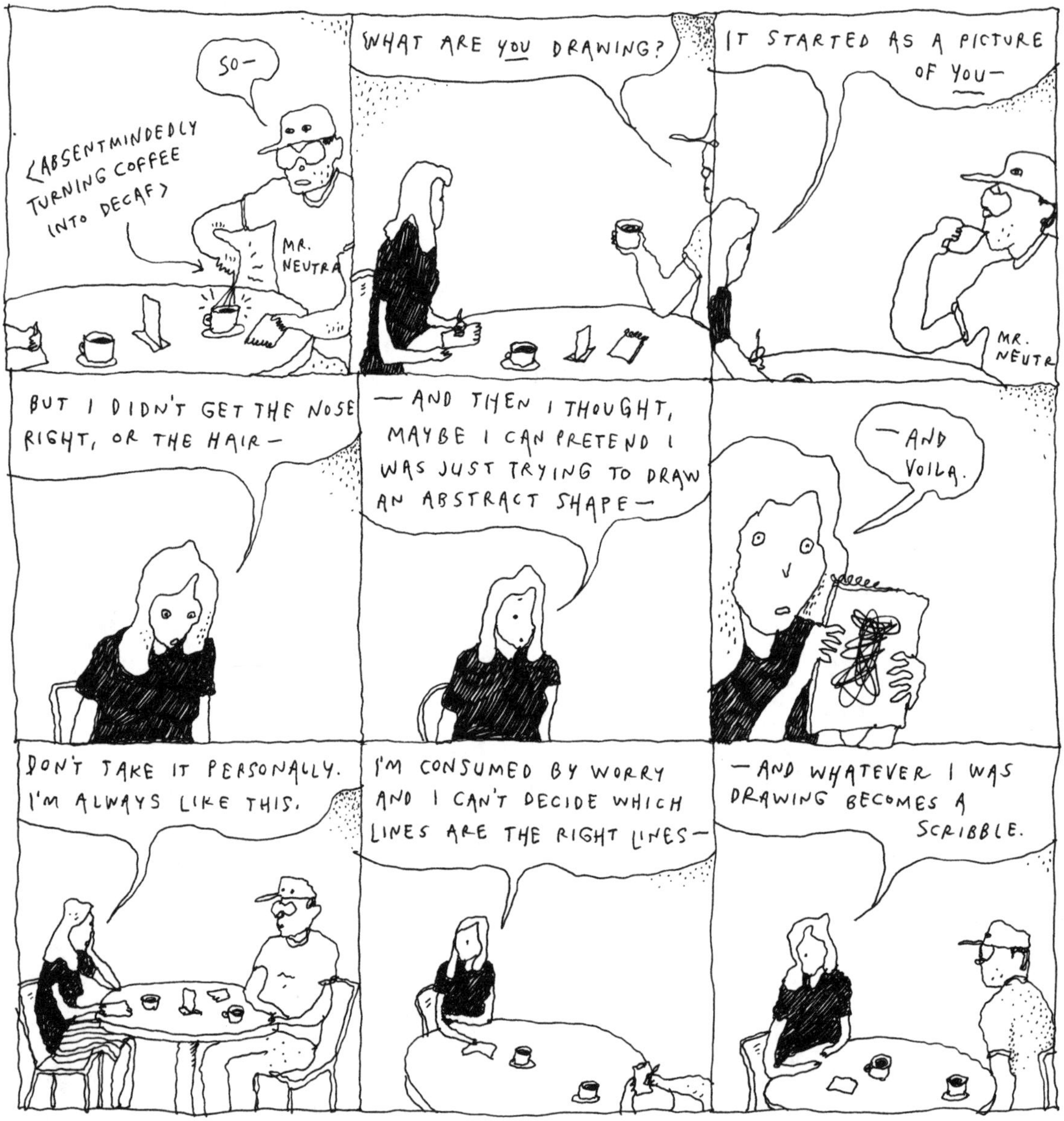
SO—
<ABSENTMINDEDLY TURNING COFFEE INTO DECAF>
MR. NEUTRA
WHAT ARE YOU DRAWING?
IT STARTED AS A PICTURE OF YOU—
MR. NEUTR
BUT I DIDN'T GET THE NOSE RIGHT, OR THE HAIR—
—AND THEN I THOUGHT, MAYBE I CAN PRETEND I WAS JUST TRYING TO DRAW AN ABSTRACT SHAPE—
—AND VOILA.
DON'T TAKE IT PERSONALLY. I'M ALWAYS LIKE THIS.
I'M CONSUMED BY WORRY AND I CAN'T DECIDE WHICH LINES ARE THE RIGHT LINES—
—AND WHATEVER I WAS DRAWING BECOMES A SCRIBBLE.

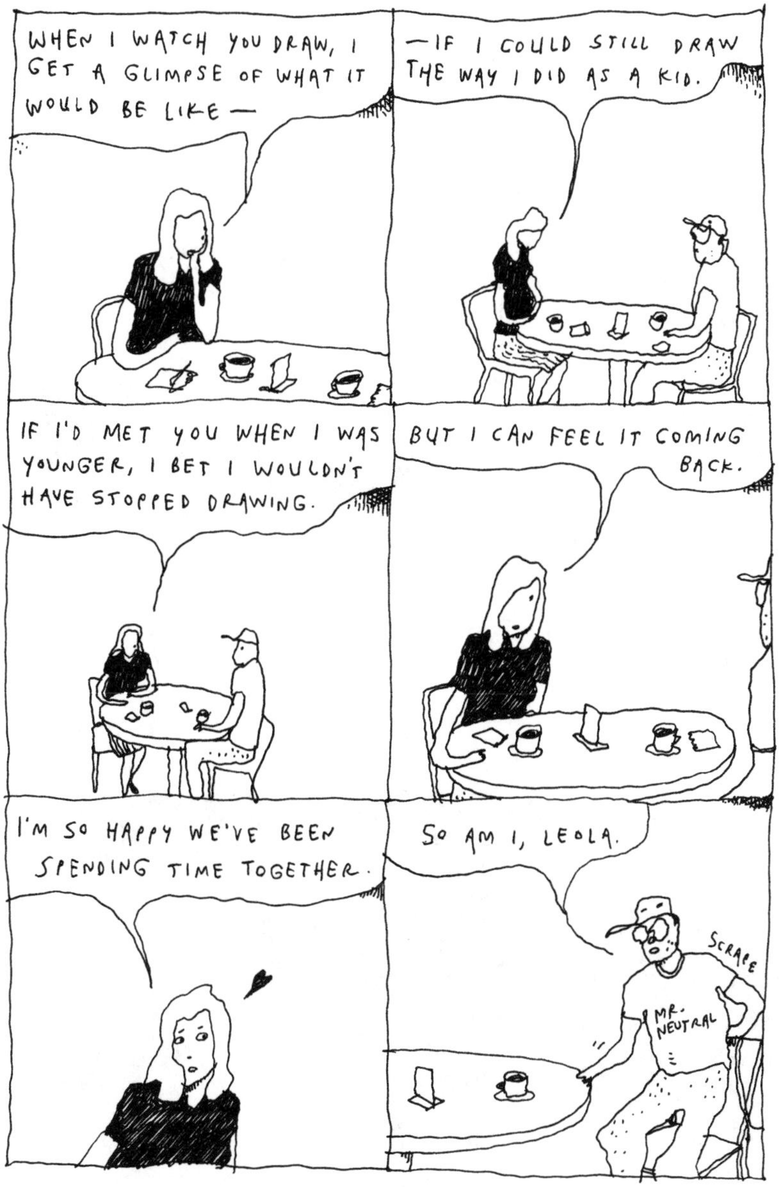
WHEN I WATCH YOU DRAW, I GET A GLIMPSE OF WHAT IT WOULD BE LIKE—
—IF I COULD STILL DRAW THE WAY I DID AS A KID.
IF I'D MET YOU WHEN I WAS YOUNGER, I BET I WOULDN'T HAVE STOPPED DRAWING.
BUT I CAN FEEL IT COMING BACK.
I'M SO HAPPY WE'VE BEEN SPENDING TIME TOGETHER.
SO AM I, LEOLA.
SCRAPE
MR. NEUTRAL

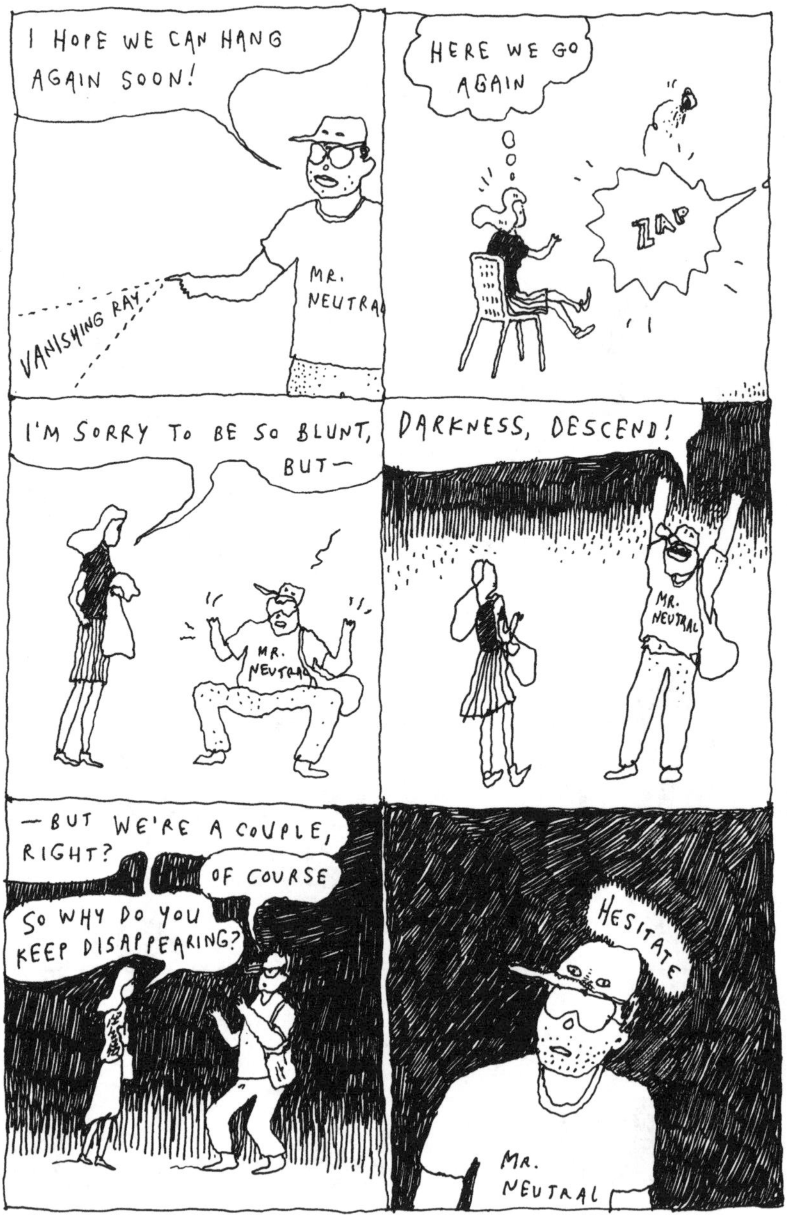
I HOPE WE CAN HANG AGAIN SOON!
VANISHING RAY
MR. NEUTRAL
HERE WE GO AGAIN
ZAP
I'M SORRY TO BE SO BLUNT, BUT—
MR. NEUTRAL
DARKNESS, DESCEND!
MR. NEUTRAL
—BUT WE'RE A COUPLE, RIGHT?
OF COURSE
SO WHY DO YOU KEEP DISAPPEARING?
HESITATE
MR. NEUTRAL

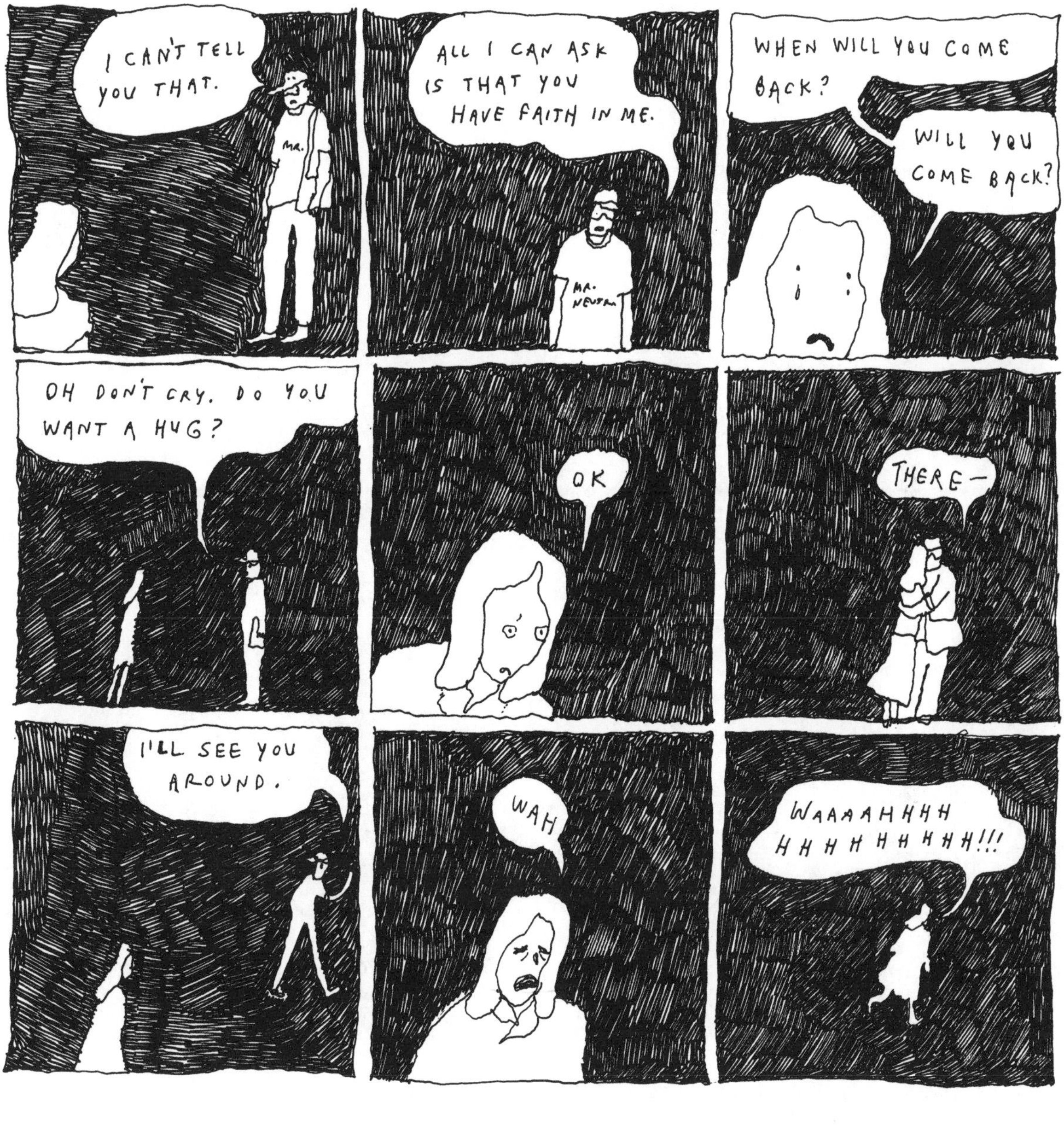
I CAN'T TELL YOU THAT.
MR.
ALL I CAN ASK IS THAT YOU HAVE FAITH IN ME.
MR. NEUTRA
WHEN WILL YOU COME BACK?
WILL YOU COME BACK?
OH DON'T CRY. DO YOU WANT A HUG?
OK
THERE—
I'LL SEE YOU AROUND.
WAH
WAAAAHHHH HHHHHHHHH!!!

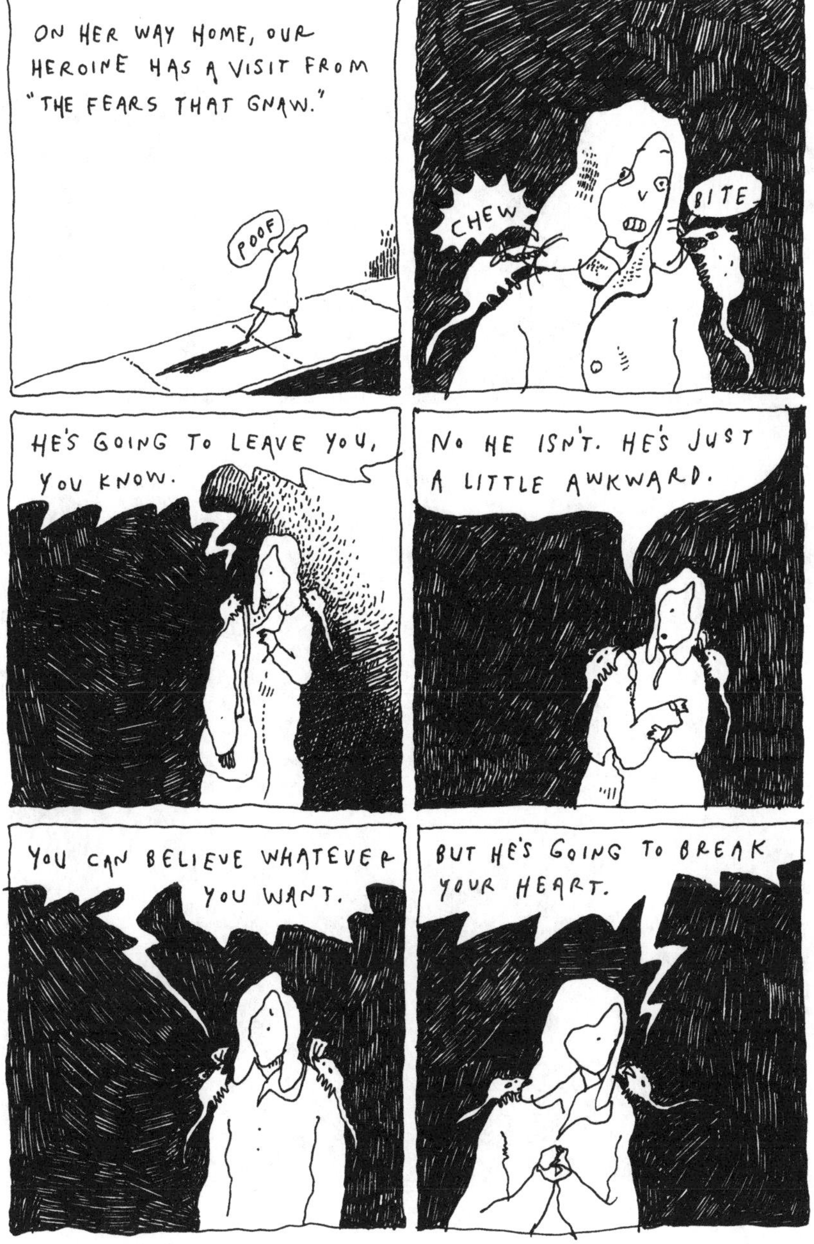
ON HER WAY HOME, OUR HEROINE HAS A VISIT FROM "THE FEARS THAT GNAW."
POOF
CHEW
BITE
HE'S GOING TO LEAVE YOU, YOU KNOW.
NO HE ISN'T. HE'S JUST A LITTLE AWKWARD.
YOU CAN BELIEVE WHATEVER YOU WANT.
BUT HE'S GOING TO BREAK YOUR HEART.

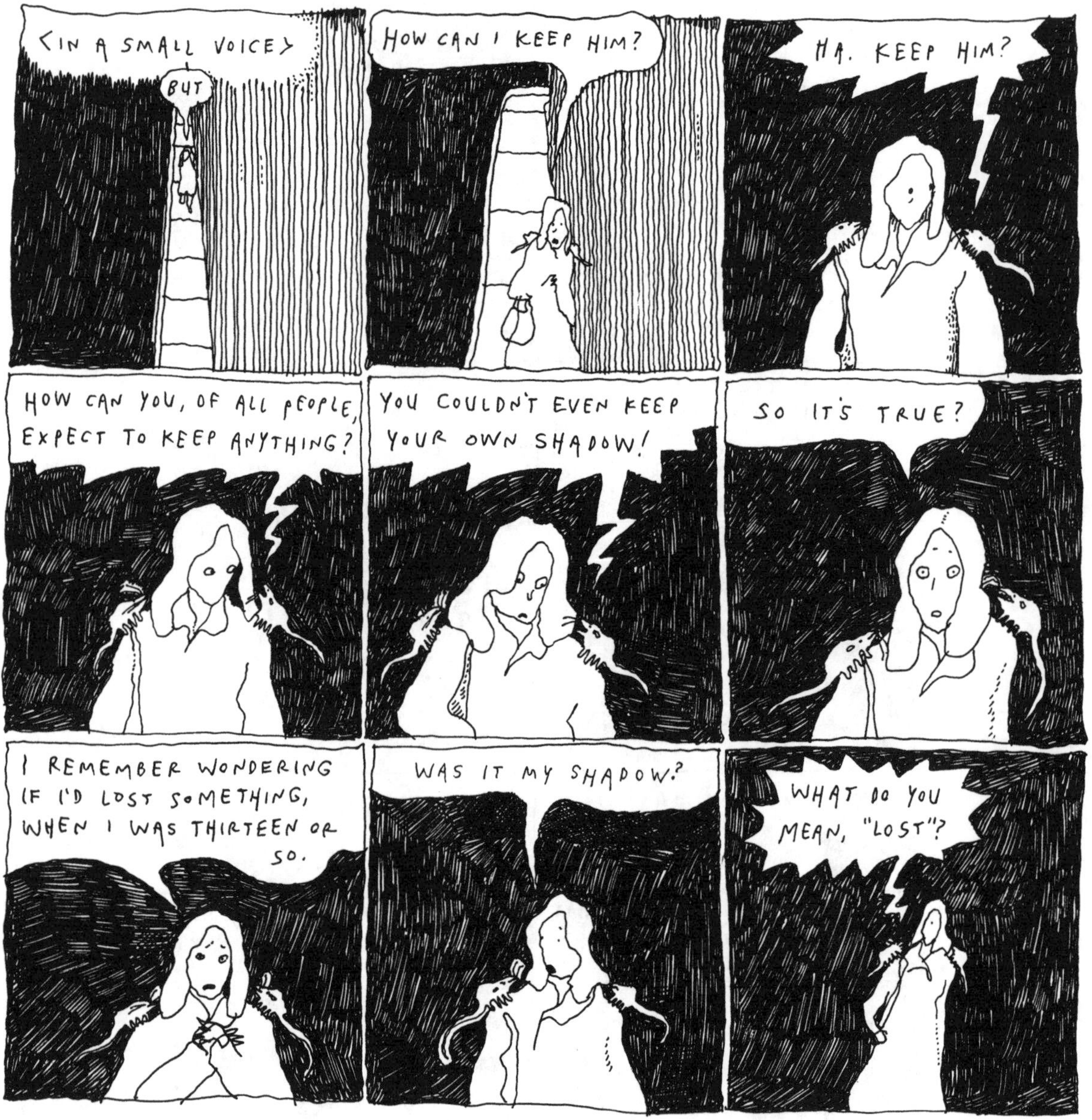
<IN A SMALL VOICE>
BUT
HOW CAN I KEEP HIM?
HA. KEEP HIM?
HOW CAN YOU, OF ALL PEOPLE, EXPECT TO KEEP ANYTHING?
YOU COULDN'T EVEN KEEP YOUR OWN SHADOW!
SO IT'S TRUE?
I REMEMBER WONDERING IF I'D LOST SOMETHING, WHEN I WAS THIRTEEN OR SO.
WAS IT MY SHADOW?
WHAT DO YOU MEAN, "LOST"?

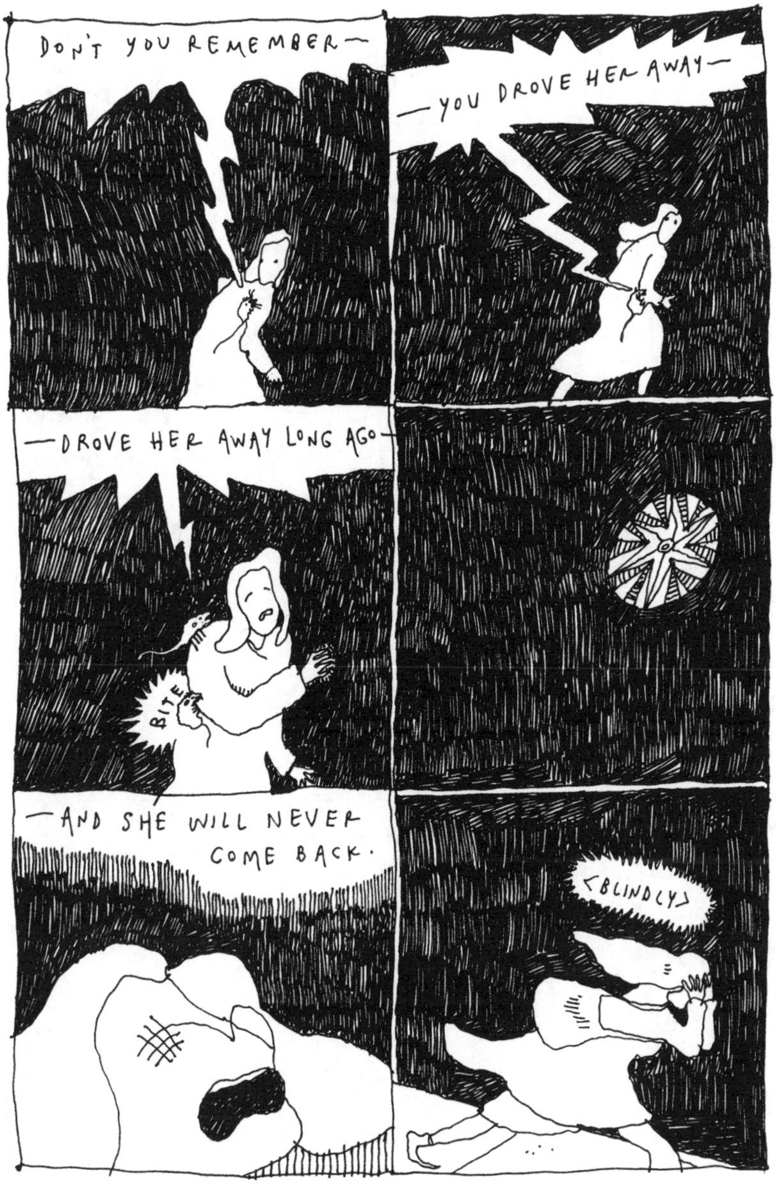
DON'T YOU REMEMBER—
—YOU DROVE HER AWAY—
—DROVE HER AWAY LONG AGO—
BITE
—AND SHE WILL NEVER COME BACK.
<BLINDLY>

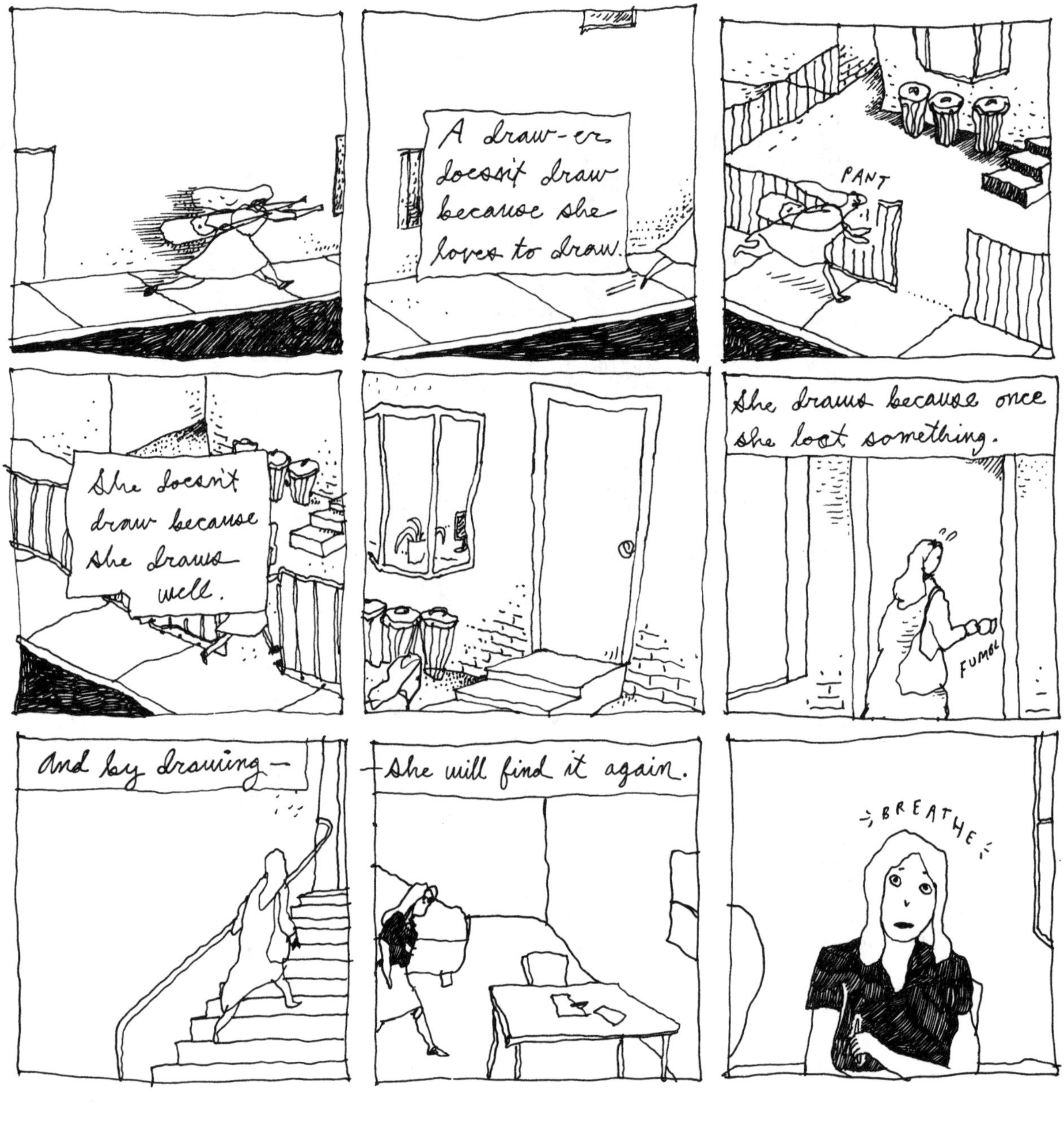
A draw-er doesn't draw because she loves to draw.
PANT
She doesn't draw because she draws well.
She draws because once she lost something.
FUMBL
And by drawing—
—she will find it again.
BREATHE

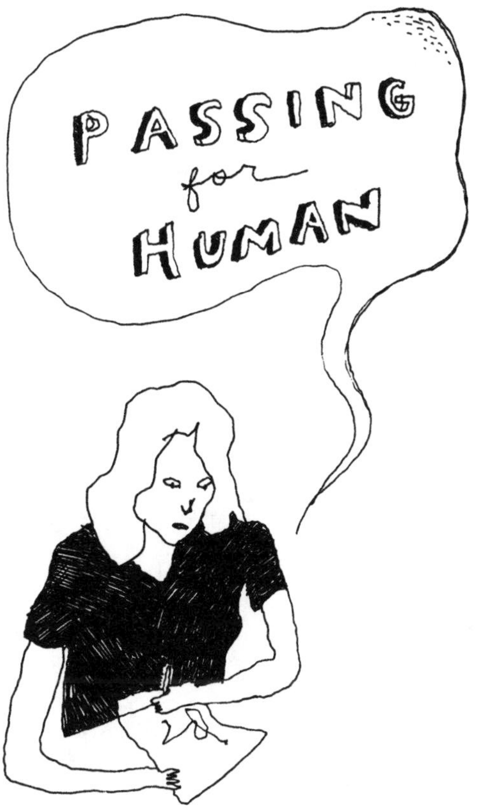
PASSING
for
HUMAN

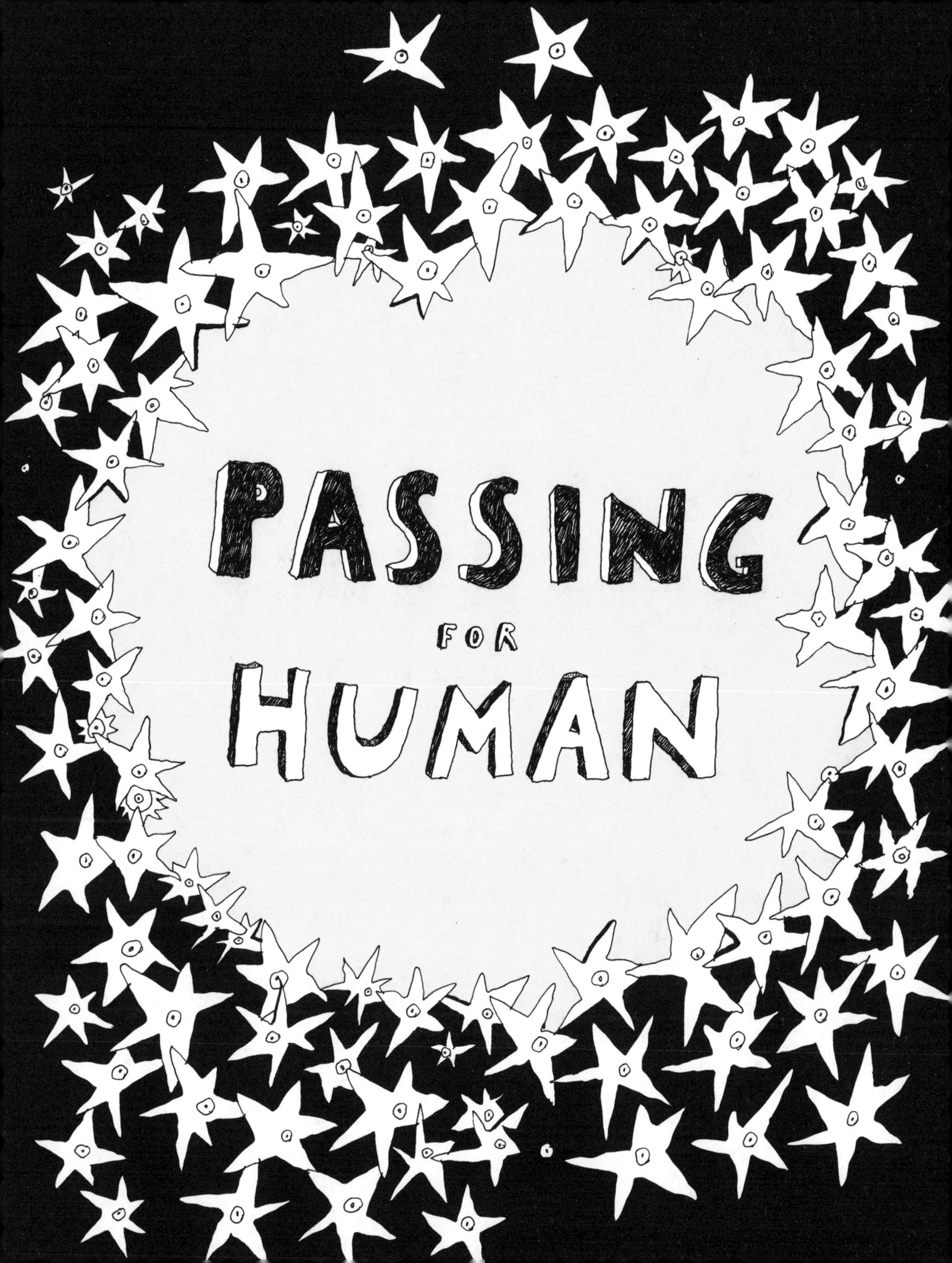
PASSING
FOR
HUMAN

"ONLY CONNECT THE PROSE AND THE PASSION, AND BOTH WILL BE EXALTED, AND HUMAN LOVE WILL BE SEEN AT ITS HIGHEST. LIVE IN FRAGMENTS NO LONGER."

— E. M. FORSTER, HOWARDS END

CHAPTER 1

.

Ruth and Boaz

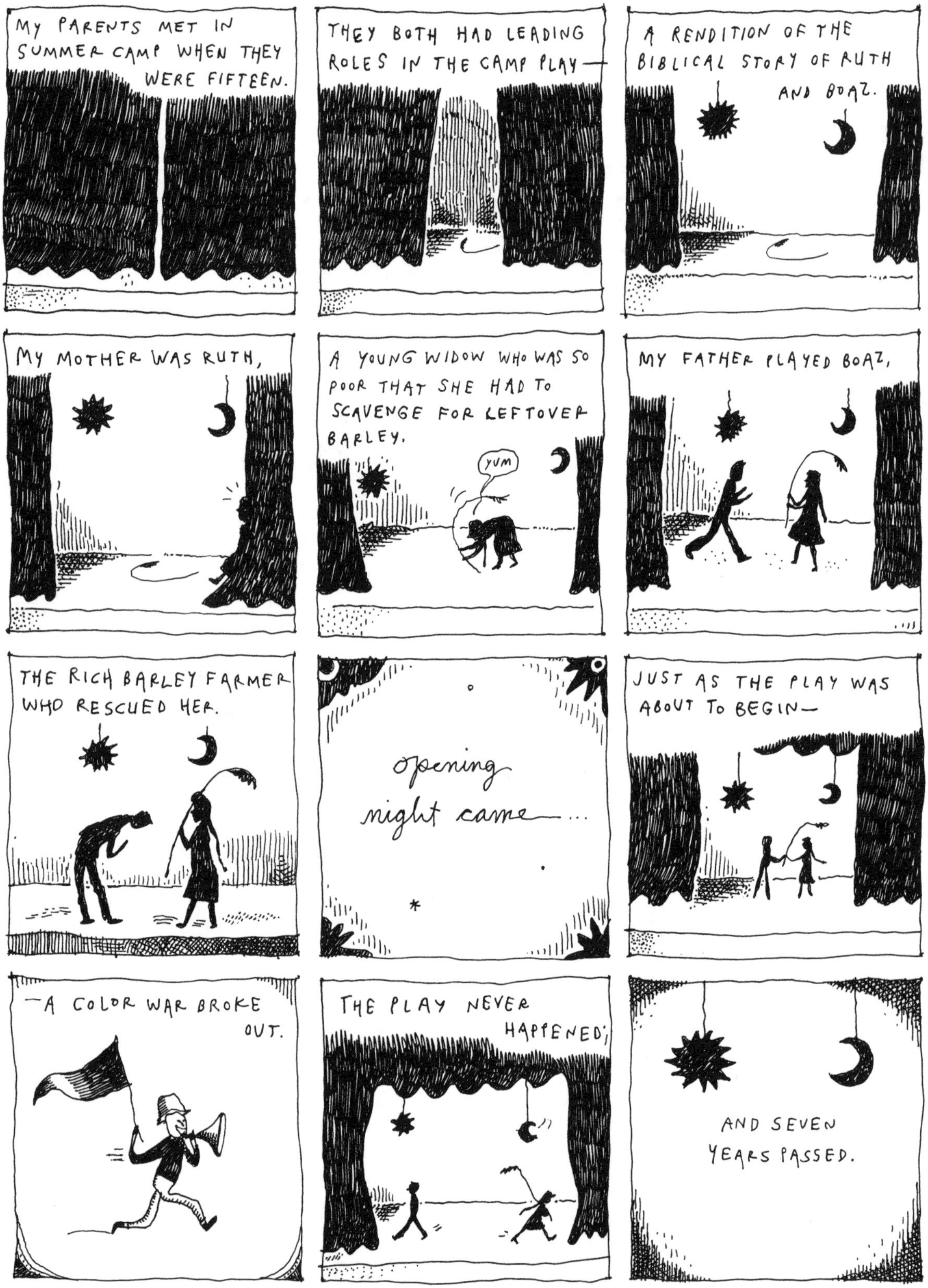
MY PARENTS MET IN SUMMER CAMP WHEN THEY WERE FIFTEEN.
THEY BOTH HAD LEADING ROLES IN THE CAMP PLAY—
A RENDITION OF THE BIBLICAL STORY OF RUTH AND BOAZ.
MY MOTHER WAS RUTH,
A YOUNG WIDOW WHO WAS SO POOR THAT SHE HAD TO SCAVENGE FOR LEFTOVER BARLEY.
YUM
MY FATHER PLAYED BOAZ,
THE RICH BARLEY FARMER WHO RESCUED HER.
opening night came...
JUST AS THE PLAY WAS ABOUT TO BEGIN—
—A COLOR WAR BROKE OUT.
THE PLAY NEVER HAPPENED;
AND SEVEN YEARS PASSED.

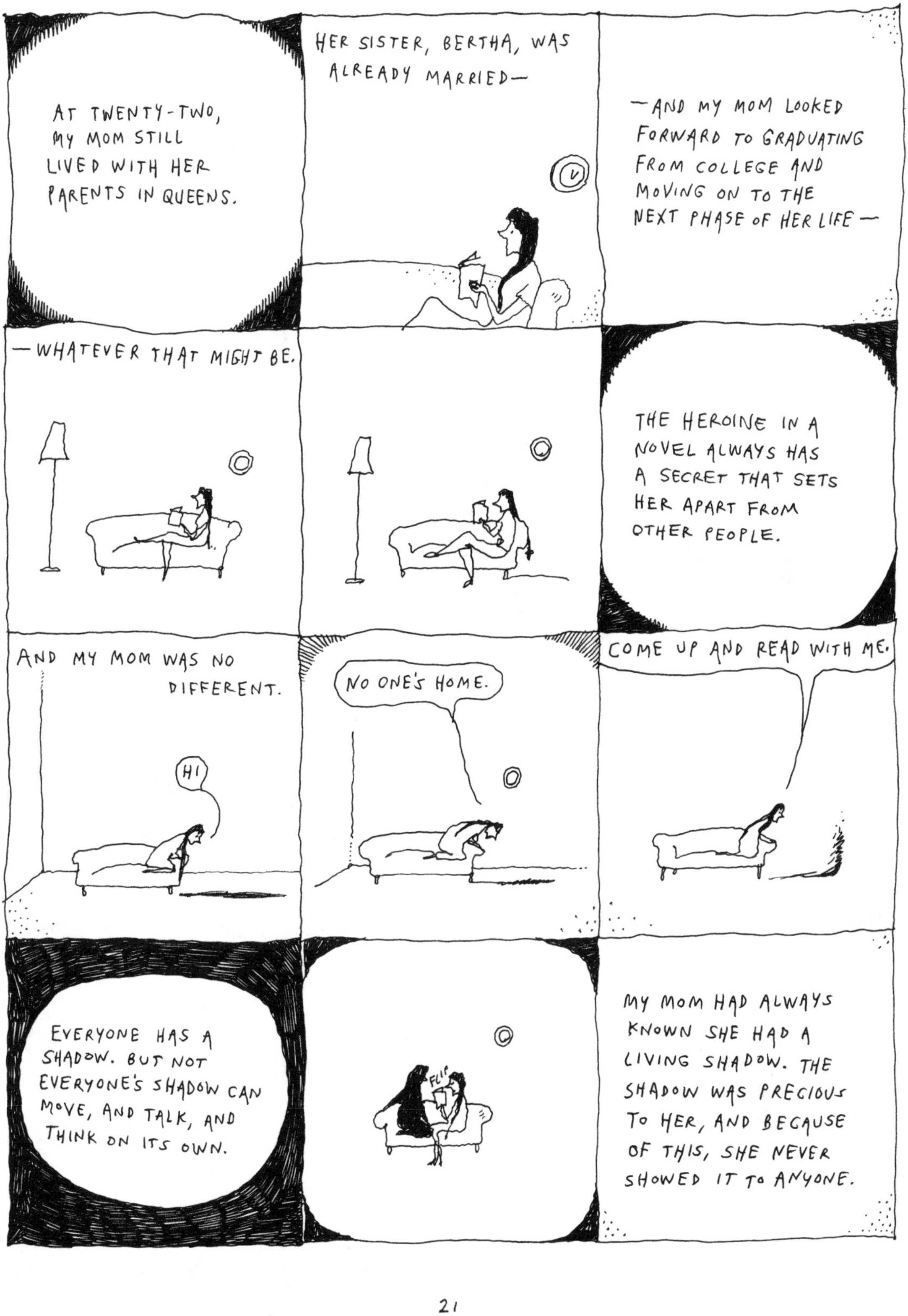
AT TWENTY-TWO, MY MOM STILL LIVED WITH HER PARENTS IN QUEENS.
HER SISTER, BERTHA, WAS ALREADY MARRIED—
—AND MY MOM LOOKED FORWARD TO GRADUATING FROM COLLEGE AND MOVING ON TO THE NEXT PHASE OF HER LIFE—
—WHATEVER THAT MIGHT BE.
THE HEROINE IN A NOVEL ALWAYS HAS A SECRET THAT SETS HER APART FROM OTHER PEOPLE.
AND MY MOM WAS NO DIFFERENT.
HI
NO ONE'S HOME.
COME UP AND READ WITH ME.
EVERYONE HAS A SHADOW. BUT NOT EVERYONE'S SHADOW CAN MOVE, AND TALK, AND THINK ON ITS OWN.
FLIP
MY MOM HAD ALWAYS KNOWN SHE HAD A LIVING SHADOW. THE SHADOW WAS PRECIOUS TO HER, AND BECAUSE OF THIS, SHE NEVER SHOWED IT TO ANYONE.

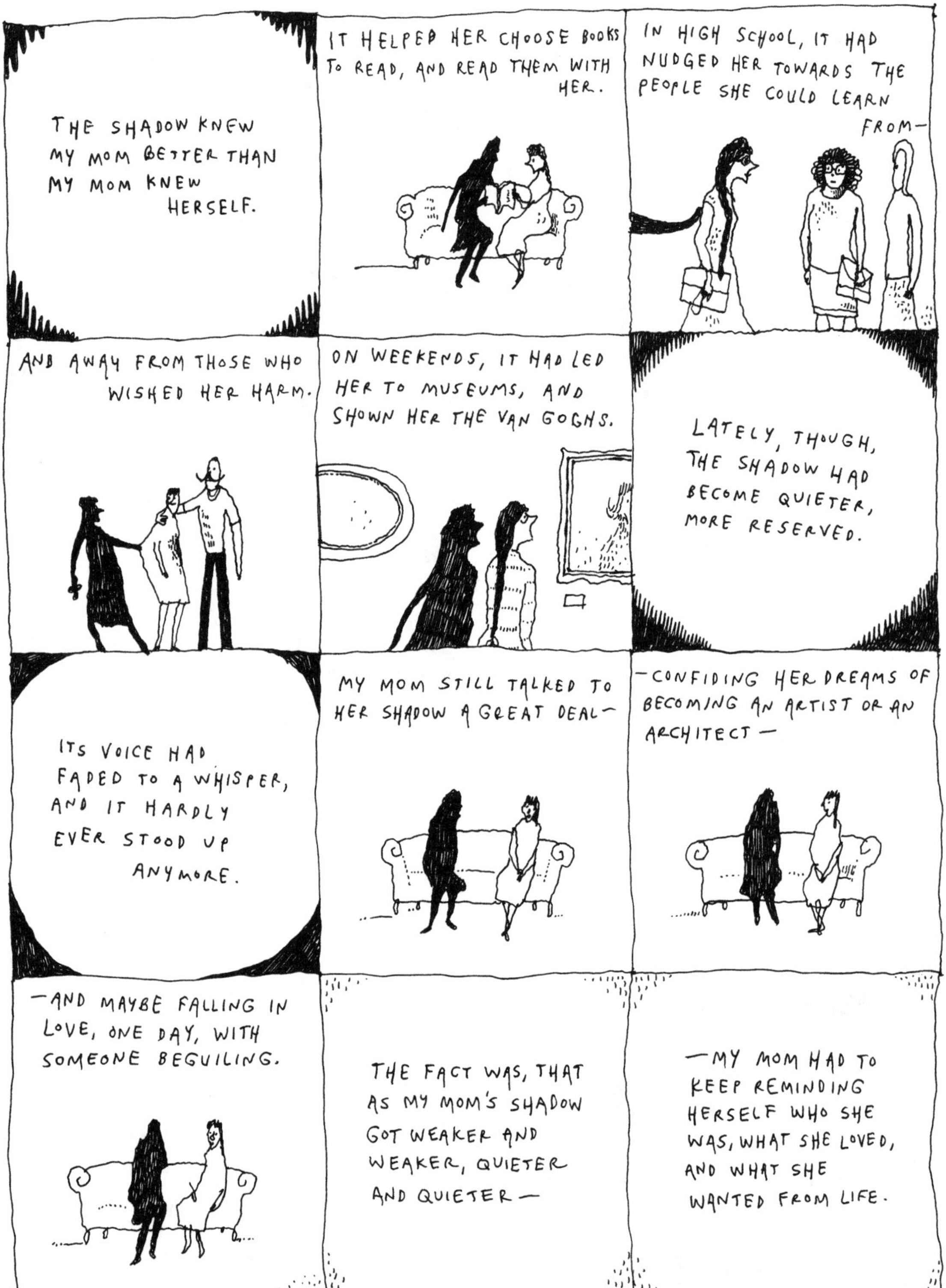
THE SHADOW KNEW MY MOM BETTER THAN MY MOM KNEW HERSELF.
IT HELPED HER CHOOSE BOOKS TO READ, AND READ THEM WITH HER.
IN HIGH SCHOOL, IT HAD NUDGED HER TOWARDS THE PEOPLE SHE COULD LEARN FROM—
AND AWAY FROM THOSE WHO WISHED HER HARM.
ON WEEKENDS, IT HAD LED HER TO MUSEUMS, AND SHOWN HER THE VAN GOGHS.
LATELY, THOUGH, THE SHADOW HAD BECOME QUIETER, MORE RESERVED.
ITS VOICE HAD FADED TO A WHISPER, AND IT HARDLY EVER STOOD UP ANYMORE.
MY MOM STILL TALKED TO HER SHADOW A GREAT DEAL—
—CONFIDING HER DREAMS OF BECOMING AN ARTIST OR AN ARCHITECT—
—AND MAYBE FALLING IN LOVE, ONE DAY, WITH SOMEONE BEGUILING.
THE FACT WAS, THAT AS MY MOM'S SHADOW GOT WEAKER AND WEAKER, QUIETER AND QUIETER—
—MY MOM HAD TO KEEP REMINDING HERSELF WHO SHE WAS, WHAT SHE LOVED, AND WHAT SHE WANTED FROM LIFE.

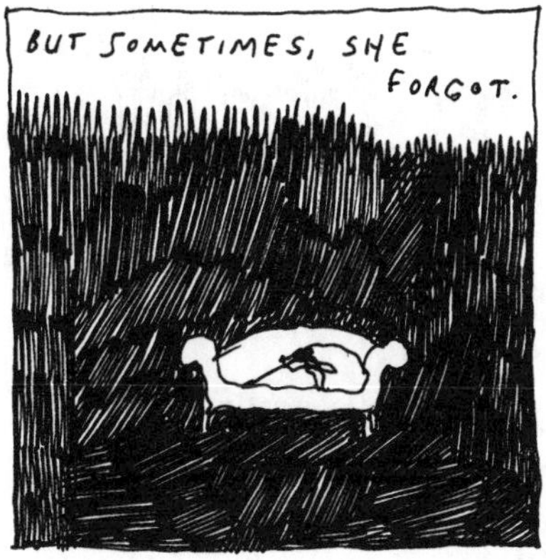
BUT SOMETIMES, SHE FORGOT.

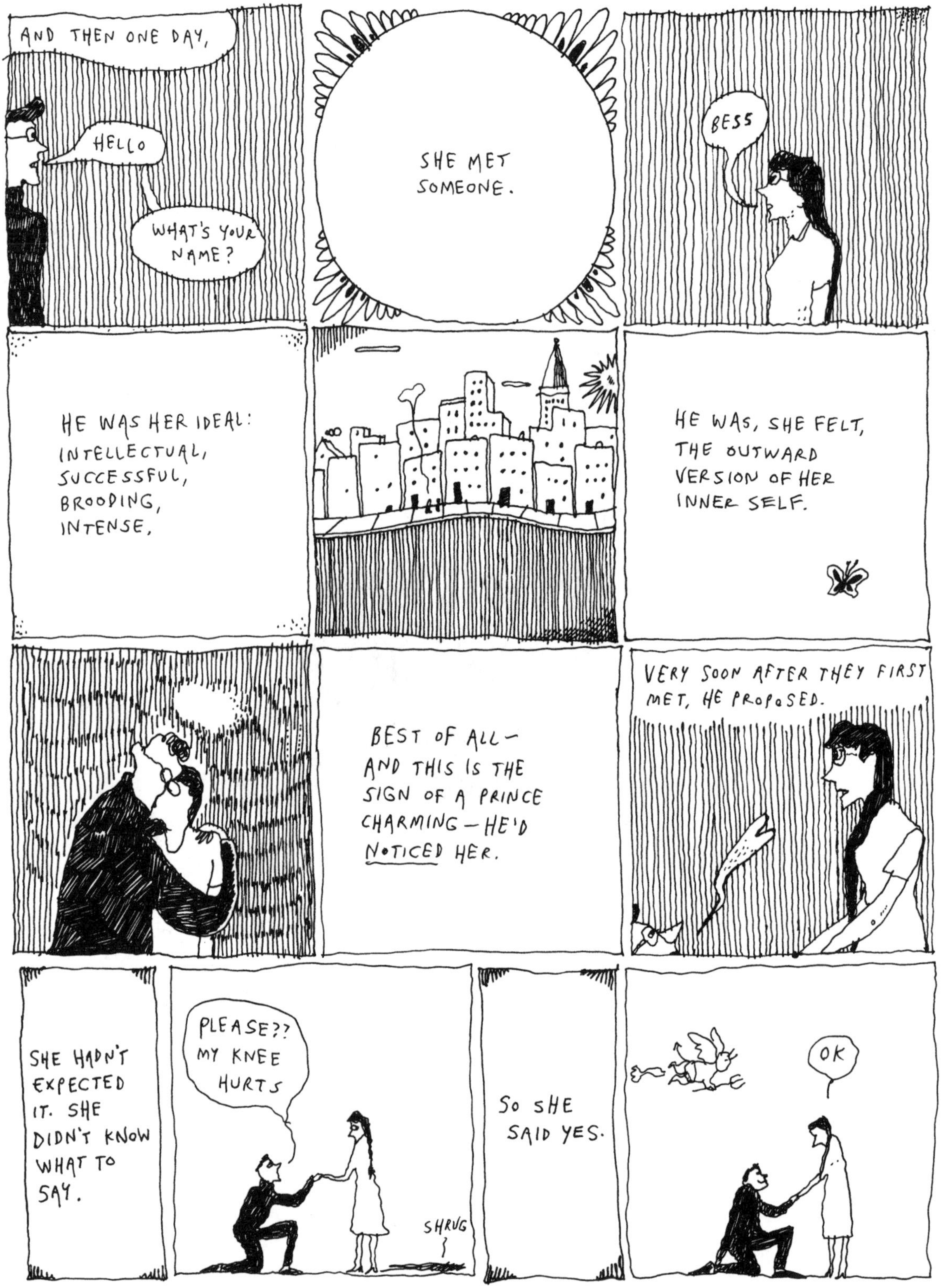
AND THEN ONE DAY,
HELLO
WHAT'S YOUR NAME?
SHE MET SOMEONE.
BESS
HE WAS HER IDEAL: INTELLECTUAL, SUCCESSFUL, BROODING, INTENSE,
HE WAS, SHE FELT, THE OUTWARD VERSION OF HER INNER SELF.
BEST OF ALL— AND THIS IS THE SIGN OF A PRINCE CHARMING—HE'D NOTICED HER.
VERY SOON AFTER THEY FIRST MET, HE PROPOSED.
SHE HADN'T EXPECTED IT. SHE DIDN'T KNOW WHAT TO SAY.
PLEASE?? MY KNEE HURTS
SHRUG
SO SHE SAID YES.
OK

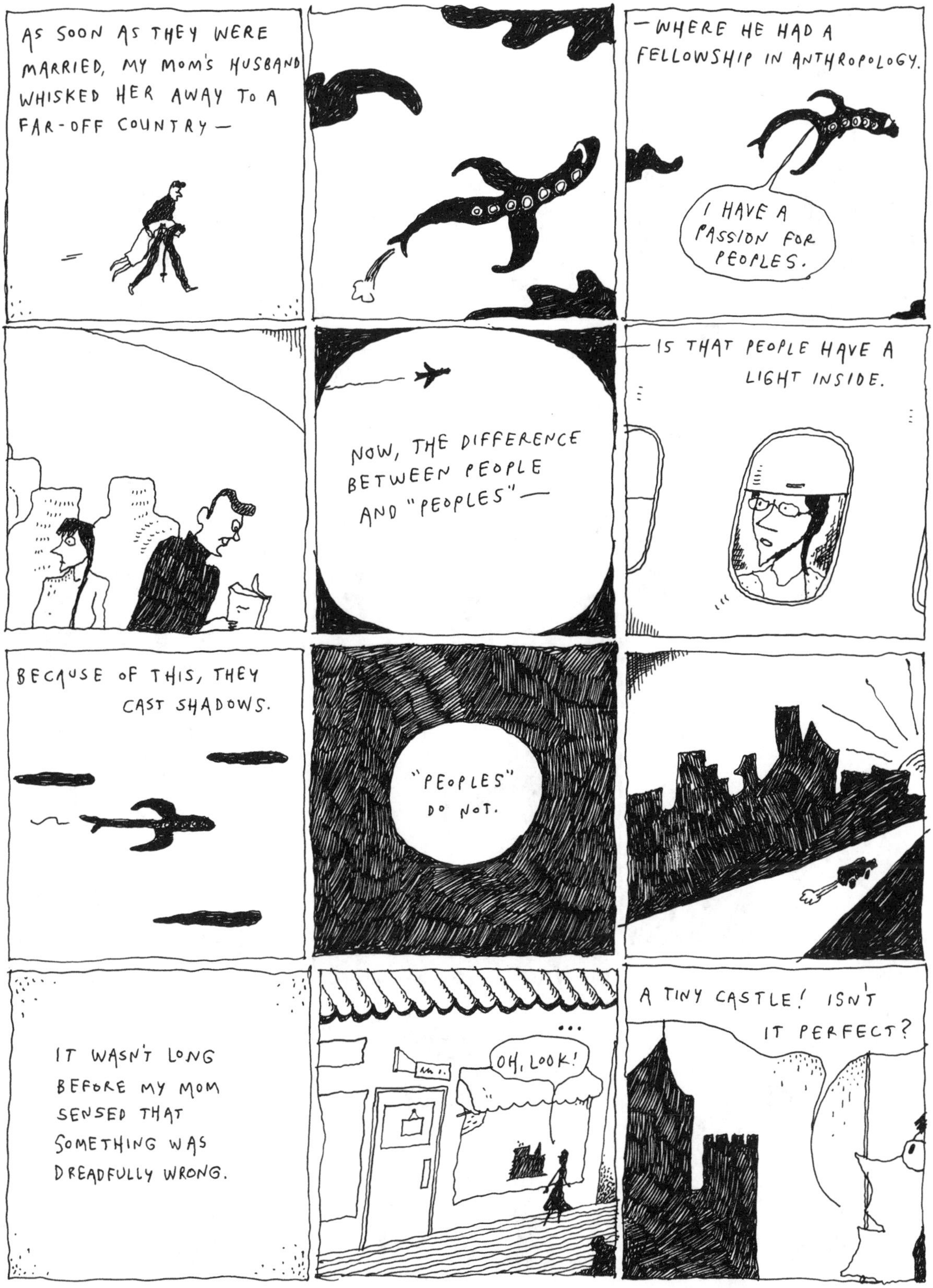
AS SOON AS THEY WERE MARRIED, MY MOM'S HUSBAND WHISKED HER AWAY TO A FAR-OFF COUNTRY—
—WHERE HE HAD A FELLOWSHIP IN ANTHROPOLOGY.
I HAVE A PASSION FOR PEOPLES.
NOW, THE DIFFERENCE BETWEEN PEOPLE AND "PEOPLES"—
—IS THAT PEOPLE HAVE A LIGHT INSIDE.
BECAUSE OF THIS, THEY CAST SHADOWS.
"PEOPLES" DO NOT.
IT WASN'T LONG BEFORE MY MOM SENSED THAT SOMETHING WAS DREADFULLY WRONG.
OH, LOOK!
A TINY CASTLE! ISN'T IT PERFECT?

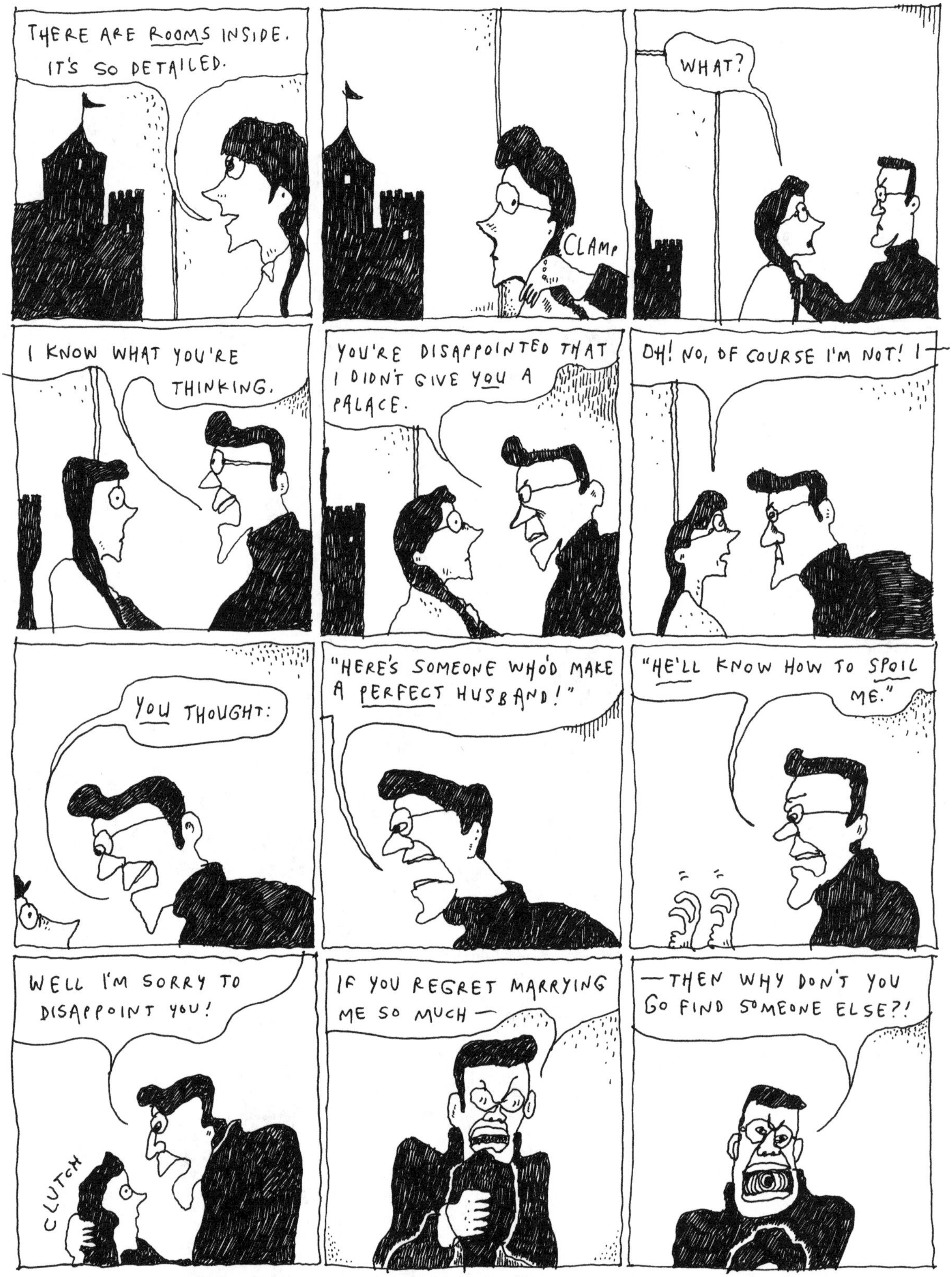
THERE ARE ROOMS INSIDE. IT'S SO DETAILED.
CLAMP
WHAT?
I KNOW WHAT YOU'RE THINKING.
YOU'RE DISAPPOINTED THAT I DIDN'T GIVE YOU A PALACE.
OH! NO, OF COURSE I'M NOT! I—
YOU THOUGHT:
"HERE'S SOMEONE WHO'D MAKE A PERFECT HUSBAND!"
"HE'LL KNOW HOW TO SPOIL ME."
WELL I'M SORRY TO DISAPPOINT YOU!
CLUTCH
IF YOU REGRET MARRYING ME SO MUCH—
—THEN WHY DON'T YOU GO FIND SOMEONE ELSE?!

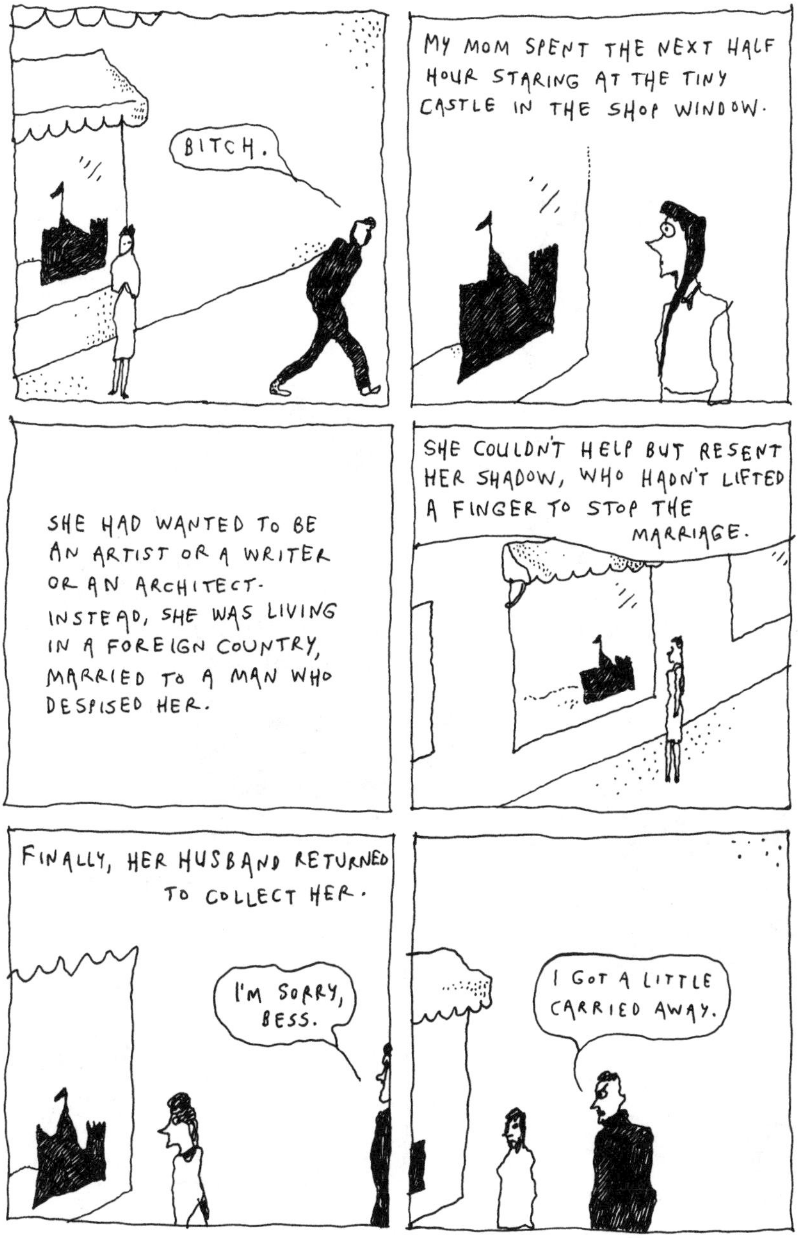
BITCH.
MY MOM SPENT THE NEXT HALF HOUR STARING AT THE TINY CASTLE IN THE SHOP WINDOW.
SHE HAD WANTED TO BE AN ARTIST OR A WRITER OR AN ARCHITECT. INSTEAD, SHE WAS LIVING IN A FOREIGN COUNTRY, MARRIED TO A MAN WHO DESPISED HER.
SHE COULDN'T HELP BUT RESENT HER SHADOW, WHO HADN'T LIFTED A FINGER TO STOP THE MARRIAGE.
FINALLY, HER HUSBAND RETURNED TO COLLECT HER.
I'M SORRY, BESS.
I GOT A LITTLE CARRIED AWAY.

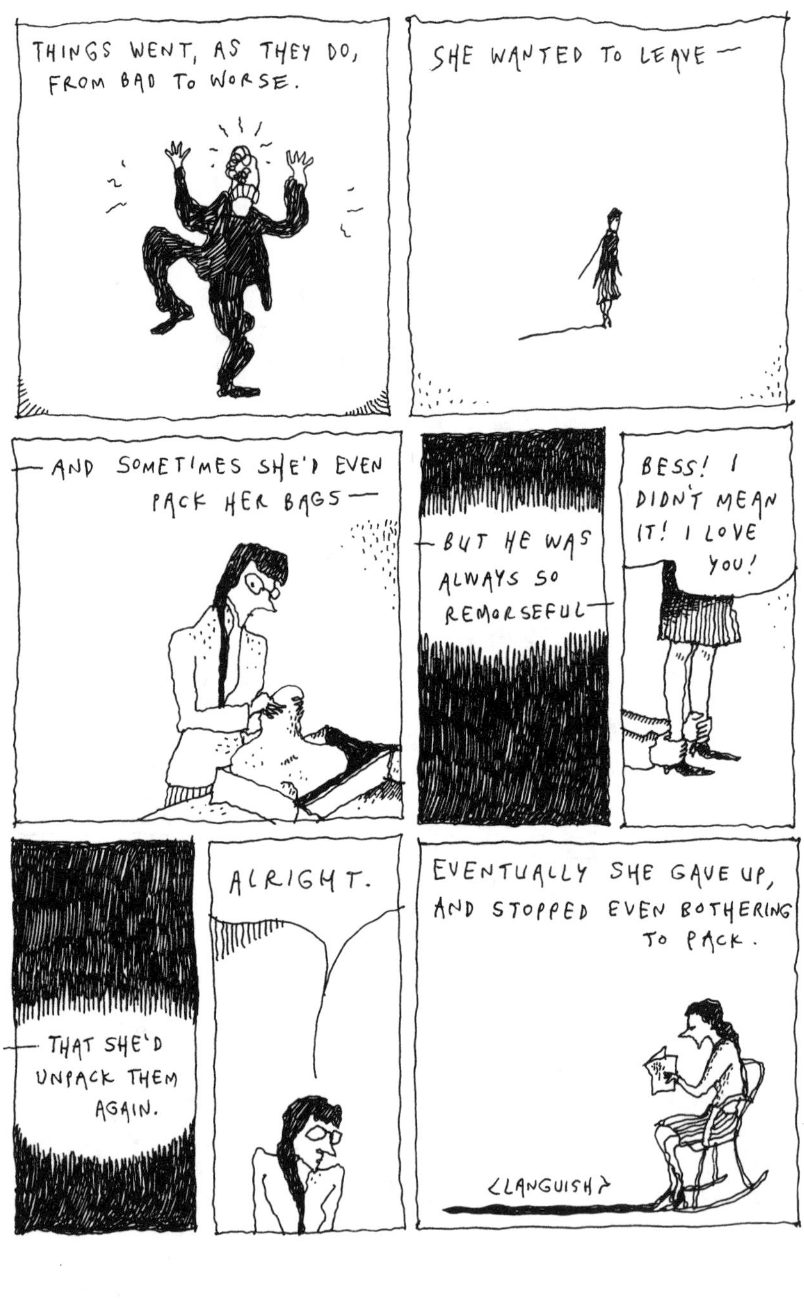
THINGS WENT, AS THEY DO, FROM BAD TO WORSE.
SHE WANTED TO LEAVE —
— AND SOMETIMES SHE'D EVEN PACK HER BAGS —
— BUT HE WAS ALWAYS SO REMORSEFUL —
BESS! I DIDN'T MEAN IT! I LOVE YOU!
— THAT SHE'D UNPACK THEM AGAIN.
ALRIGHT.
EVENTUALLY SHE GAVE UP, AND STOPPED EVEN BOTHERING TO PACK.
<LANGUISH>

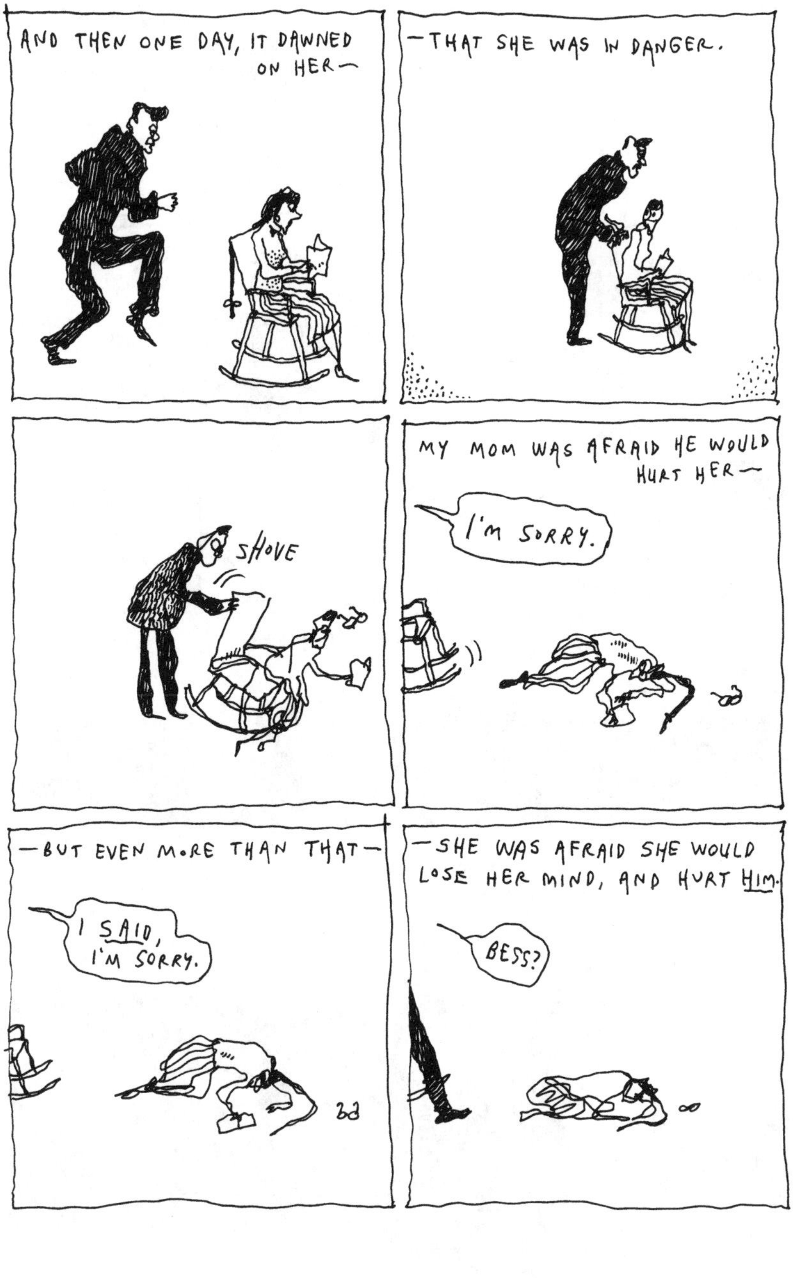
AND THEN ONE DAY, IT DAWNED ON HER—
—THAT SHE WAS IN DANGER.
SHOVE
MY MOM WAS AFRAID HE WOULD HURT HER—
I'M SORRY.
—BUT EVEN MORE THAN THAT—
I SAID, I'M SORRY.
—SHE WAS AFRAID SHE WOULD LOSE HER MIND, AND HURT HIM.
BESS?

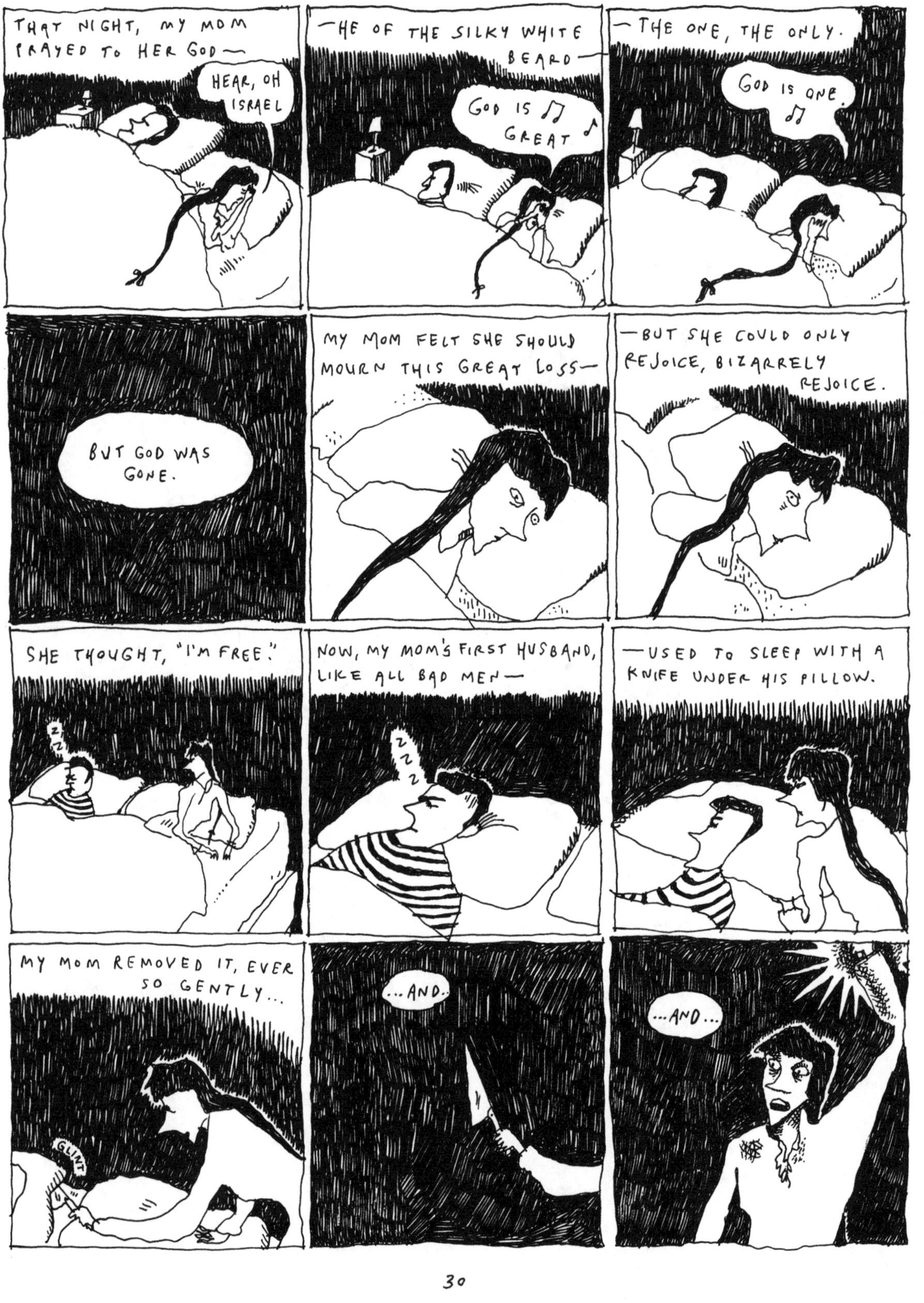
THAT NIGHT, MY MOM PRAYED TO HER GOD—
HEAR, OH ISRAEL
—HE OF THE SILKY WHITE BEARD—
GOD IS GREAT
—THE ONE, THE ONLY.
GOD IS ONE.
BUT GOD WAS GONE.
MY MOM FELT SHE SHOULD MOURN THIS GREAT LOSS—
—BUT SHE COULD ONLY REJOICE, BIZARRELY REJOICE.
SHE THOUGHT, "I'M FREE."
Z Z
NOW, MY MOM'S FIRST HUSBAND, LIKE ALL BAD MEN—
Z Z Z
—USED TO SLEEP WITH A KNIFE UNDER HIS PILLOW.
MY MOM REMOVED IT, EVER SO GENTLY...
GLINT
...AND...
...AND...

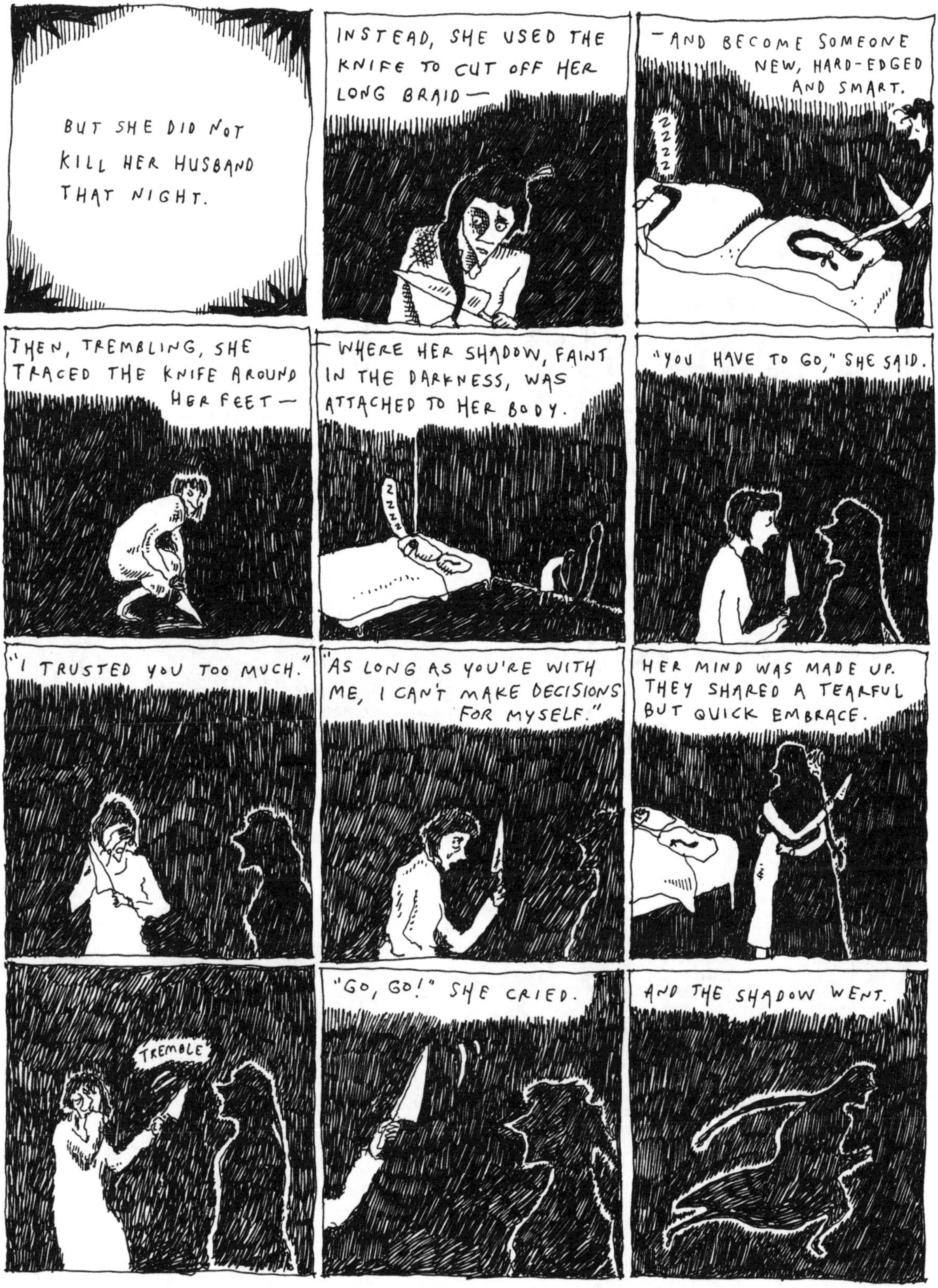
BUT SHE DID NOT KILL HER HUSBAND THAT NIGHT.
INSTEAD, SHE USED THE KNIFE TO CUT OFF HER LONG BRAID—
—AND BECOME SOMEONE NEW, HARD-EDGED AND SMART.
ZZZZ
THEN, TREMBLING, SHE TRACED THE KNIFE AROUND HER FEET—
—WHERE HER SHADOW, FAINT IN THE DARKNESS, WAS ATTACHED TO HER BODY.
ZZZZ
"YOU HAVE TO GO," SHE SAID.
"I TRUSTED YOU TOO MUCH."
"AS LONG AS YOU'RE WITH ME, I CAN'T MAKE DECISIONS FOR MYSELF."
HER MIND WAS MADE UP. THEY SHARED A TEARFUL BUT QUICK EMBRACE.
TREMBLE
"GO, GO!" SHE CRIED.
AND THE SHADOW WENT.

WHATEVER HAD BEEN KEEPING MY MOM FROM LEAVING HER HUSBAND WAS GONE NOW.

SHE SIMPLY WALKED OUT THE DOOR.

TEN MINUTES LATER, SHE WAS IN A CAB.

TWO HOURS LATER, SHE WAS ON A PLANE.

A WEEK LATER, SHE HAD A NEW JOB—

—AND AN APARTMENT THAT WAS SMALL, BUT HERS.

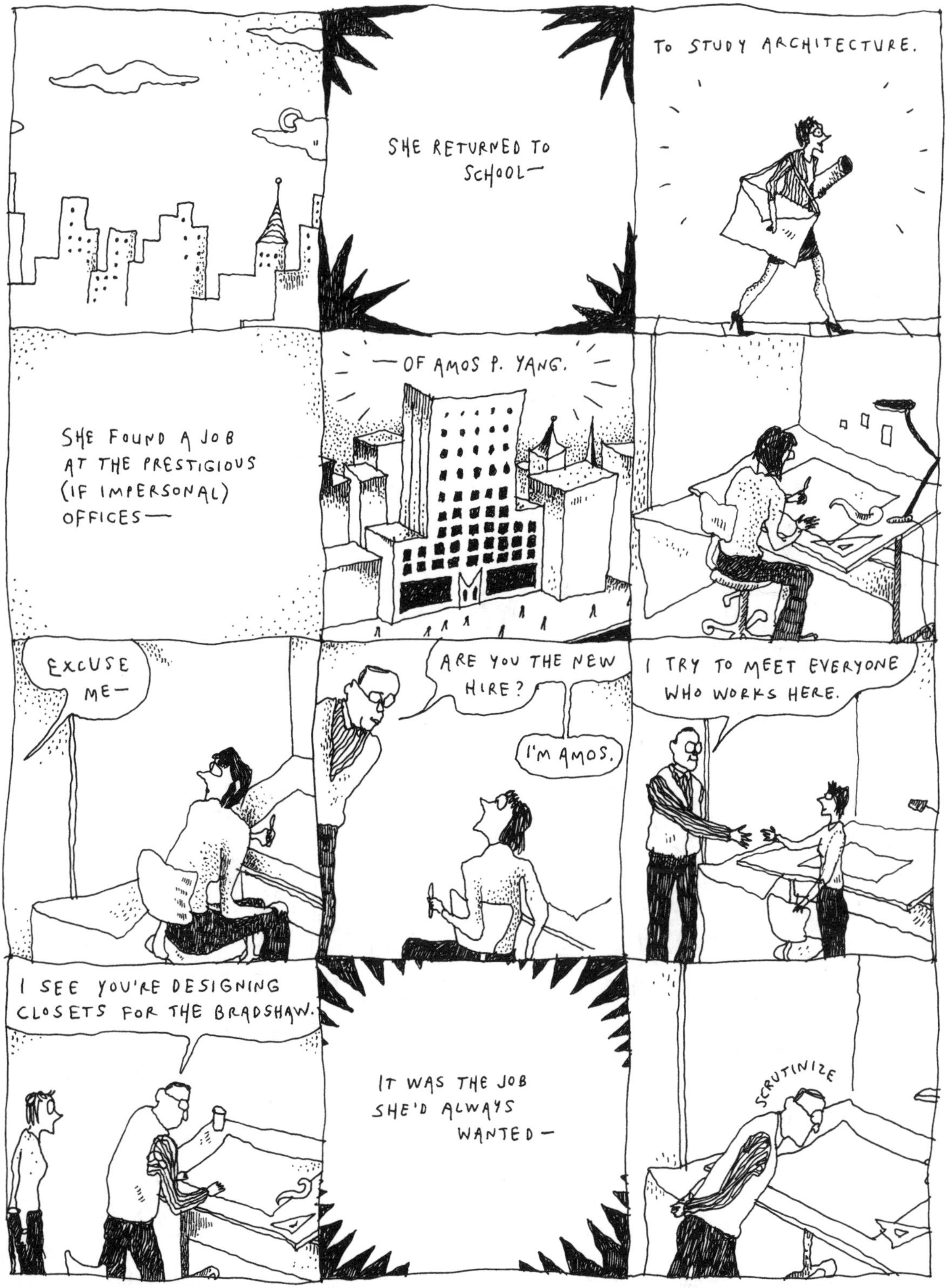
SHE RETURNED TO SCHOOL—
TO STUDY ARCHITECTURE.
SHE FOUND A JOB AT THE PRESTIGIOUS (IF IMPERSONAL) OFFICES—
—OF AMOS P. YANG.
EXCUSE ME—
ARE YOU THE NEW HIRE?
I'M AMOS.
I TRY TO MEET EVERYONE WHO WORKS HERE.
I SEE YOU'RE DESIGNING CLOSETS FOR THE BRADSHAW.
IT WAS THE JOB SHE'D ALWAYS WANTED—
SCRUTINIZE

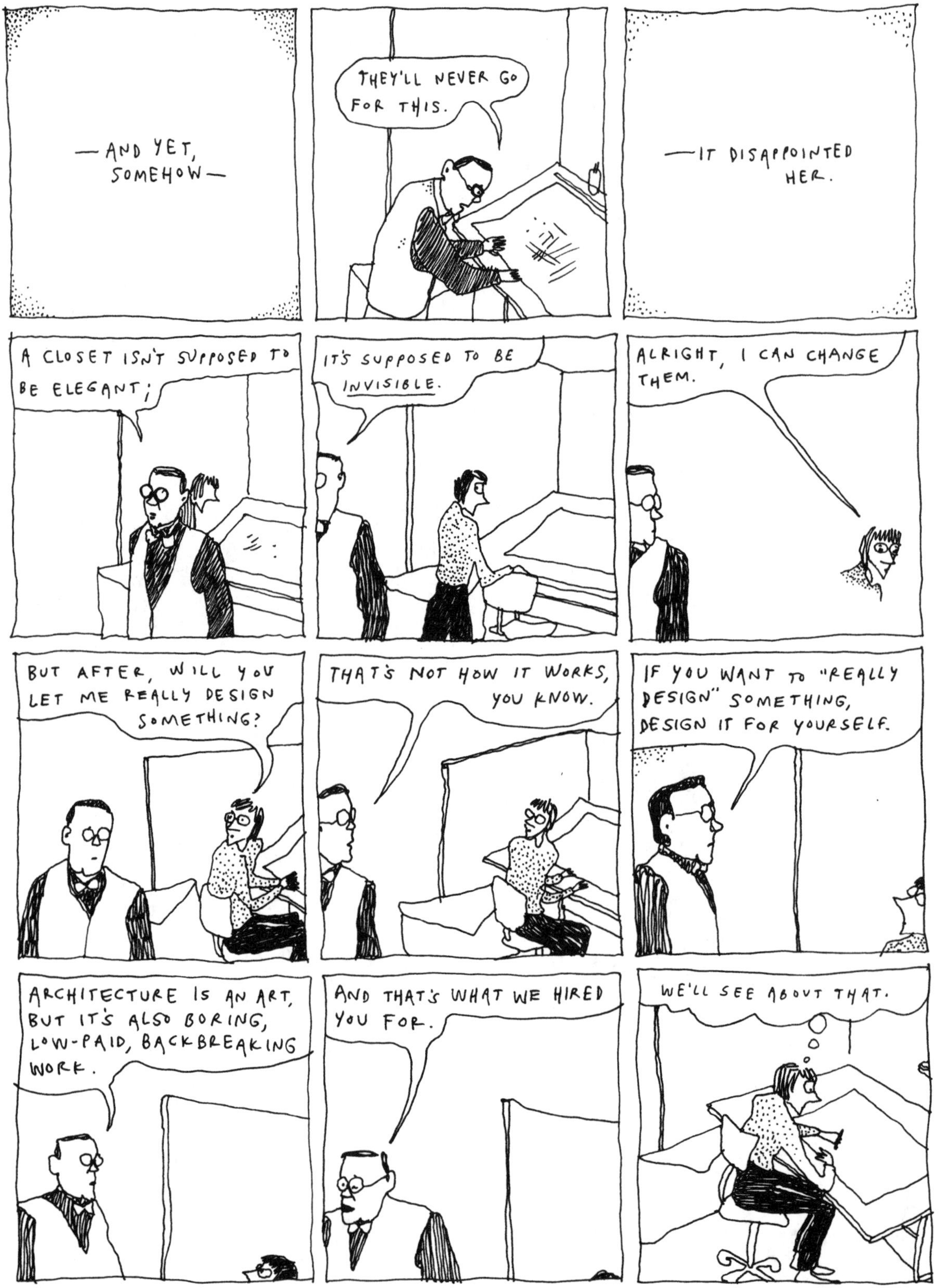
—AND YET, SOMEHOW—
THEY'LL NEVER GO FOR THIS.
—IT DISAPPOINTED HER.
A CLOSET ISN'T SUPPOSED TO BE ELEGANT;
IT'S SUPPOSED TO BE INVISIBLE.
ALRIGHT, I CAN CHANGE THEM.
BUT AFTER, WILL YOU LET ME REALLY DESIGN SOMETHING?
THAT'S NOT HOW IT WORKS, YOU KNOW.
IF YOU WANT TO "REALLY DESIGN" SOMETHING, DESIGN IT FOR YOURSELF.
ARCHITECTURE IS AN ART, BUT IT'S ALSO BORING, LOW-PAID, BACKBREAKING WORK.
AND THAT'S WHAT WE HIRED YOU FOR.
WE'LL SEE ABOUT THAT.

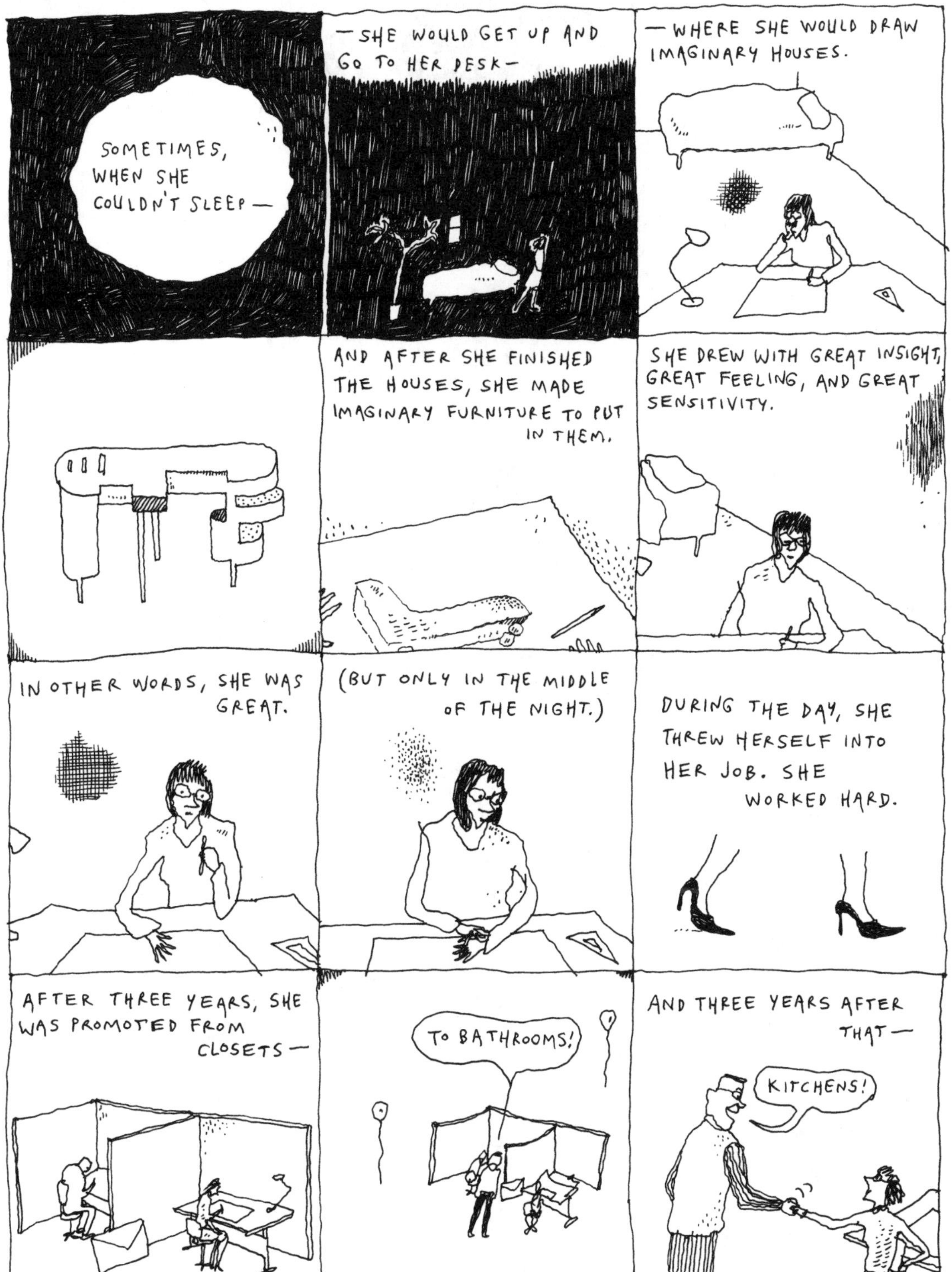
SOMETIMES, WHEN SHE COULDN'T SLEEP—
—SHE WOULD GET UP AND GO TO HER DESK—
—WHERE SHE WOULD DRAW IMAGINARY HOUSES.
AND AFTER SHE FINISHED THE HOUSES, SHE MADE IMAGINARY FURNITURE TO PUT IN THEM.
SHE DREW WITH GREAT INSIGHT, GREAT FEELING, AND GREAT SENSITIVITY.
IN OTHER WORDS, SHE WAS GREAT.
(BUT ONLY IN THE MIDDLE OF THE NIGHT.)
DURING THE DAY, SHE THREW HERSELF INTO HER JOB. SHE WORKED HARD.
AFTER THREE YEARS, SHE WAS PROMOTED FROM CLOSETS—
TO BATHROOMS!
AND THREE YEARS AFTER THAT—
KITCHENS!

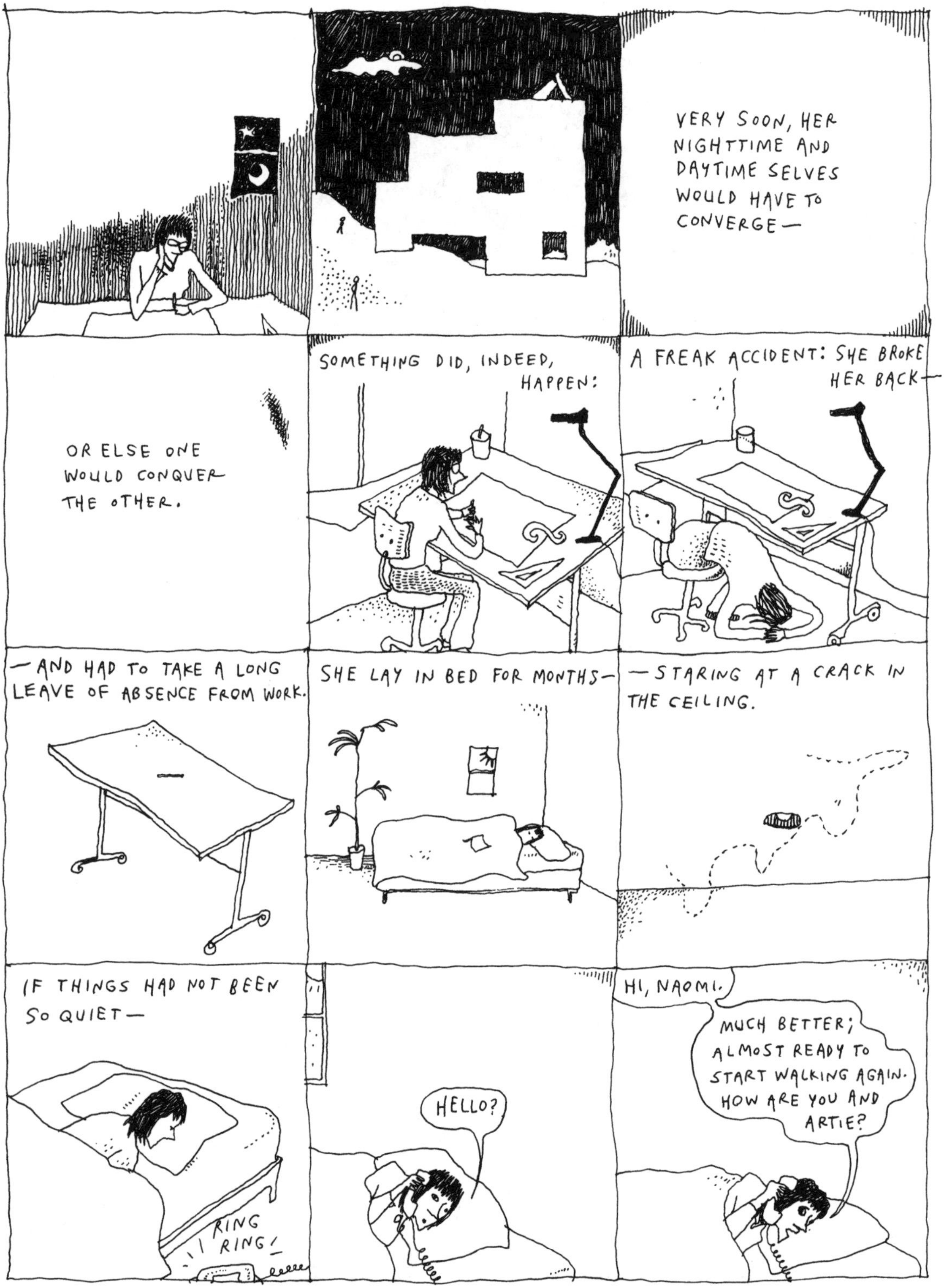
VERY SOON, HER NIGHTTIME AND DAYTIME SELVES WOULD HAVE TO CONVERGE—
OR ELSE ONE WOULD CONQUER THE OTHER.
SOMETHING DID, INDEED, HAPPEN:
A FREAK ACCIDENT: SHE BROKE HER BACK—
—AND HAD TO TAKE A LONG LEAVE OF ABSENCE FROM WORK.
SHE LAY IN BED FOR MONTHS—
—STARING AT A CRACK IN THE CEILING.
IF THINGS HAD NOT BEEN SO QUIET—
RING RING!
HELLO?
HI, NAOMI.
MUCH BETTER; ALMOST READY TO START WALKING AGAIN. HOW ARE YOU AND ARTIE?

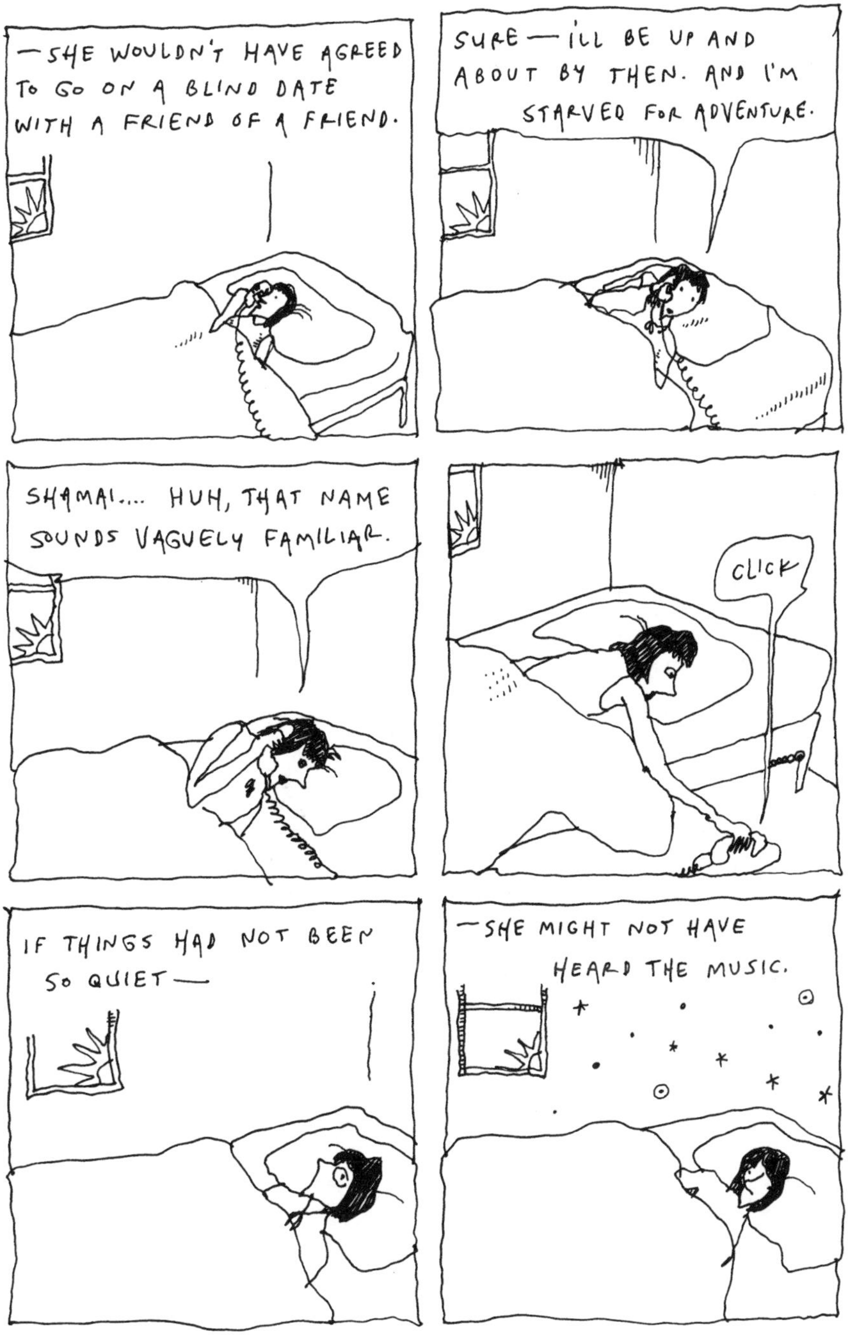
—SHE WOULDN'T HAVE AGREED TO GO ON A BLIND DATE WITH A FRIEND OF A FRIEND.
SURE—I'LL BE UP AND ABOUT BY THEN. AND I'M STARVED FOR ADVENTURE.
SHAMAI.... HUH, THAT NAME SOUNDS VAGUELY FAMILIAR.
CLICK
IF THINGS HAD NOT BEEN SO QUIET—
—SHE MIGHT NOT HAVE HEARD THE MUSIC.

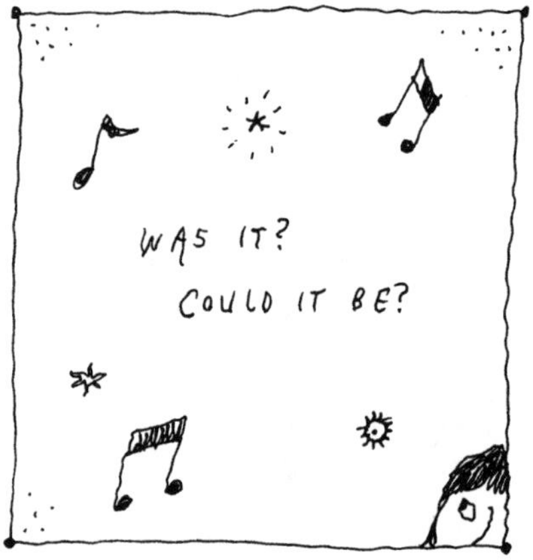
WAS IT?
COULD IT BE?

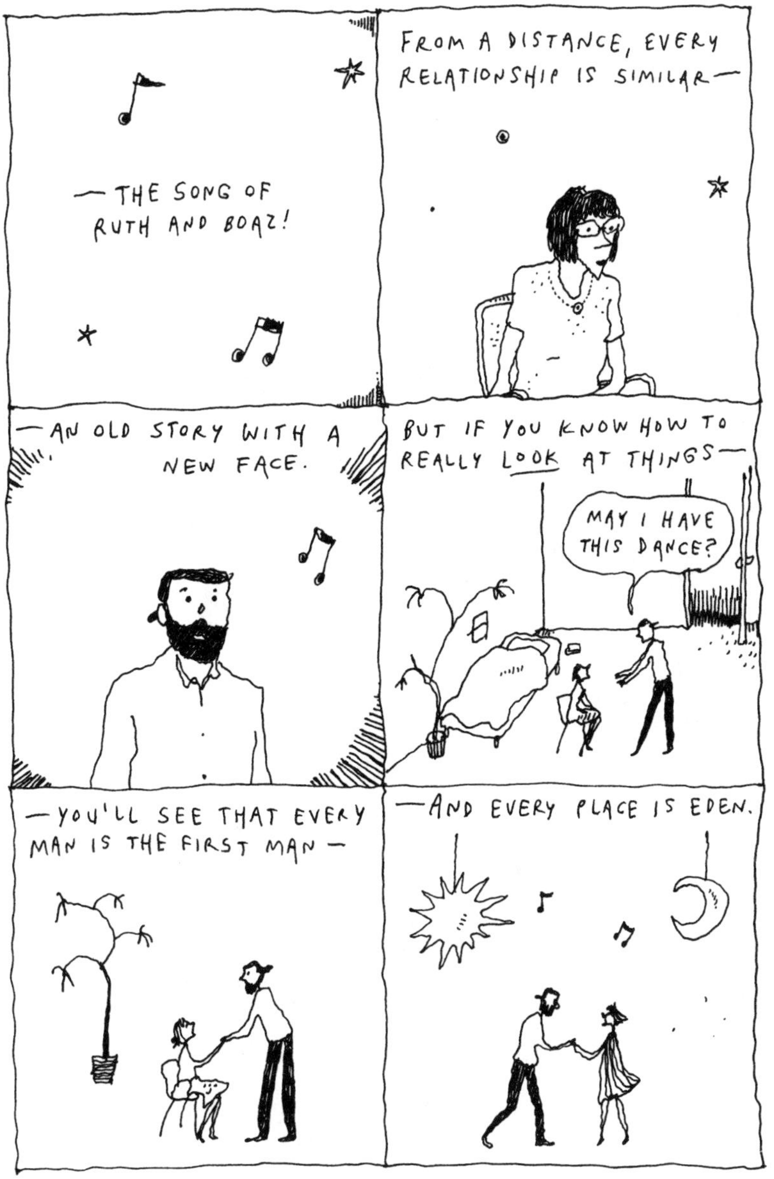
—THE SONG OF RUTH AND BOAZ!
FROM A DISTANCE, EVERY RELATIONSHIP IS SIMILAR—
—AN OLD STORY WITH A NEW FACE.
BUT IF YOU KNOW HOW TO REALLY LOOK AT THINGS—
MAY I HAVE THIS DANCE?
—YOU'LL SEE THAT EVERY MAN IS THE FIRST MAN—
—AND EVERY PLACE IS EDEN.

CREATION

(AN INTERLUDE)

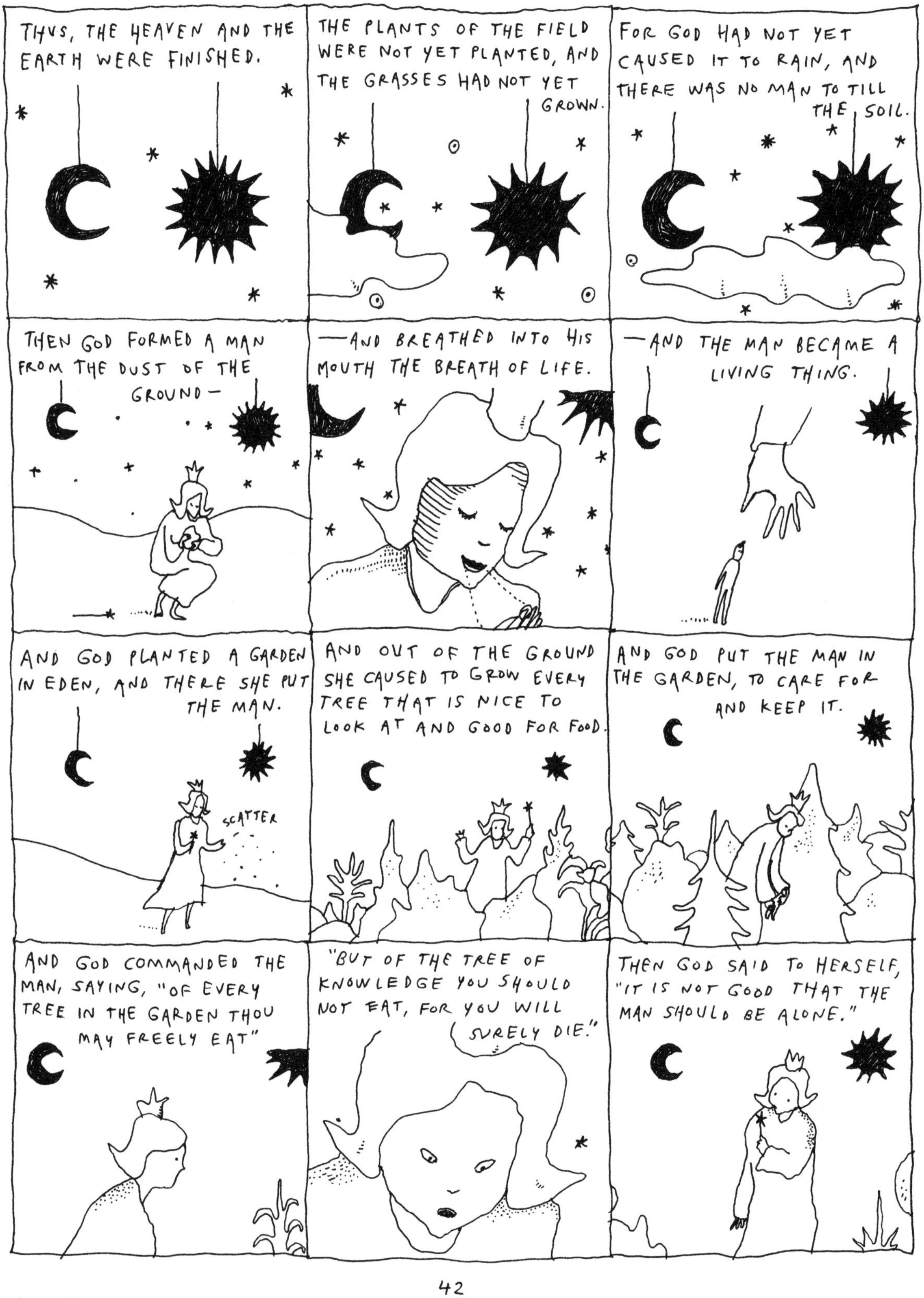
THUS, THE HEAVEN AND THE EARTH WERE FINISHED.
THE PLANTS OF THE FIELD WERE NOT YET PLANTED, AND THE GRASSES HAD NOT YET GROWN.
FOR GOD HAD NOT YET CAUSED IT TO RAIN, AND THERE WAS NO MAN TO TILL THE SOIL.
THEN GOD FORMED A MAN FROM THE DUST OF THE GROUND—
—AND BREATHED INTO HIS MOUTH THE BREATH OF LIFE.
—AND THE MAN BECAME A LIVING THING.
AND GOD PLANTED A GARDEN IN EDEN, AND THERE SHE PUT THE MAN.
SCATTER
AND OUT OF THE GROUND SHE CAUSED TO GROW EVERY TREE THAT IS NICE TO LOOK AT AND GOOD FOR FOOD.
AND GOD PUT THE MAN IN THE GARDEN, TO CARE FOR AND KEEP IT.
AND GOD COMMANDED THE MAN, SAYING, "OF EVERY TREE IN THE GARDEN THOU MAY FREELY EAT"
"BUT OF THE TREE OF KNOWLEDGE YOU SHOULD NOT EAT, FOR YOU WILL SURELY DIE."
THEN GOD SAID TO HERSELF, "IT IS NOT GOOD THAT THE MAN SHOULD BE ALONE."

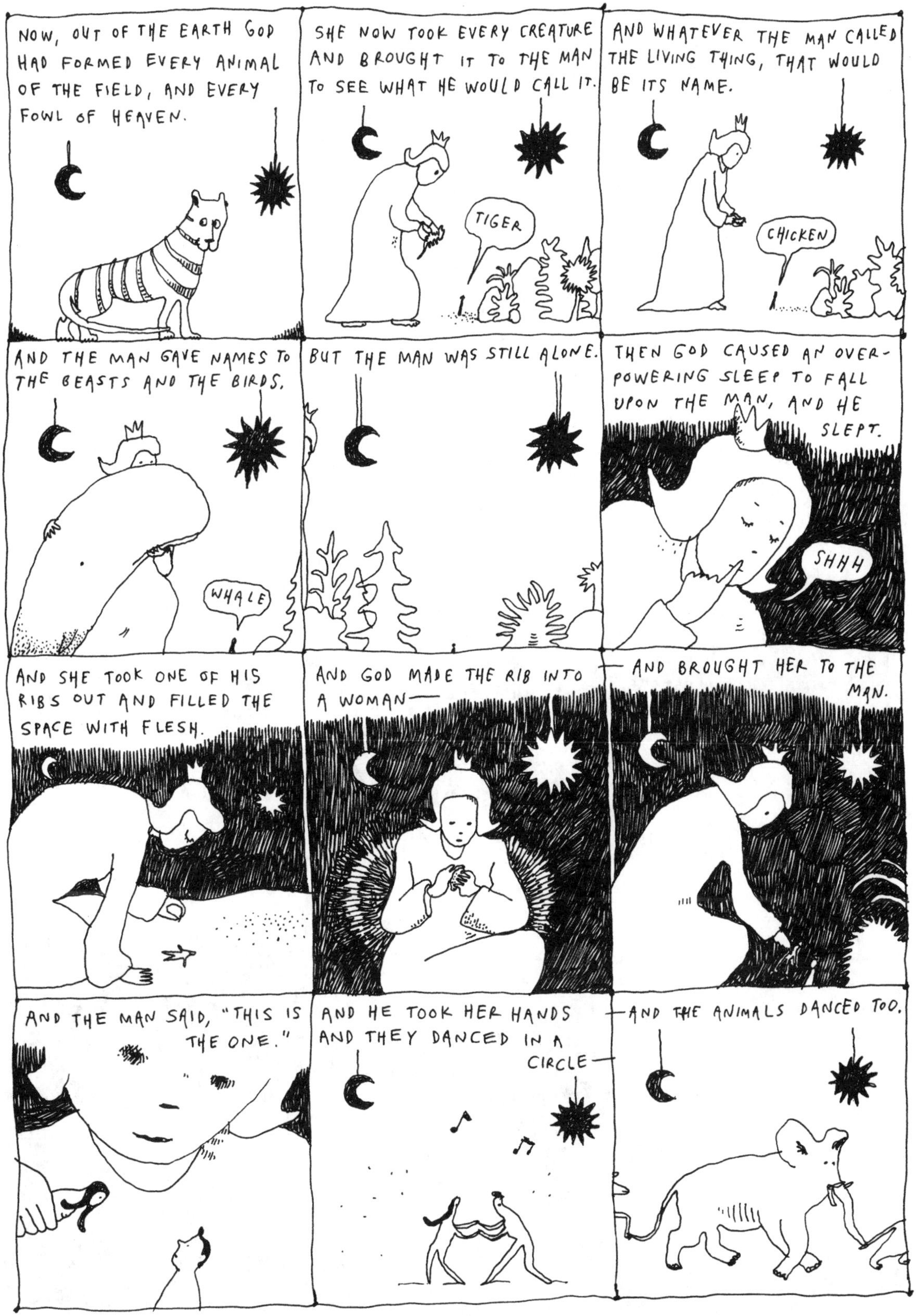
NOW, OUT OF THE EARTH GOD HAD FORMED EVERY ANIMAL OF THE FIELD, AND EVERY FOWL OF HEAVEN.
SHE NOW TOOK EVERY CREATURE AND BROUGHT IT TO THE MAN TO SEE WHAT HE WOULD CALL IT.
TIGER
AND WHATEVER THE MAN CALLED THE LIVING THING, THAT WOULD BE ITS NAME.
CHICKEN
AND THE MAN GAVE NAMES TO THE BEASTS AND THE BIRDS.
WHALE
BUT THE MAN WAS STILL ALONE.
THEN GOD CAUSED AN OVER-POWERING SLEEP TO FALL UPON THE MAN, AND HE SLEPT.
SHHH
AND SHE TOOK ONE OF HIS RIBS OUT AND FILLED THE SPACE WITH FLESH.
AND GOD MADE THE RIB INTO A WOMAN—
—AND BROUGHT HER TO THE MAN.
AND THE MAN SAID, "THIS IS THE ONE."
AND HE TOOK HER HANDS AND THEY DANCED IN A CIRCLE—
—AND THE ANIMALS DANCED TOO.

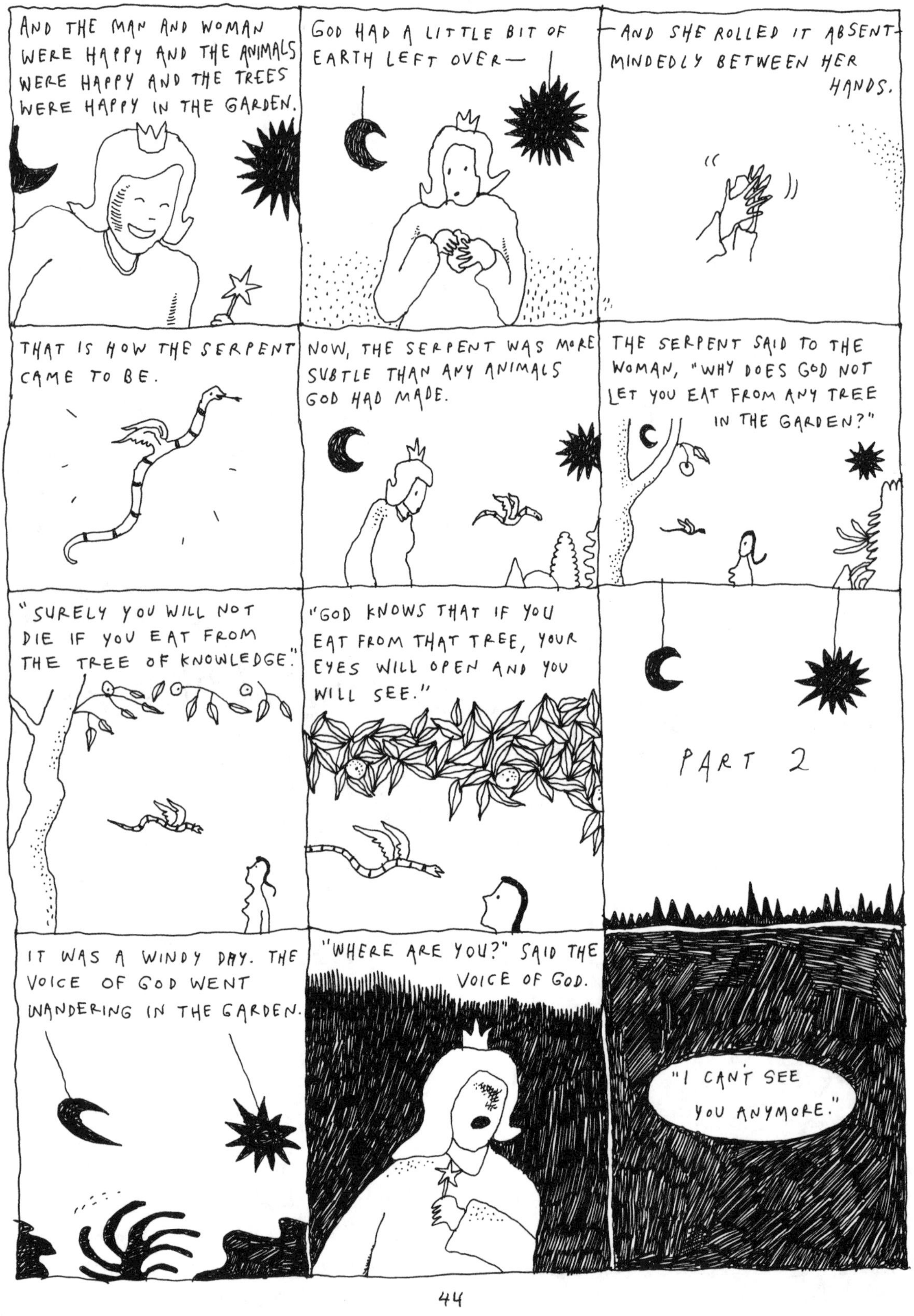

AND THE MAN AND WOMAN WERE HAPPY AND THE ANIMALS WERE HAPPY AND THE TREES WERE HAPPY IN THE GARDEN.
GOD HAD A LITTLE BIT OF EARTH LEFT OVER—
—AND SHE ROLLED IT ABSENT-MINDEDLY BETWEEN HER HANDS.
THAT IS HOW THE SERPENT CAME TO BE.
NOW, THE SERPENT WAS MORE SUBTLE THAN ANY ANIMALS GOD HAD MADE.
THE SERPENT SAID TO THE WOMAN, "WHY DOES GOD NOT LET YOU EAT FROM ANY TREE IN THE GARDEN?"
"SURELY YOU WILL NOT DIE IF YOU EAT FROM THE TREE OF KNOWLEDGE."
"GOD KNOWS THAT IF YOU EAT FROM THAT TREE, YOUR EYES WILL OPEN AND YOU WILL SEE."
PART 2
IT WAS A WINDY DAY. THE VOICE OF GOD WENT WANDERING IN THE GARDEN.
"WHERE ARE YOU?" SAID THE VOICE OF GOD.
"I CAN'T SEE YOU ANYMORE."

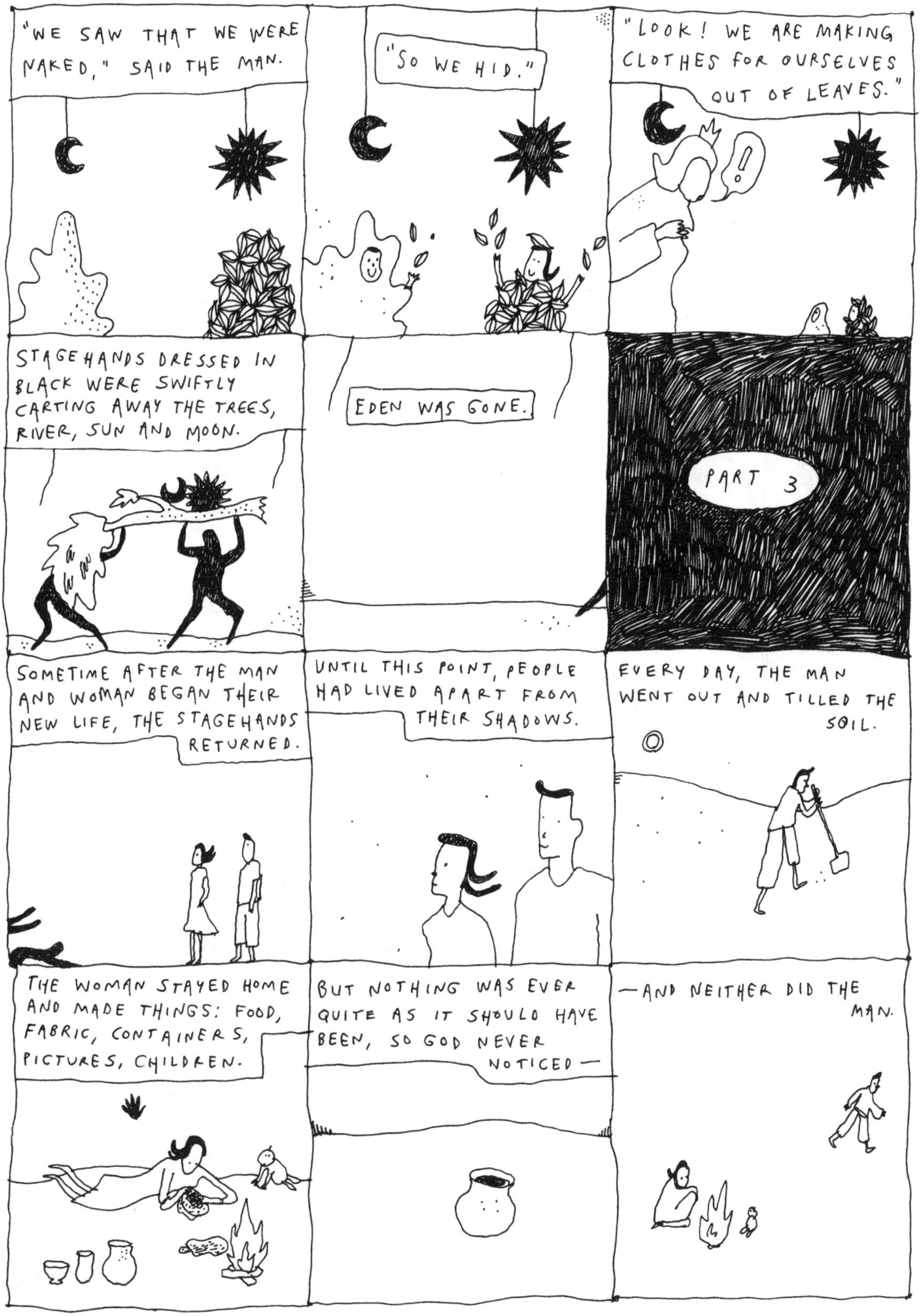

"WE SAW THAT WE WERE NAKED," SAID THE MAN.
"SO WE HID."
"LOOK! WE ARE MAKING CLOTHES FOR OURSELVES OUT OF LEAVES."
!
STAGEHANDS DRESSED IN BLACK WERE SWIFTLY CARTING AWAY THE TREES, RIVER, SUN AND MOON.
EDEN WAS GONE.
PART 3
SOMETIME AFTER THE MAN AND WOMAN BEGAN THEIR NEW LIFE, THE STAGEHANDS RETURNED.
UNTIL THIS POINT, PEOPLE HAD LIVED APART FROM THEIR SHADOWS.
EVERY DAY, THE MAN WENT OUT AND TILLED THE SOIL.
THE WOMAN STAYED HOME AND MADE THINGS: FOOD, FABRIC, CONTAINERS, PICTURES, CHILDREN.
BUT NOTHING WAS EVER QUITE AS IT SHOULD HAVE BEEN, SO GOD NEVER NOTICED—
—AND NEITHER DID THE MAN.

THE SNAKE FORGOT HOW TO FLY IN THE AIR. NOW IT FLIES ON THE GROUND.

IT USED TO BE AN IDEA. NOW IT IS AN ANIMAL.

PLOP

AND SOMETIMES, ON A WINDY DAY —

— YOU CAN STILL HEAR THE VOICE OF GOD.

I AM LISTENING

AND WHEN YOU DO, YOU WILL KNOW THAT YOU ARE STANDING —

— WHERE THE GARDEN USED TO BE.

I AM HERE

END OF INTERLUDE.

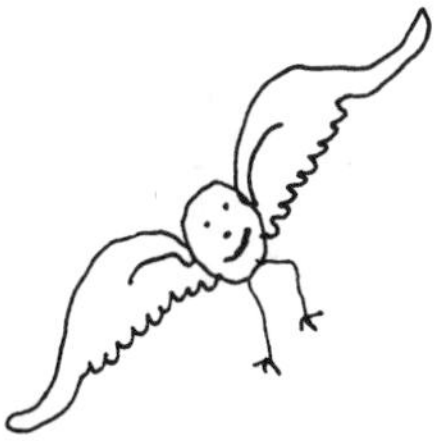

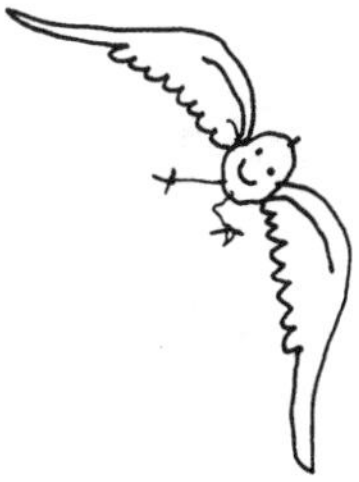

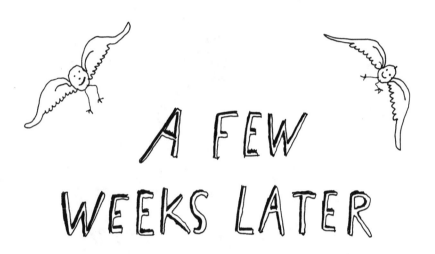

A FEW WEEKS LATER

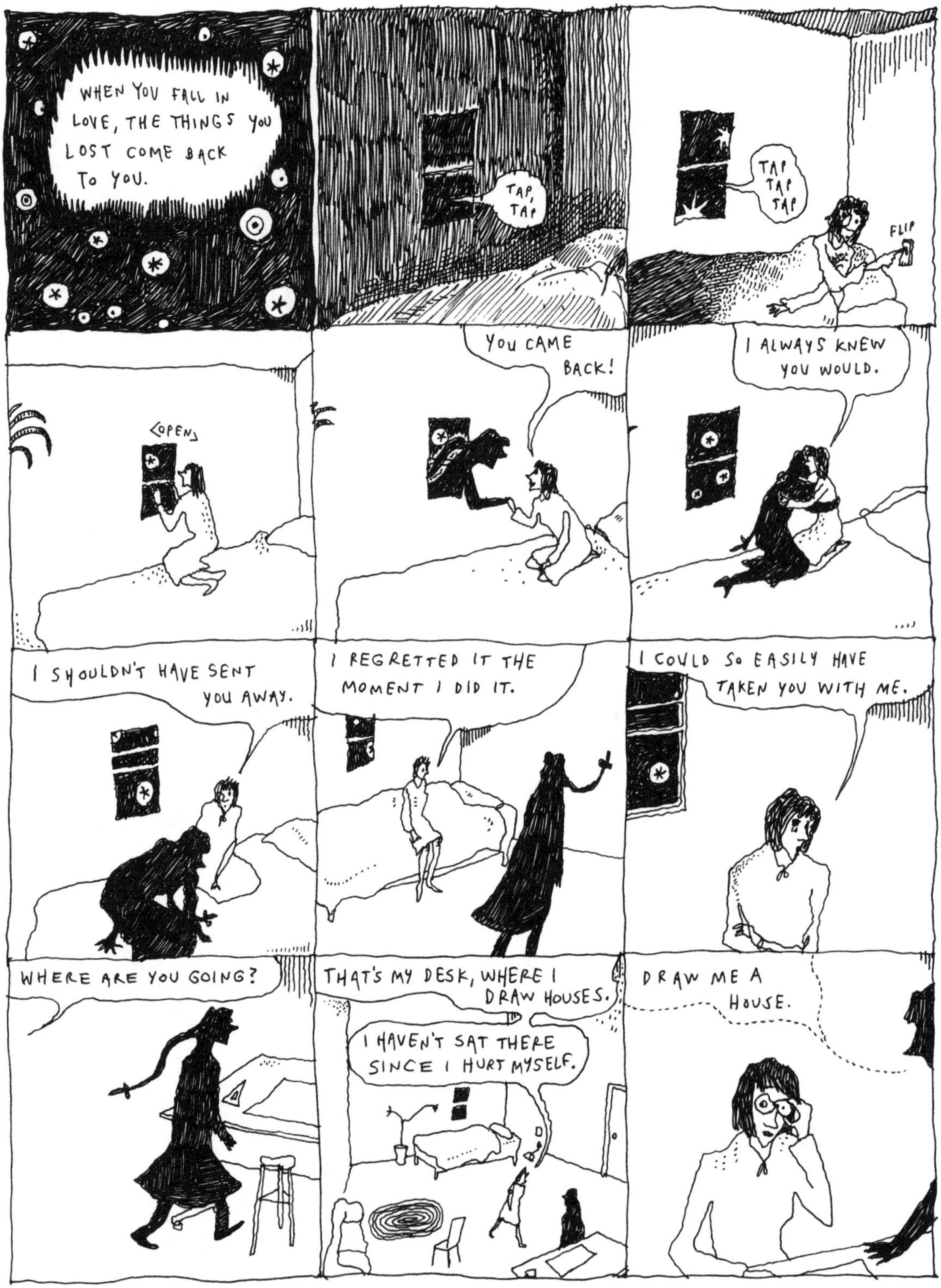
WHEN YOU FALL IN LOVE, THE THINGS YOU LOST COME BACK TO YOU.
TAP, TAP
TAP TAP TAP
FLIP
<OPEN>
YOU CAME BACK!
I ALWAYS KNEW YOU WOULD.
I SHOULDN'T HAVE SENT YOU AWAY.
I REGRETTED IT THE MOMENT I DID IT.
I COULD SO EASILY HAVE TAKEN YOU WITH ME.
WHERE ARE YOU GOING?
THAT'S MY DESK, WHERE I DRAW HOUSES.
I HAVEN'T SAT THERE SINCE I HURT MYSELF.
DRAW ME A HOUSE.

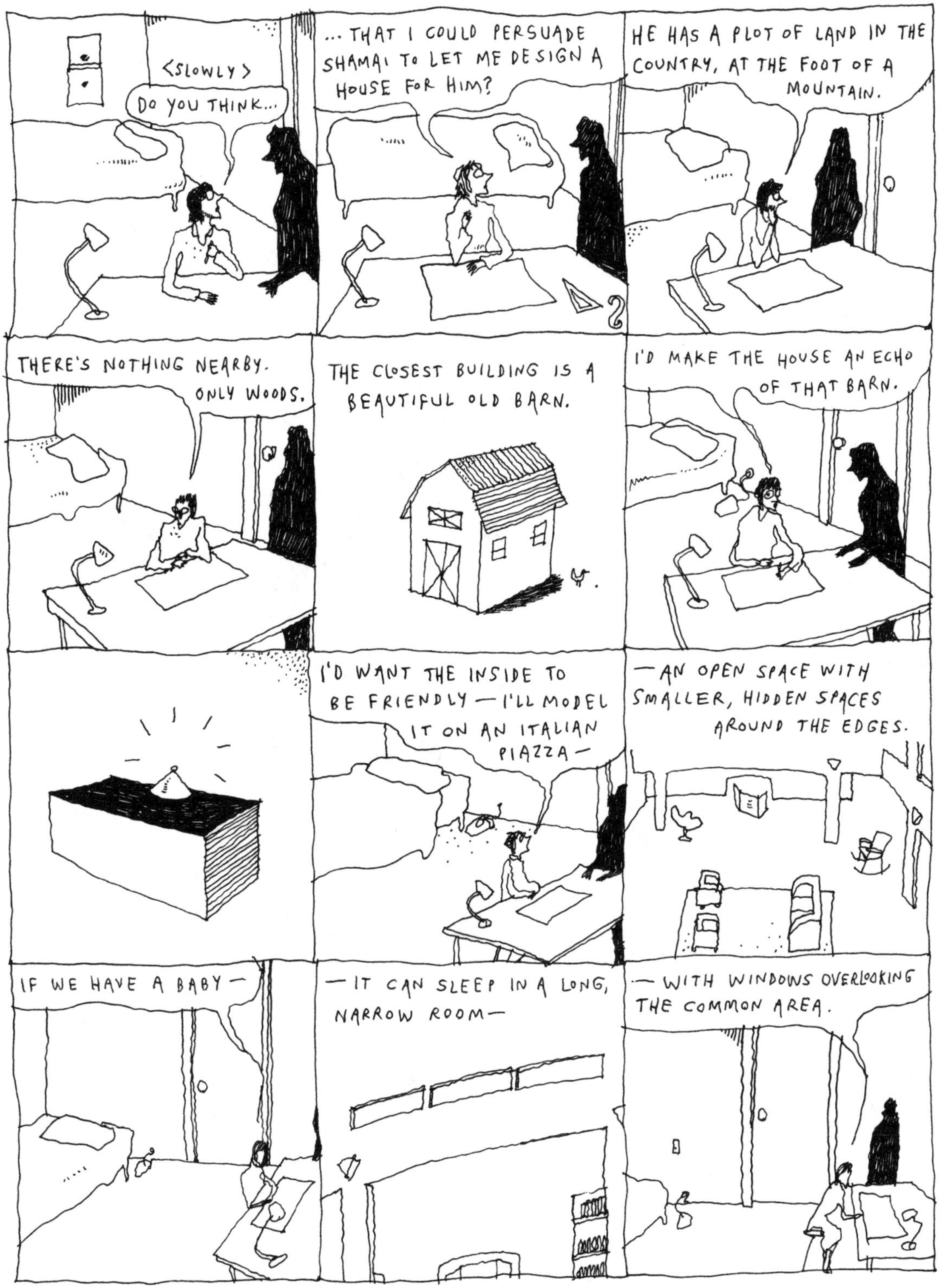
<SLOWLY>
DO YOU THINK...
...THAT I COULD PERSUADE SHAMAI TO LET ME DESIGN A HOUSE FOR HIM?
HE HAS A PLOT OF LAND IN THE COUNTRY, AT THE FOOT OF A MOUNTAIN.
THERE'S NOTHING NEARBY. ONLY WOODS.
THE CLOSEST BUILDING IS A BEAUTIFUL OLD BARN.
I'D MAKE THE HOUSE AN ECHO OF THAT BARN.
I'D WANT THE INSIDE TO BE FRIENDLY—I'LL MODEL IT ON AN ITALIAN PIAZZA—
—AN OPEN SPACE WITH SMALLER, HIDDEN SPACES AROUND THE EDGES.
IF WE HAVE A BABY—
—IT CAN SLEEP IN A LONG, NARROW ROOM—
—WITH WINDOWS OVERLOOKING THE COMMON AREA.

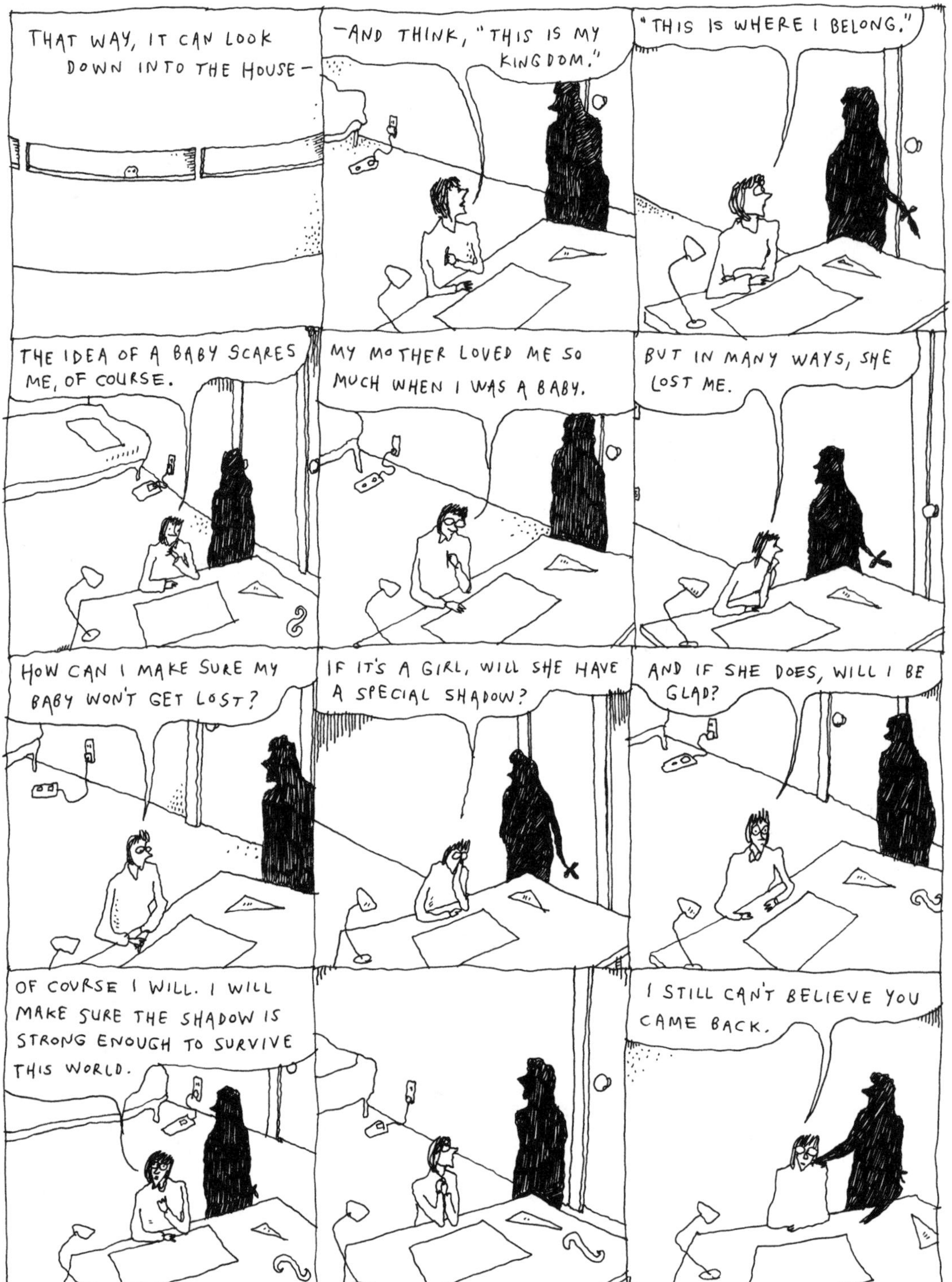
THAT WAY, IT CAN LOOK DOWN INTO THE HOUSE—
—AND THINK, "THIS IS MY KINGDOM."
"THIS IS WHERE I BELONG."
THE IDEA OF A BABY SCARES ME, OF COURSE.
MY MOTHER LOVED ME SO MUCH WHEN I WAS A BABY.
BUT IN MANY WAYS, SHE LOST ME.
HOW CAN I MAKE SURE MY BABY WON'T GET LOST?
IF IT'S A GIRL, WILL SHE HAVE A SPECIAL SHADOW?
AND IF SHE DOES, WILL I BE GLAD?
OF COURSE I WILL. I WILL MAKE SURE THE SHADOW IS STRONG ENOUGH TO SURVIVE THIS WORLD.
I STILL CAN'T BELIEVE YOU CAME BACK.

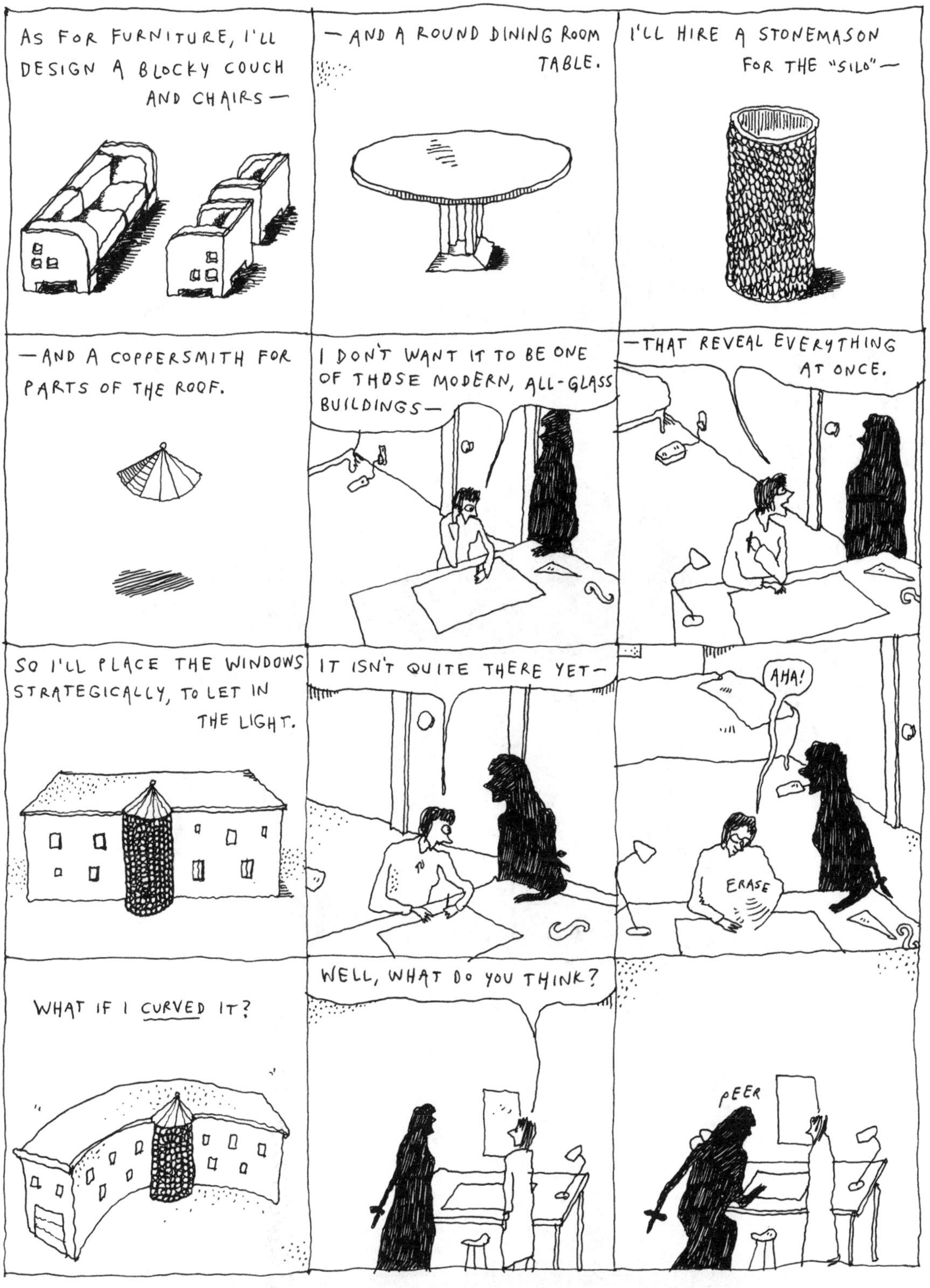
AS FOR FURNITURE, I'LL DESIGN A BLOCKY COUCH AND CHAIRS—
—AND A ROUND DINING ROOM TABLE.
I'LL HIRE A STONEMASON FOR THE "SILO"—
—AND A COPPERSMITH FOR PARTS OF THE ROOF.
I DON'T WANT IT TO BE ONE OF THOSE MODERN, ALL-GLASS BUILDINGS—
—THAT REVEAL EVERYTHING AT ONCE.
SO I'LL PLACE THE WINDOWS STRATEGICALLY, TO LET IN THE LIGHT.
IT ISN'T QUITE THERE YET—
AHA!
ERASE
WHAT IF I CURVED IT?
WELL, WHAT DO YOU THINK?
PEER

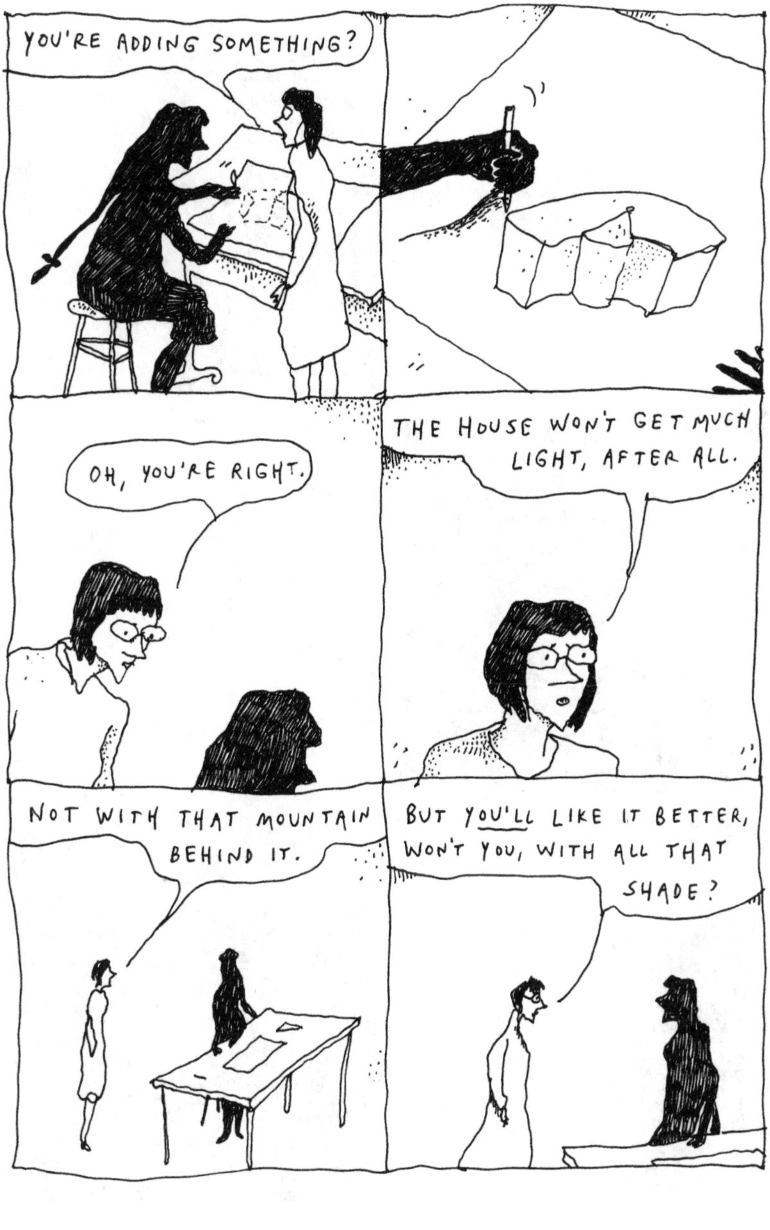
YOU'RE ADDING SOMETHING?
OH, YOU'RE RIGHT.
THE HOUSE WON'T GET MUCH LIGHT, AFTER ALL.
NOT WITH THAT MOUNTAIN BEHIND IT.
BUT YOU'LL LIKE IT BETTER, WON'T YOU, WITH ALL THAT SHADE?

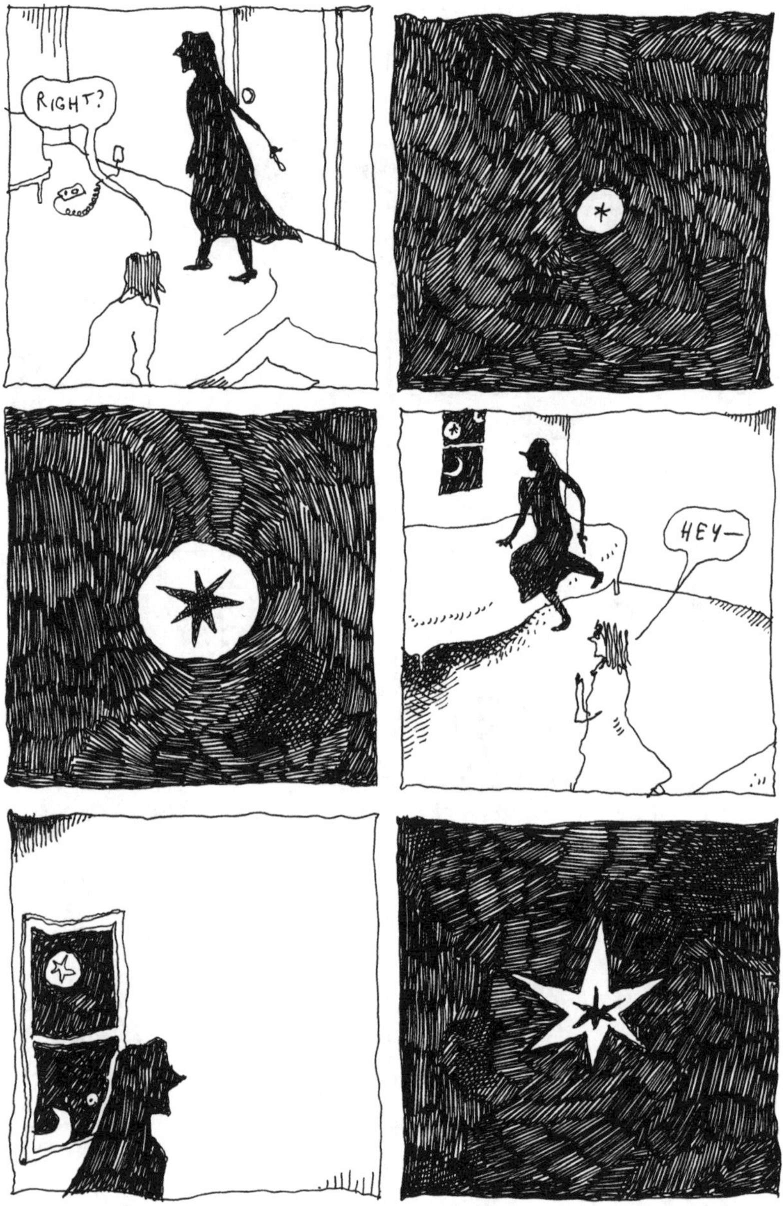
RIGHT?
HEY—

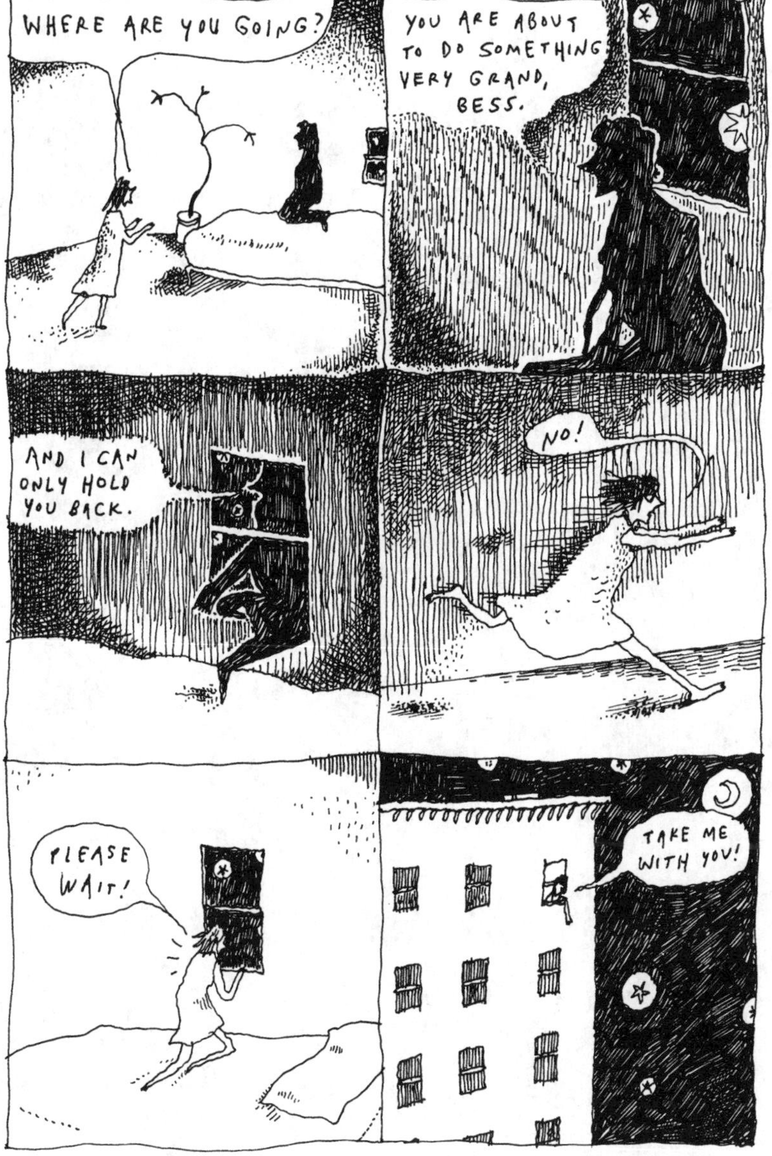
WHERE ARE YOU GOING?
YOU ARE ABOUT TO DO SOMETHING VERY GRAND, BESS.
AND I CAN ONLY HOLD YOU BACK.
NO!
PLEASE WAIT!
TAKE ME WITH YOU!

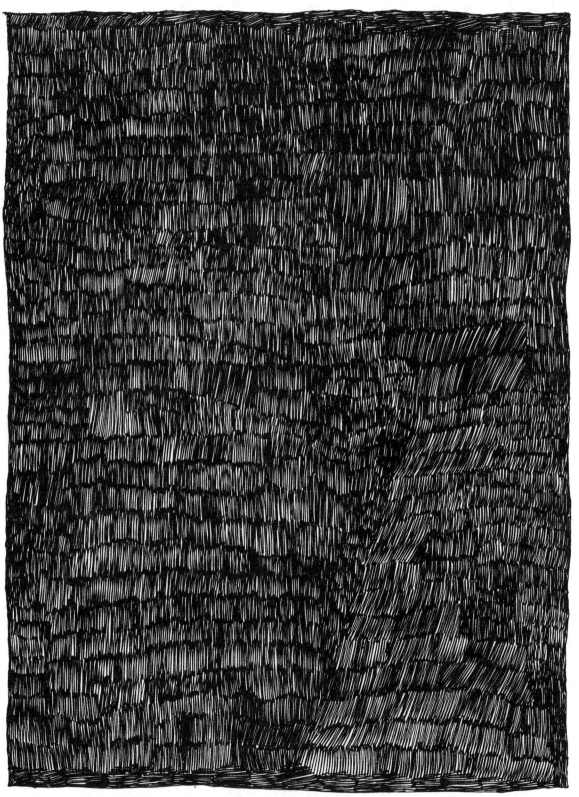

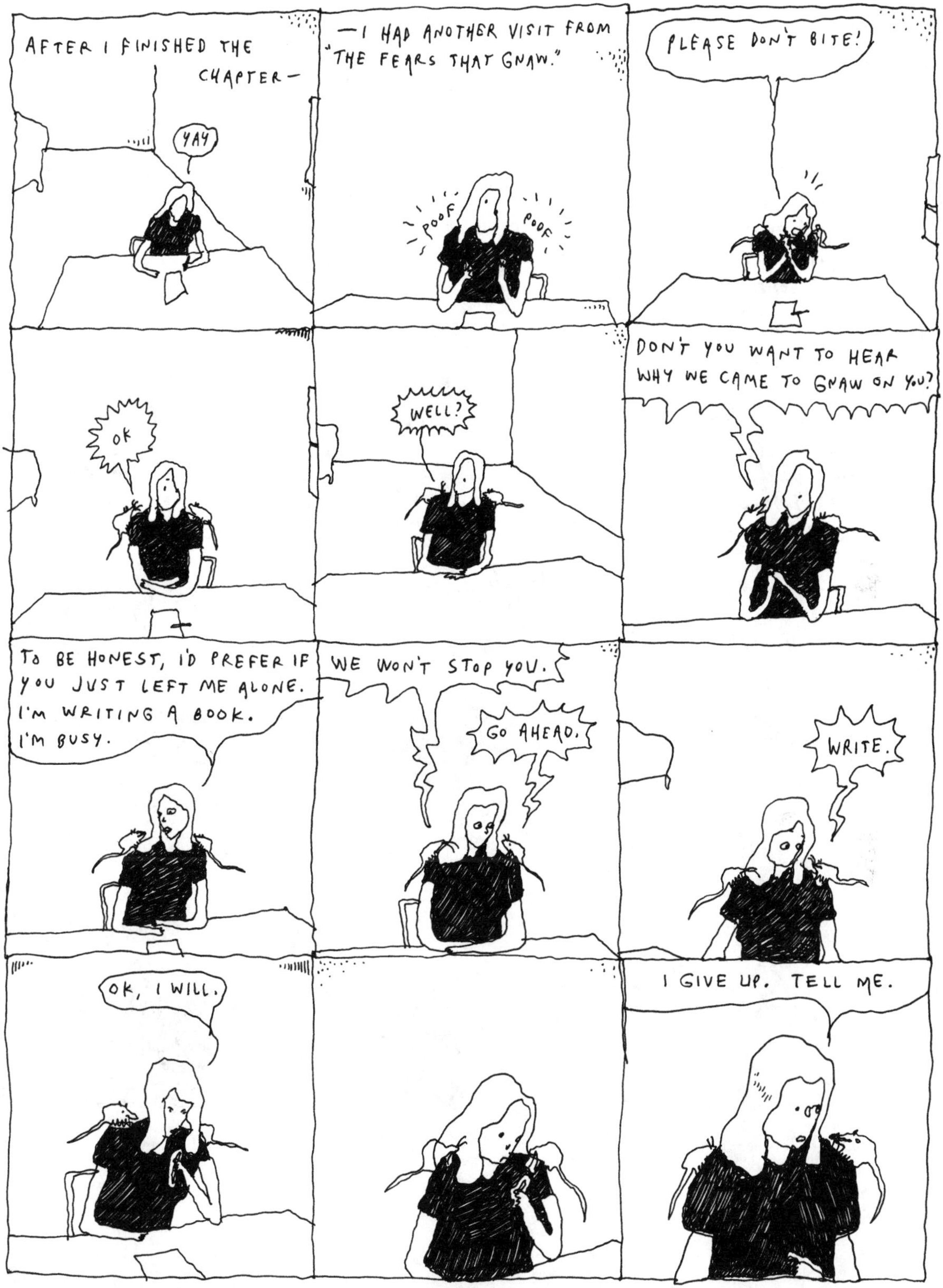
AFTER I FINISHED THE CHAPTER—
YAY
—I HAD ANOTHER VISIT FROM "THE FEARS THAT GNAW."
POOF
POOF
PLEASE DON'T BITE!
OK
WELL?
DON'T YOU WANT TO HEAR WHY WE CAME TO GNAW ON YOU?
TO BE HONEST, I'D PREFER IF YOU JUST LEFT ME ALONE. I'M WRITING A BOOK. I'M BUSY.
WE WON'T STOP YOU.
GO AHEAD.
WRITE.
OK, I WILL.
I GIVE UP. TELL ME.

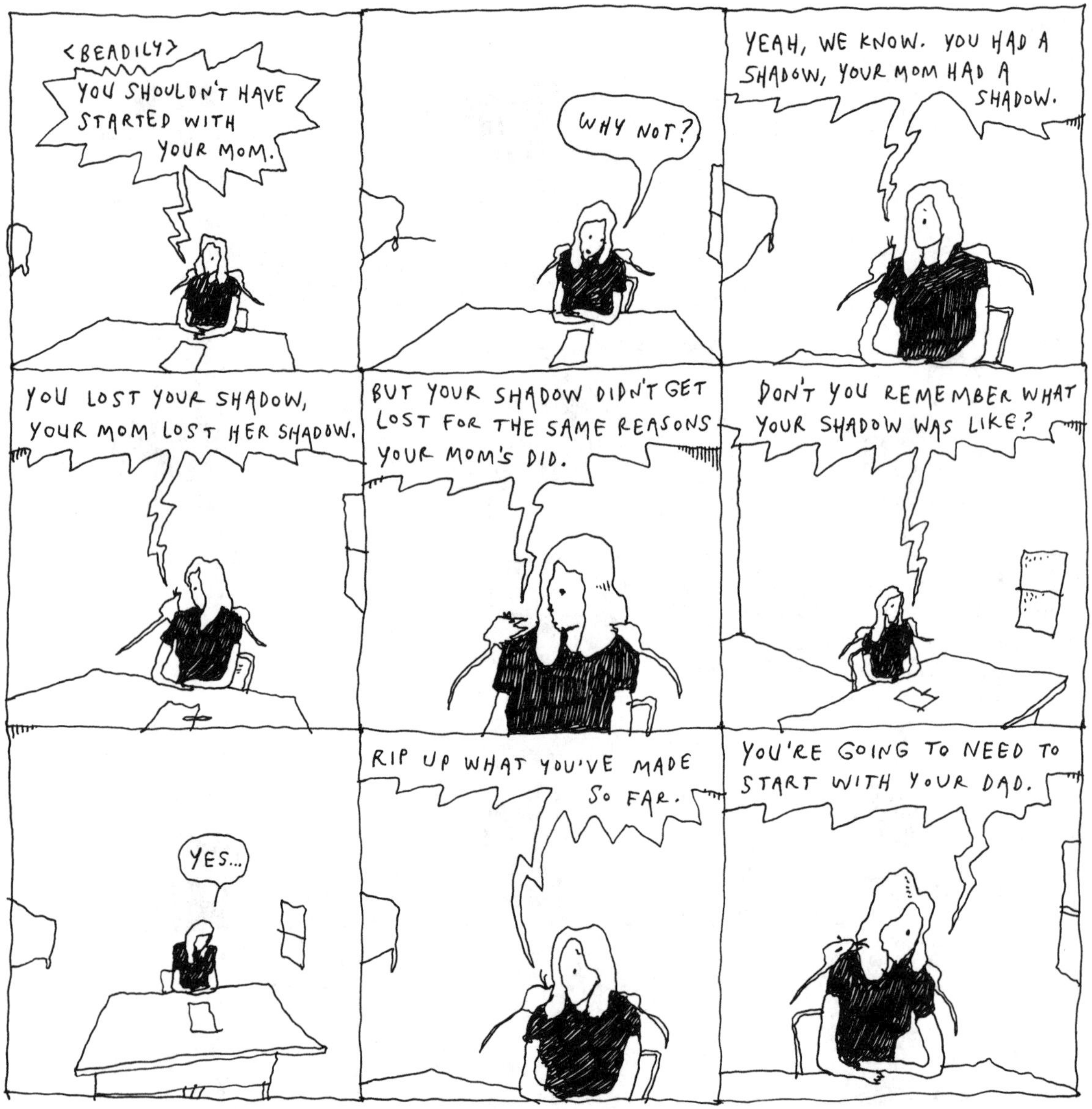
<BEADILY>
YOU SHOULDN'T HAVE STARTED WITH YOUR MOM.
WHY NOT?
YEAH, WE KNOW. YOU HAD A SHADOW, YOUR MOM HAD A SHADOW.
YOU LOST YOUR SHADOW, YOUR MOM LOST HER SHADOW.
BUT YOUR SHADOW DIDN'T GET LOST FOR THE SAME REASONS YOUR MOM'S DID.
DON'T YOU REMEMBER WHAT YOUR SHADOW WAS LIKE?
YES...
RIP UP WHAT YOU'VE MADE SO FAR.
YOU'RE GOING TO NEED TO START WITH YOUR DAD.

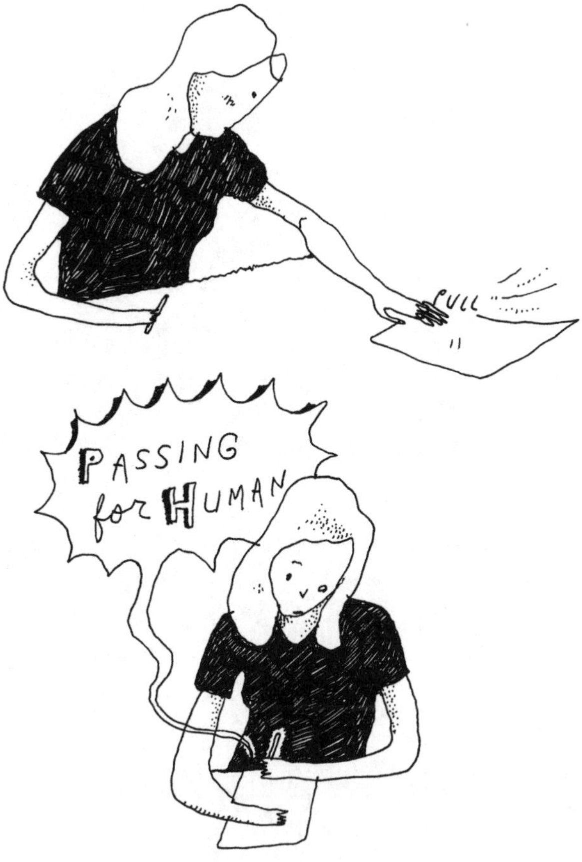
PULL
PASSING for HUMAN

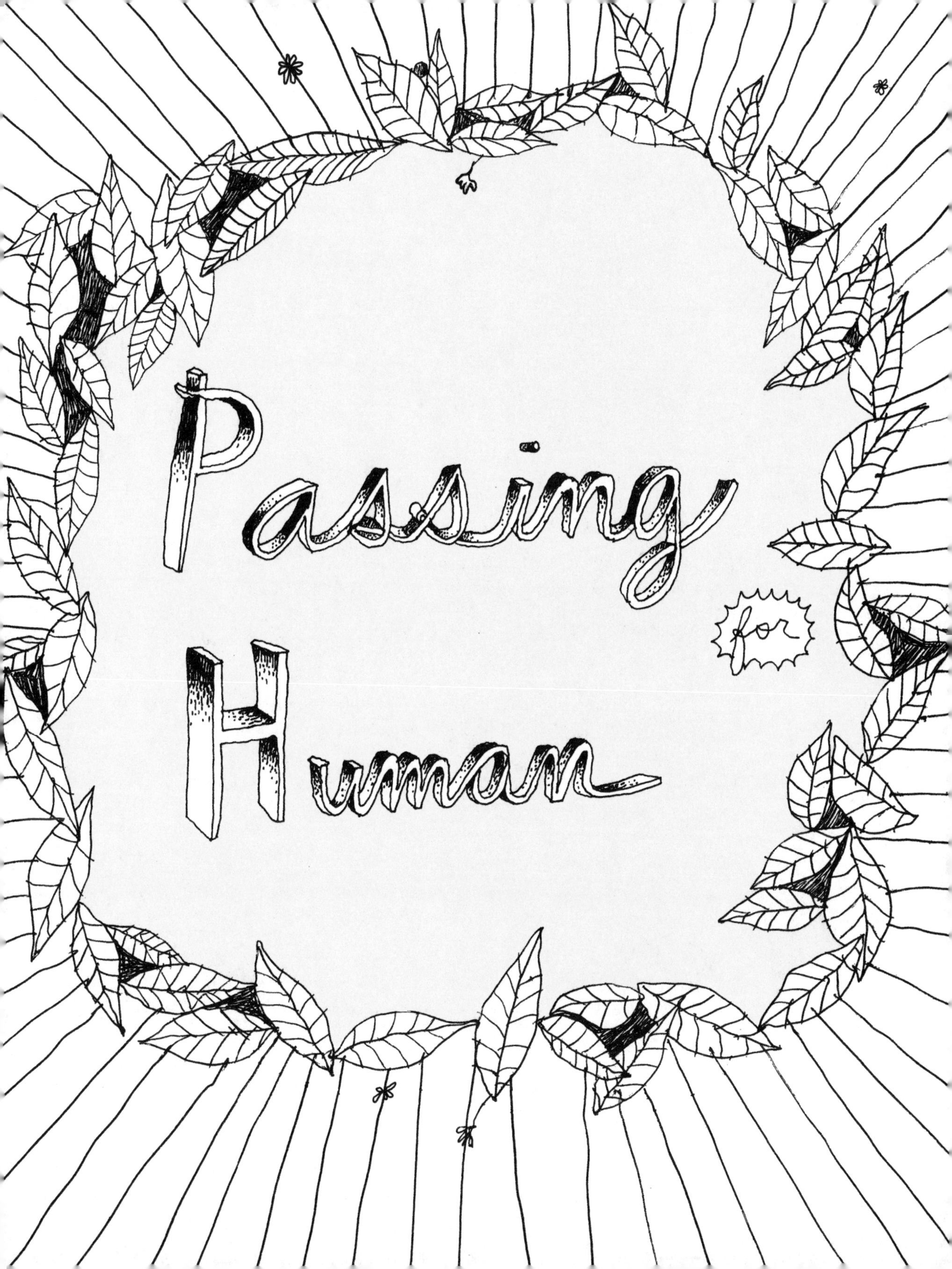
Passing
for
Human

"I'M NOBODY! WHO ARE YOU?
ARE YOU — NOBODY — TOO?
THEN THERE'S A PAIR OF US!
DON'T TELL! THEY'D ADVERTISE — YOU KNOW!"

—EMILY DICKINSON

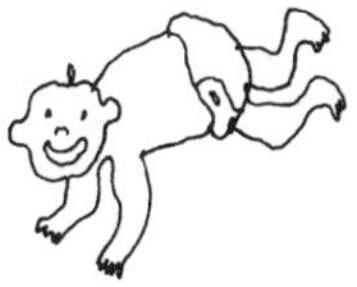

CHAPTER 1
DAD

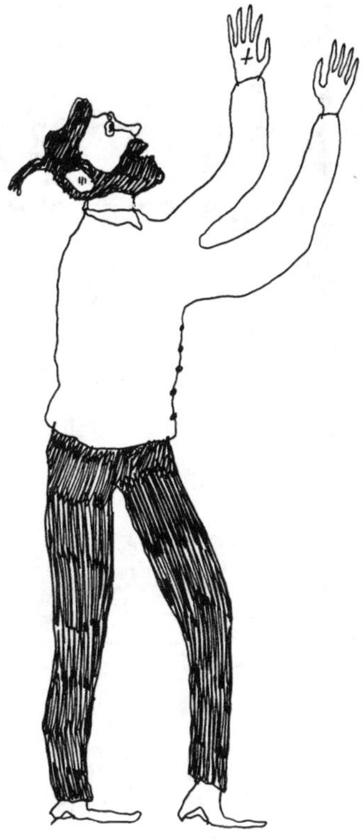

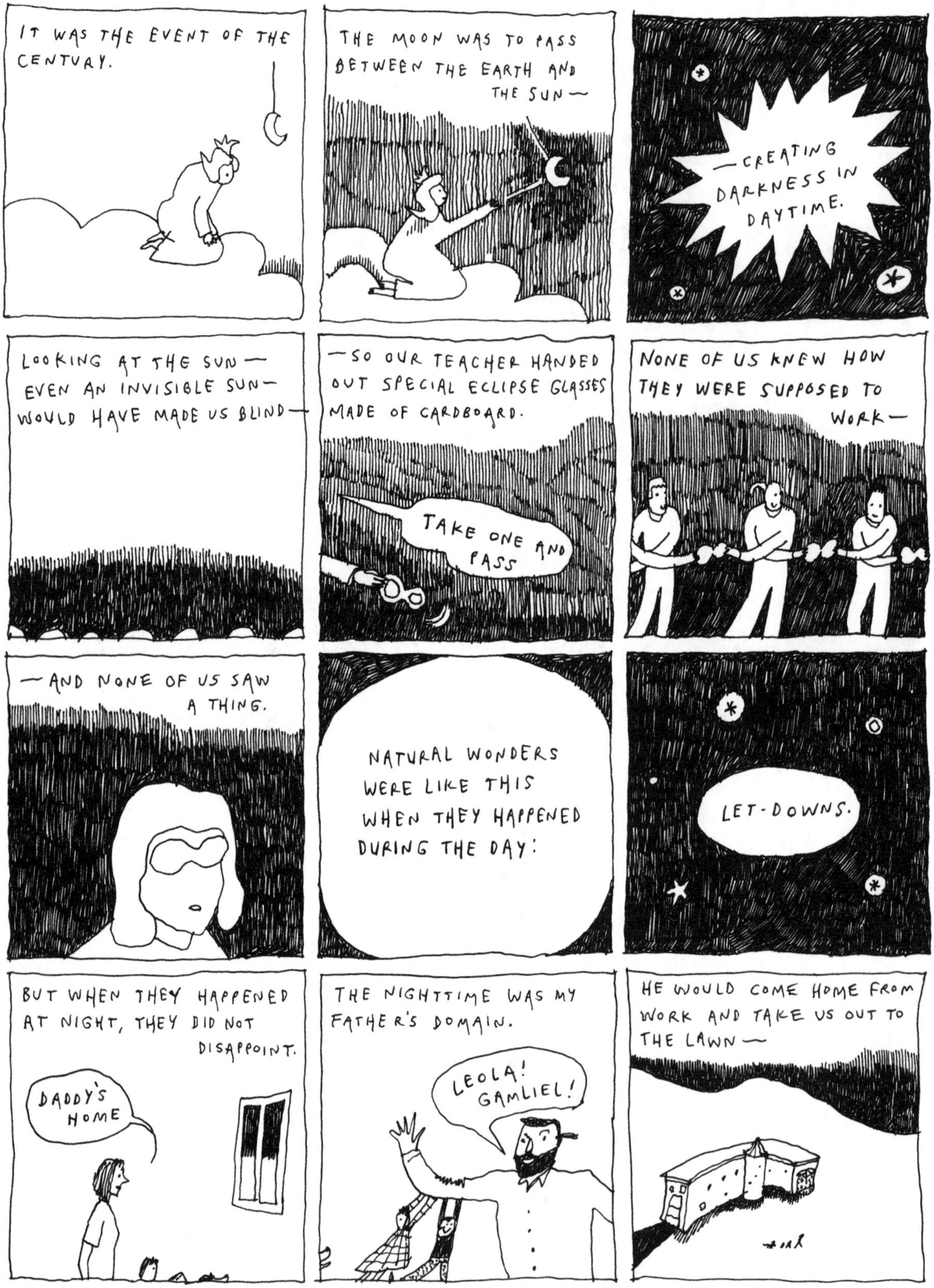
IT WAS THE EVENT OF THE CENTURY.
THE MOON WAS TO PASS BETWEEN THE EARTH AND THE SUN—
—CREATING DARKNESS IN DAYTIME.
LOOKING AT THE SUN— EVEN AN INVISIBLE SUN— WOULD HAVE MADE US BLIND—
—SO OUR TEACHER HANDED OUT SPECIAL ECLIPSE GLASSES MADE OF CARDBOARD.
TAKE ONE AND PASS
NONE OF US KNEW HOW THEY WERE SUPPOSED TO WORK—
—AND NONE OF US SAW A THING.
NATURAL WONDERS WERE LIKE THIS WHEN THEY HAPPENED DURING THE DAY:
LET-DOWNS.
BUT WHEN THEY HAPPENED AT NIGHT, THEY DID NOT DISAPPOINT.
DADDY'S HOME
THE NIGHTTIME WAS MY FATHER'S DOMAIN.
LEOLA! GAMLIEL!
HE WOULD COME HOME FROM WORK AND TAKE US OUT TO THE LAWN—

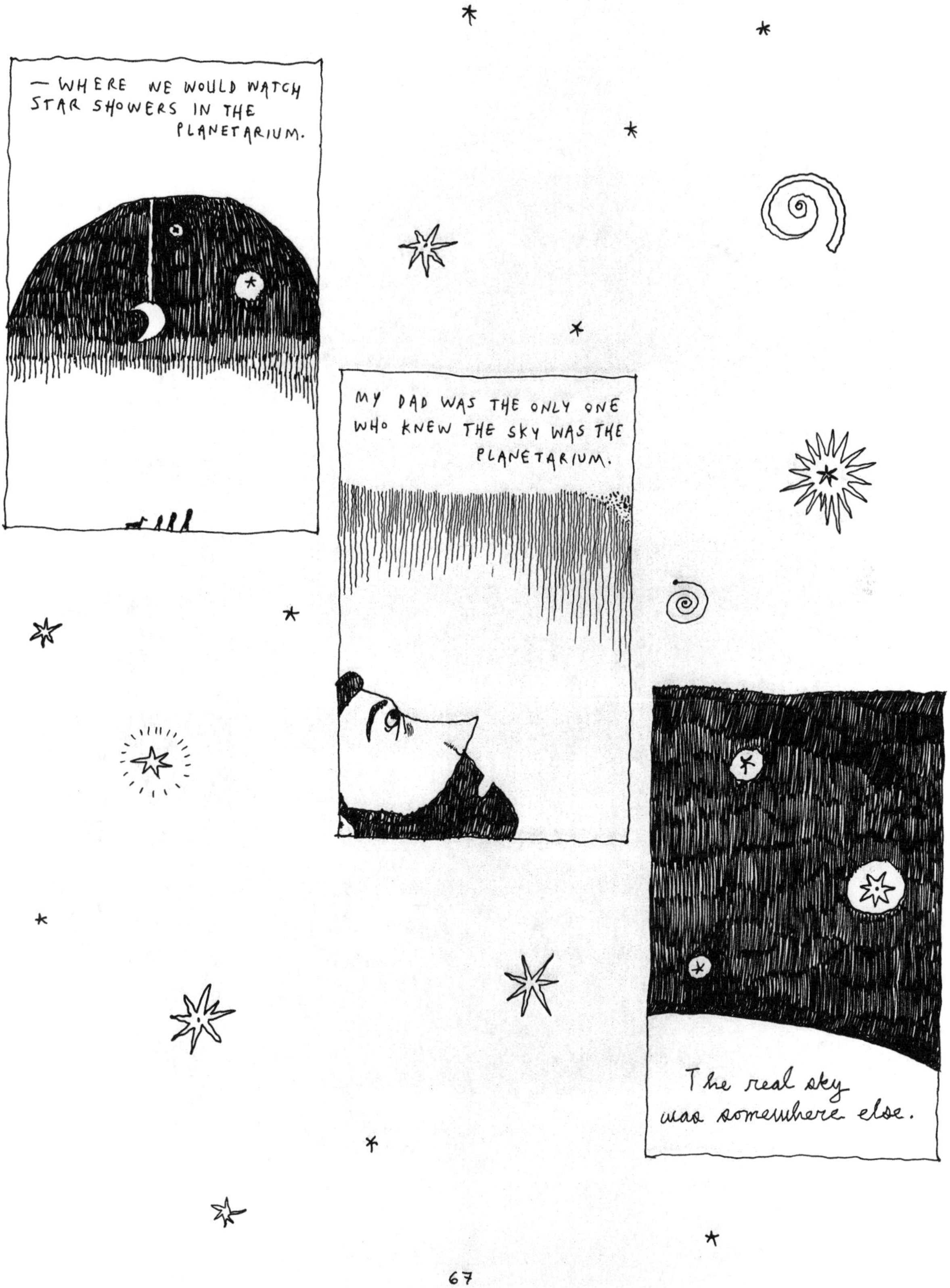
—WHERE WE WOULD WATCH STAR SHOWERS IN THE PLANETARIUM.
MY DAD WAS THE ONLY ONE WHO KNEW THE SKY WAS THE PLANETARIUM.
The real sky was somewhere else.

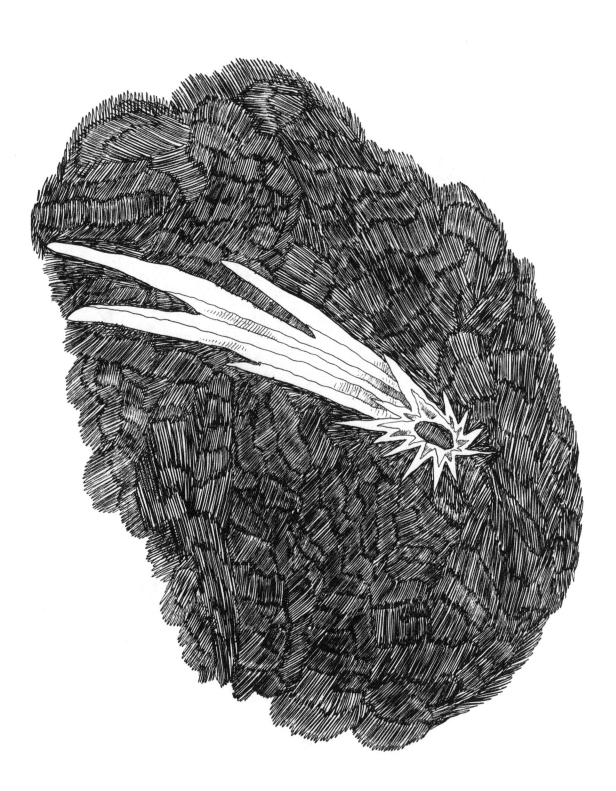

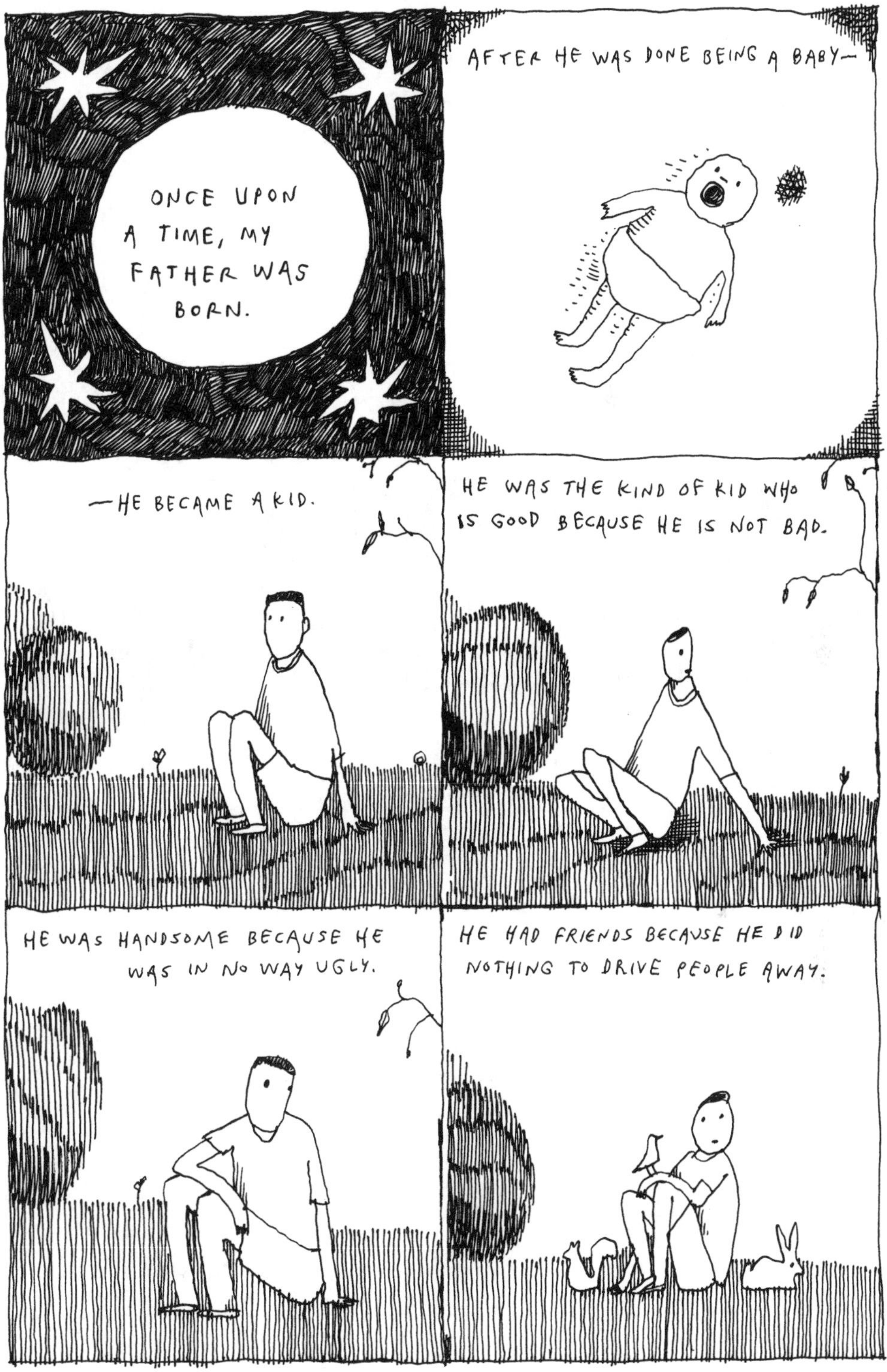
ONCE UPON A TIME, MY FATHER WAS BORN.
AFTER HE WAS DONE BEING A BABY—
—HE BECAME A KID.
HE WAS THE KIND OF KID WHO IS GOOD BECAUSE HE IS NOT BAD.
HE WAS HANDSOME BECAUSE HE WAS IN NO WAY UGLY.
HE HAD FRIENDS BECAUSE HE DID NOTHING TO DRIVE PEOPLE AWAY.

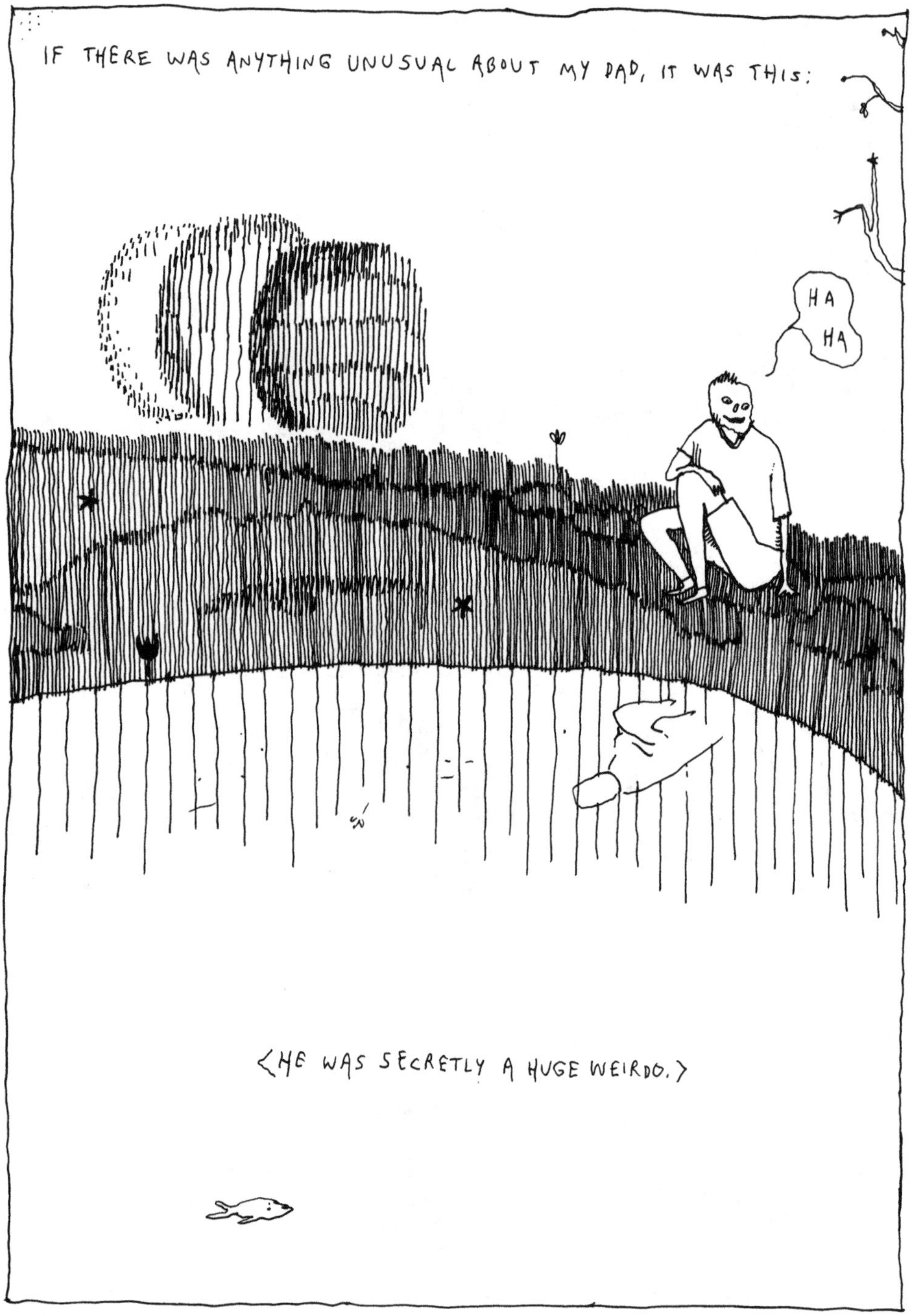
IF THERE WAS ANYTHING UNUSUAL ABOUT MY DAD, IT WAS THIS:
HA HA
<HE WAS SECRETLY A HUGE WEIRDO.>

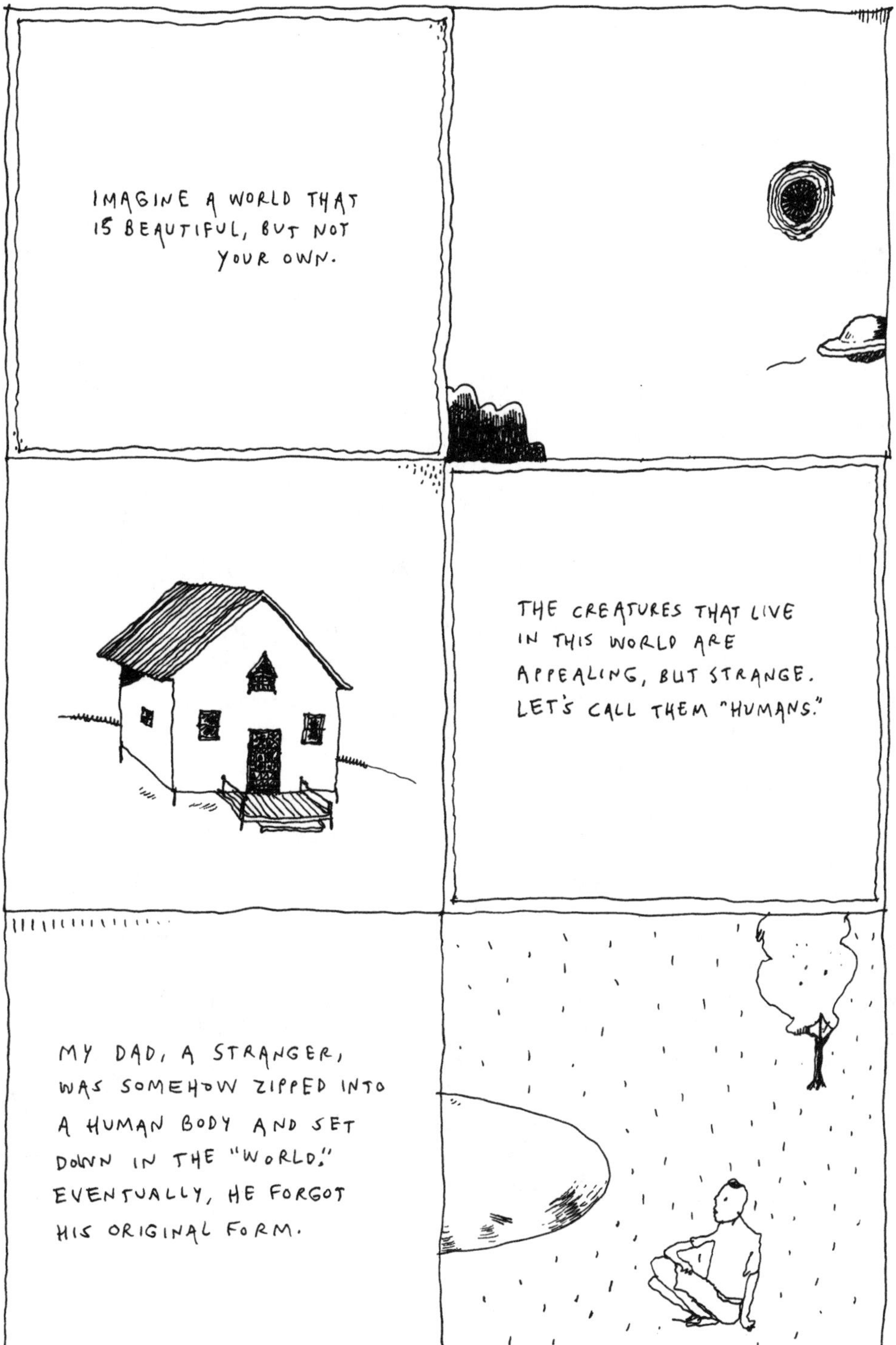
IMAGINE A WORLD THAT IS BEAUTIFUL, BUT NOT YOUR OWN.
THE CREATURES THAT LIVE IN THIS WORLD ARE APPEALING, BUT STRANGE. LET'S CALL THEM "HUMANS."
MY DAD, A STRANGER, WAS SOMEHOW ZIPPED INTO A HUMAN BODY AND SET DOWN IN THE "WORLD." EVENTUALLY, HE FORGOT HIS ORIGINAL FORM.

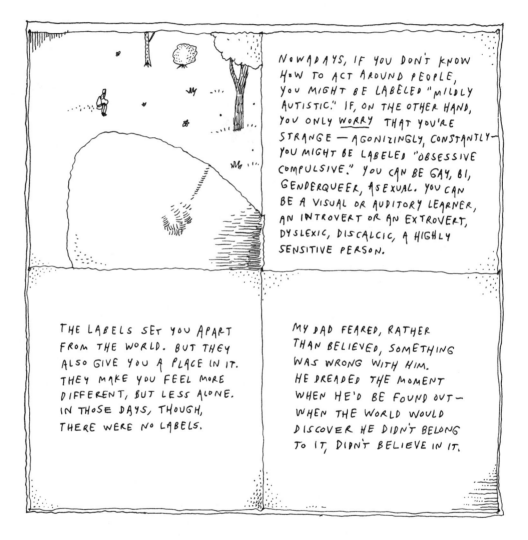

NOWADAYS, IF YOU DON'T KNOW HOW TO ACT AROUND PEOPLE, YOU MIGHT BE LABELED "MILDLY AUTISTIC." IF, ON THE OTHER HAND, YOU ONLY <u>WORRY</u> THAT YOU'RE STRANGE — AGONIZINGLY, CONSTANTLY — YOU MIGHT BE LABELED "OBSESSIVE COMPULSIVE." YOU CAN BE GAY, BI, GENDERQUEER, ASEXUAL. YOU CAN BE A VISUAL OR AUDITORY LEARNER, AN INTROVERT OR AN EXTROVERT, DYSLEXIC, DISCALCIC, A HIGHLY SENSITIVE PERSON.

THE LABELS SET YOU APART FROM THE WORLD. BUT THEY ALSO GIVE YOU A PLACE IN IT. THEY MAKE YOU FEEL MORE DIFFERENT, BUT LESS ALONE. IN THOSE DAYS, THOUGH, THERE WERE NO LABELS.

MY DAD FEARED, RATHER THAN BELIEVED, SOMETHING WAS WRONG WITH HIM. HE DREADED THE MOMENT WHEN HE'D BE FOUND OUT — WHEN THE WORLD WOULD DISCOVER HE DIDN'T BELONG TO IT, DIDN'T BELIEVE IN IT.

HE KNEW THAT WHATEVER LIFE IT WAS HE
WAS NOW LIVING WAS ONLY TEMPORARY—

—A MOMENT OF REPRIEVE BEFORE HE'D BE FOUND
OUT AND BANISHED TO SOME SMALL, DARK
CORNER OF CIVILIZATION.

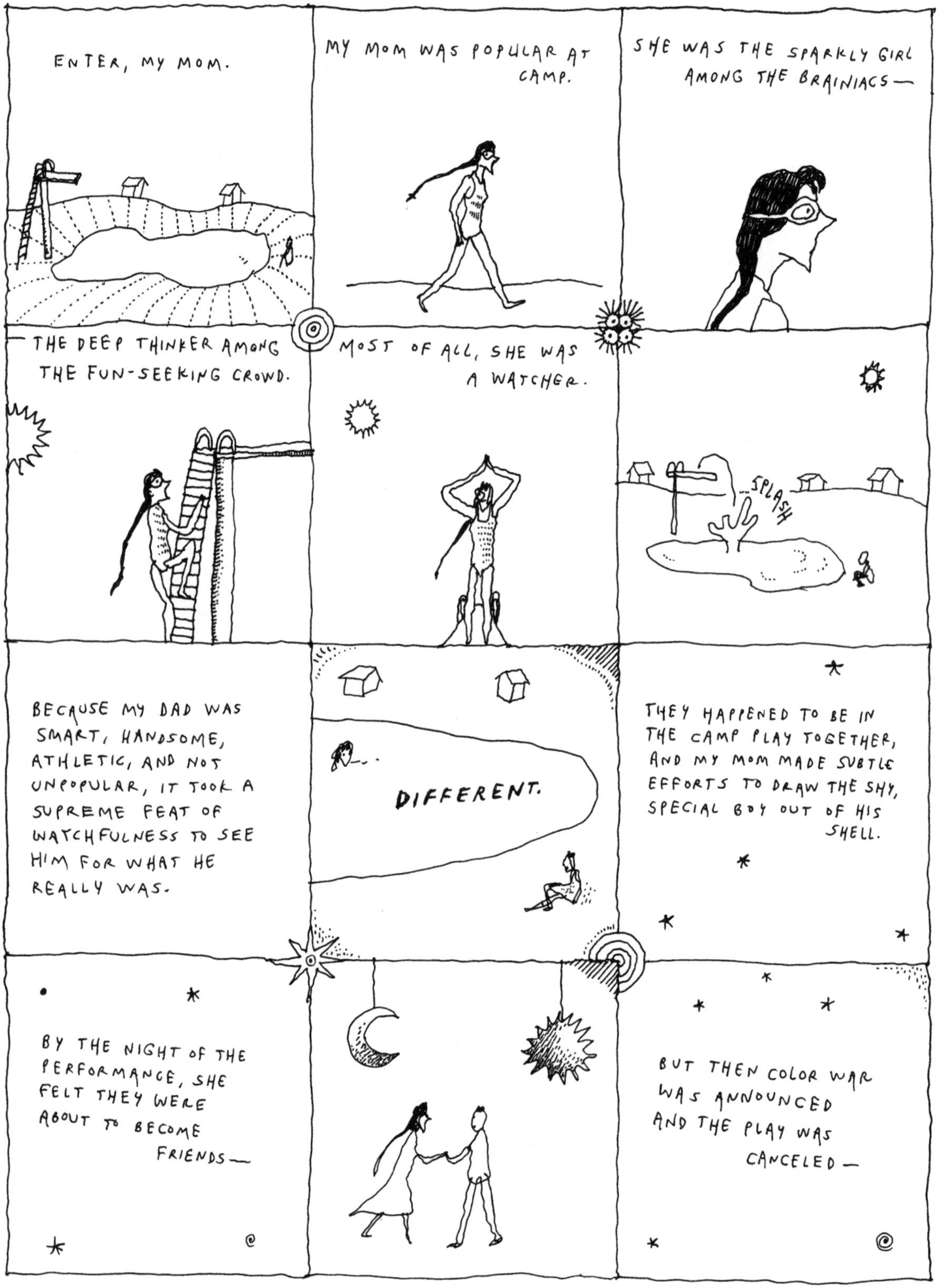
ENTER, MY MOM.
MY MOM WAS POPULAR AT CAMP.
SHE WAS THE SPARKLY GIRL AMONG THE BRAINIACS—
—THE DEEP THINKER AMONG THE FUN-SEEKING CROWD.
MOST OF ALL, SHE WAS A WATCHER.
SPLASH
BECAUSE MY DAD WAS SMART, HANDSOME, ATHLETIC, AND NOT UNPOPULAR, IT TOOK A SUPREME FEAT OF WATCHFULNESS TO SEE HIM FOR WHAT HE REALLY WAS.
DIFFERENT.
THEY HAPPENED TO BE IN THE CAMP PLAY TOGETHER, AND MY MOM MADE SUBTLE EFFORTS TO DRAW THE SHY, SPECIAL BOY OUT OF HIS SHELL.
BY THE NIGHT OF THE PERFORMANCE, SHE FELT THEY WERE ABOUT TO BECOME FRIENDS—
BUT THEN COLOR WAR WAS ANNOUNCED AND THE PLAY WAS CANCELED—

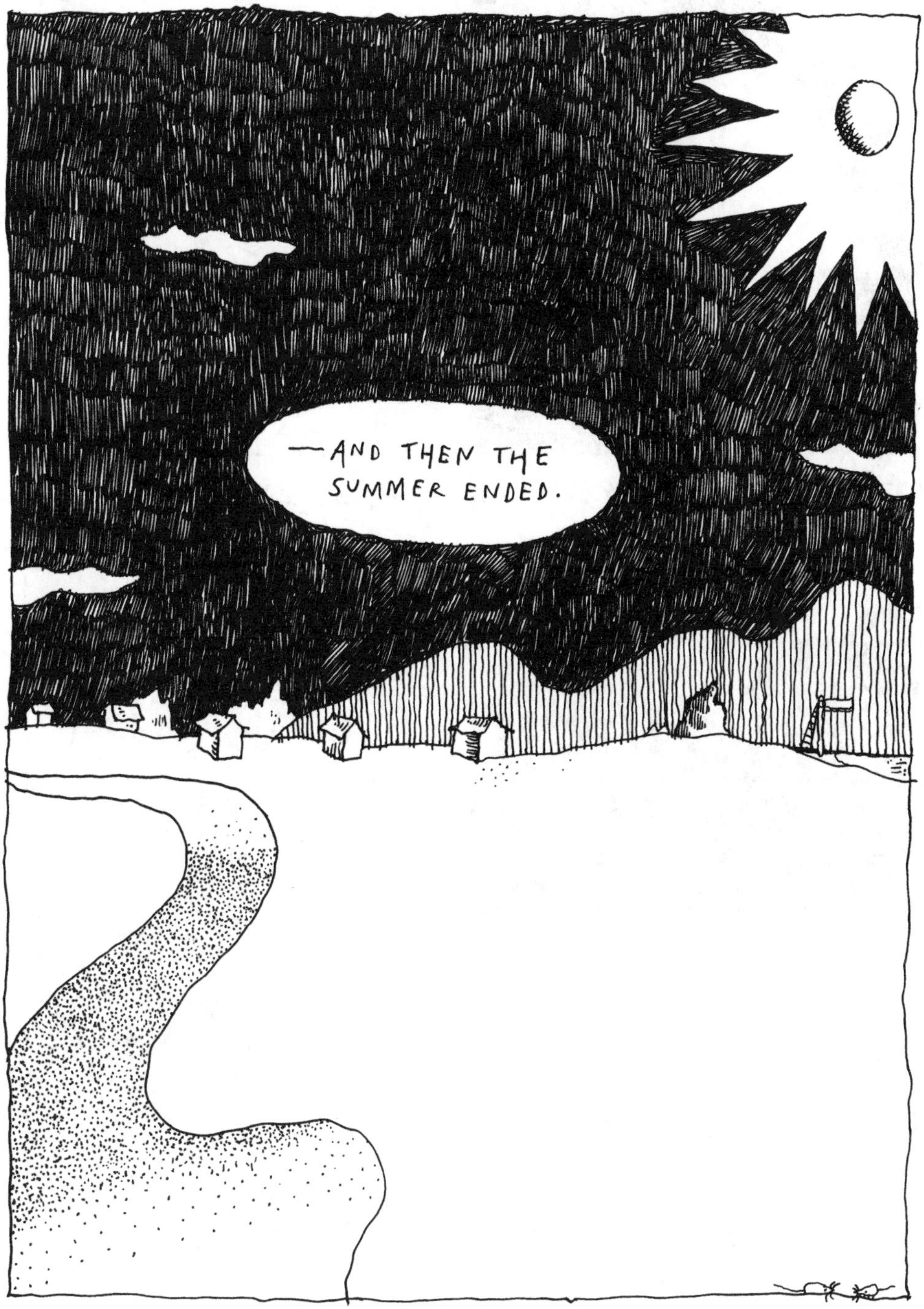
—AND THEN THE SUMMER ENDED.

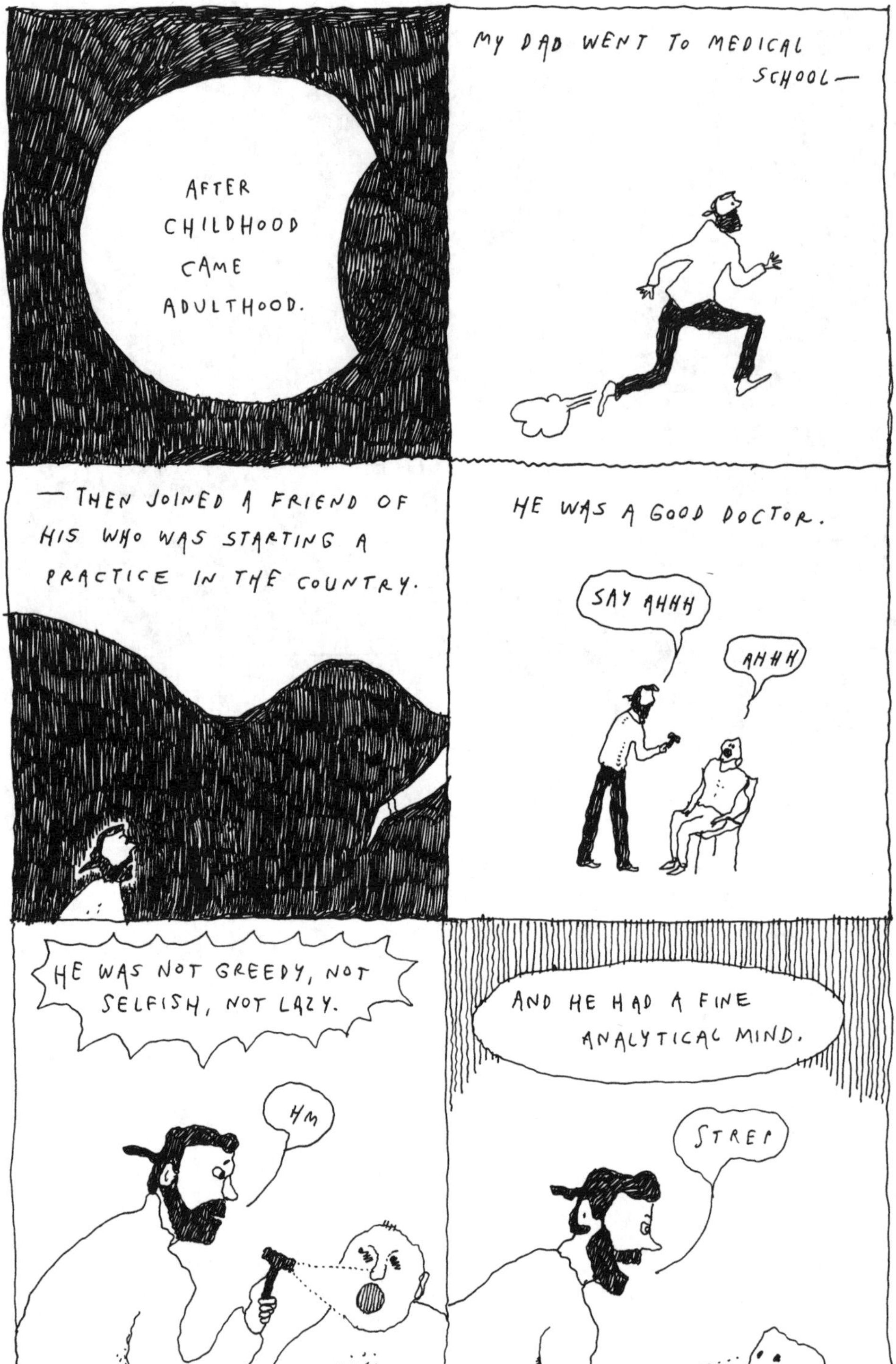
AFTER CHILDHOOD CAME ADULTHOOD.
MY DAD WENT TO MEDICAL SCHOOL—
—THEN JOINED A FRIEND OF HIS WHO WAS STARTING A PRACTICE IN THE COUNTRY.
HE WAS A GOOD DOCTOR.
SAY AHHH
AHHH
HE WAS NOT GREEDY, NOT SELFISH, NOT LAZY.
HM
AND HE HAD A FINE ANALYTICAL MIND.
STREP

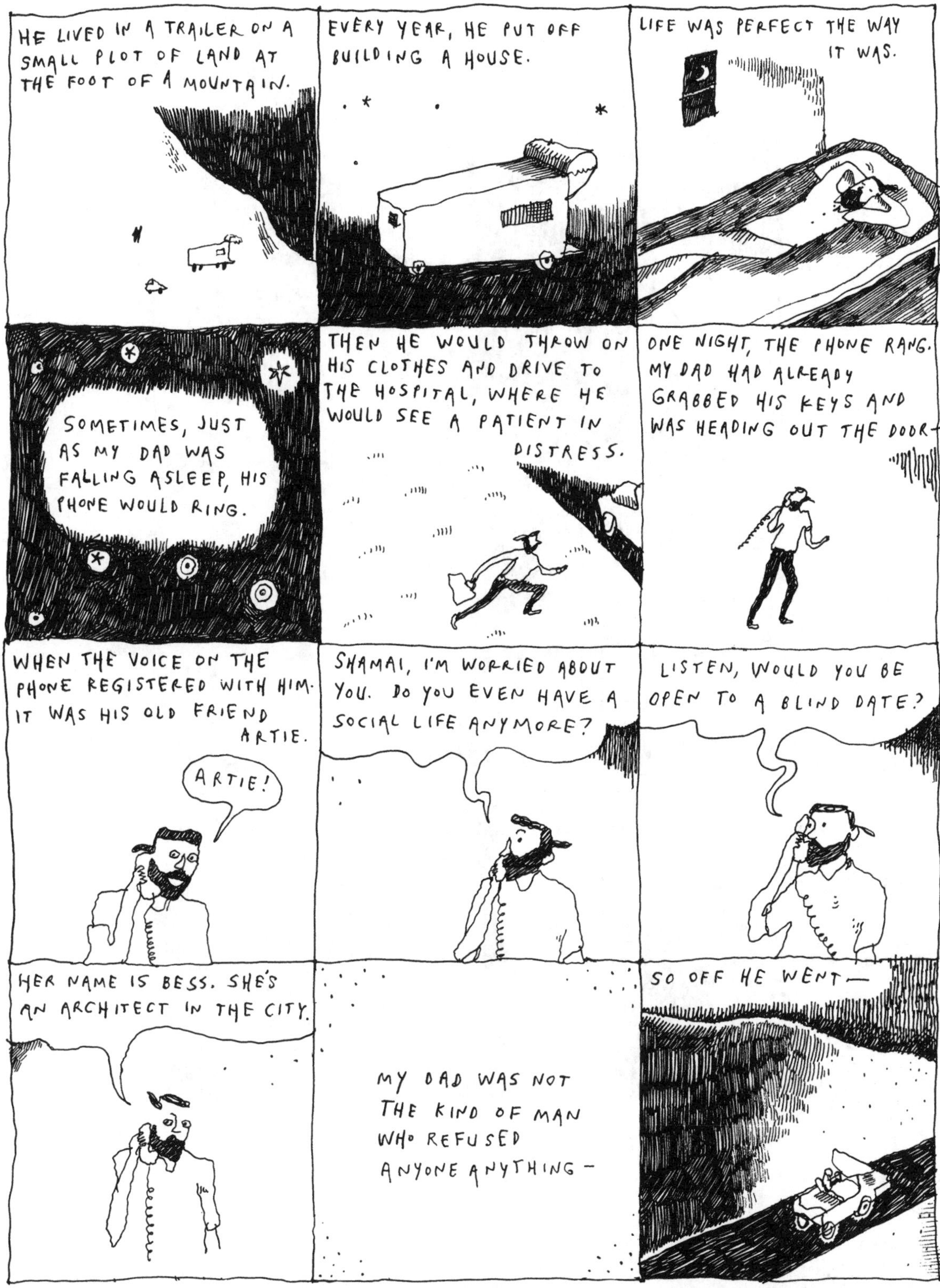
HE LIVED IN A TRAILER ON A SMALL PLOT OF LAND AT THE FOOT OF A MOUNTAIN.
EVERY YEAR, HE PUT OFF BUILDING A HOUSE.
LIFE WAS PERFECT THE WAY IT WAS.
SOMETIMES, JUST AS MY DAD WAS FALLING ASLEEP, HIS PHONE WOULD RING.
THEN HE WOULD THROW ON HIS CLOTHES AND DRIVE TO THE HOSPITAL, WHERE HE WOULD SEE A PATIENT IN DISTRESS.
ONE NIGHT, THE PHONE RANG. MY DAD HAD ALREADY GRABBED HIS KEYS AND WAS HEADING OUT THE DOOR—
WHEN THE VOICE ON THE PHONE REGISTERED WITH HIM. IT WAS HIS OLD FRIEND ARTIE.
ARTIE!
SHAMAI, I'M WORRIED ABOUT YOU. DO YOU EVEN HAVE A SOCIAL LIFE ANYMORE?
LISTEN, WOULD YOU BE OPEN TO A BLIND DATE?
HER NAME IS BESS. SHE'S AN ARCHITECT IN THE CITY.
MY DAD WAS NOT THE KIND OF MAN WHO REFUSED ANYONE ANYTHING—
SO OFF HE WENT—

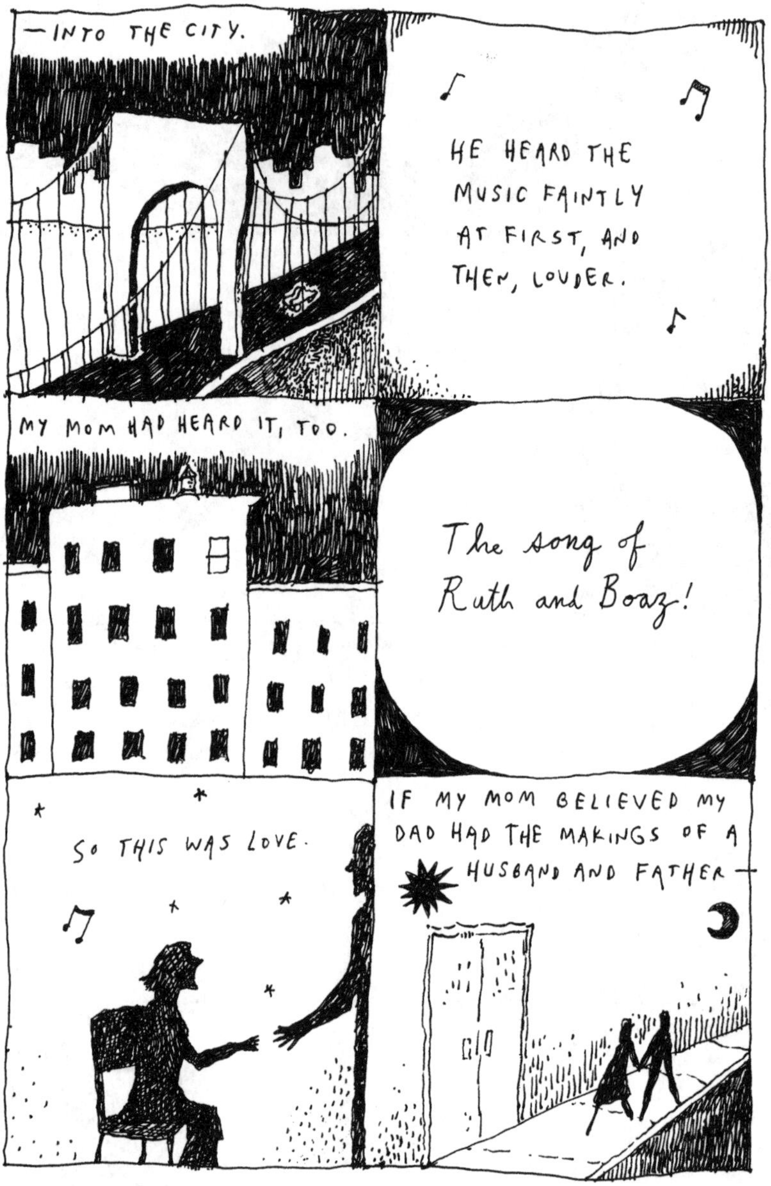
—INTO THE CITY.
HE HEARD THE MUSIC FAINTLY AT FIRST, AND THEN, LOUDER.
MY MOM HAD HEARD IT, TOO.
The song of Ruth and Boaz!
SO THIS WAS LOVE.
IF MY MOM BELIEVED MY DAD HAD THE MAKINGS OF A HUSBAND AND FATHER—

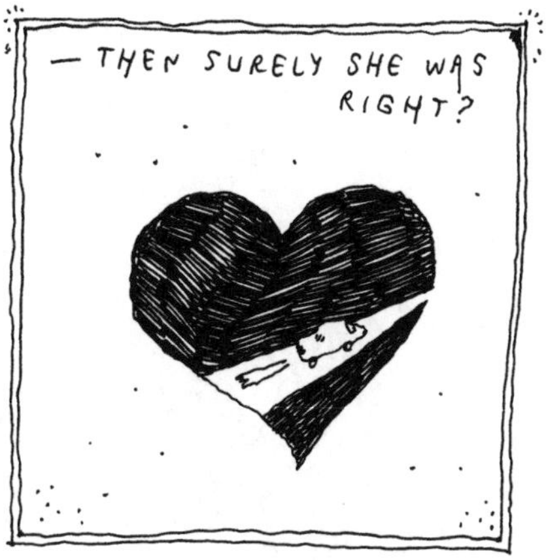
— THEN SURELY SHE WAS RIGHT?

IF YOU INTEND TO CREATE A WORLD—

—YOU NEED TO LEAVE THE REAL WORLD BEHIND.

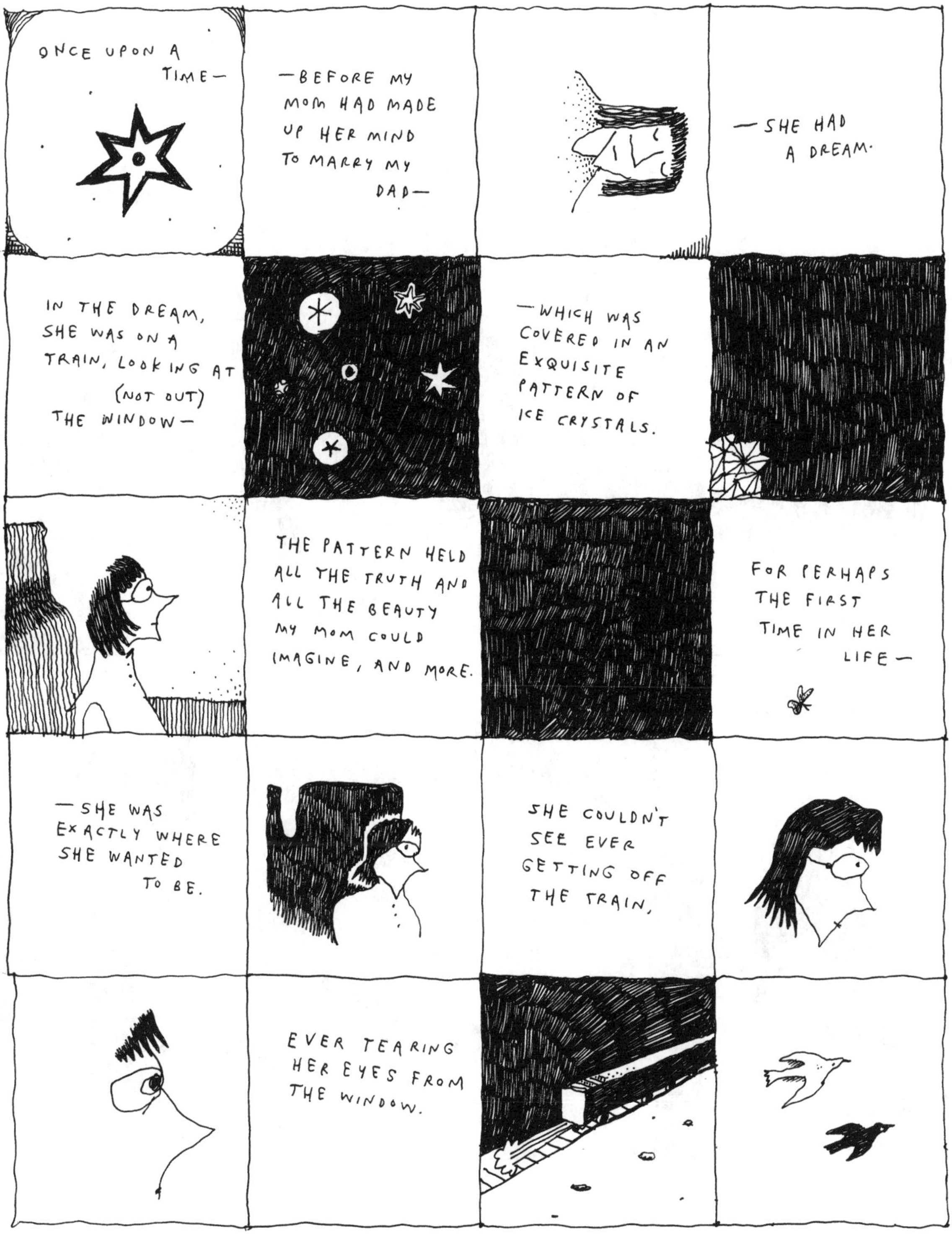
ONCE UPON A TIME—
—BEFORE MY MOM HAD MADE UP HER MIND TO MARRY MY DAD—
—SHE HAD A DREAM.
IN THE DREAM, SHE WAS ON A TRAIN, LOOKING AT (NOT OUT) THE WINDOW—
—WHICH WAS COVERED IN AN EXQUISITE PATTERN OF ICE CRYSTALS.
THE PATTERN HELD ALL THE TRUTH AND ALL THE BEAUTY MY MOM COULD IMAGINE, AND MORE.
FOR PERHAPS THE FIRST TIME IN HER LIFE—
—SHE WAS EXACTLY WHERE SHE WANTED TO BE.
SHE COULDN'T SEE EVER GETTING OFF THE TRAIN,
EVER TEARING HER EYES FROM THE WINDOW.

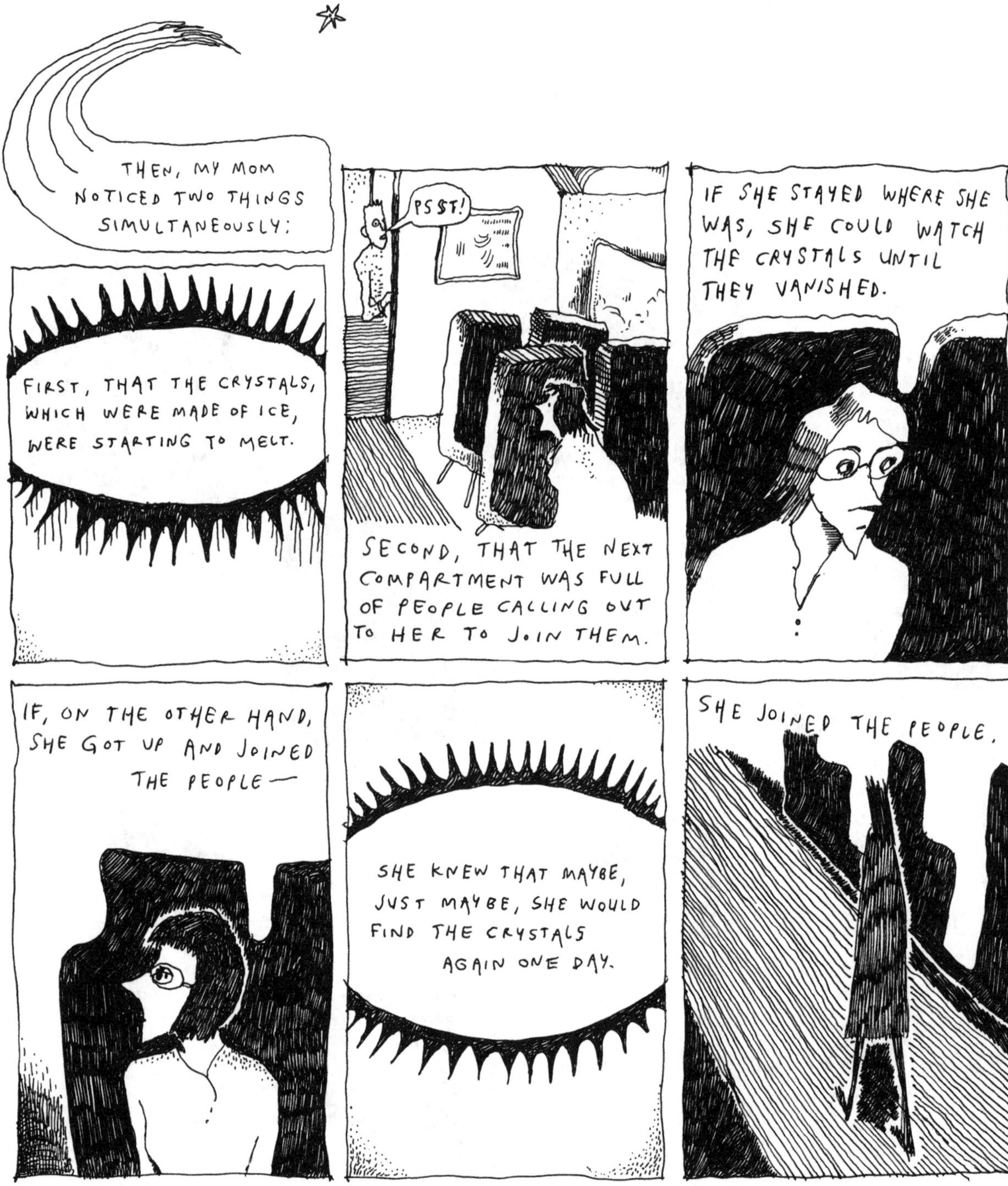
THEN, MY MOM NOTICED TWO THINGS SIMULTANEOUSLY:
FIRST, THAT THE CRYSTALS, WHICH WERE MADE OF ICE, WERE STARTING TO MELT.
PSSST!
SECOND, THAT THE NEXT COMPARTMENT WAS FULL OF PEOPLE CALLING OUT TO HER TO JOIN THEM.
IF SHE STAYED WHERE SHE WAS, SHE COULD WATCH THE CRYSTALS UNTIL THEY VANISHED.
IF, ON THE OTHER HAND, SHE GOT UP AND JOINED THE PEOPLE—
SHE KNEW THAT MAYBE, JUST MAYBE, SHE WOULD FIND THE CRYSTALS AGAIN ONE DAY.
SHE JOINED THE PEOPLE.

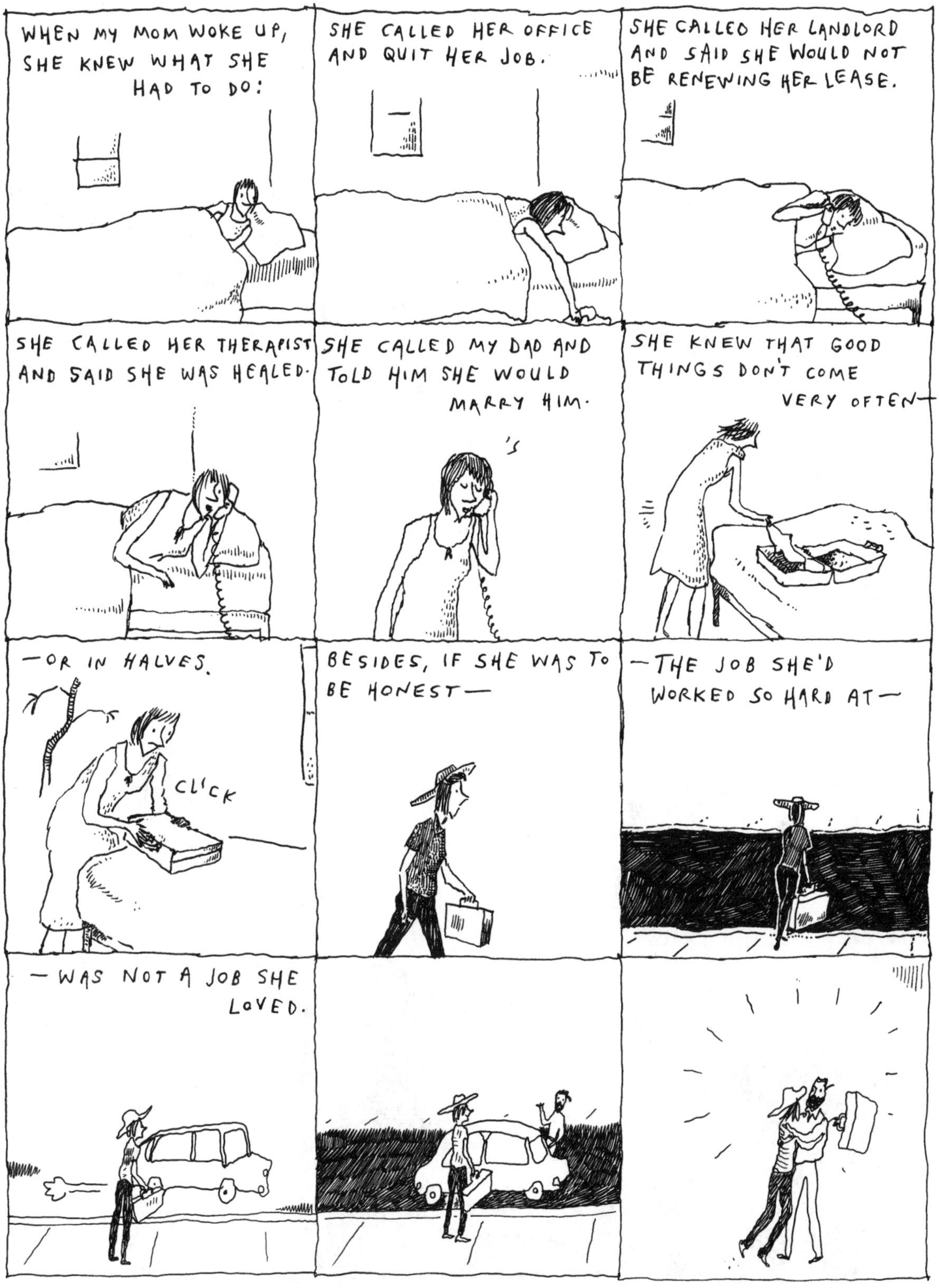
WHEN MY MOM WOKE UP, SHE KNEW WHAT SHE HAD TO DO:
SHE CALLED HER OFFICE AND QUIT HER JOB.
SHE CALLED HER LANDLORD AND SAID SHE WOULD NOT BE RENEWING HER LEASE.
SHE CALLED HER THERAPIST AND SAID SHE WAS HEALED.
SHE CALLED MY DAD AND TOLD HIM SHE WOULD MARRY HIM.
SHE KNEW THAT GOOD THINGS DON'T COME VERY OFTEN—
—OR IN HALVES.
CLICK
BESIDES, IF SHE WAS TO BE HONEST—
—THE JOB SHE'D WORKED SO HARD AT—
—WAS NOT A JOB SHE LOVED.

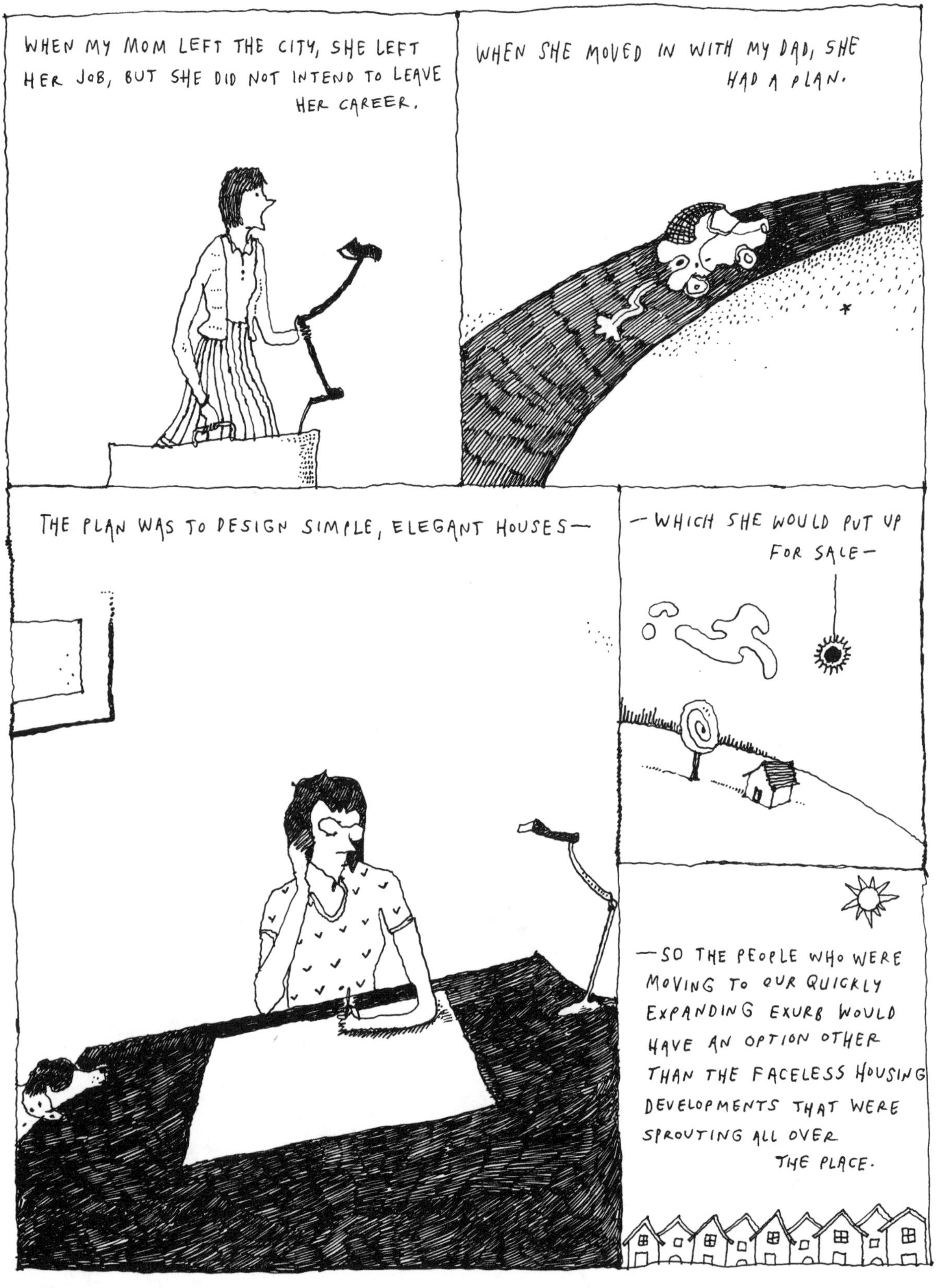
WHEN MY MOM LEFT THE CITY, SHE LEFT HER JOB, BUT SHE DID NOT INTEND TO LEAVE HER CAREER.
WHEN SHE MOVED IN WITH MY DAD, SHE HAD A PLAN.
THE PLAN WAS TO DESIGN SIMPLE, ELEGANT HOUSES—
—WHICH SHE WOULD PUT UP FOR SALE—
—SO THE PEOPLE WHO WERE MOVING TO OUR QUICKLY EXPANDING EXURB WOULD HAVE AN OPTION OTHER THAN THE FACELESS HOUSING DEVELOPMENTS THAT WERE SPROUTING ALL OVER THE PLACE.

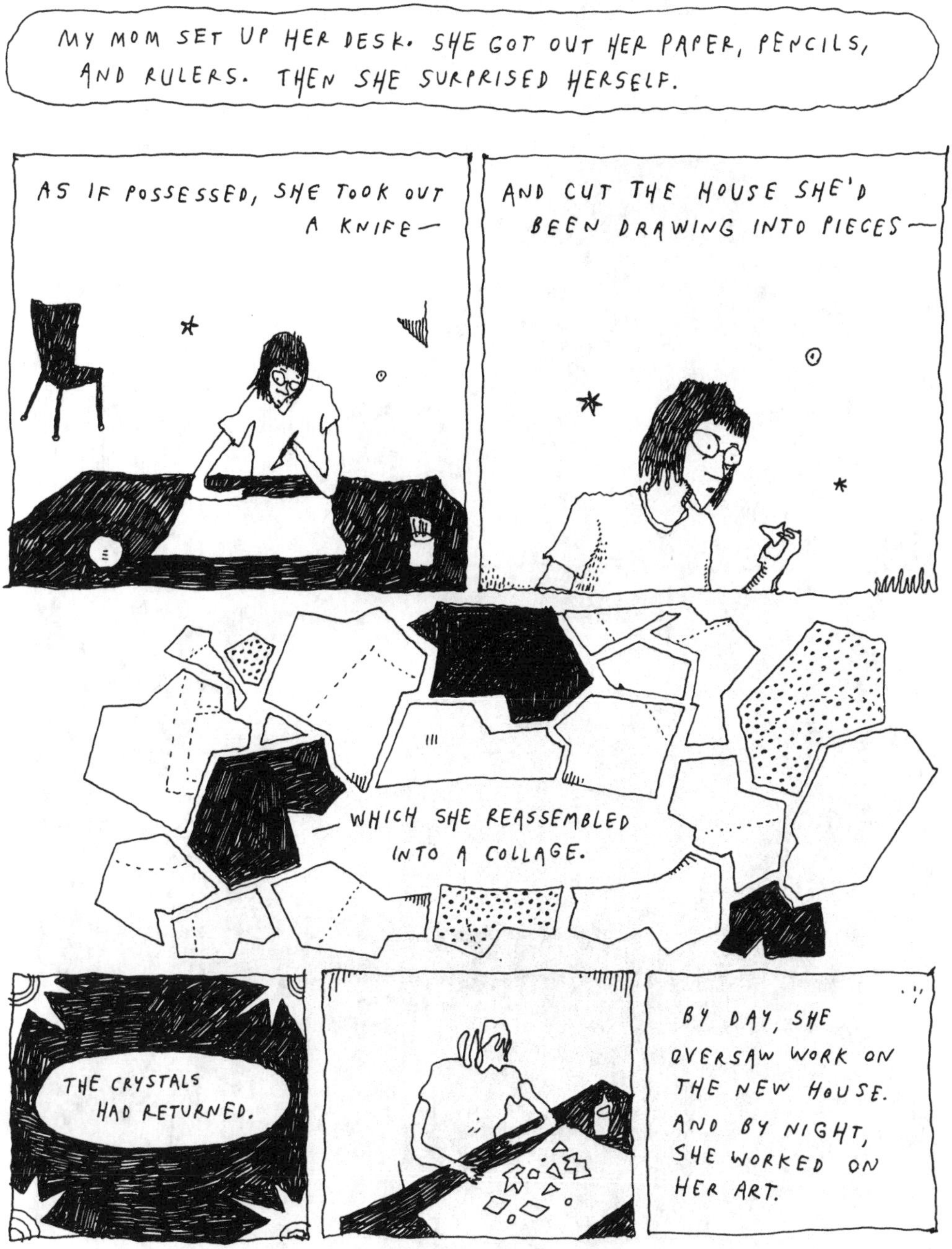
MY MOM SET UP HER DESK. SHE GOT OUT HER PAPER, PENCILS, AND RULERS. THEN SHE SURPRISED HERSELF.
AS IF POSSESSED, SHE TOOK OUT A KNIFE—
AND CUT THE HOUSE SHE'D BEEN DRAWING INTO PIECES—
—WHICH SHE REASSEMBLED INTO A COLLAGE.
THE CRYSTALS HAD RETURNED.
BY DAY, SHE OVERSAW WORK ON THE NEW HOUSE.
AND BY NIGHT, SHE WORKED ON HER ART.

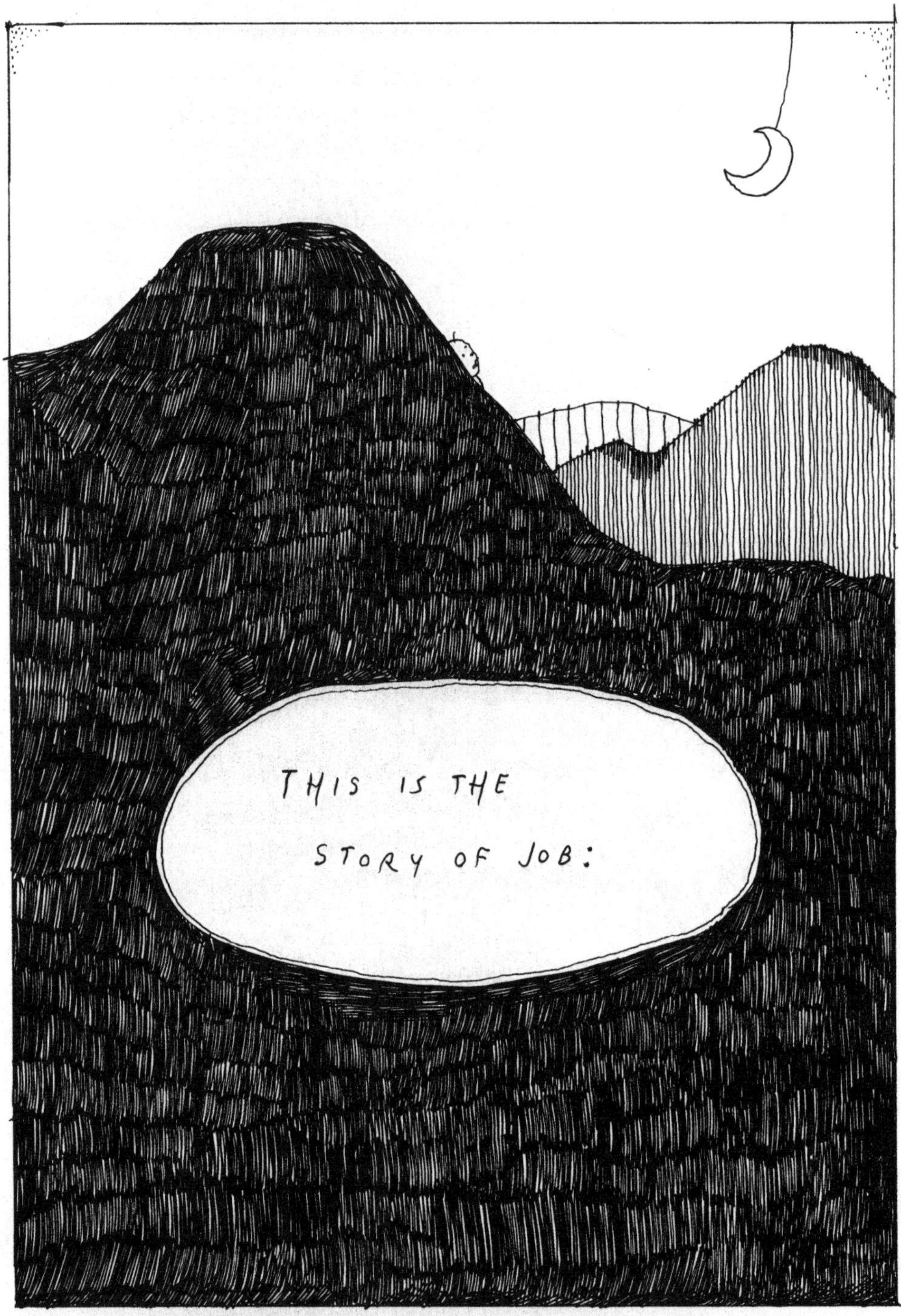
THIS IS THE
STORY OF JOB:

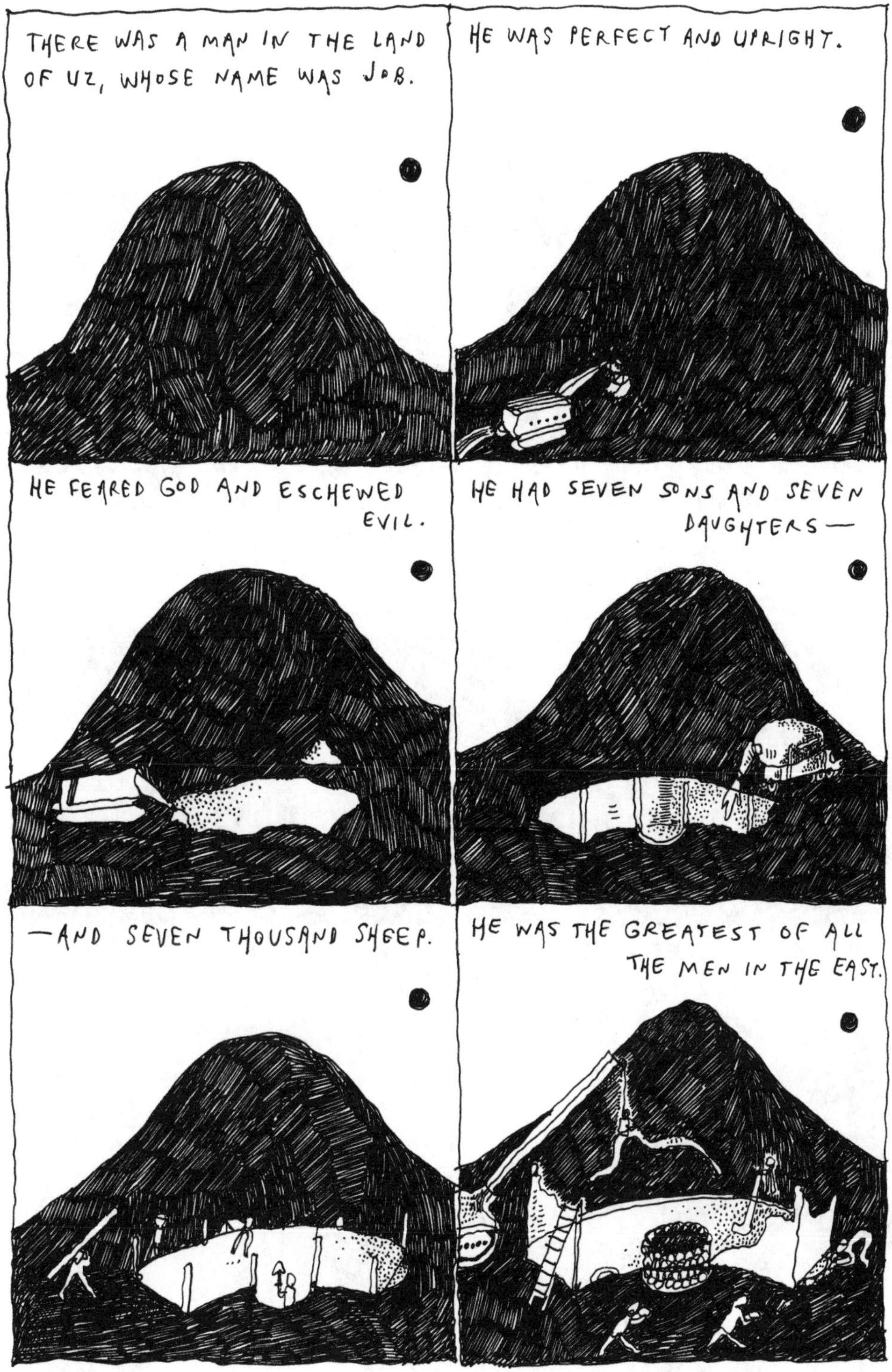

THERE WAS A MAN IN THE LAND OF UZ, WHOSE NAME WAS JOB.
HE WAS PERFECT AND UPRIGHT.
HE FEARED GOD AND ESCHEWED EVIL.
HE HAD SEVEN SONS AND SEVEN DAUGHTERS—
—AND SEVEN THOUSAND SHEEP.
HE WAS THE GREATEST OF ALL THE MEN IN THE EAST.

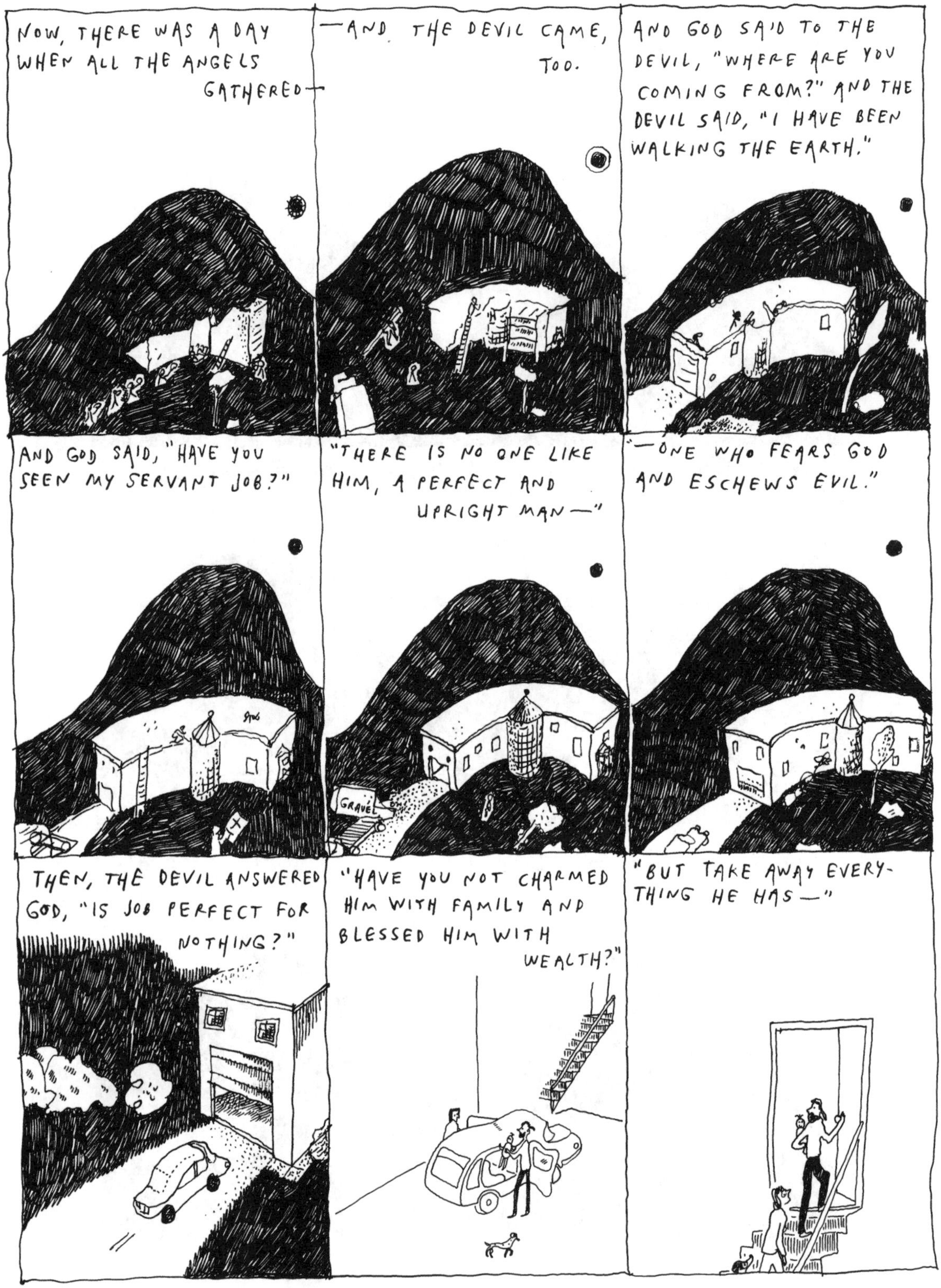
NOW, THERE WAS A DAY WHEN ALL THE ANGELS GATHERED—
—AND THE DEVIL CAME, TOO.
AND GOD SAID TO THE DEVIL, "WHERE ARE YOU COMING FROM?" AND THE DEVIL SAID, "I HAVE BEEN WALKING THE EARTH."
AND GOD SAID, "HAVE YOU SEEN MY SERVANT JOB?"
"THERE IS NO ONE LIKE HIM, A PERFECT AND UPRIGHT MAN—"
GRAVEL
"—ONE WHO FEARS GOD AND ESCHEWS EVIL."
THEN, THE DEVIL ANSWERED GOD, "IS JOB PERFECT FOR NOTHING?"
"HAVE YOU NOT CHARMED HIM WITH FAMILY AND BLESSED HIM WITH WEALTH?"
"BUT TAKE AWAY EVERYTHING HE HAS—"

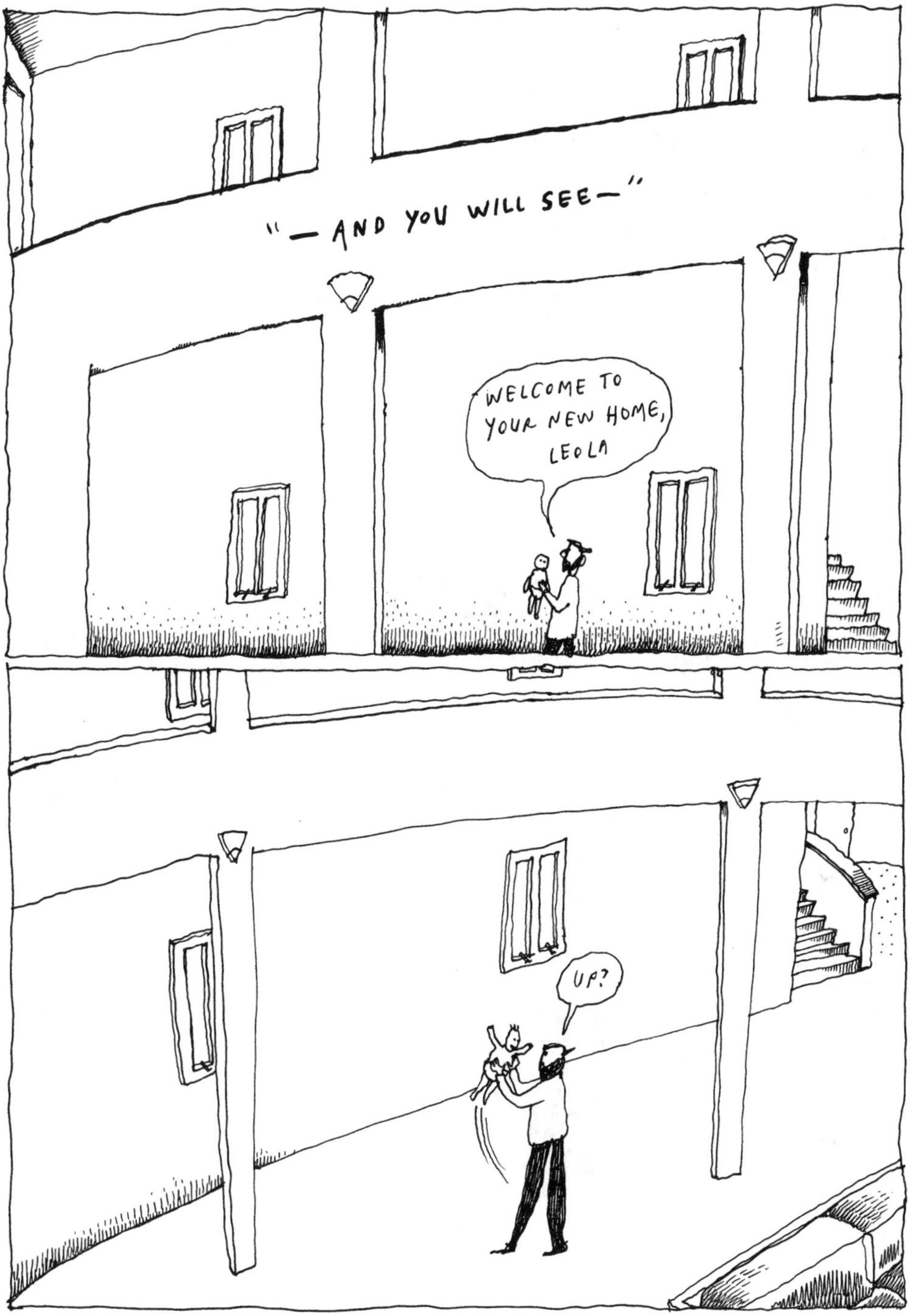
"—AND YOU WILL SEE—"
WELCOME TO YOUR NEW HOME, LEOLA
UP?

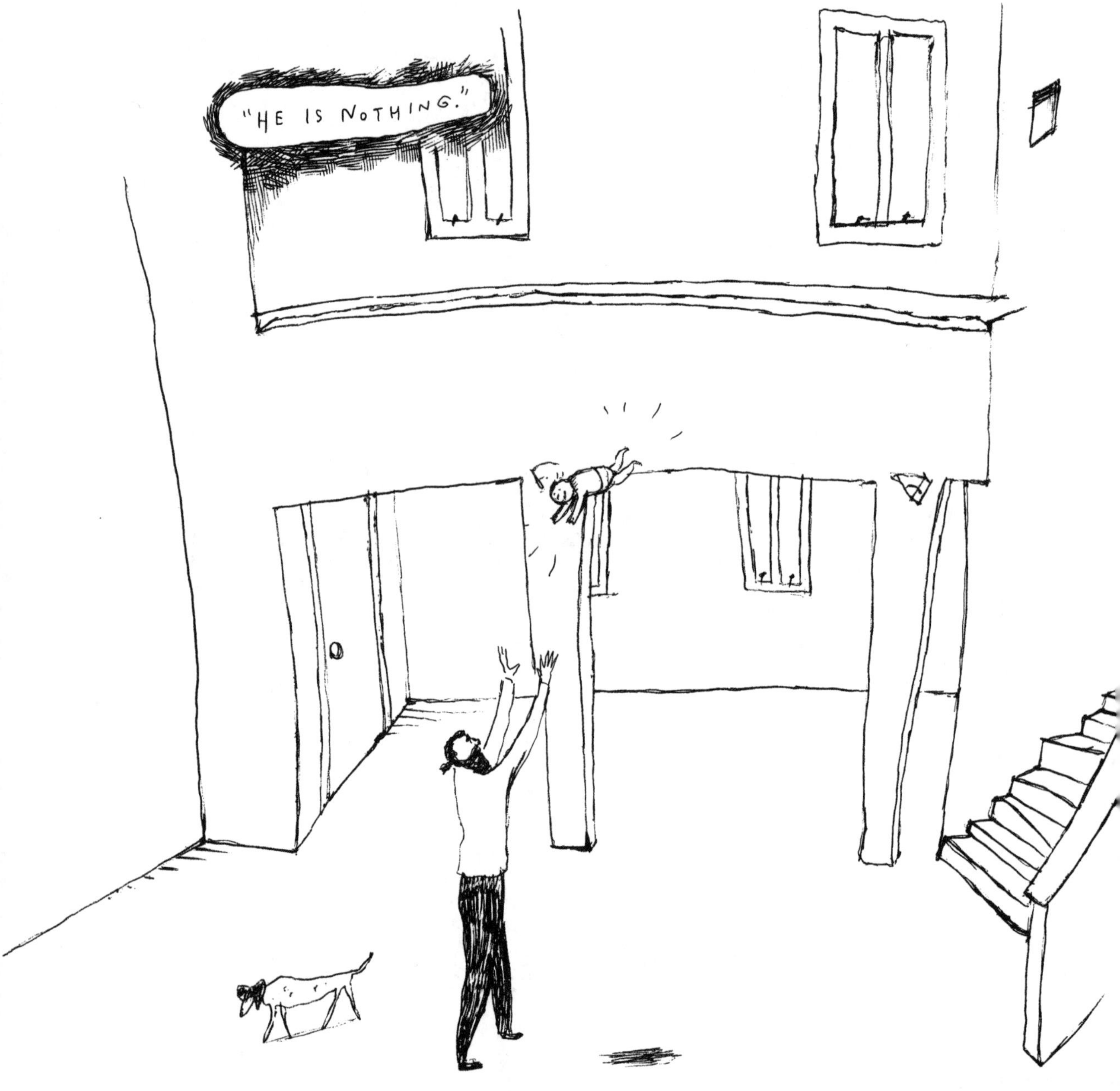
"HE IS NOTHING."

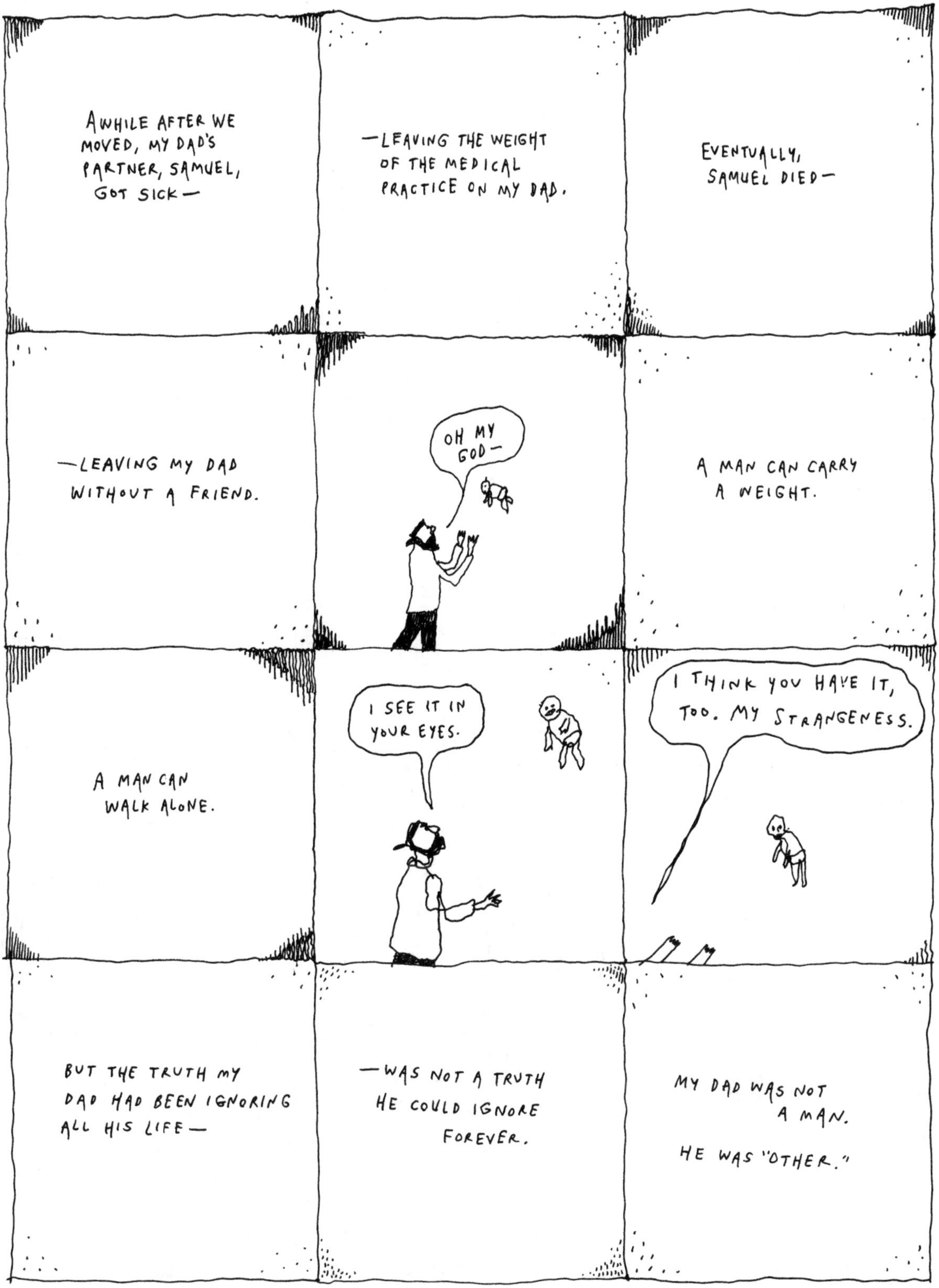
AWHILE AFTER WE MOVED, MY DAD'S PARTNER, SAMUEL, GOT SICK—
—LEAVING THE WEIGHT OF THE MEDICAL PRACTICE ON MY DAD.
EVENTUALLY, SAMUEL DIED—
—LEAVING MY DAD WITHOUT A FRIEND.
OH MY GOD—
A MAN CAN CARRY A WEIGHT.
A MAN CAN WALK ALONE.
I SEE IT IN YOUR EYES.
I THINK YOU HAVE IT, TOO. MY STRANGENESS.
BUT THE TRUTH MY DAD HAD BEEN IGNORING ALL HIS LIFE—
—WAS NOT A TRUTH HE COULD IGNORE FOREVER.
MY DAD WAS NOT A MAN.
HE WAS "OTHER."

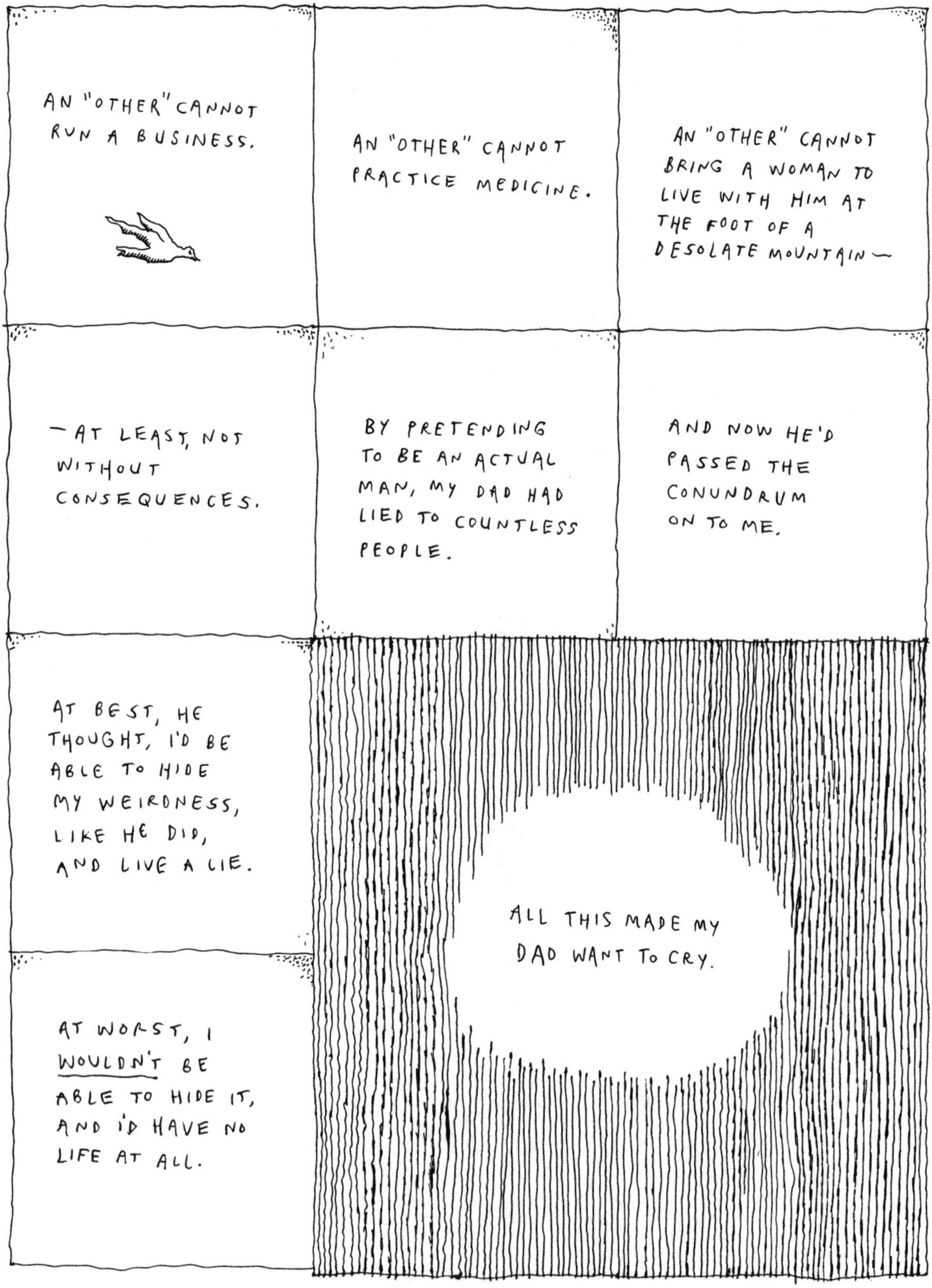
AN "OTHER" CANNOT RUN A BUSINESS.
AN "OTHER" CANNOT PRACTICE MEDICINE.
AN "OTHER" CANNOT BRING A WOMAN TO LIVE WITH HIM AT THE FOOT OF A DESOLATE MOUNTAIN—
—AT LEAST, NOT WITHOUT CONSEQUENCES.
BY PRETENDING TO BE AN ACTUAL MAN, MY DAD HAD LIED TO COUNTLESS PEOPLE.
AND NOW HE'D PASSED THE CONUNDRUM ON TO ME.
AT BEST, HE THOUGHT, I'D BE ABLE TO HIDE MY WEIRDNESS, LIKE HE DID, AND LIVE A LIE.
AT WORST, I WOULDN'T BE ABLE TO HIDE IT, AND I'D HAVE NO LIFE AT ALL.
ALL THIS MADE MY DAD WANT TO CRY.

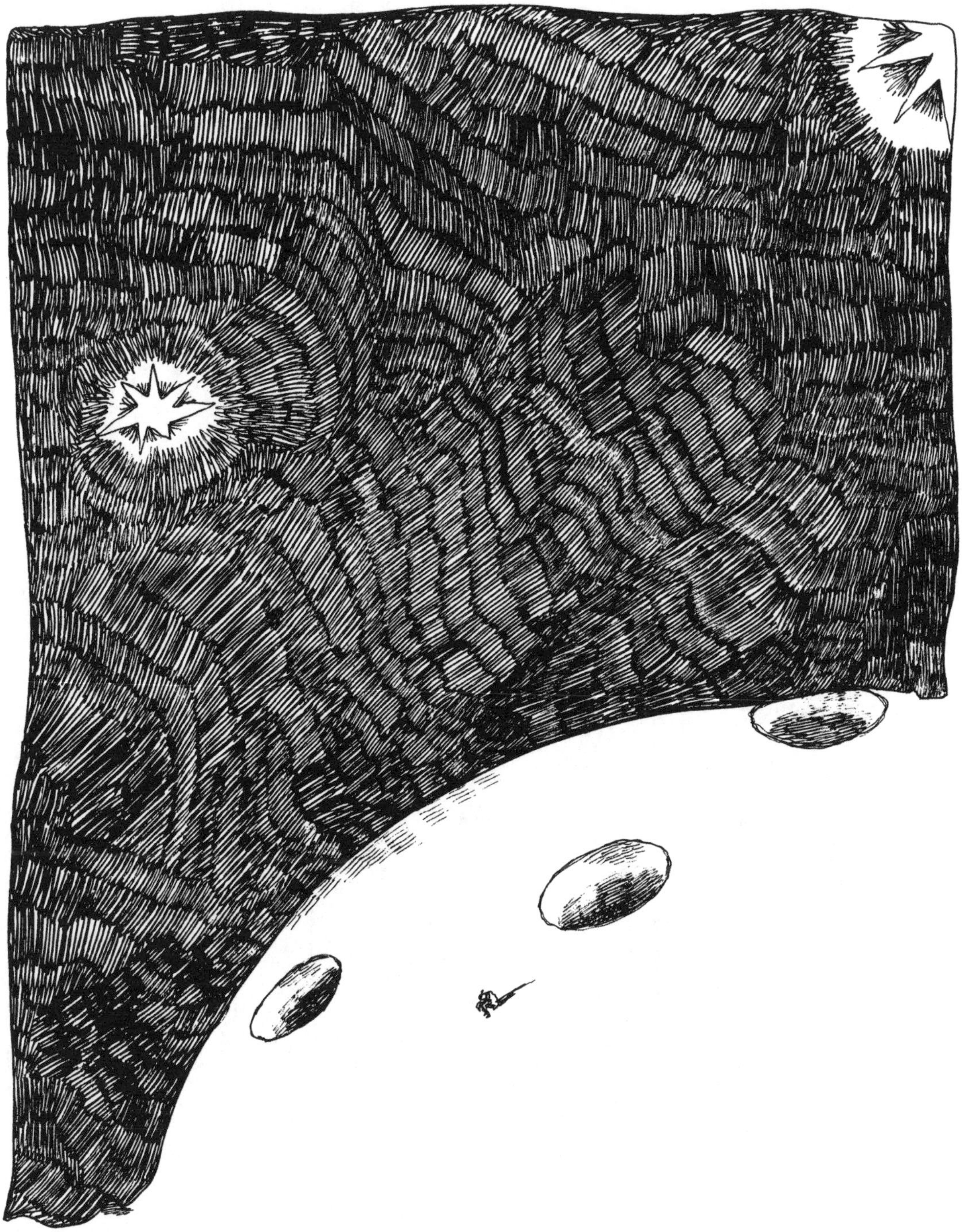

NOW, THE TEARS
OF MEN ARE
CORROSIVE.

THEY BURN
THROUGH THE
SOCIAL FABRIC.

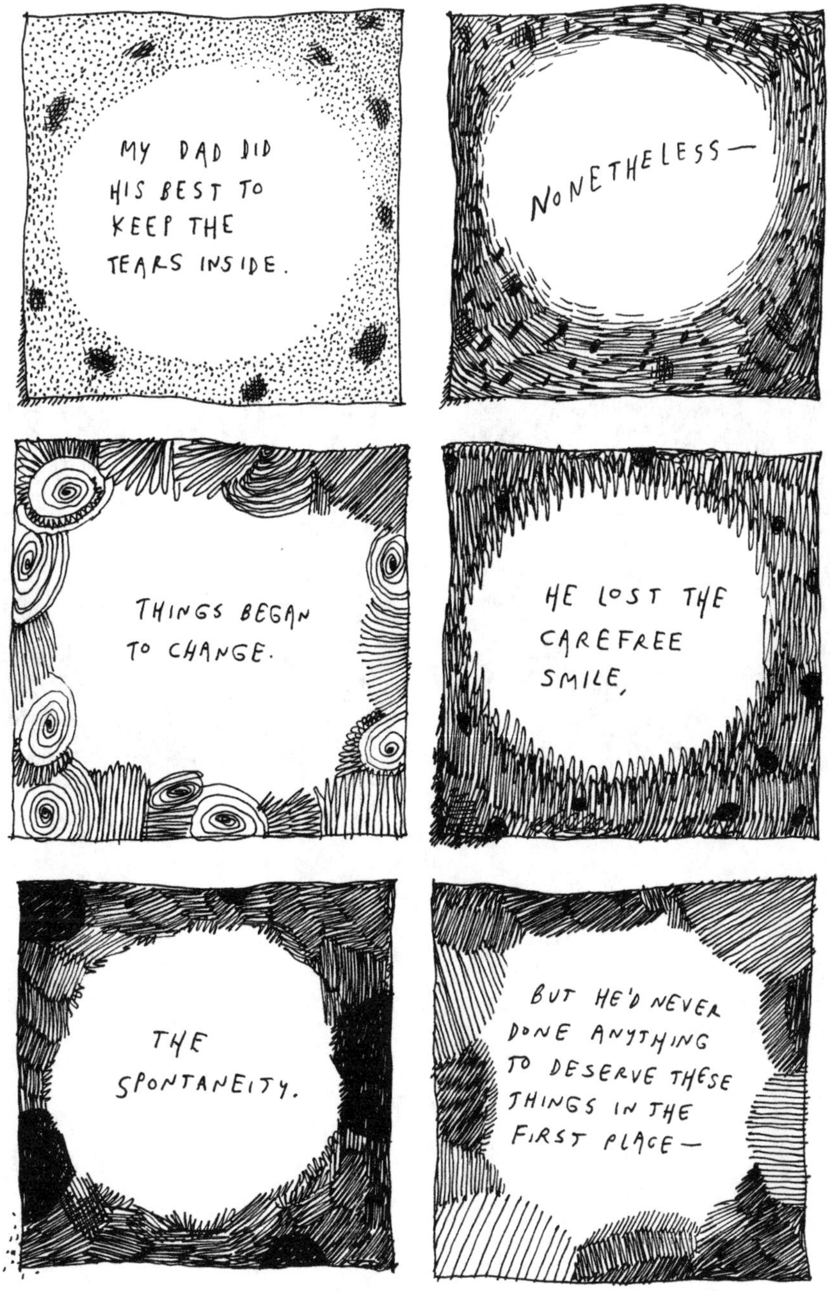
MY DAD DID HIS BEST TO KEEP THE TEARS INSIDE.
NONETHELESS—
THINGS BEGAN TO CHANGE.
HE LOST THE CAREFREE SMILE,
THE SPONTANEITY.
BUT HE'D NEVER DONE ANYTHING TO DESERVE THESE THINGS IN THE FIRST PLACE—

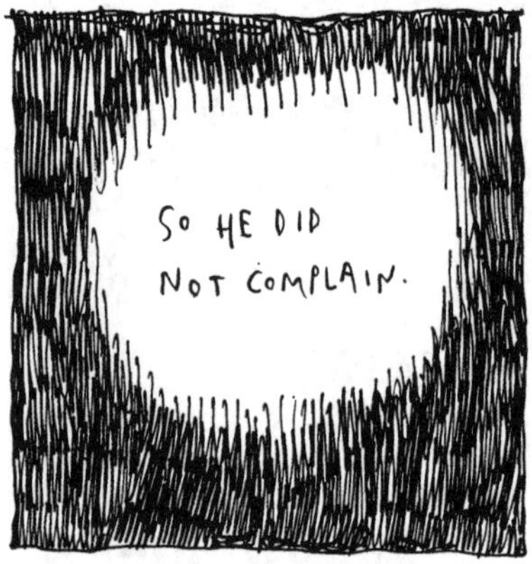
SO HE DID
NOT COMPLAIN.
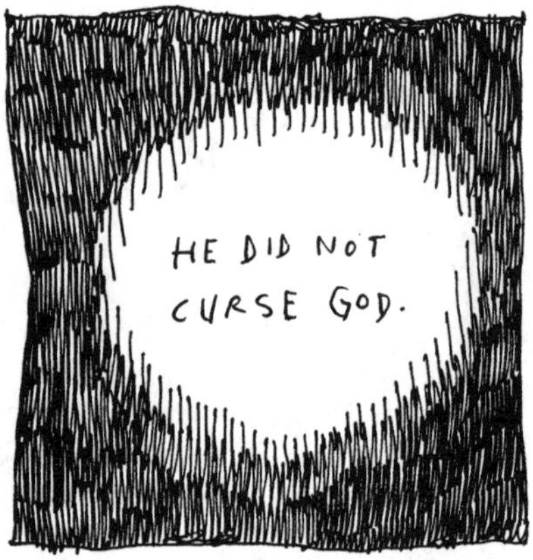
HE DID NOT
CURSE GOD.

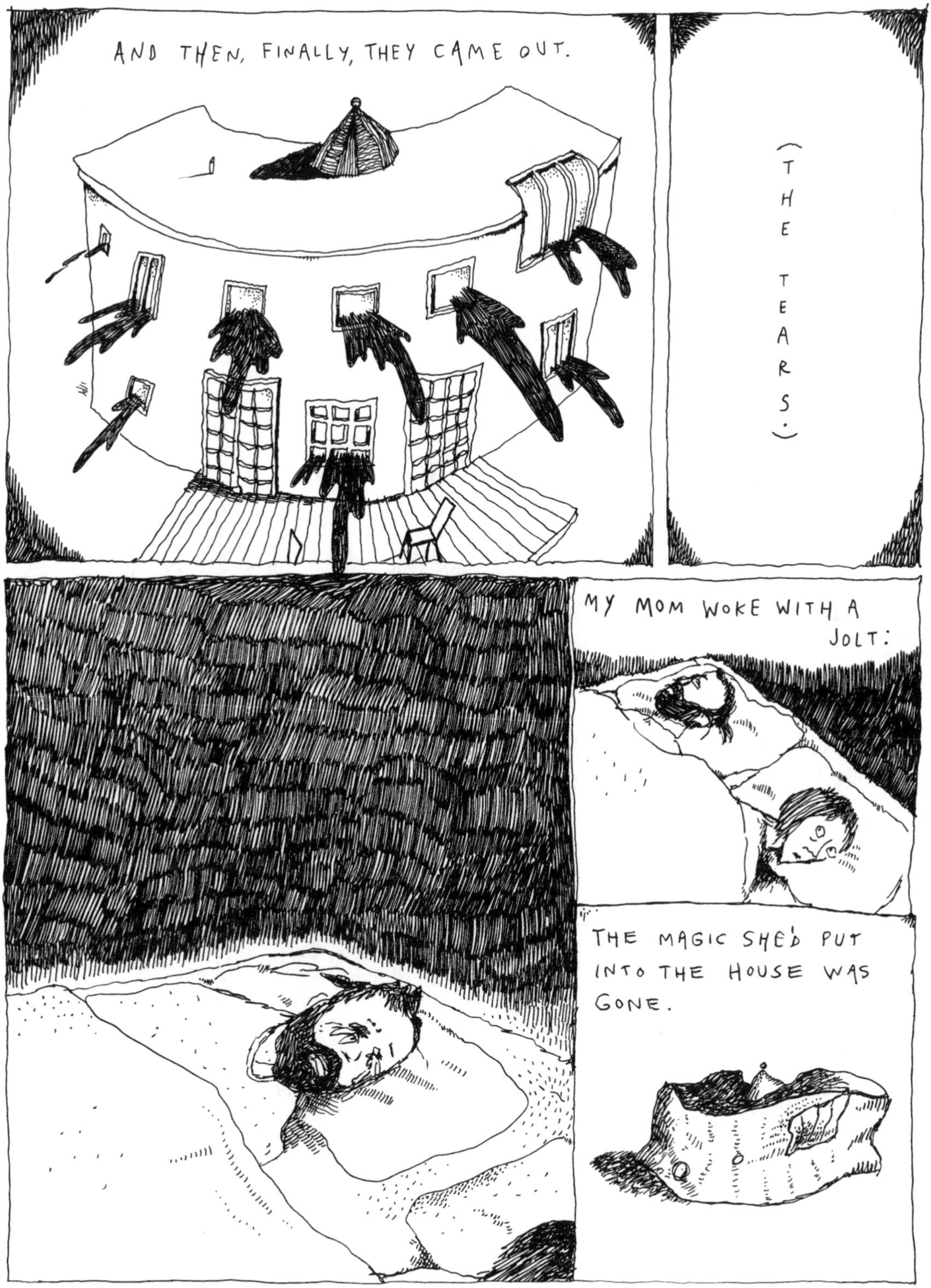
AND THEN, FINALLY, THEY CAME OUT.
(THE TEARS.)
MY MOM WOKE WITH A JOLT:
THE MAGIC SHE'D PUT INTO THE HOUSE WAS GONE.

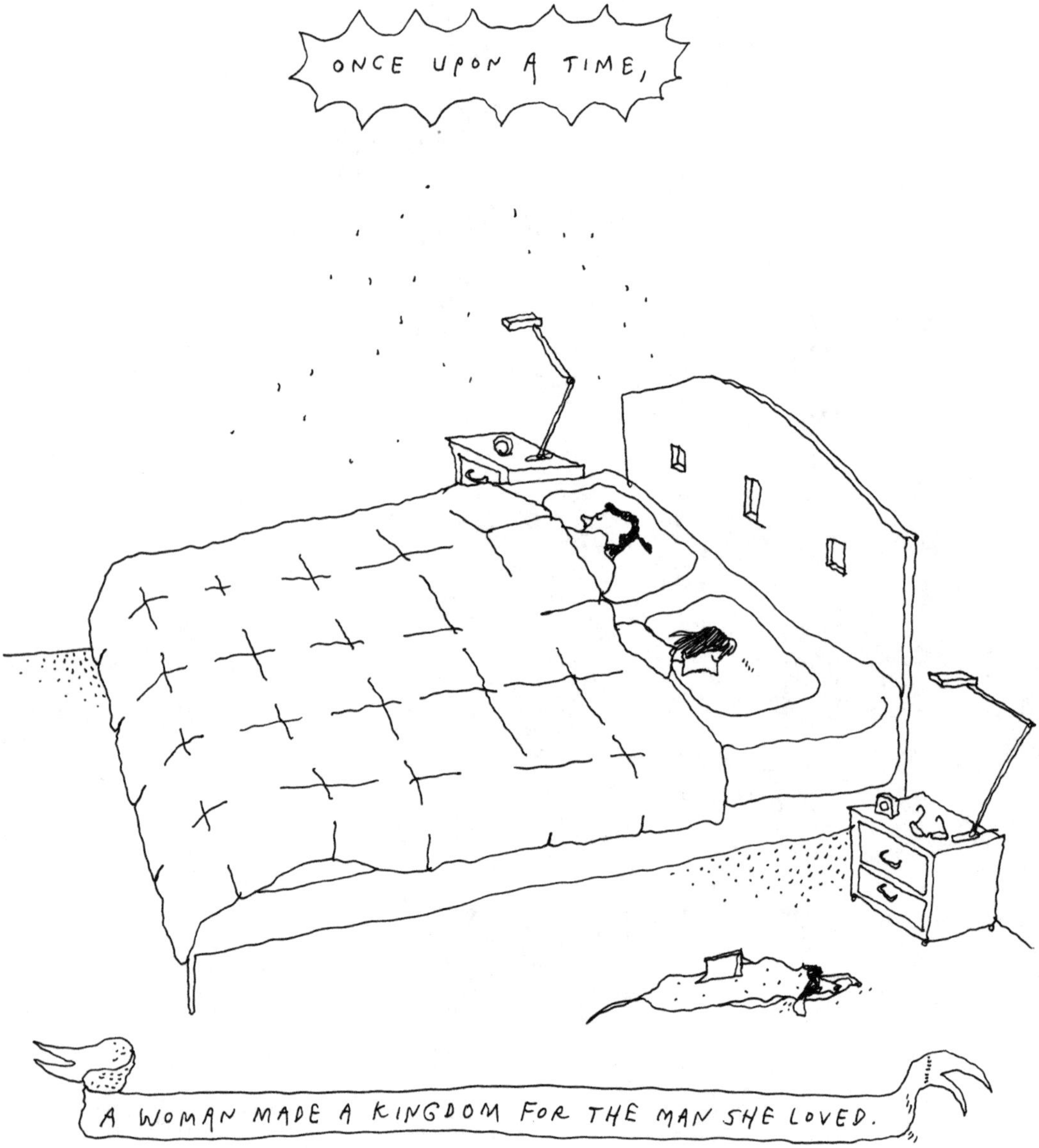
ONCE UPON A TIME,
A WOMAN MADE A KINGDOM FOR THE MAN SHE LOVED.

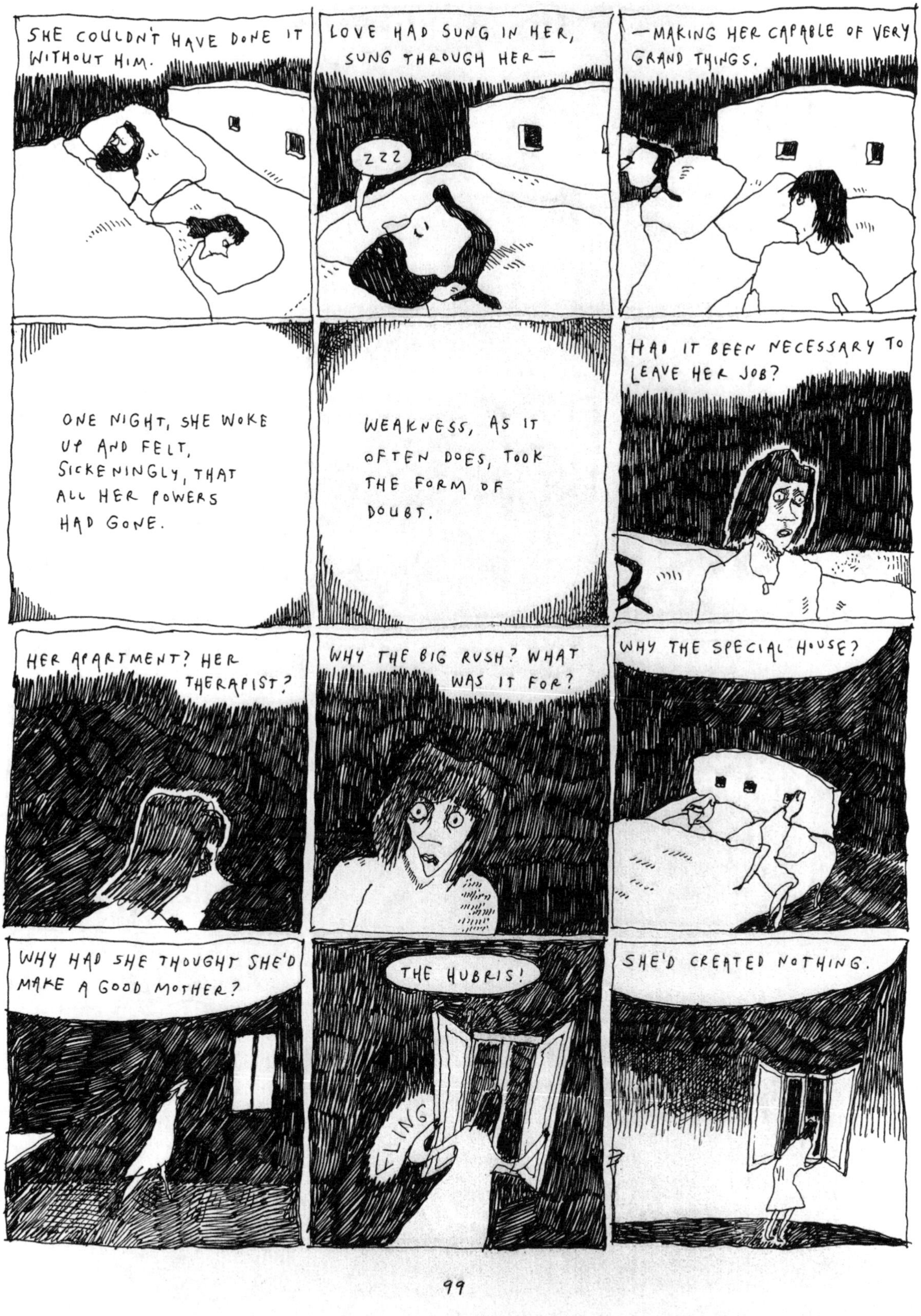
SHE COULDN'T HAVE DONE IT WITHOUT HIM.
LOVE HAD SUNG IN HER, SUNG THROUGH HER—
ZZZ
—MAKING HER CAPABLE OF VERY GRAND THINGS.
ONE NIGHT, SHE WOKE UP AND FELT, SICKENINGLY, THAT ALL HER POWERS HAD GONE.
WEAKNESS, AS IT OFTEN DOES, TOOK THE FORM OF DOUBT.
HAD IT BEEN NECESSARY TO LEAVE HER JOB?
HER APARTMENT? HER THERAPIST?
WHY THE BIG RUSH? WHAT WAS IT FOR?
WHY THE SPECIAL HOUSE?
WHY HAD SHE THOUGHT SHE'D MAKE A GOOD MOTHER?
THE HUBRIS!
FLING
SHE'D CREATED NOTHING.

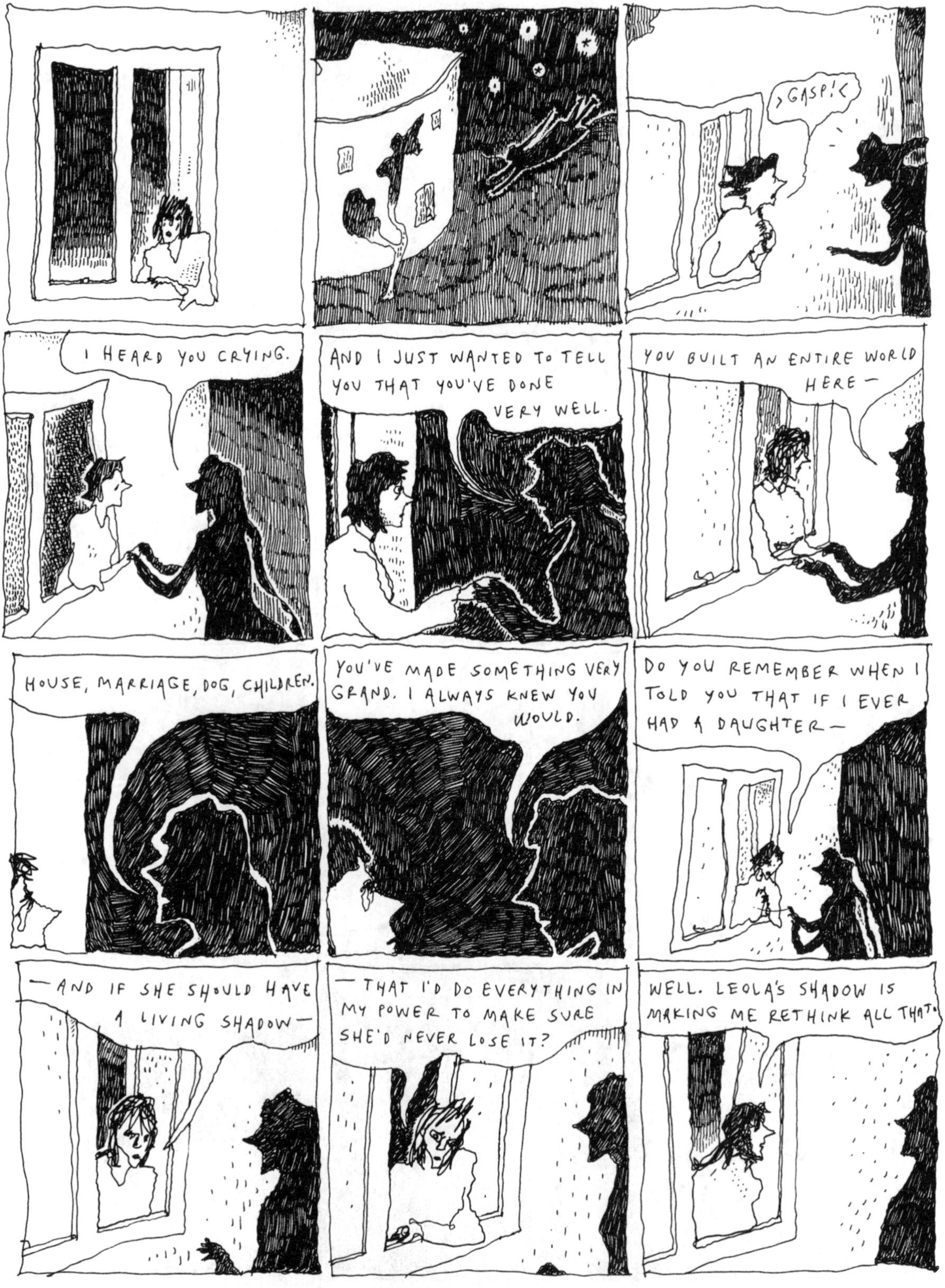
>GASP!<
I HEARD YOU CRYING.
AND I JUST WANTED TO TELL YOU THAT YOU'VE DONE VERY WELL.
YOU BUILT AN ENTIRE WORLD HERE—
HOUSE, MARRIAGE, DOG, CHILDREN.
YOU'VE MADE SOMETHING VERY GRAND. I ALWAYS KNEW YOU WOULD.
DO YOU REMEMBER WHEN I TOLD YOU THAT IF I EVER HAD A DAUGHTER—
—AND IF SHE SHOULD HAVE A LIVING SHADOW—
—THAT I'D DO EVERYTHING IN MY POWER TO MAKE SURE SHE'D NEVER LOSE IT?
WELL. LEOLA'S SHADOW IS MAKING ME RETHINK ALL THAT.

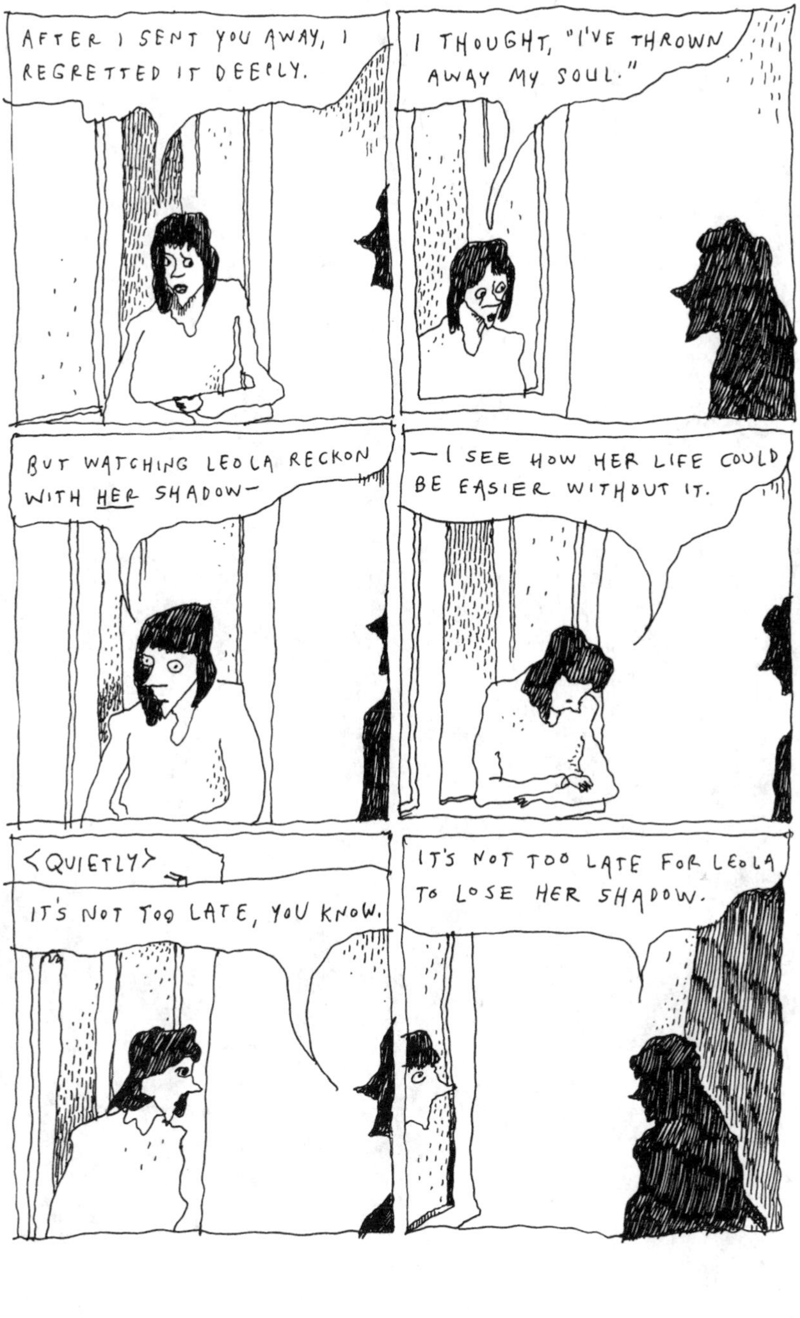
AFTER I SENT YOU AWAY, I REGRETTED IT DEEPLY.
I THOUGHT, "I'VE THROWN AWAY MY SOUL."
BUT WATCHING LEOLA RECKON WITH HER SHADOW—
—I SEE HOW HER LIFE COULD BE EASIER WITHOUT IT.
<QUIETLY>
IT'S NOT TOO LATE, YOU KNOW.
IT'S NOT TOO LATE FOR LEOLA TO LOSE HER SHADOW.

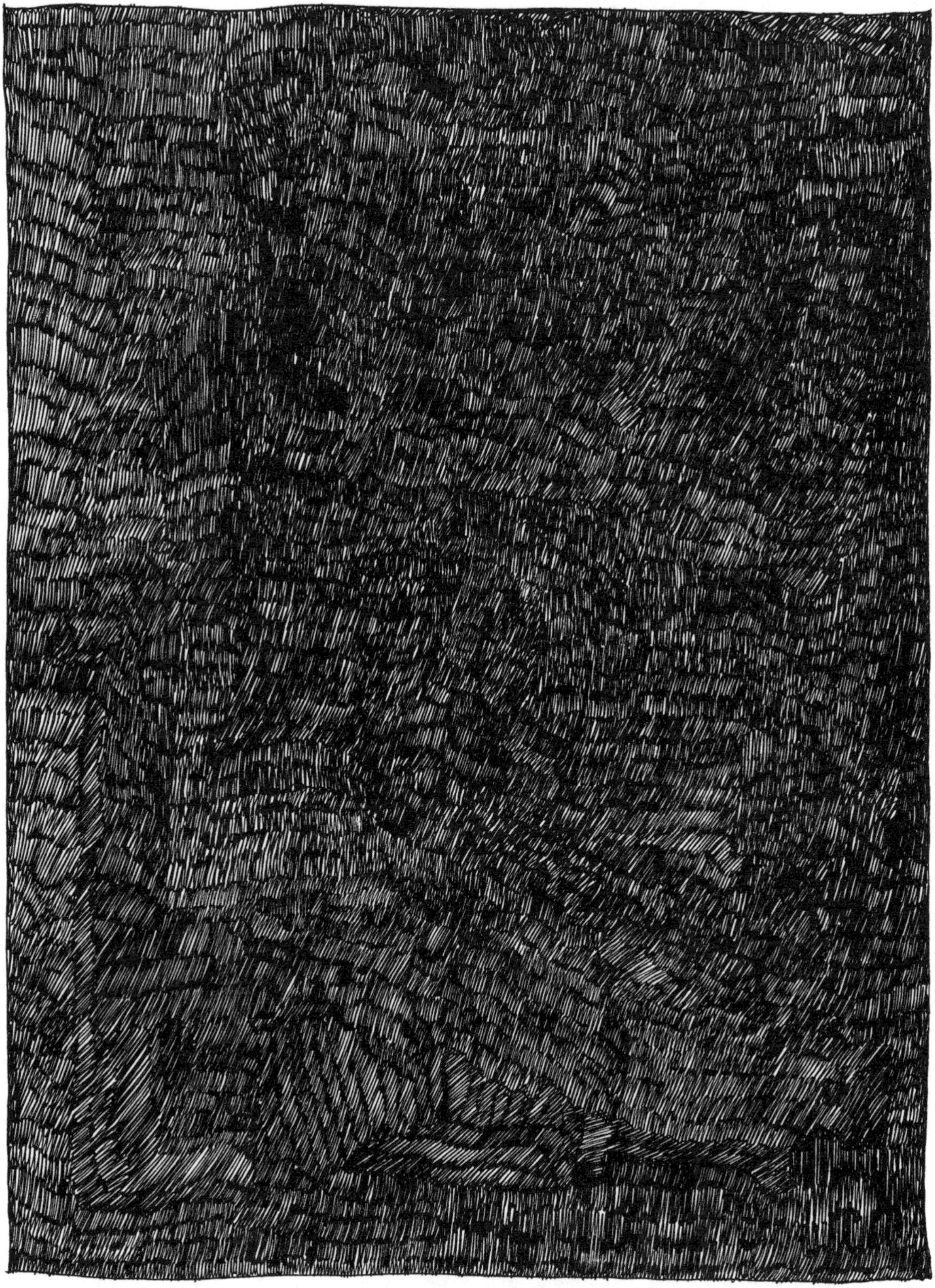

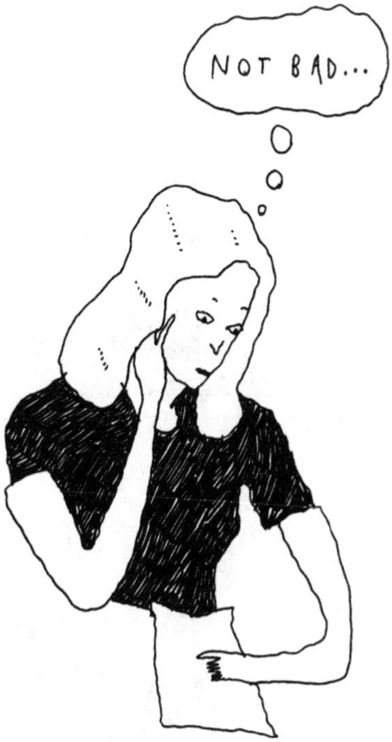
NOT BAD...

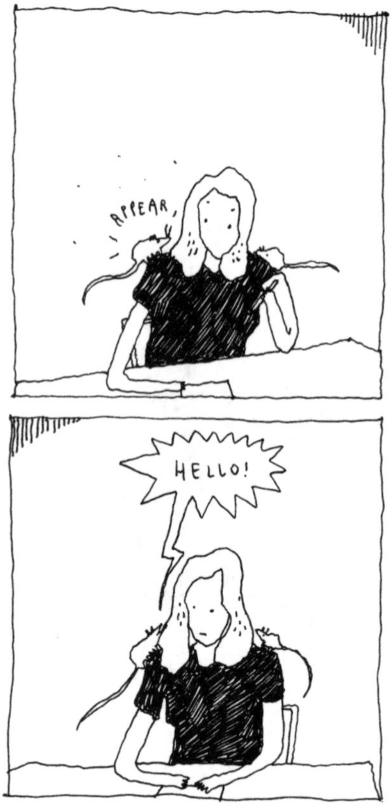
APPEAR
HELLO!

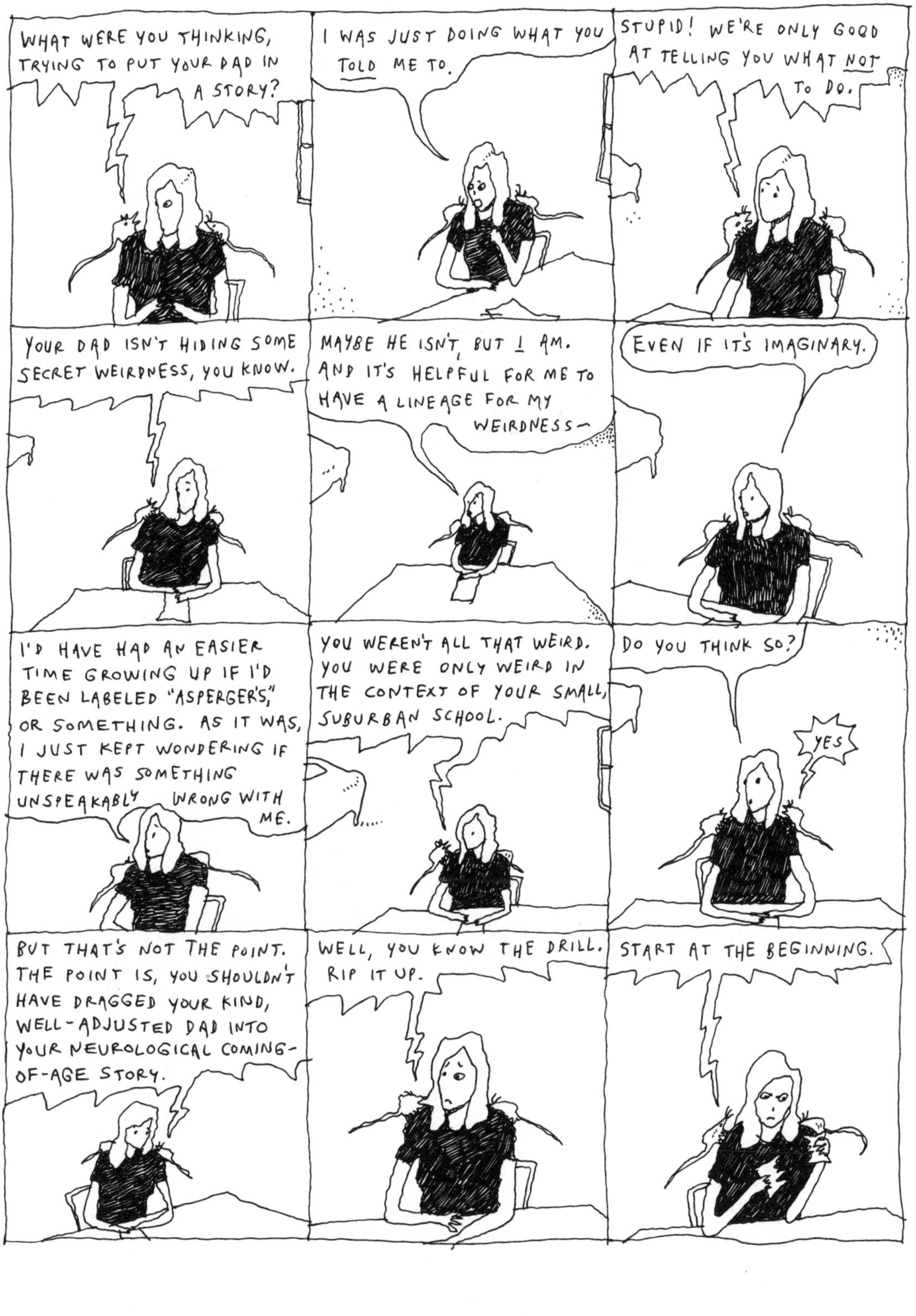
WHAT WERE YOU THINKING, TRYING TO PUT YOUR DAD IN A STORY?
I WAS JUST DOING WHAT YOU TOLD ME TO.
STUPID! WE'RE ONLY GOOD AT TELLING YOU WHAT NOT TO DO.
YOUR DAD ISN'T HIDING SOME SECRET WEIRDNESS, YOU KNOW.
MAYBE HE ISN'T, BUT I AM. AND IT'S HELPFUL FOR ME TO HAVE A LINEAGE FOR MY WEIRDNESS—
EVEN IF IT'S IMAGINARY.
I'D HAVE HAD AN EASIER TIME GROWING UP IF I'D BEEN LABELED "ASPERGER'S," OR SOMETHING. AS IT WAS, I JUST KEPT WONDERING IF THERE WAS SOMETHING UNSPEAKABLY WRONG WITH ME.
YOU WEREN'T ALL THAT WEIRD. YOU WERE ONLY WEIRD IN THE CONTEXT OF YOUR SMALL, SUBURBAN SCHOOL.
DO YOU THINK SO?
YES
BUT THAT'S NOT THE POINT. THE POINT IS, YOU SHOULDN'T HAVE DRAGGED YOUR KIND, WELL-ADJUSTED DAD INTO YOUR NEUROLOGICAL COMING-OF-AGE STORY.
WELL, YOU KNOW THE DRILL. RIP IT UP.
START AT THE BEGINNING.

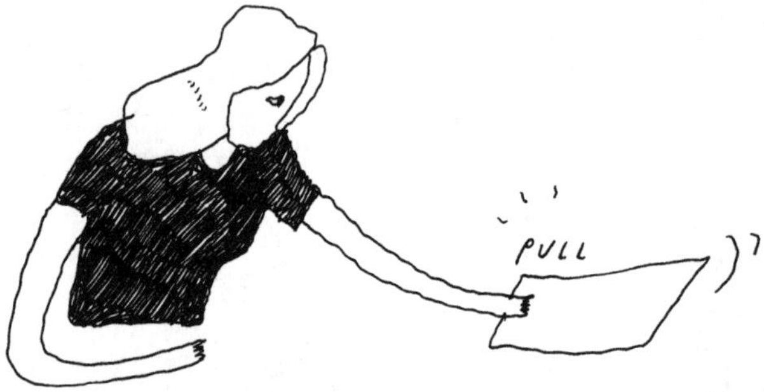
PULL

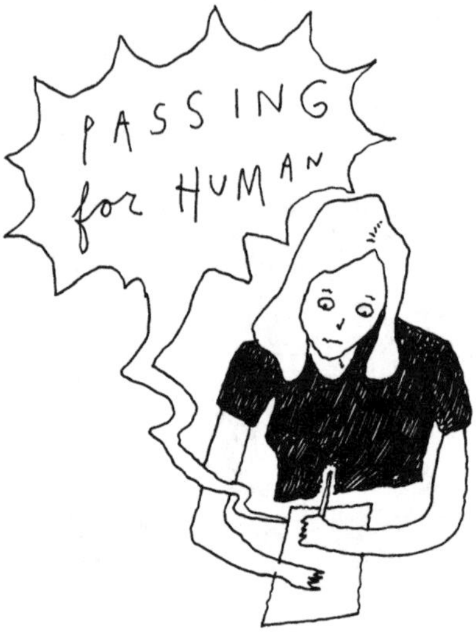
PASSING for HUMAN

PASSING *for* HUMAN

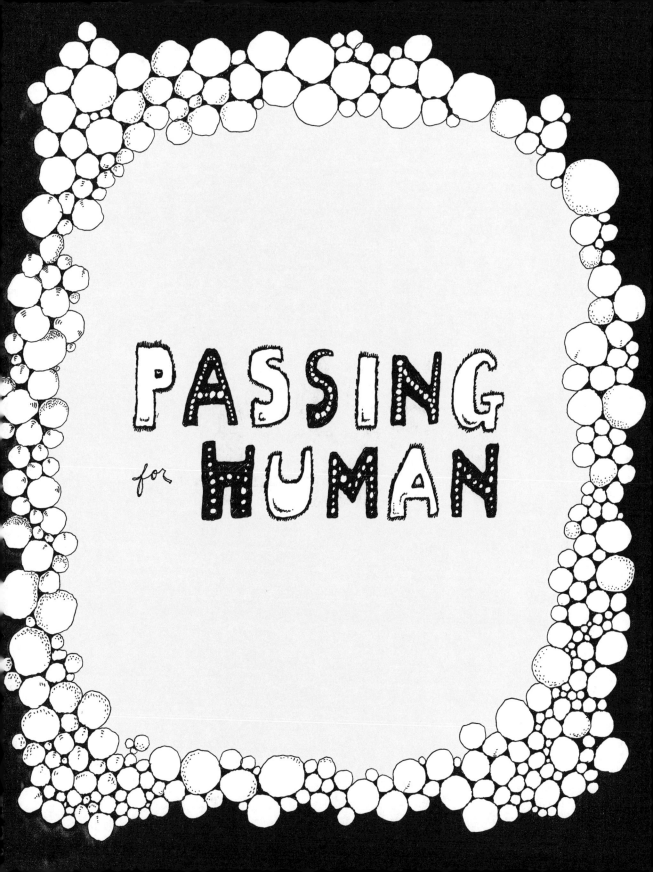

"HER WISH WAS GRANTED:
SHE BECAME A HUMAN.
THE PRICE WAS THAT EVERY STEP
SHE TOOK WAS LIKE WALKING ON KNIVES."

— ANDREW SOLOMON, *FAR FROM THE TREE*

CHAPTER 1

Paradise Lost

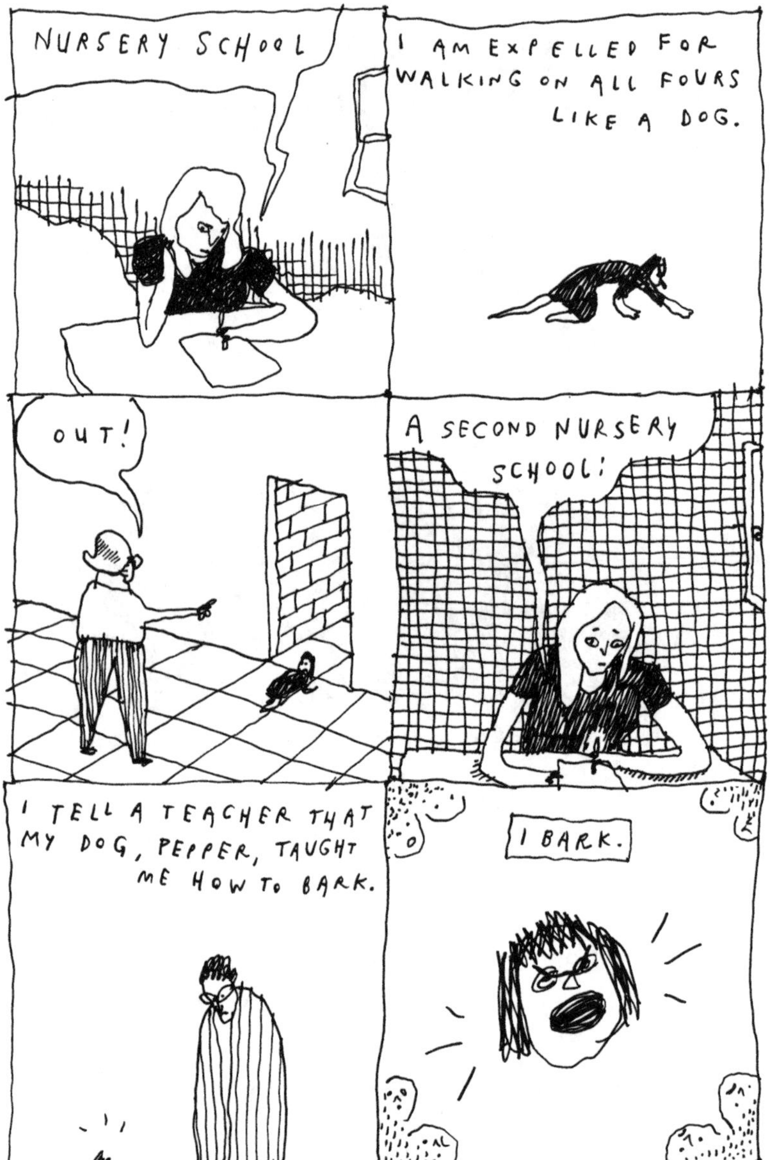
NURSERY SCHOOL
I AM EXPELLED FOR WALKING ON ALL FOURS LIKE A DOG.
OUT!
A SECOND NURSERY SCHOOL:
I TELL A TEACHER THAT MY DOG, PEPPER, TAUGHT ME HOW TO BARK.
I BARK.

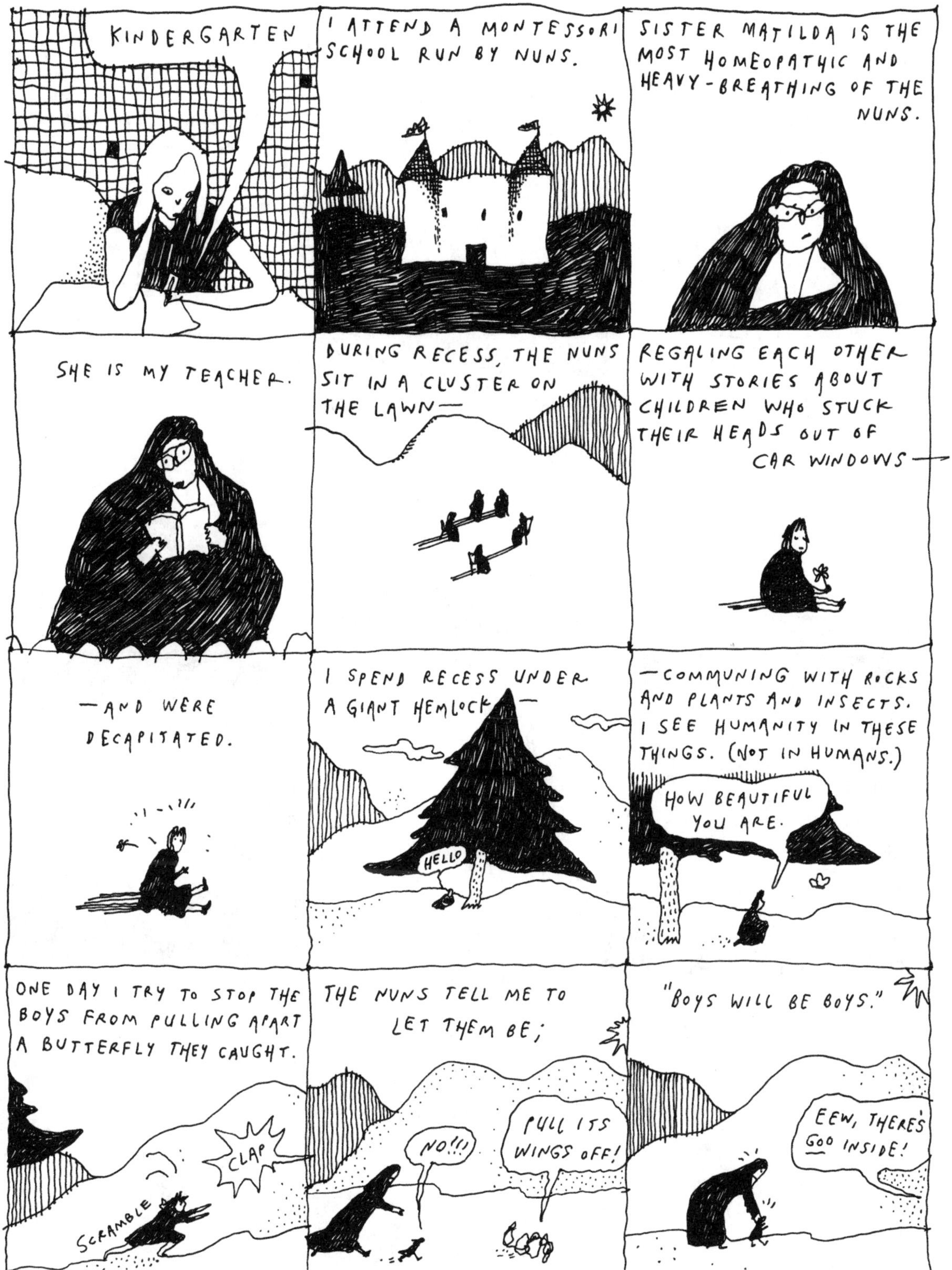
KINDERGARTEN
I ATTEND A MONTESSORI SCHOOL RUN BY NUNS.
SISTER MATILDA IS THE MOST HOMEOPATHIC AND HEAVY-BREATHING OF THE NUNS.
SHE IS MY TEACHER.
DURING RECESS, THE NUNS SIT IN A CLUSTER ON THE LAWN—
REGALING EACH OTHER WITH STORIES ABOUT CHILDREN WHO STUCK THEIR HEADS OUT OF CAR WINDOWS—
—AND WERE DECAPITATED.
I SPEND RECESS UNDER A GIANT HEMLOCK—
HELLO
—COMMUNING WITH ROCKS AND PLANTS AND INSECTS. I SEE HUMANITY IN THESE THINGS. (NOT IN HUMANS.)
HOW BEAUTIFUL YOU ARE.
ONE DAY I TRY TO STOP THE BOYS FROM PULLING APART A BUTTERFLY THEY CAUGHT.
CLAP
SCRAMBLE
THE NUNS TELL ME TO LET THEM BE;
NO!!!
PULL ITS WINGS OFF!
"BOYS WILL BE BOYS."
EEW, THERE'S GOO INSIDE!

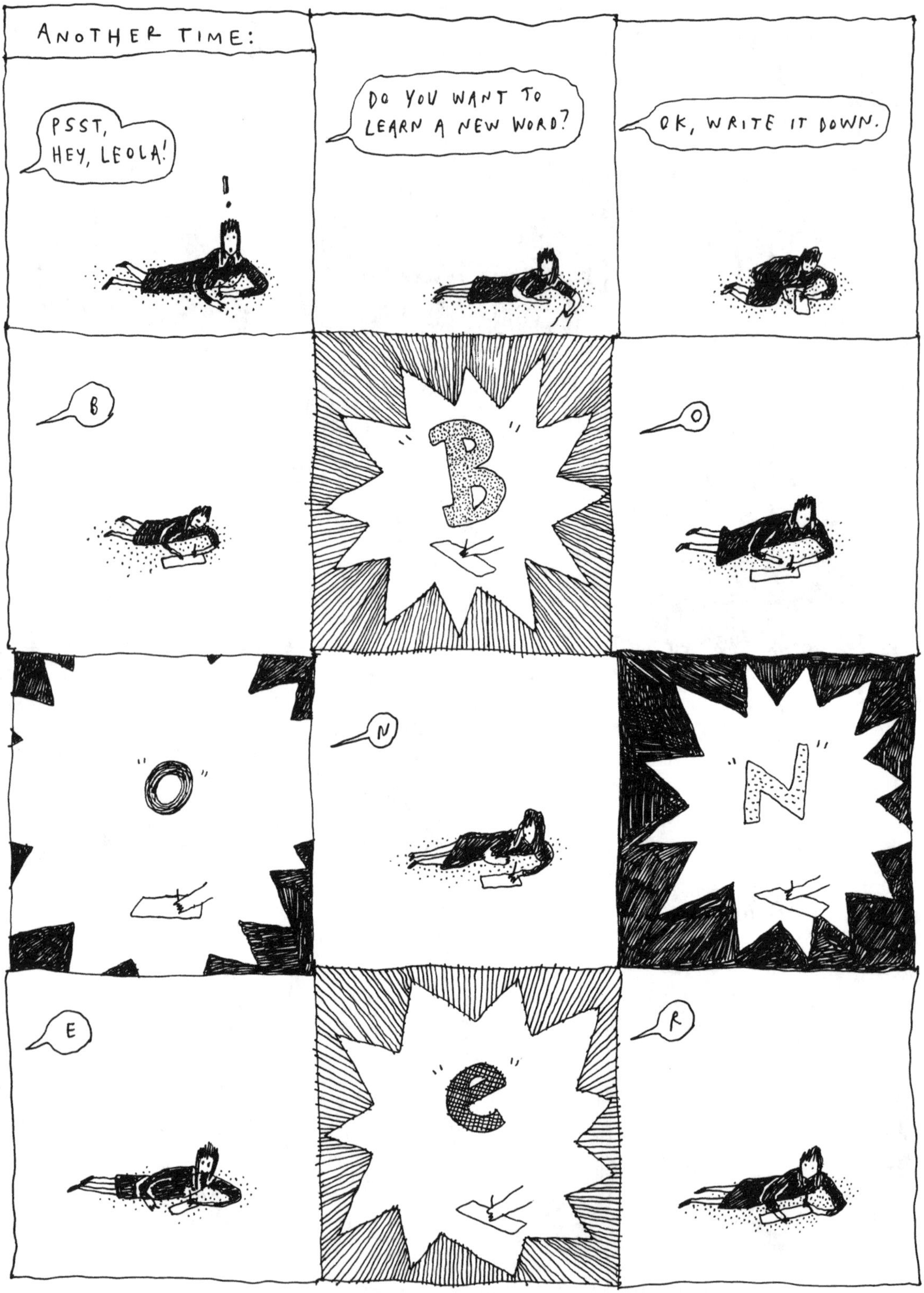
ANOTHER TIME:
PSST, HEY, LEOLA!
!
DO YOU WANT TO LEARN A NEW WORD?
OK, WRITE IT DOWN.
B
"B"
O
"O"
N
"N"
E
"e"
R

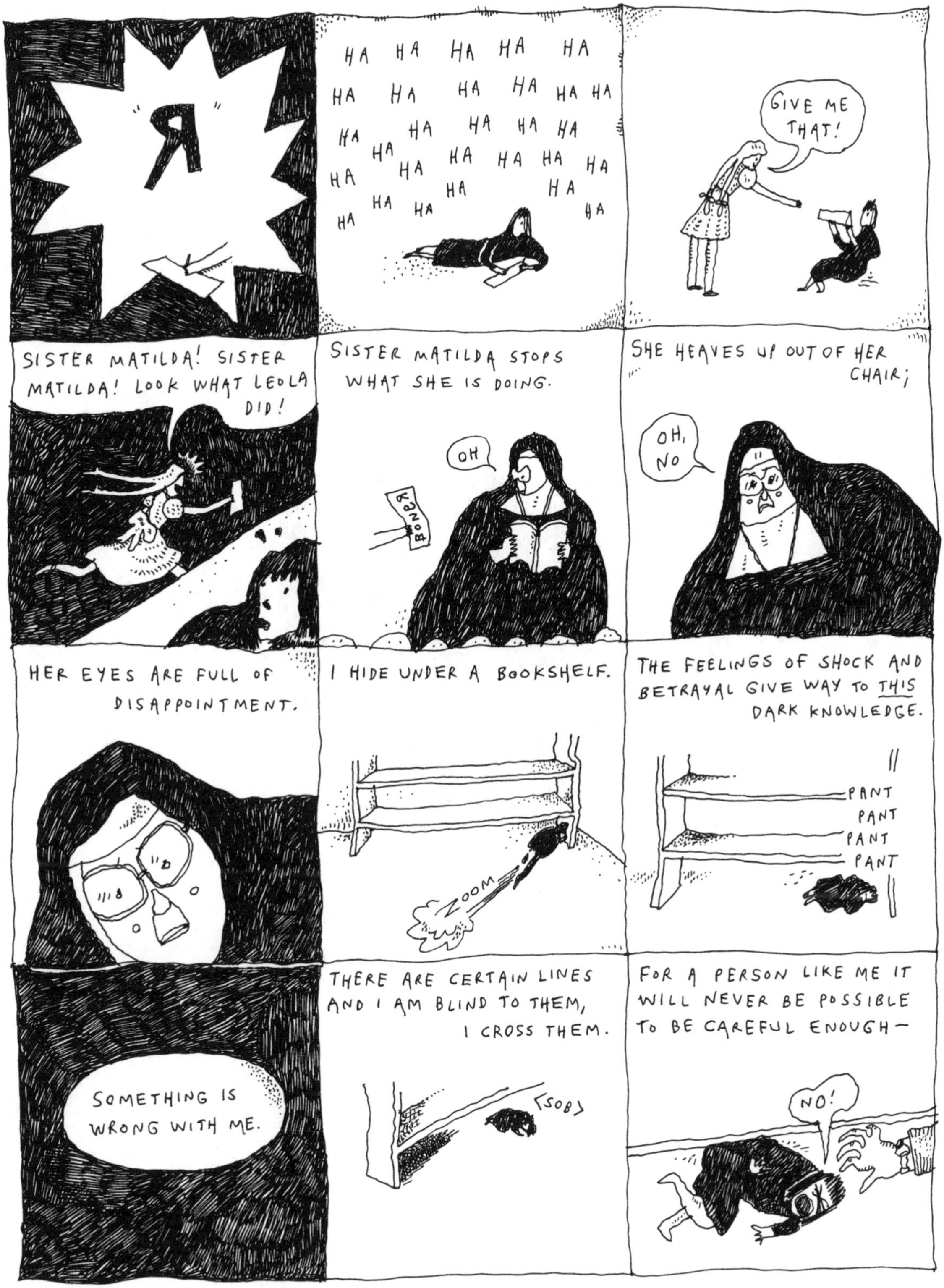
"R"
HA HA HA HA HA HA HA HA HA HA HA HA HA HA HA HA HA HA HA HA HA HA HA HA HA HA HA HA HA HA HA HA
GIVE ME THAT!
SISTER MATILDA! SISTER MATILDA! LOOK WHAT LEOLA DID!
SISTER MATILDA STOPS WHAT SHE IS DOING.
OH
BONER
SHE HEAVES UP OUT OF HER CHAIR;
OH, NO
HER EYES ARE FULL OF DISAPPOINTMENT.
I HIDE UNDER A BOOKSHELF.
ZOOM
THE FEELINGS OF SHOCK AND BETRAYAL GIVE WAY TO THIS DARK KNOWLEDGE.
PANT PANT PANT PANT
SOMETHING IS WRONG WITH ME.
THERE ARE CERTAIN LINES AND I AM BLIND TO THEM, I CROSS THEM.
[SOB]
FOR A PERSON LIKE ME IT WILL NEVER BE POSSIBLE TO BE CAREFUL ENOUGH—
NO!

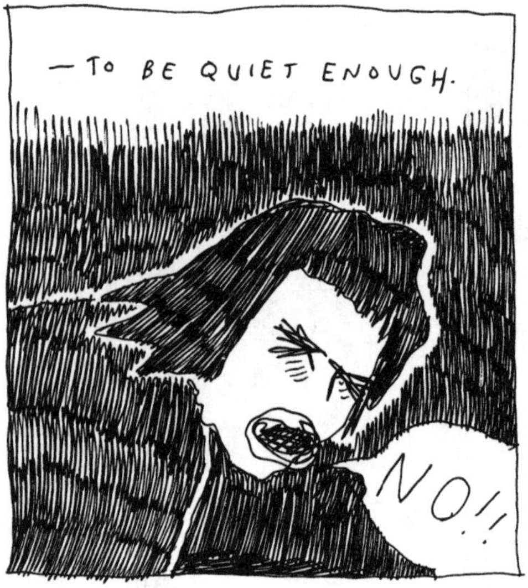
—TO BE QUIET ENOUGH.
NO!!

OVER THE SUMMER, MY MOM MAKES ME A PAPER REPLICA OF OUR HOUSE.

IT'S COMPLETELY COMPLETE —

WITH A TINY MOM, A TINY DAD, A TINY GAMLIEL, A TINY PEPPER, AND A TINY ME.

I'D GIVE ANYTHING TO BE ABLE TO SEE THAT TINY HOUSE NOW.

BUT IT'S STILL IN ME, IN A WAY.

THE REAL HOUSE IS, TOO.

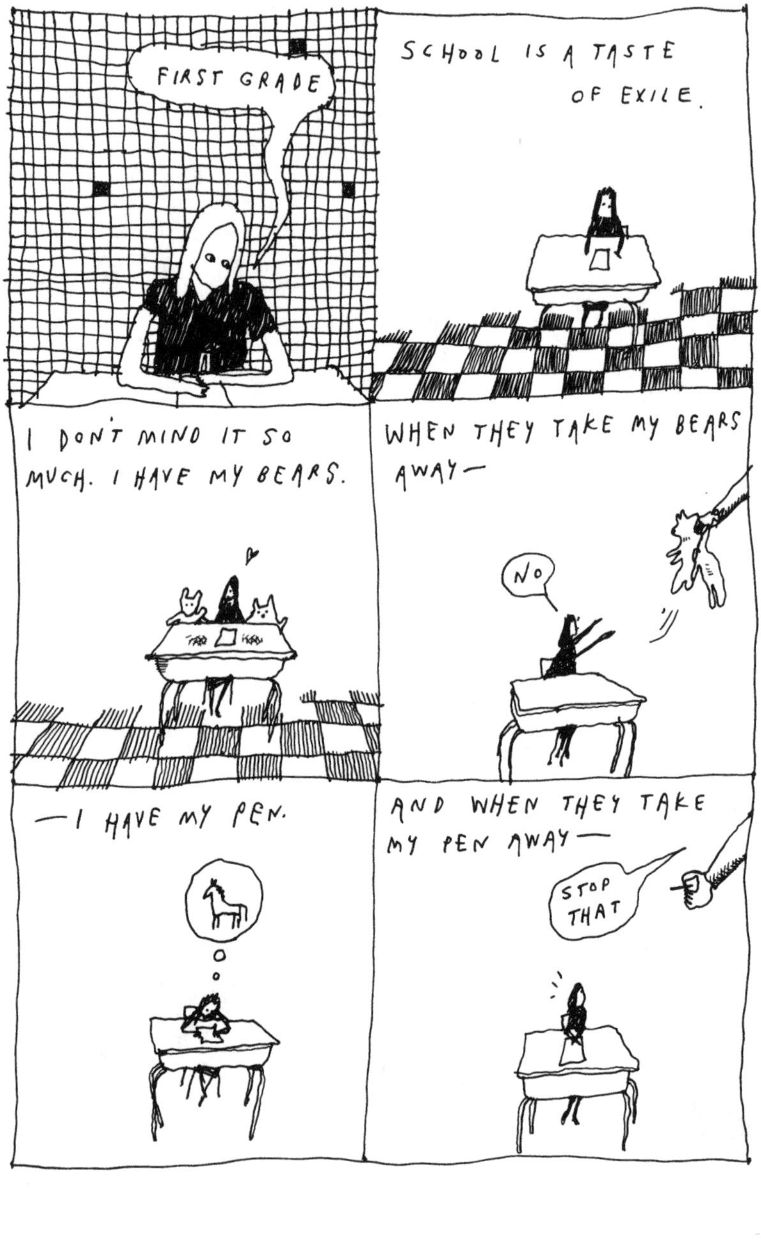
FIRST GRADE
SCHOOL IS A TASTE OF EXILE.
I DON'T MIND IT SO MUCH. I HAVE MY BEARS.
WHEN THEY TAKE MY BEARS AWAY—
NO
—I HAVE MY PEN.
AND WHEN THEY TAKE MY PEN AWAY—
STOP THAT

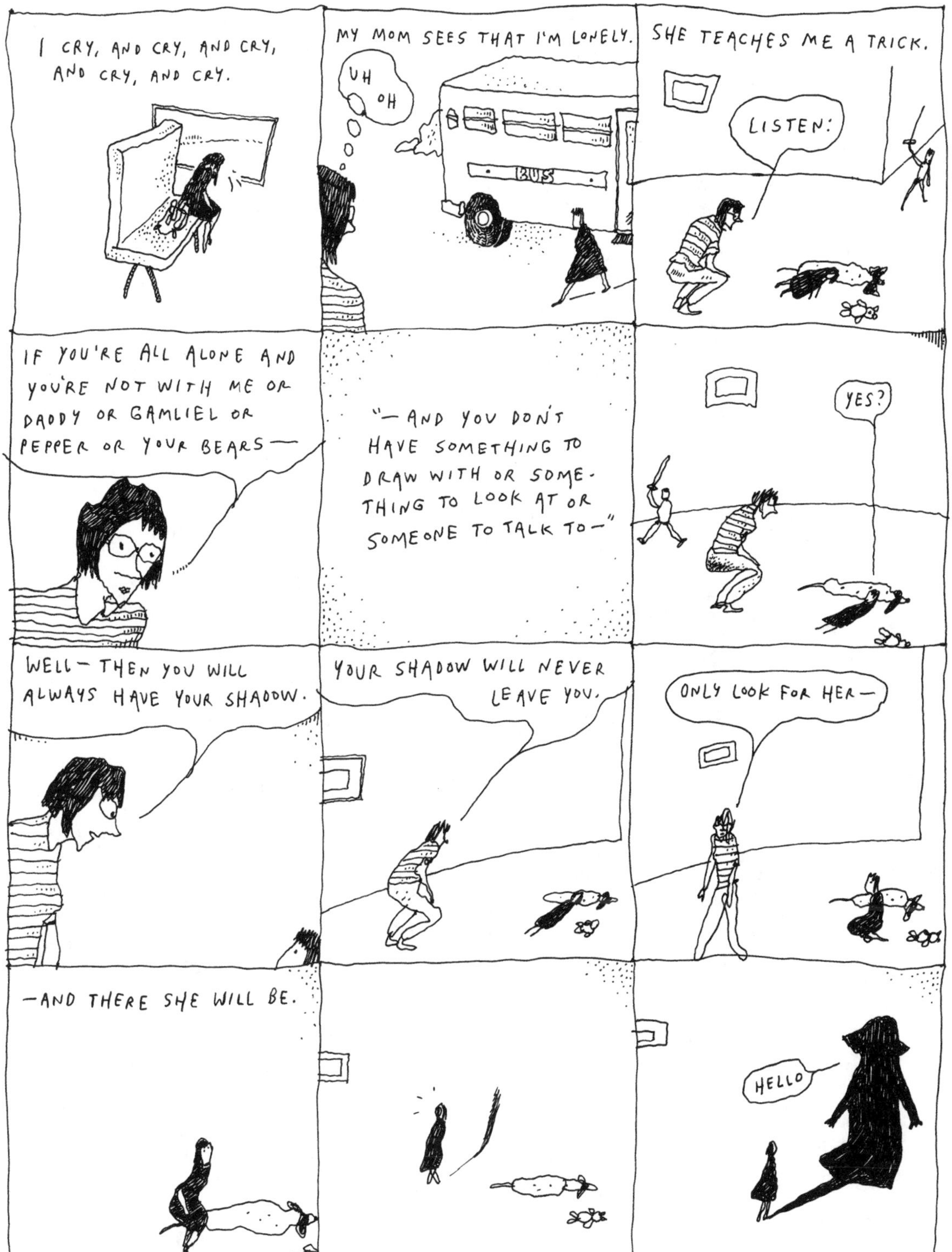
I CRY, AND CRY, AND CRY, AND CRY, AND CRY.
MY MOM SEES THAT I'M LONELY.
UH OH
BUS
SHE TEACHES ME A TRICK.
LISTEN:
IF YOU'RE ALL ALONE AND YOU'RE NOT WITH ME OR DADDY OR GAMLIEL OR PEPPER OR YOUR BEARS—
"—AND YOU DON'T HAVE SOMETHING TO DRAW WITH OR SOMETHING TO LOOK AT OR SOMEONE TO TALK TO—"
YES?
WELL—THEN YOU WILL ALWAYS HAVE YOUR SHADOW.
YOUR SHADOW WILL NEVER LEAVE YOU.
ONLY LOOK FOR HER—
—AND THERE SHE WILL BE.
HELLO

THE ELEMENTARY SCHOOL HIERARCHY

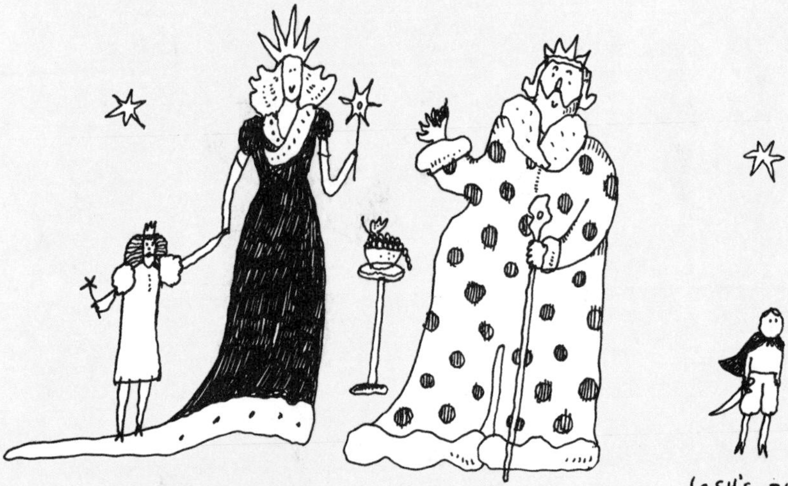

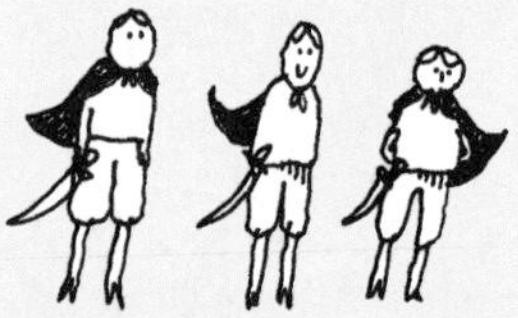

AT THE TOP WAS MANDY, THE MOST POPULAR GIRL. SHE HAD DOMINION OVER EVERY LIFE FORM IN OUR CLASS, WITH THE HELP OF HER ADVISOR, TIFF—

—AND HER COUSIN, JOSH, WHO WAS THE BIGGEST, LOUDEST, AND MOST POPULAR BOY.

JOSH'S THREE MANSERVANTS WERE ALL NAMED JOSH. JOSH THE ATHLETIC, JOSH THE CHARMING, AND JOSH THE CLOWN.

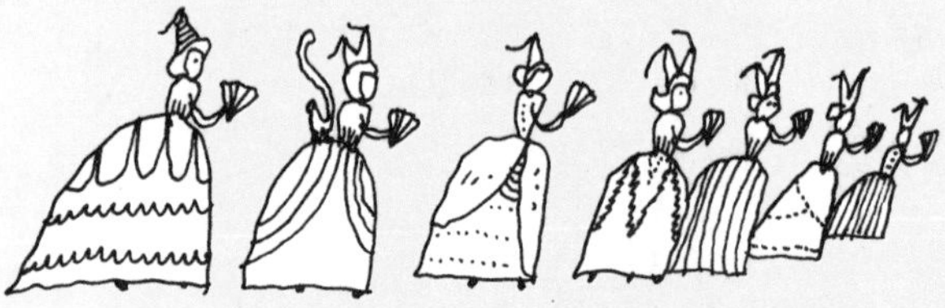

MANDY AND TIFF WERE WAITED UPON BY SEVEN MAIDENS: MELISSA, JEN, RACHEL, ALLY, RACHEL II, SHULI, AND SARAH.

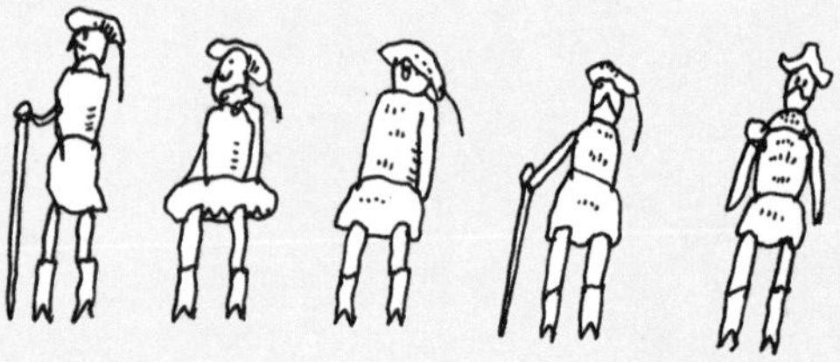

THE COOL NON-JOSH BOYS WERE NAMED JAKE, JEREMY, JONATHAN, NATHAN, AND ALON.

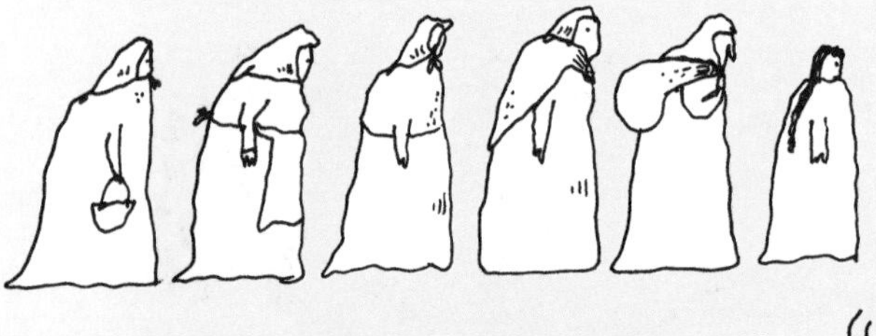

THE GIRLS WHO <u>WISHED</u> THEY WERE COOL WERE ILANA, AVIVA, STEPHANIE, DASHA, SVETLANA, AND BETH.

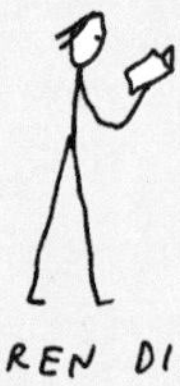

(LAUREN DIDN'T WANT TO BE COOL. SHE LIKED SCIENCE FICTION.)

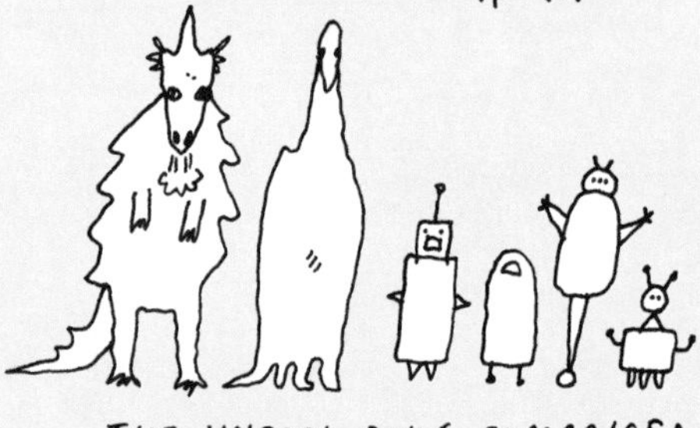

THE UNCOOL BOYS COMPRISED TWO BULLIES (OFER AND ANATOLE) AND FOUR NERDS: DANNY, DAVID, ILAN, AND ARI.

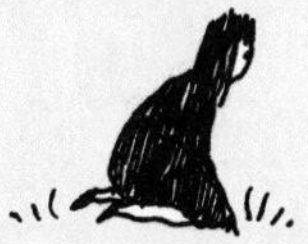

I WAS OVER HERE.

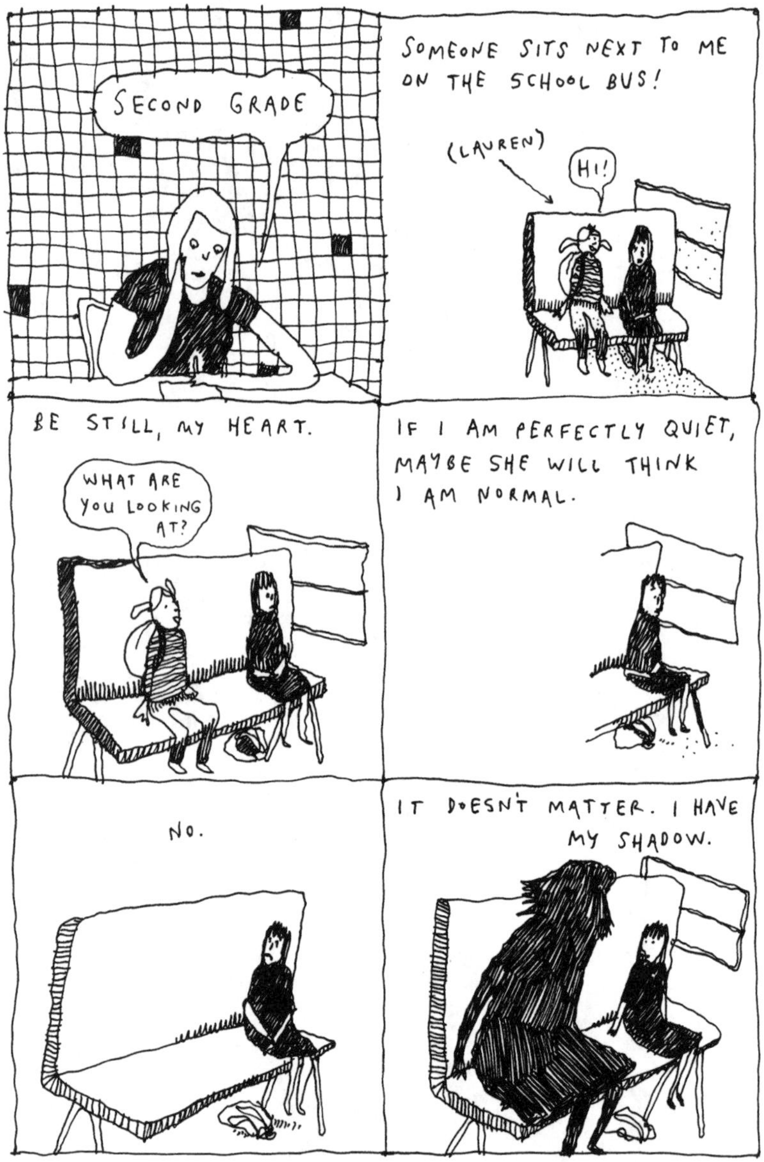
SECOND GRADE
SOMEONE SITS NEXT TO ME ON THE SCHOOL BUS!
(LAUREN)
HI!
BE STILL, MY HEART.
WHAT ARE YOU LOOKING AT?
IF I AM PERFECTLY QUIET, MAYBE SHE WILL THINK I AM NORMAL.
NO.
IT DOESN'T MATTER. I HAVE MY SHADOW.

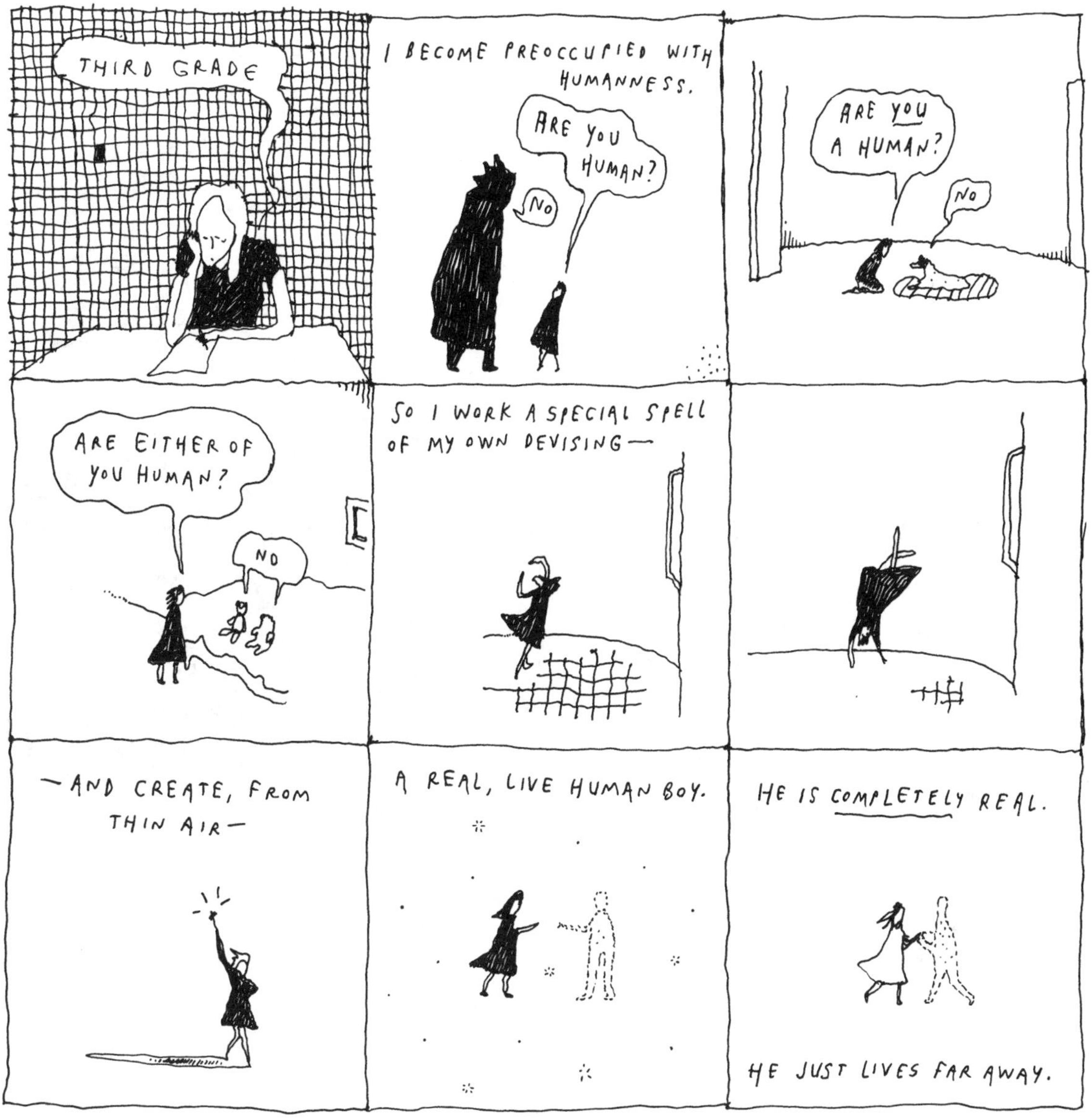
THIRD GRADE
I BECOME PREOCCUPIED WITH HUMANNESS.
ARE YOU HUMAN?
NO
ARE YOU A HUMAN?
NO
ARE EITHER OF YOU HUMAN?
NO
SO I WORK A SPECIAL SPELL OF MY OWN DEVISING—
—AND CREATE, FROM THIN AIR—
A REAL, LIVE HUMAN BOY.
HE IS COMPLETELY REAL.
HE JUST LIVES FAR AWAY.

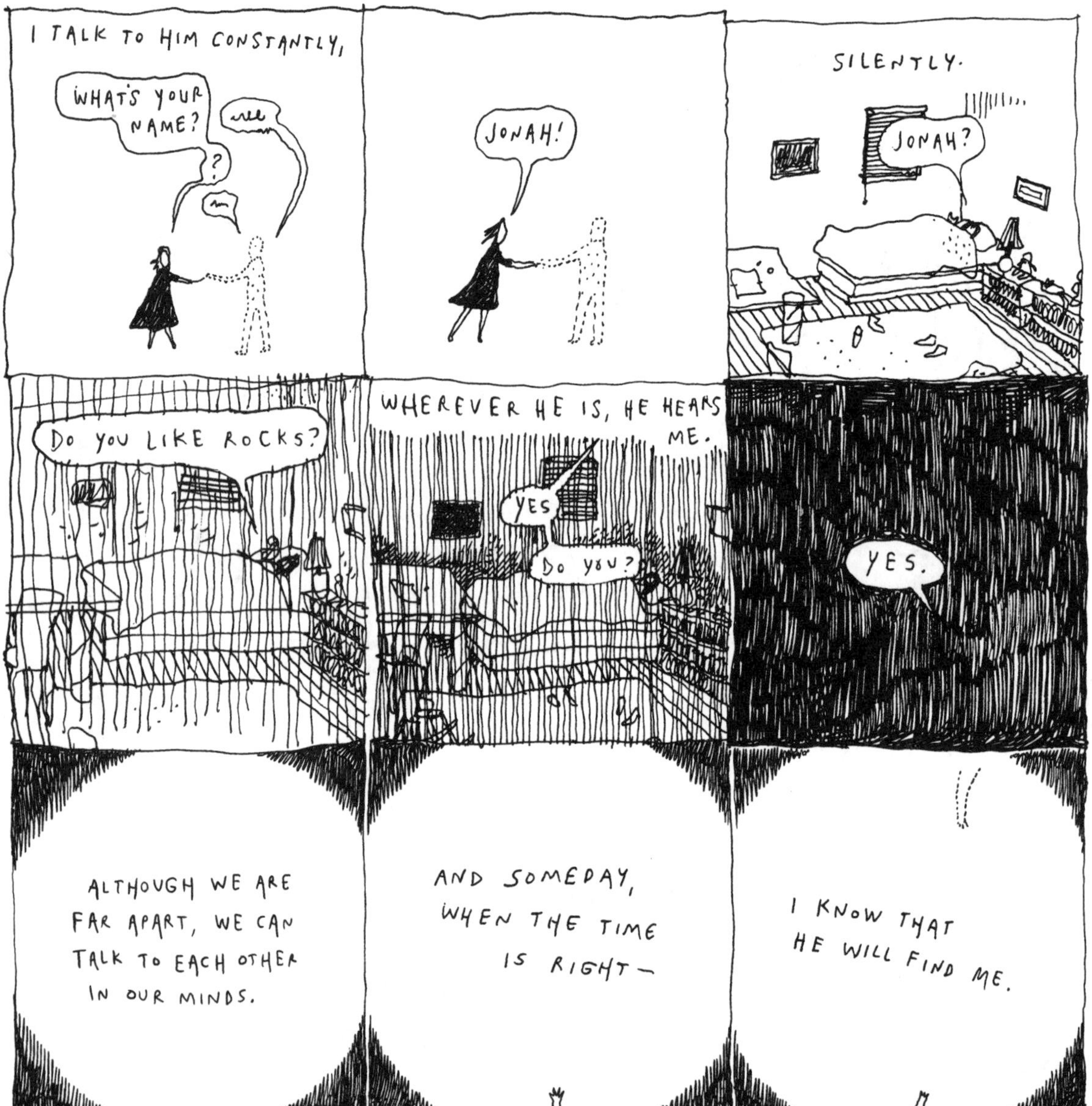
I TALK TO HIM CONSTANTLY,
WHAT'S YOUR NAME?
?
JONAH!
SILENTLY.
JONAH?
DO YOU LIKE ROCKS?
WHEREVER HE IS, HE HEARS ME.
YES
DO YOU?
YES.
ALTHOUGH WE ARE FAR APART, WE CAN TALK TO EACH OTHER IN OUR MINDS.
AND SOMEDAY, WHEN THE TIME IS RIGHT—
I KNOW THAT HE WILL FIND ME.

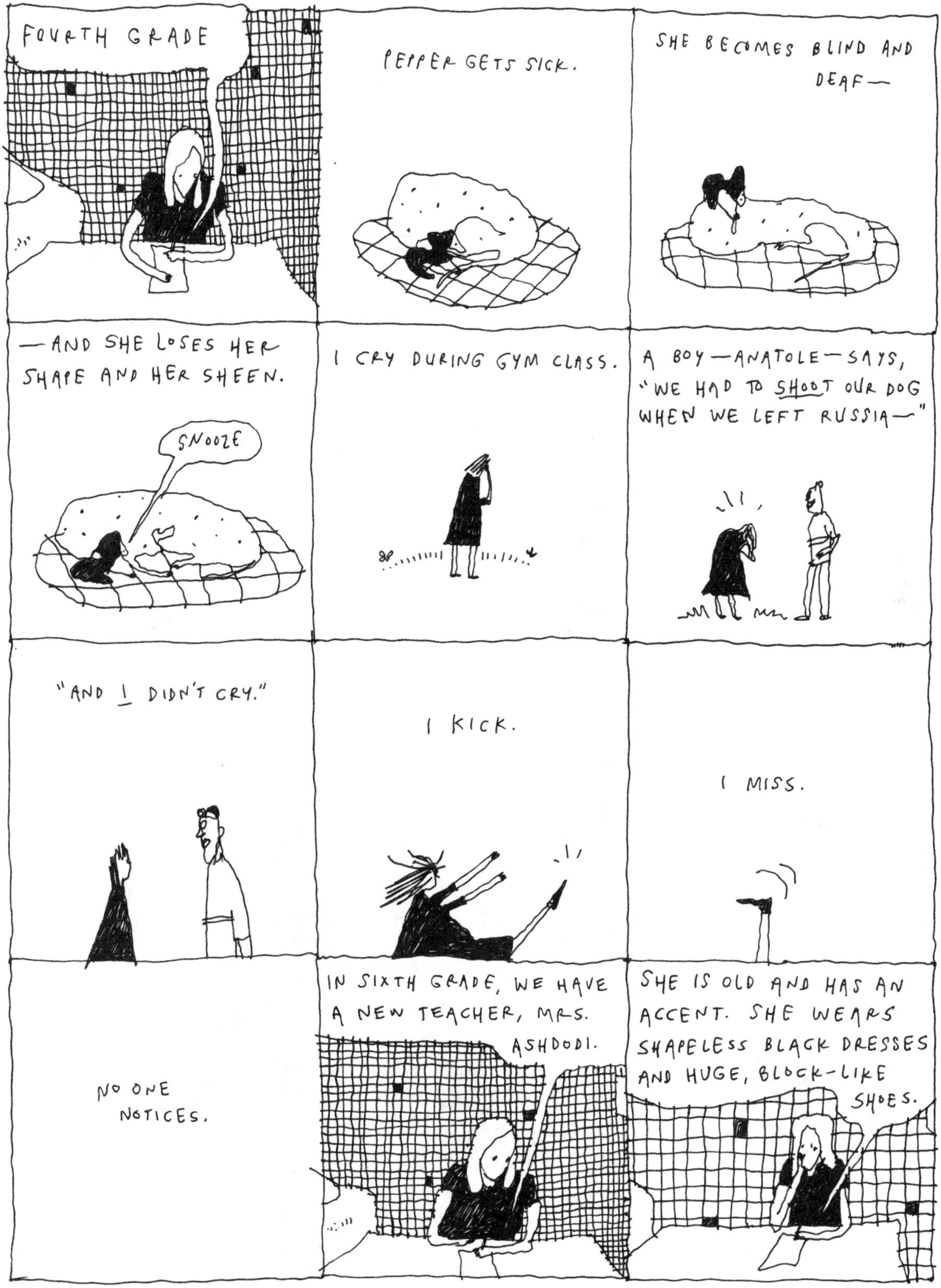
FOURTH GRADE
PEPPER GETS SICK.
SHE BECOMES BLIND AND DEAF—
—AND SHE LOSES HER SHAPE AND HER SHEEN.
SNOOZE
I CRY DURING GYM CLASS.
A BOY—ANATOLE—SAYS, "WE HAD TO SHOOT OUR DOG WHEN WE LEFT RUSSIA—"
"AND I DIDN'T CRY."
I KICK.
I MISS.
NO ONE NOTICES.
IN SIXTH GRADE, WE HAVE A NEW TEACHER, MRS. ASHDODI.
SHE IS OLD AND HAS AN ACCENT. SHE WEARS SHAPELESS BLACK DRESSES AND HUGE, BLOCK-LIKE SHOES.

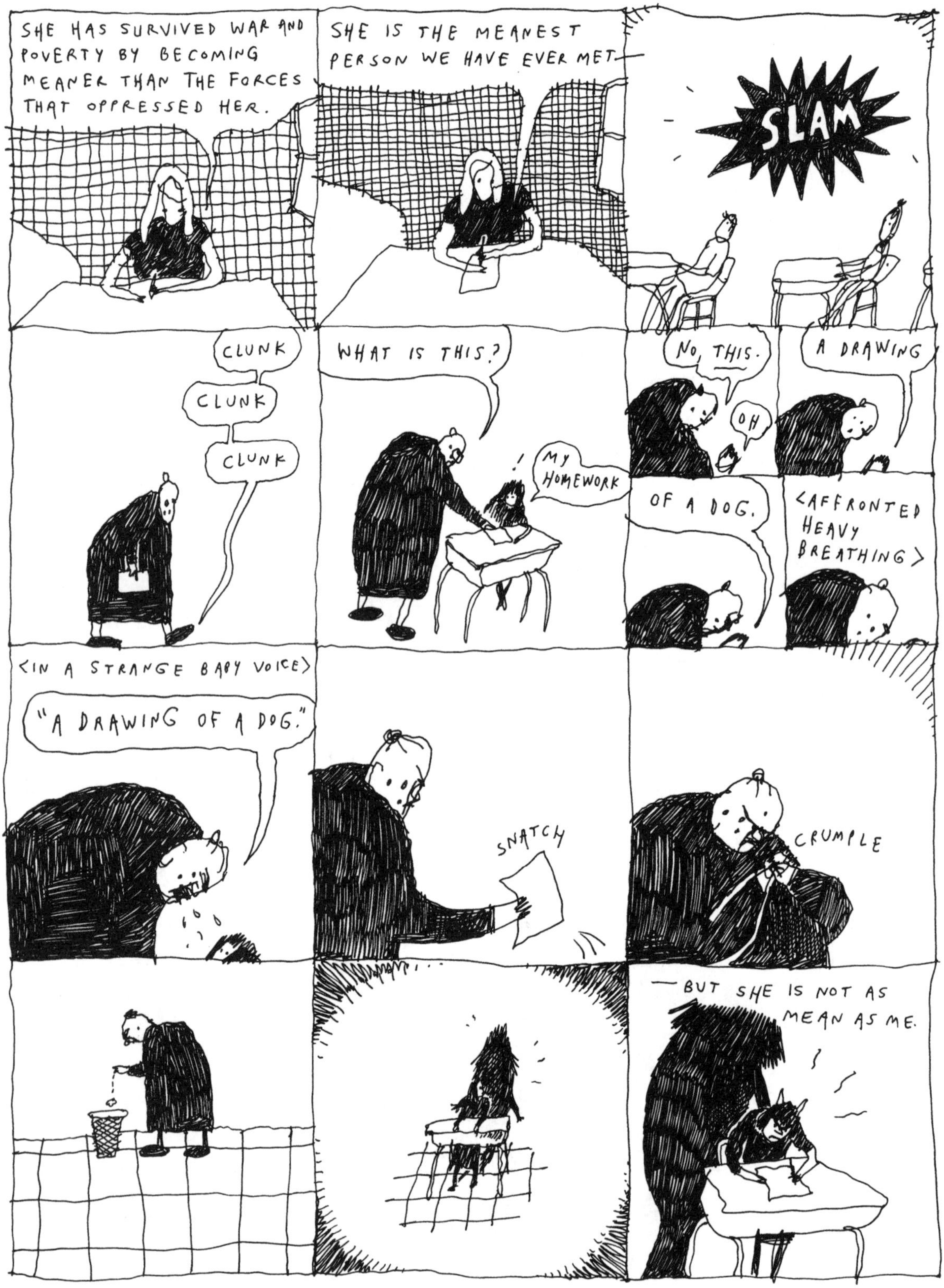
SHE HAS SURVIVED WAR AND POVERTY BY BECOMING MEANER THAN THE FORCES THAT OPPRESSED HER.
SHE IS THE MEANEST PERSON WE HAVE EVER MET—
SLAM
CLUNK
CLUNK
CLUNK
WHAT IS THIS?
MY HOMEWORK
NO, THIS.
OH
A DRAWING
OF A DOG.
<AFFRONTED HEAVY BREATHING>
<IN A STRANGE BABY VOICE>
"A DRAWING OF A DOG."
SNATCH
CRUMPLE
—BUT SHE IS NOT AS MEAN AS ME.

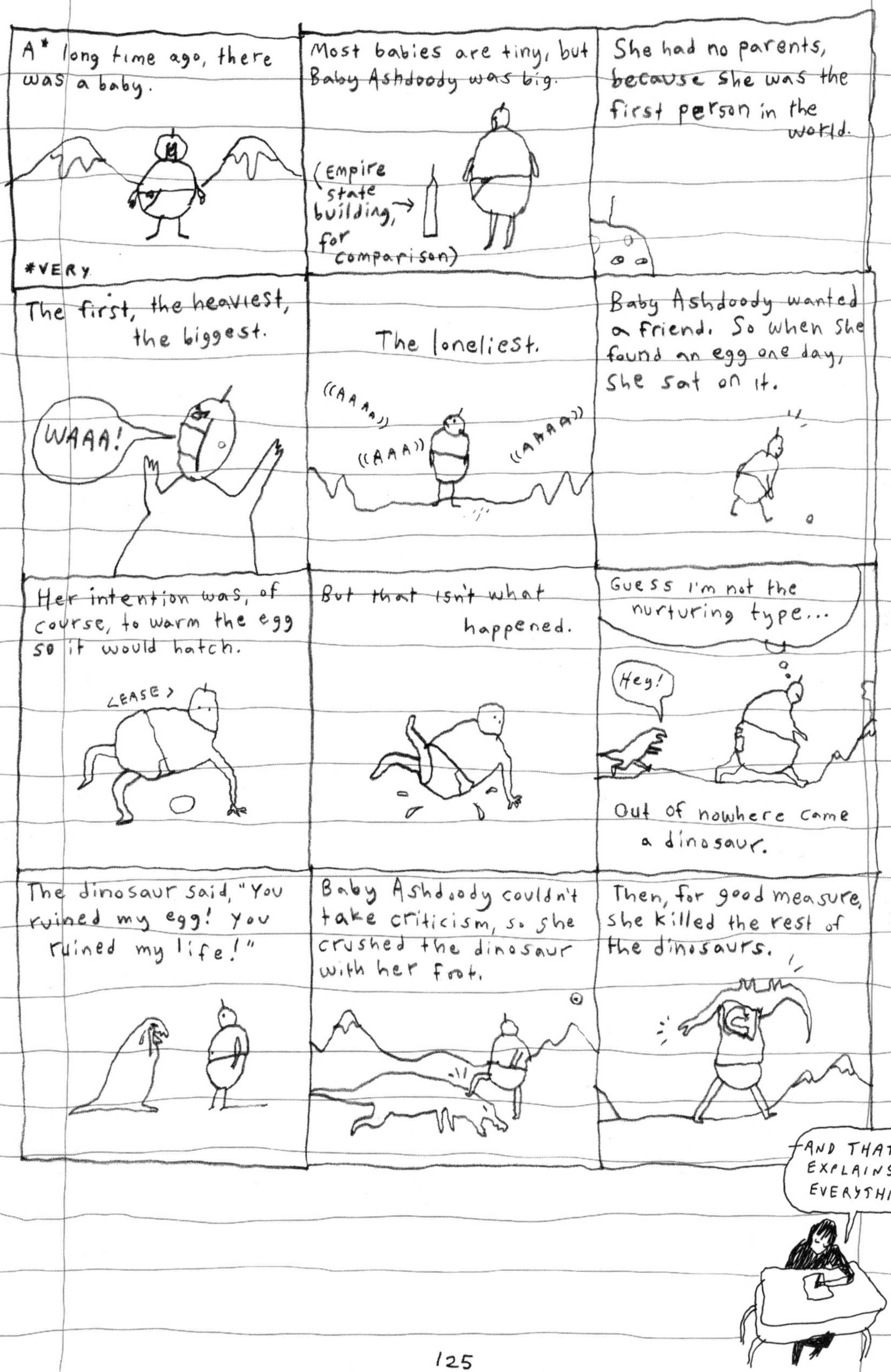
A* long time ago, there was a baby.
*VERY
Most babies are tiny, but Baby Ashdoody was big.
(Empire state building, for comparison)
She had no parents, because she was the first person in the world.
The first, the heaviest, the biggest.
WAAA!
The loneliest.
((AAAA))
((AAA))
((AAAA))
Baby Ashdoody wanted a friend. So when she found an egg one day, she sat on it.
Her intention was, of course, to warm the egg so it would hatch.
<EASE>
But that isn't what happened.
Guess I'm not the nurturing type...
Hey!
Out of nowhere came a dinosaur.
The dinosaur said, "You ruined my egg! You ruined my life!"
Baby Ashdoody couldn't take criticism, so she crushed the dinosaur with her foot.
Then, for good measure, she killed the rest of the dinosaurs.
AND THAT EXPLAINS EVERYTHING.

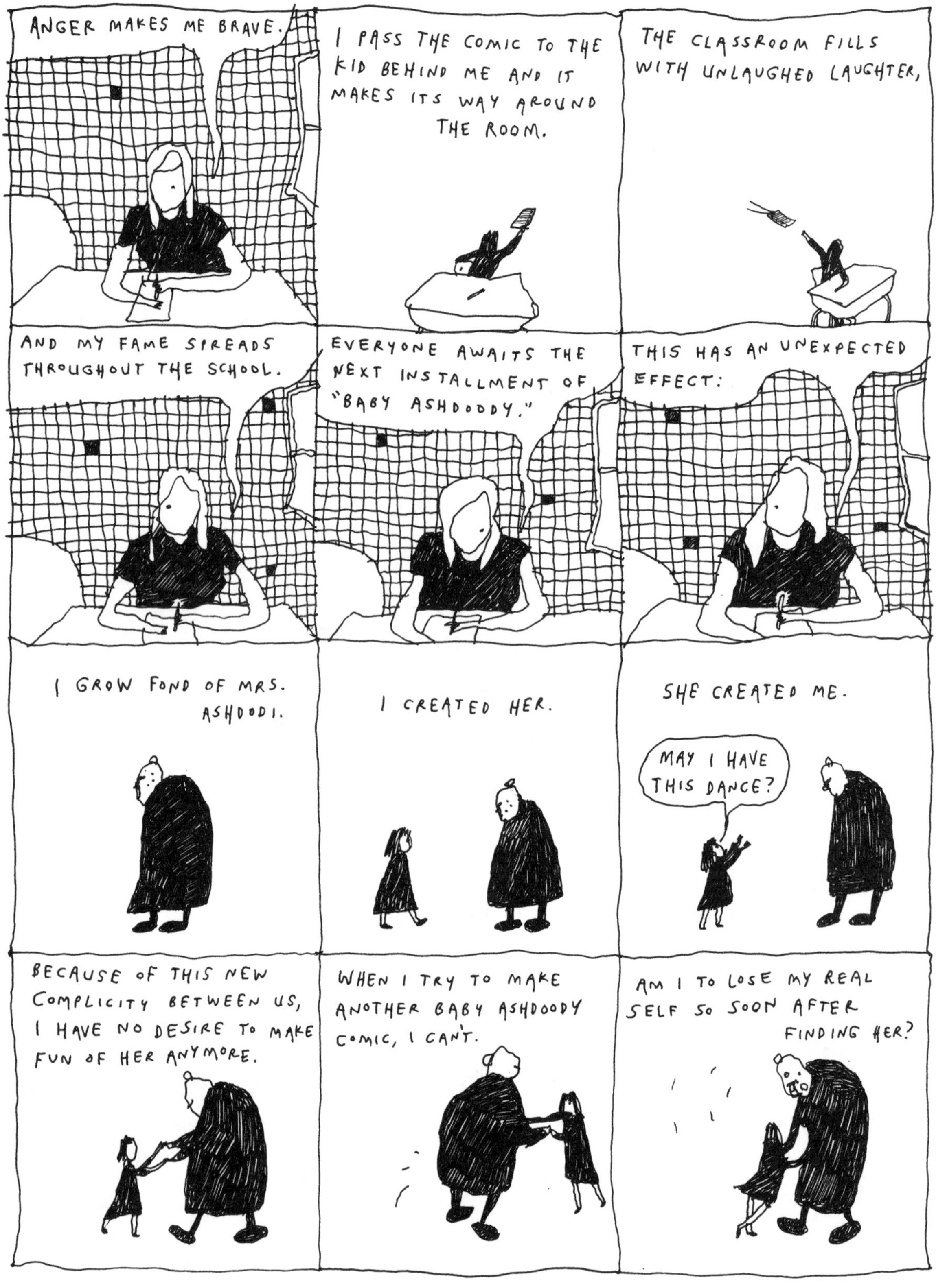
ANGER MAKES ME BRAVE.
I PASS THE COMIC TO THE KID BEHIND ME AND IT MAKES ITS WAY AROUND THE ROOM.
THE CLASSROOM FILLS WITH UNLAUGHED LAUGHTER,
AND MY FAME SPREADS THROUGHOUT THE SCHOOL.
EVERYONE AWAITS THE NEXT INSTALLMENT OF "BABY ASHDOODY."
THIS HAS AN UNEXPECTED EFFECT:
I GROW FOND OF MRS. ASHDODI.
I CREATED HER.
SHE CREATED ME.
MAY I HAVE THIS DANCE?
BECAUSE OF THIS NEW COMPLICITY BETWEEN US, I HAVE NO DESIRE TO MAKE FUN OF HER ANYMORE.
WHEN I TRY TO MAKE ANOTHER BABY ASHDOODY COMIC, I CAN'T.
AM I TO LOSE MY REAL SELF SO SOON AFTER FINDING HER?

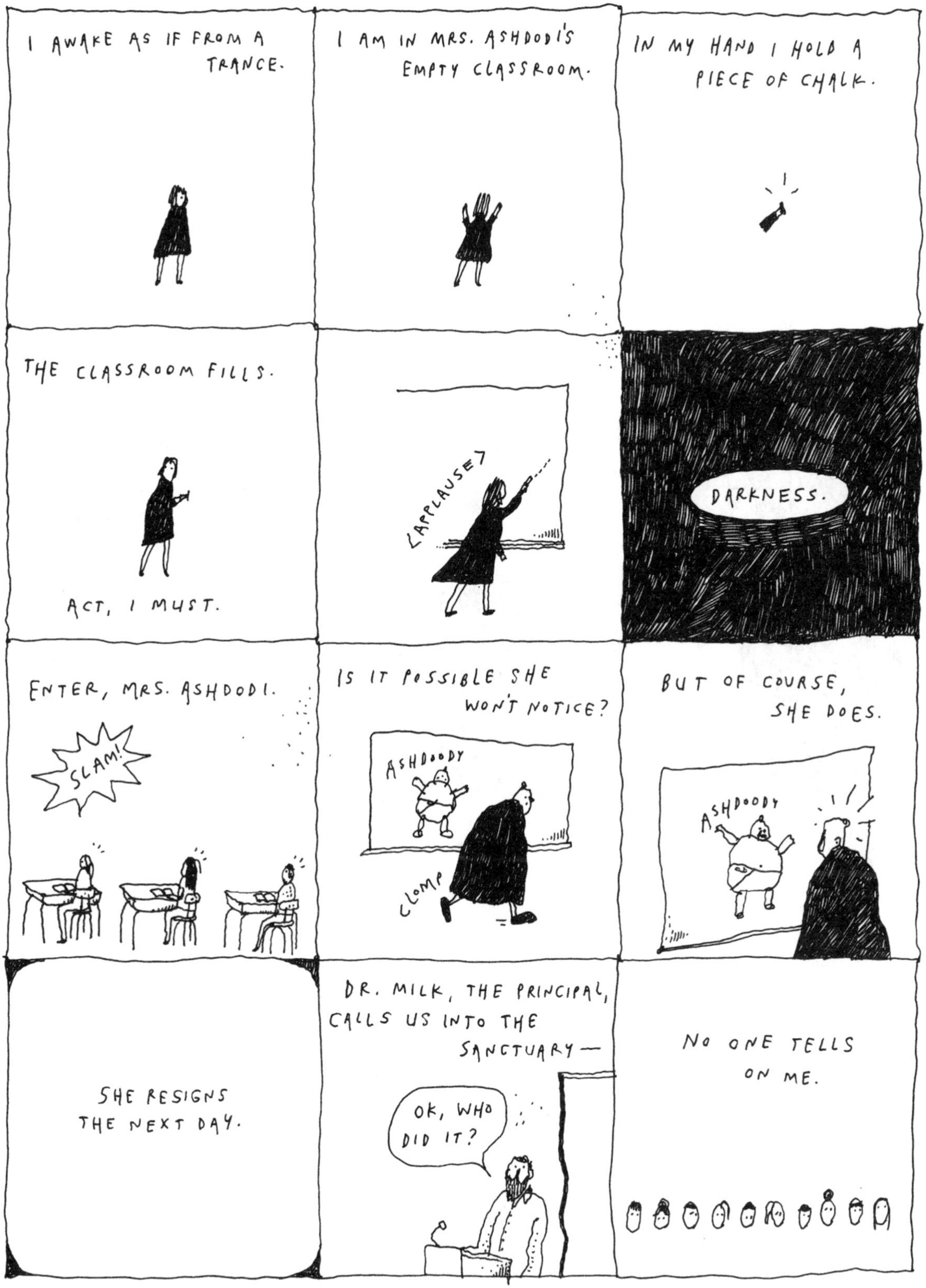
I AWAKE AS IF FROM A TRANCE.
I AM IN MRS. ASHDODI'S EMPTY CLASSROOM.
IN MY HAND I HOLD A PIECE OF CHALK.
THE CLASSROOM FILLS.
ACT, I MUST.
<APPLAUSE>
DARKNESS.
ENTER, MRS. ASHDODI.
SLAM!
IS IT POSSIBLE SHE WON'T NOTICE?
ASHDOODY
CLOMP
BUT OF COURSE, SHE DOES.
ASHDOODY
SHE RESIGNS THE NEXT DAY.
DR. MILK, THE PRINCIPAL, CALLS US INTO THE SANCTUARY—
OK, WHO DID IT?
NO ONE TELLS ON ME.

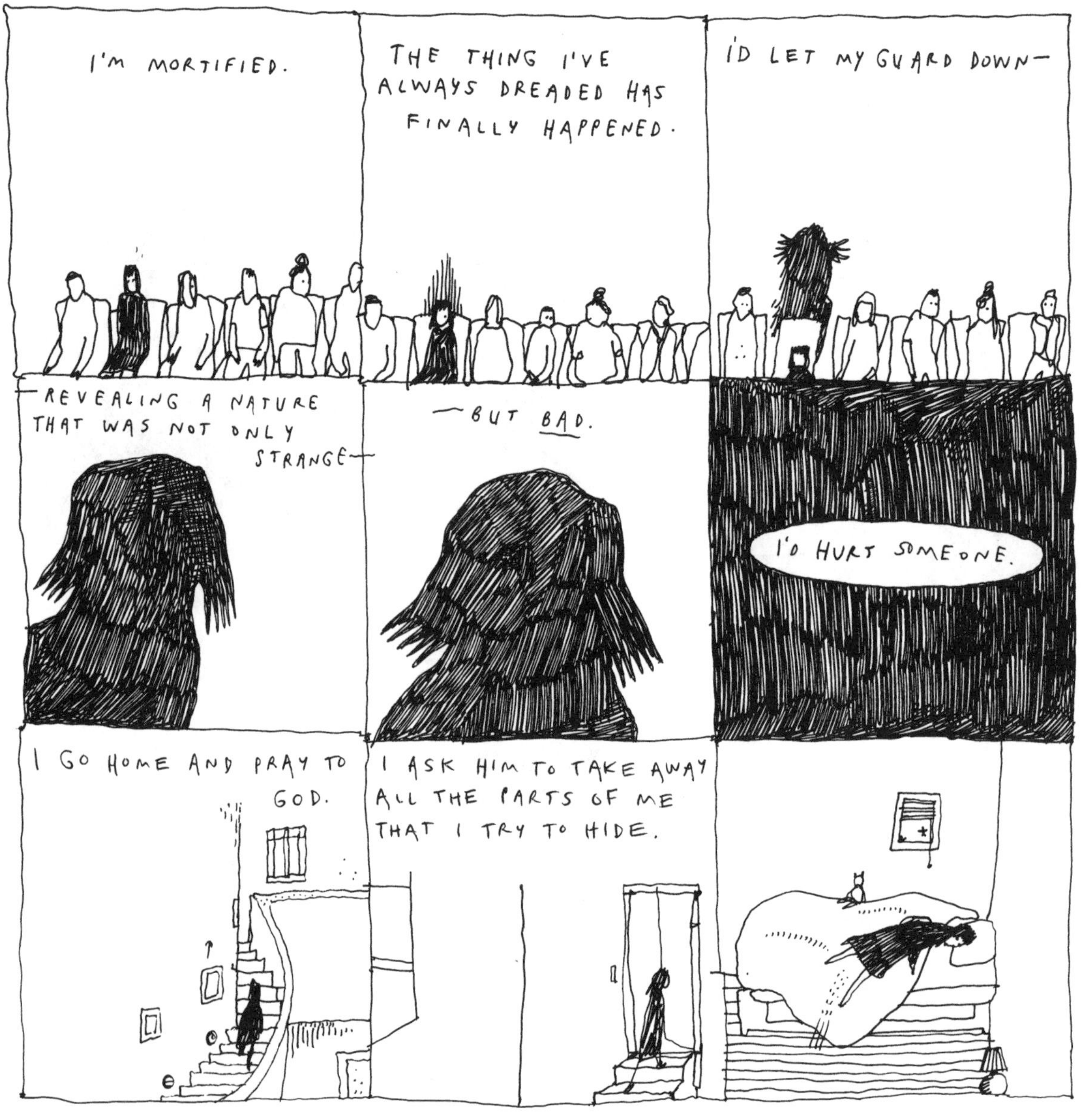
I'M MORTIFIED.
THE THING I'VE ALWAYS DREADED HAS FINALLY HAPPENED.
I'D LET MY GUARD DOWN—
—REVEALING A NATURE THAT WAS NOT ONLY STRANGE—
—BUT BAD.
I'D HURT SOMEONE.
I GO HOME AND PRAY TO GOD.
I ASK HIM TO TAKE AWAY ALL THE PARTS OF ME THAT I TRY TO HIDE.

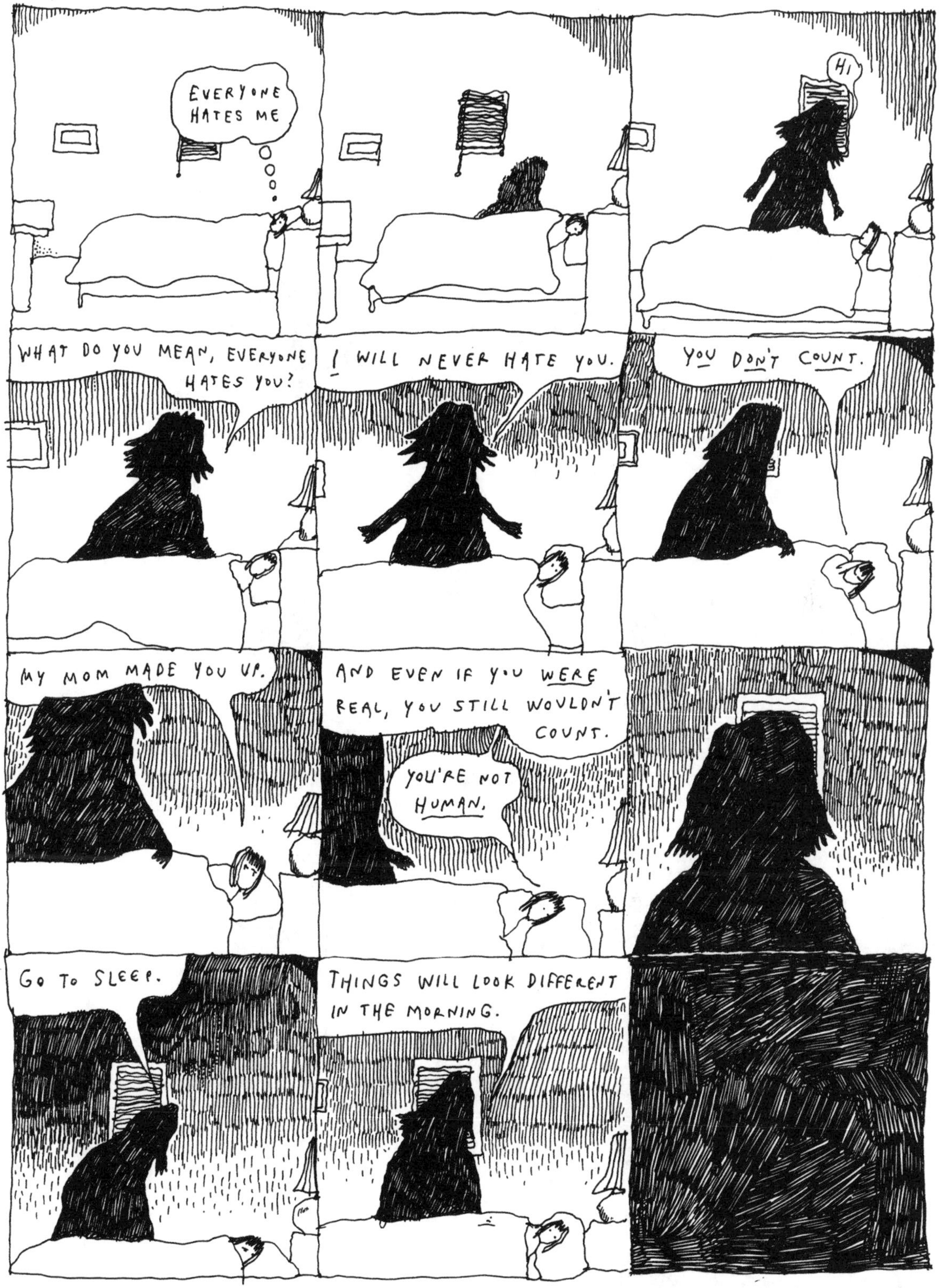
EVERYONE HATES ME
HI
WHAT DO YOU MEAN, EVERYONE HATES YOU?
I WILL NEVER HATE YOU.
YOU DON'T COUNT.
MY MOM MADE YOU UP.
AND EVEN IF YOU WERE REAL, YOU STILL WOULDN'T COUNT.
YOU'RE NOT HUMAN.
GO TO SLEEP.
THINGS WILL LOOK DIFFERENT IN THE MORNING.

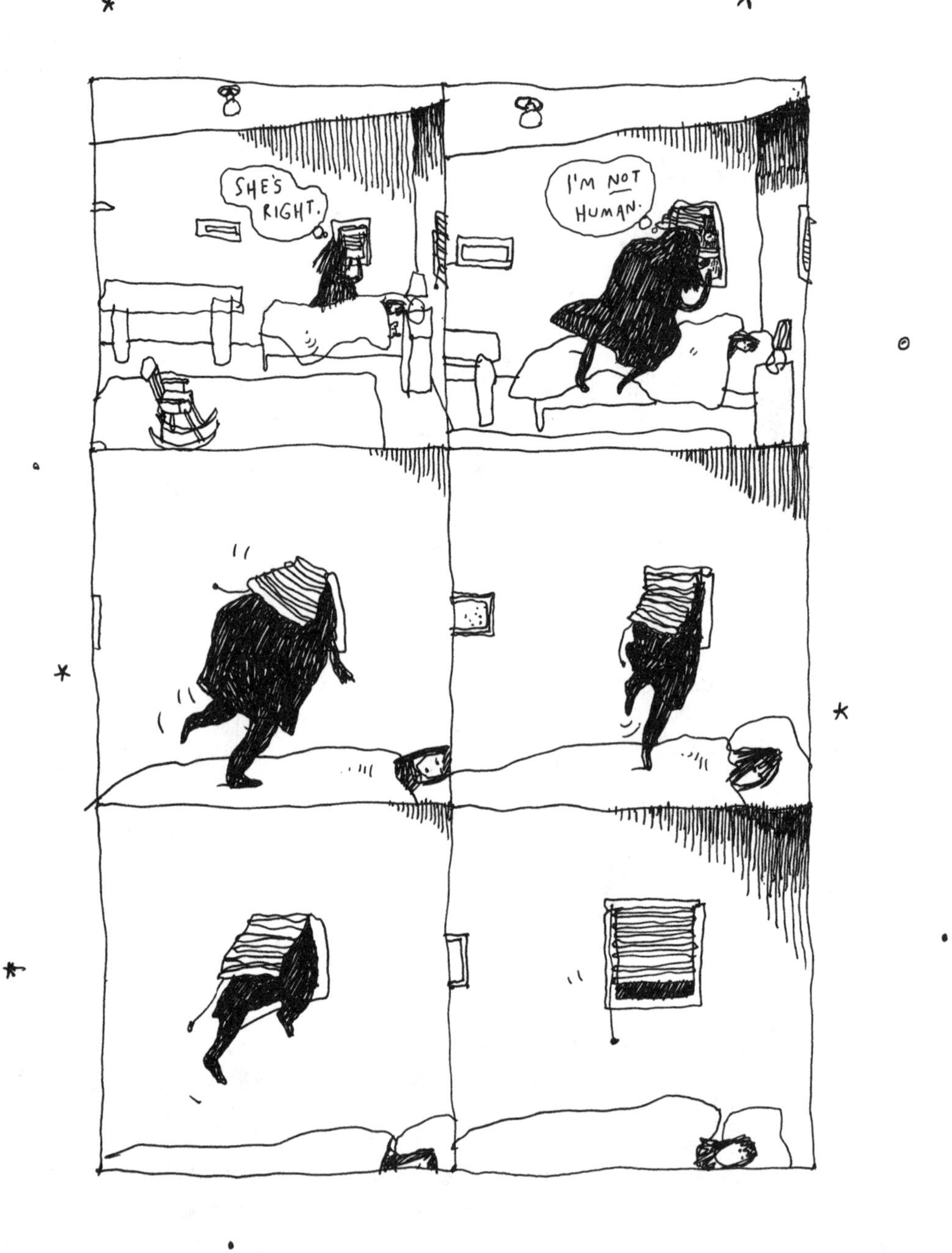
SHE'S RIGHT.
I'M NOT HUMAN.

EVERYTHING DOES LOOK DIFFERENT IN THE MORNING.

I LOOK DIFFERENT.

I GATHER UP ALL THE DRAWINGS I'VE EVER MADE—

—AND THROW THEM OUT.

THEN, I STOP EATING.

MAYBE THE PERSON I'M NOT WILL MELT AWAY, REVEALING THE PERSON I AM?

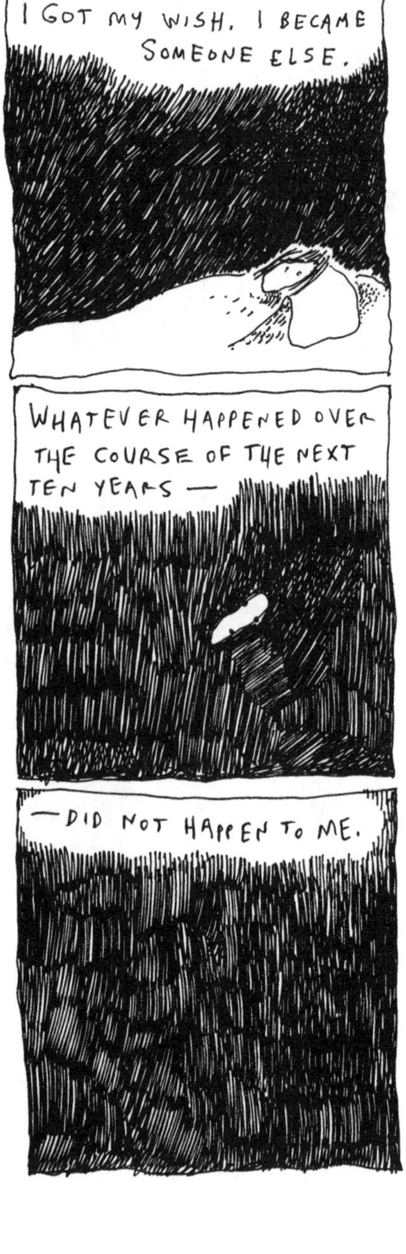
I GOT MY WISH. I BECAME SOMEONE ELSE.
WHATEVER HAPPENED OVER THE COURSE OF THE NEXT TEN YEARS —
— DID NOT HAPPEN TO ME.

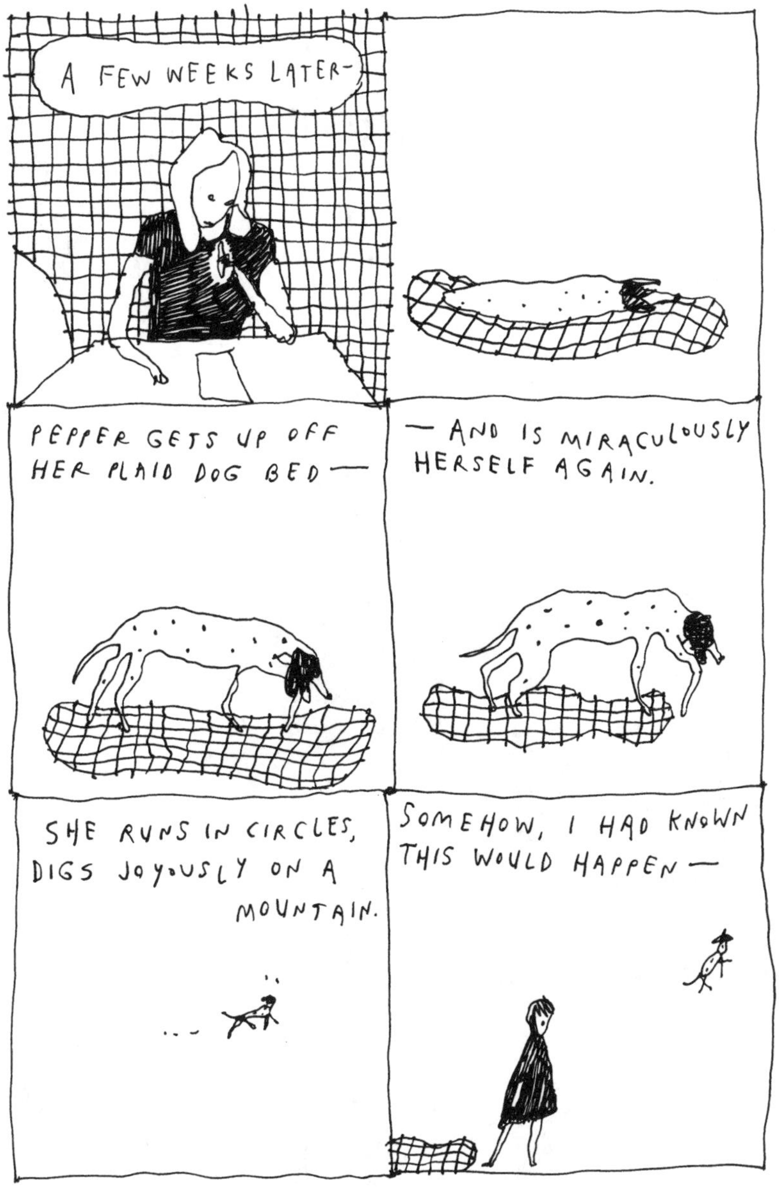
A FEW WEEKS LATER-
PEPPER GETS UP OFF HER PLAID DOG BED—
—AND IS MIRACULOUSLY HERSELF AGAIN.
SHE RUNS IN CIRCLES, DIGS JOYOUSLY ON A MOUNTAIN.
SOMEHOW, I HAD KNOWN THIS WOULD HAPPEN—

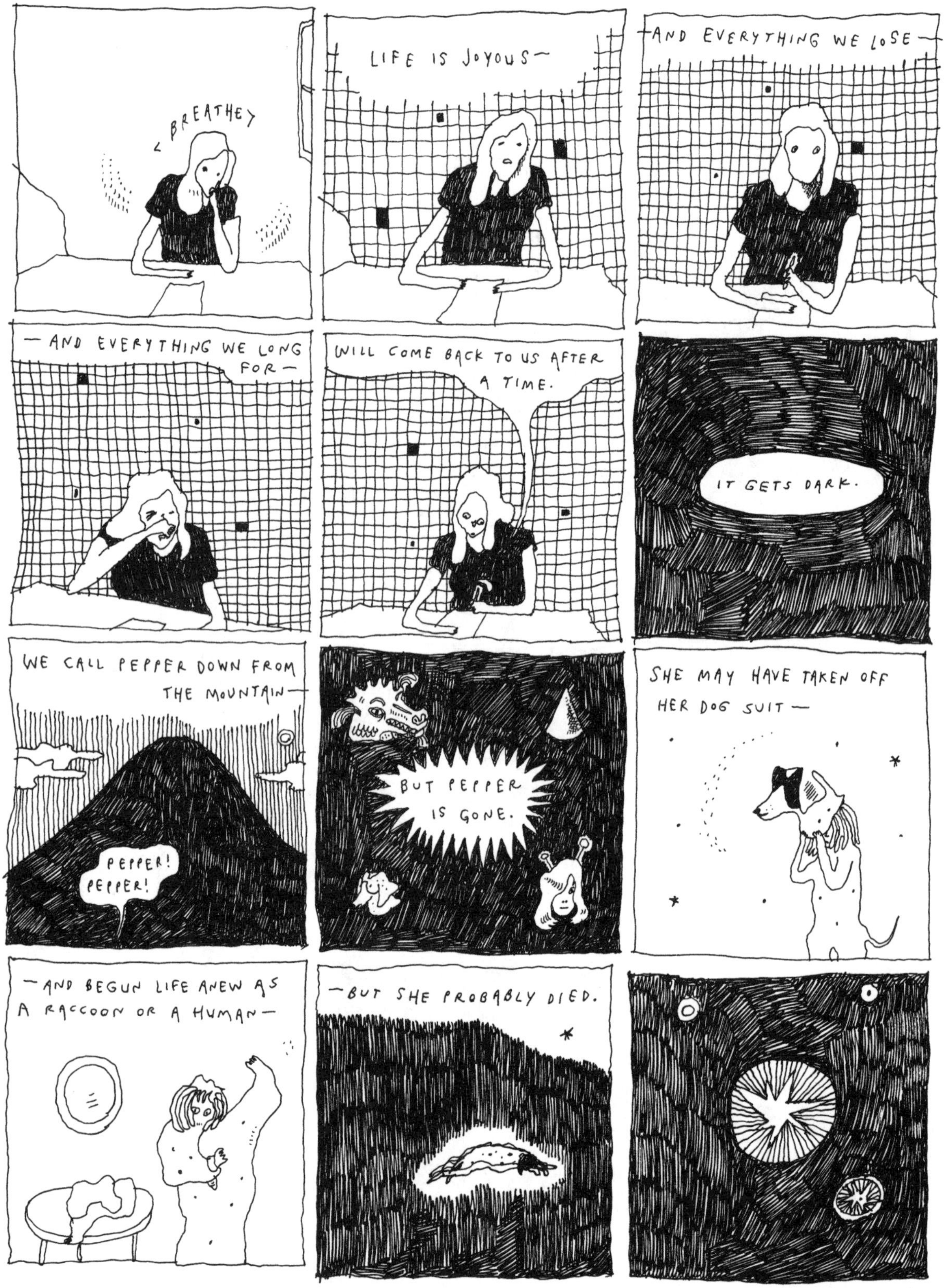
< BREATHE >
LIFE IS JOYOUS—
AND EVERYTHING WE LOSE—
—AND EVERYTHING WE LONG FOR—
WILL COME BACK TO US AFTER A TIME.
IT GETS DARK.
WE CALL PEPPER DOWN FROM THE MOUNTAIN—
PEPPER! PEPPER!
BUT PEPPER IS GONE.
SHE MAY HAVE TAKEN OFF HER DOG SUIT—
—AND BEGUN LIFE ANEW AS A RACCOON OR A HUMAN—
—BUT SHE PROBABLY DIED.

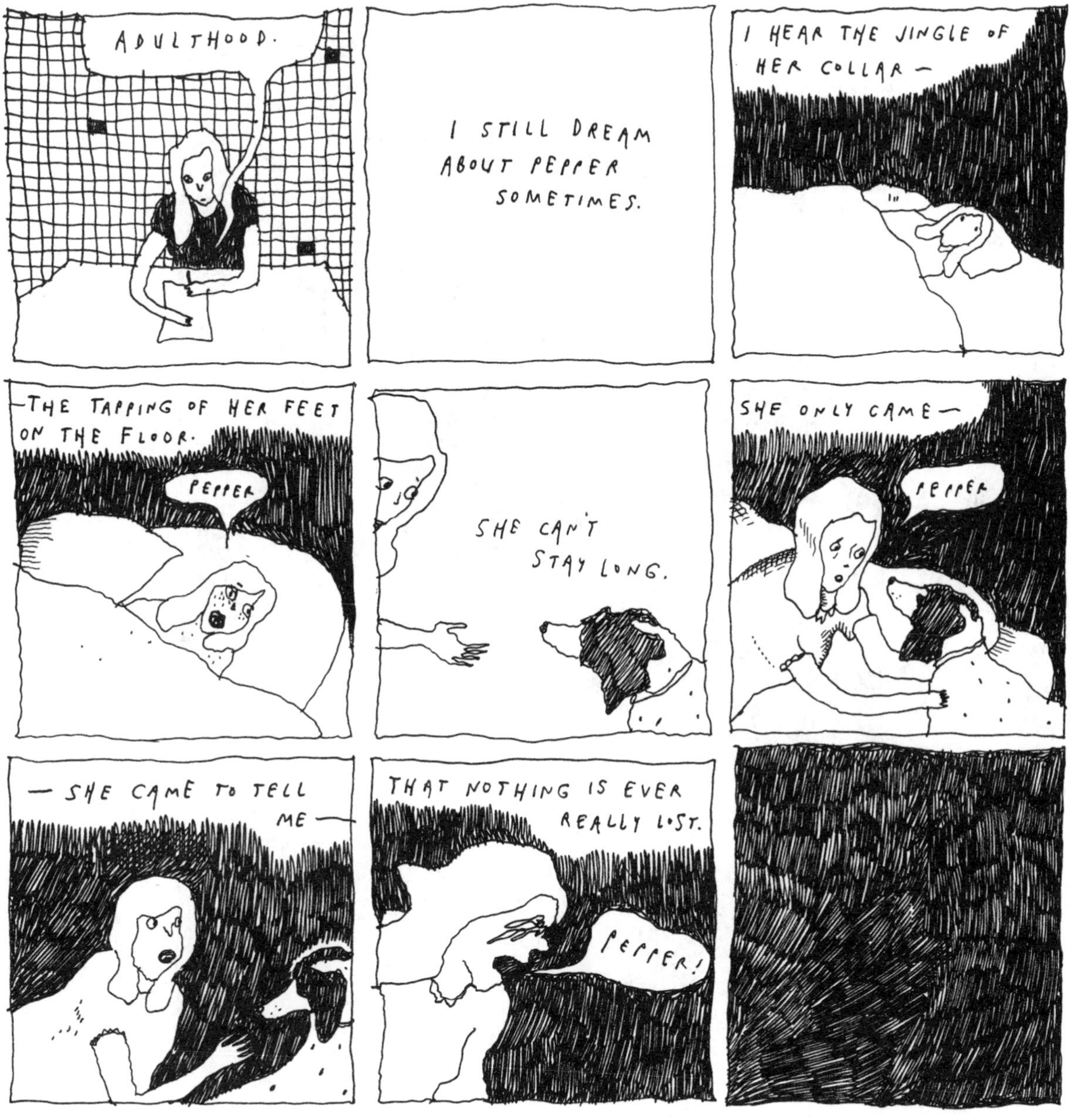
ADULTHOOD.
I STILL DREAM ABOUT PEPPER SOMETIMES.
I HEAR THE JINGLE OF HER COLLAR —
— THE TAPPING OF HER FEET ON THE FLOOR.
PEPPER
SHE CAN'T STAY LONG.
SHE ONLY CAME —
PEPPER
— SHE CAME TO TELL ME —
THAT NOTHING IS EVER REALLY LOST.
PEPPER!

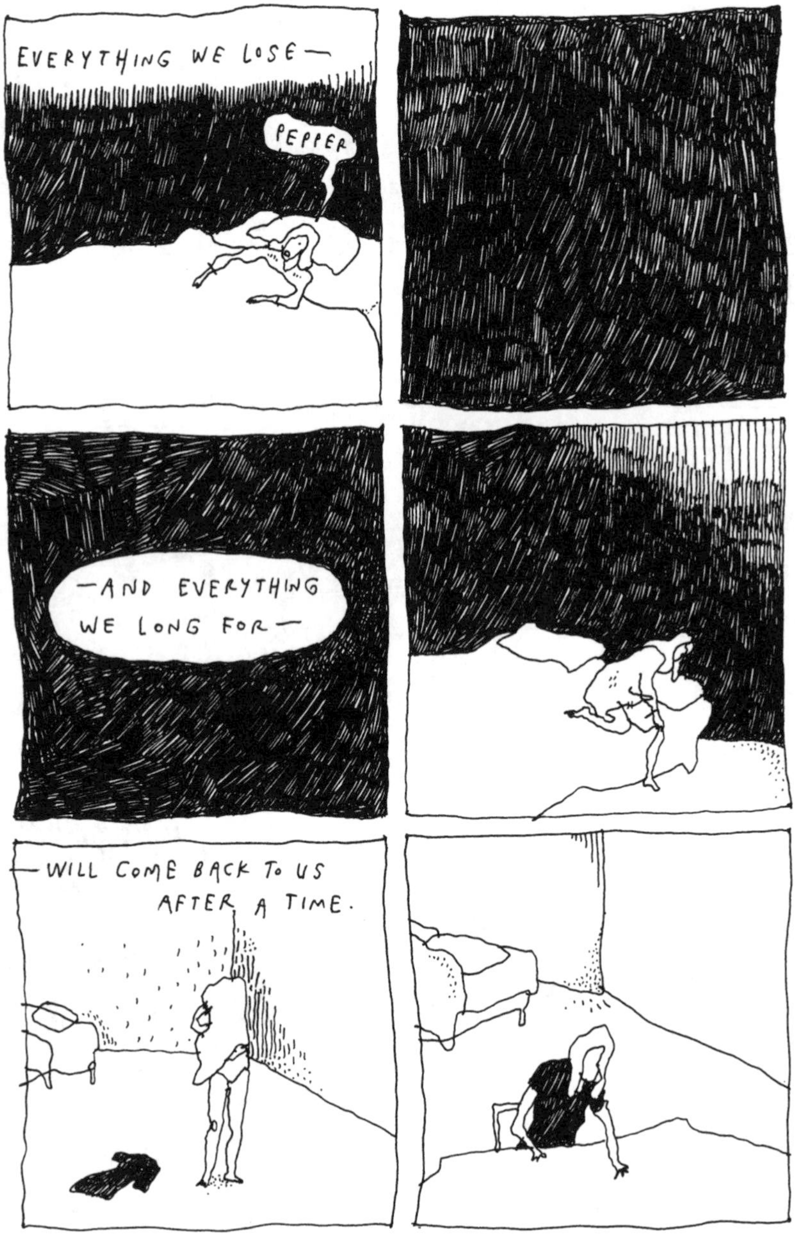
EVERYTHING WE LOSE—
PEPPER
—AND EVERYTHING WE LONG FOR—
—WILL COME BACK TO US AFTER A TIME.

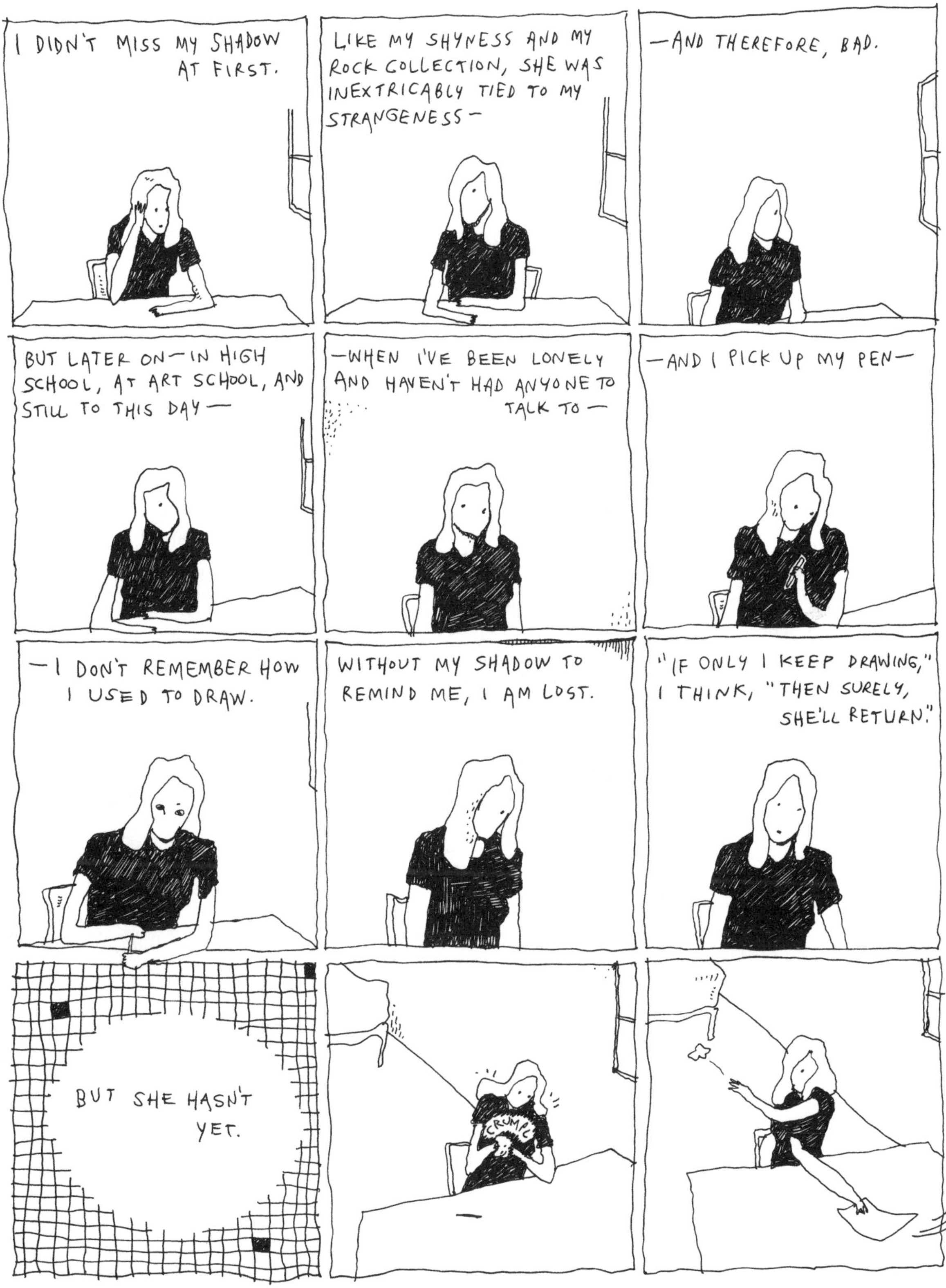
I DIDN'T MISS MY SHADOW AT FIRST.
LIKE MY SHYNESS AND MY ROCK COLLECTION, SHE WAS INEXTRICABLY TIED TO MY STRANGENESS—
—AND THEREFORE, BAD.
BUT LATER ON—IN HIGH SCHOOL, AT ART SCHOOL, AND STILL TO THIS DAY—
—WHEN I'VE BEEN LONELY AND HAVEN'T HAD ANYONE TO TALK TO—
—AND I PICK UP MY PEN—
—I DON'T REMEMBER HOW I USED TO DRAW.
WITHOUT MY SHADOW TO REMIND ME, I AM LOST.
"IF ONLY I KEEP DRAWING," I THINK, "THEN SURELY, SHE'LL RETURN."
BUT SHE HASN'T YET.
CRUMPL

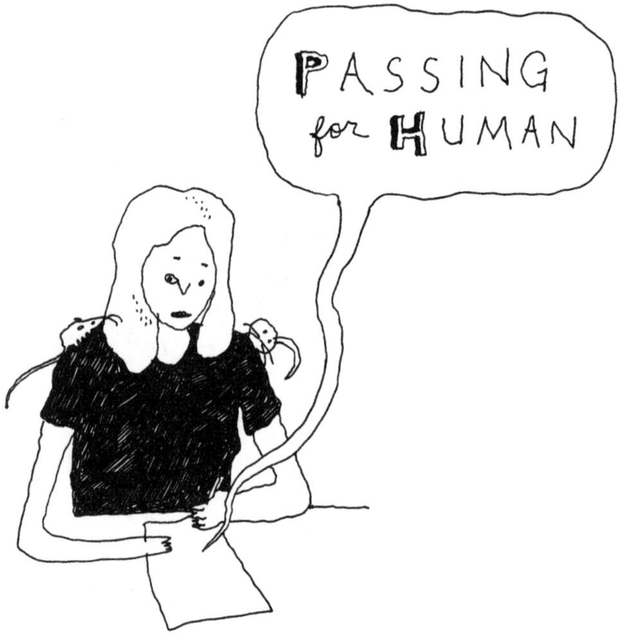
PASSING for HUMAN

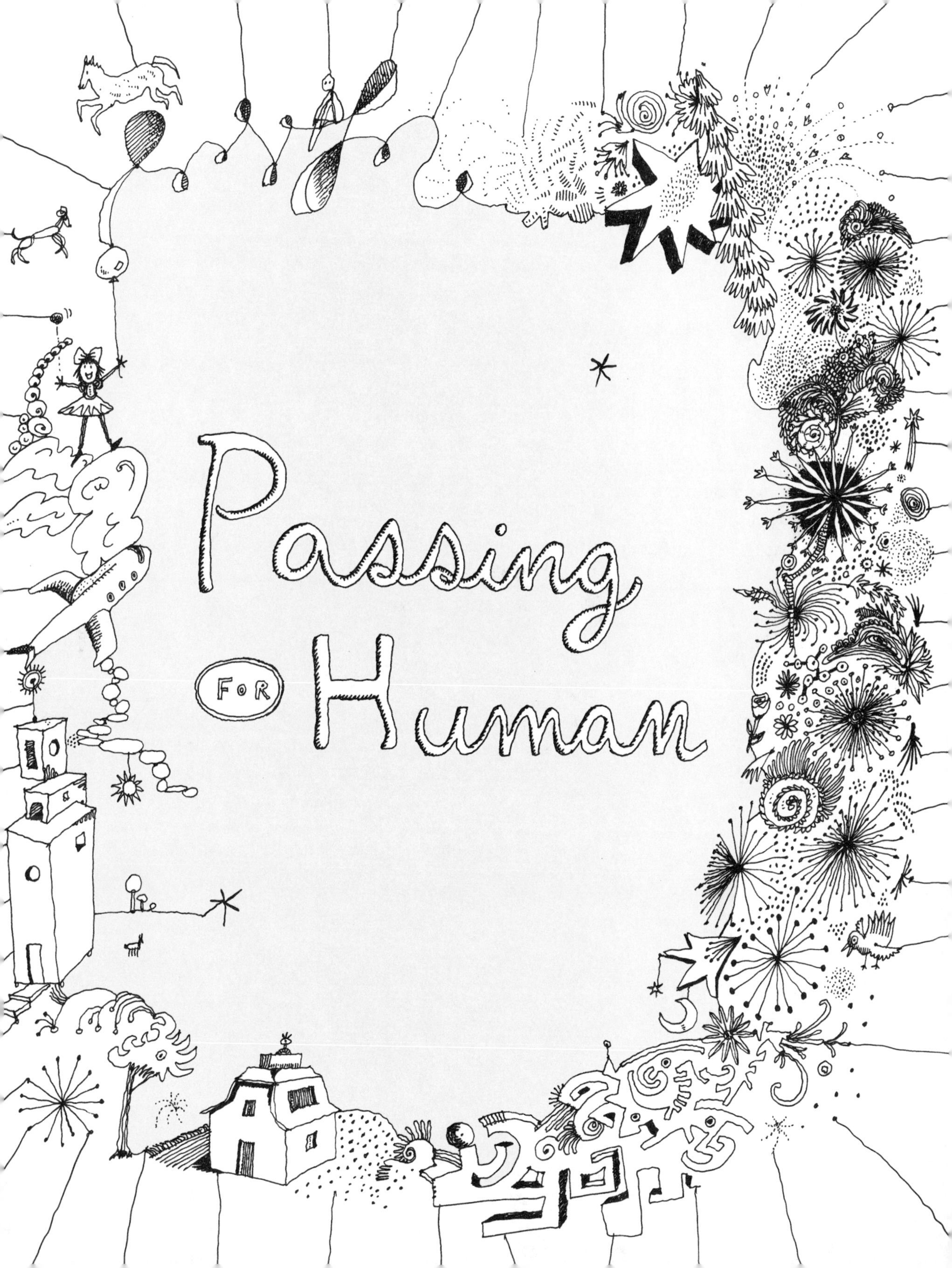
Passing
FOR
Human

"IT'S ONLY A PAPER MOON
SAILING OVER A CARDBOARD SEA
BUT IT WOULDN'T BE MAKE-BELIEVE
IF YOU BELIEVED IN ME."

—"IT'S ONLY A PAPER MOON,"
MUSIC BY HAROLD ARLEN,
LYRICS BY YIP HARBURG AND BILLY ROSE

CHAPTER 1

MR. NEUTRAL

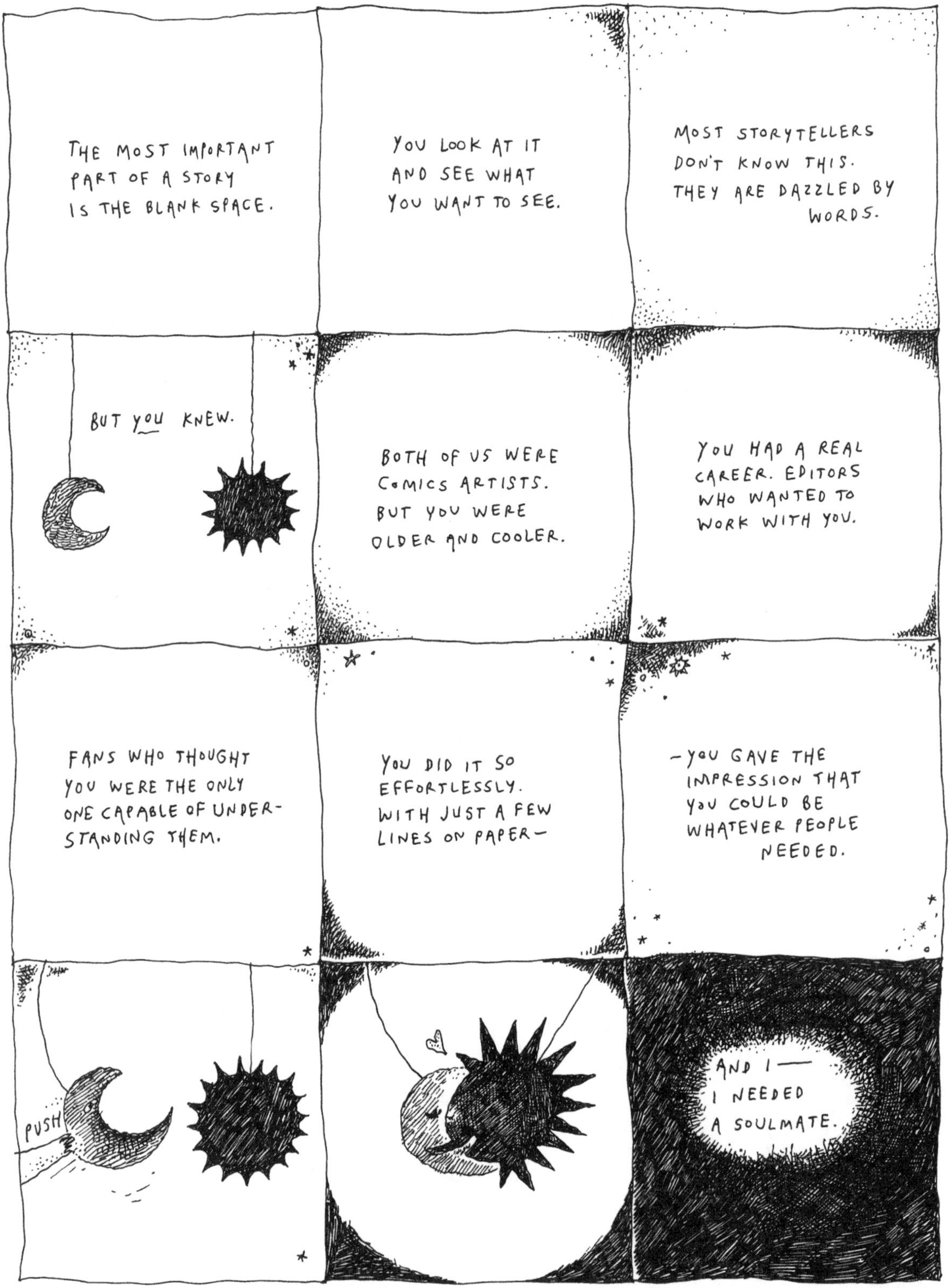
THE MOST IMPORTANT PART OF A STORY IS THE BLANK SPACE.
YOU LOOK AT IT AND SEE WHAT YOU WANT TO SEE.
MOST STORYTELLERS DON'T KNOW THIS. THEY ARE DAZZLED BY WORDS.
BUT YOU KNEW.
BOTH OF US WERE COMICS ARTISTS. BUT YOU WERE OLDER AND COOLER.
YOU HAD A REAL CAREER. EDITORS WHO WANTED TO WORK WITH YOU.
FANS WHO THOUGHT YOU WERE THE ONLY ONE CAPABLE OF UNDER-STANDING THEM.
YOU DID IT SO EFFORTLESSLY. WITH JUST A FEW LINES ON PAPER—
—YOU GAVE THE IMPRESSION THAT YOU COULD BE WHATEVER PEOPLE NEEDED.
PUSH
AND I— I NEEDED A SOULMATE.

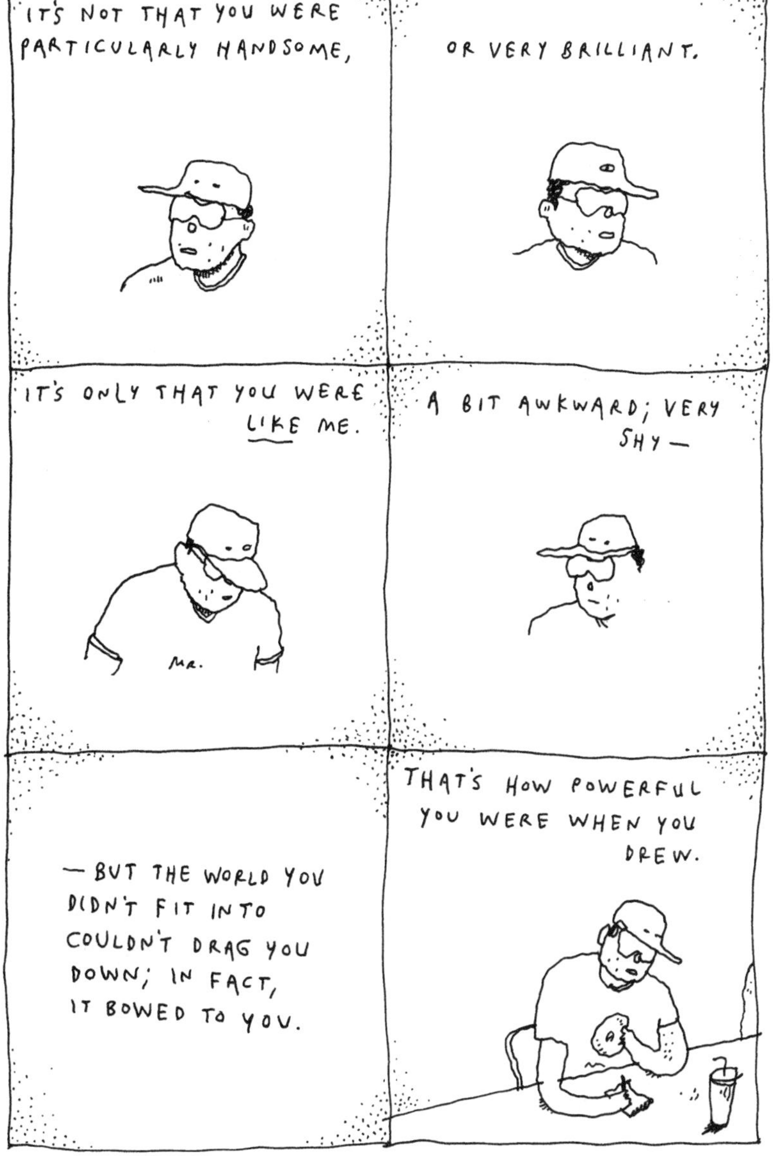
IT'S NOT THAT YOU WERE PARTICULARLY HANDSOME,
OR VERY BRILLIANT.
IT'S ONLY THAT YOU WERE LIKE ME.
MR.
A BIT AWKWARD; VERY SHY—
—BUT THE WORLD YOU DIDN'T FIT INTO COULDN'T DRAG YOU DOWN; IN FACT, IT BOWED TO YOU.
THAT'S HOW POWERFUL YOU WERE WHEN YOU DREW.

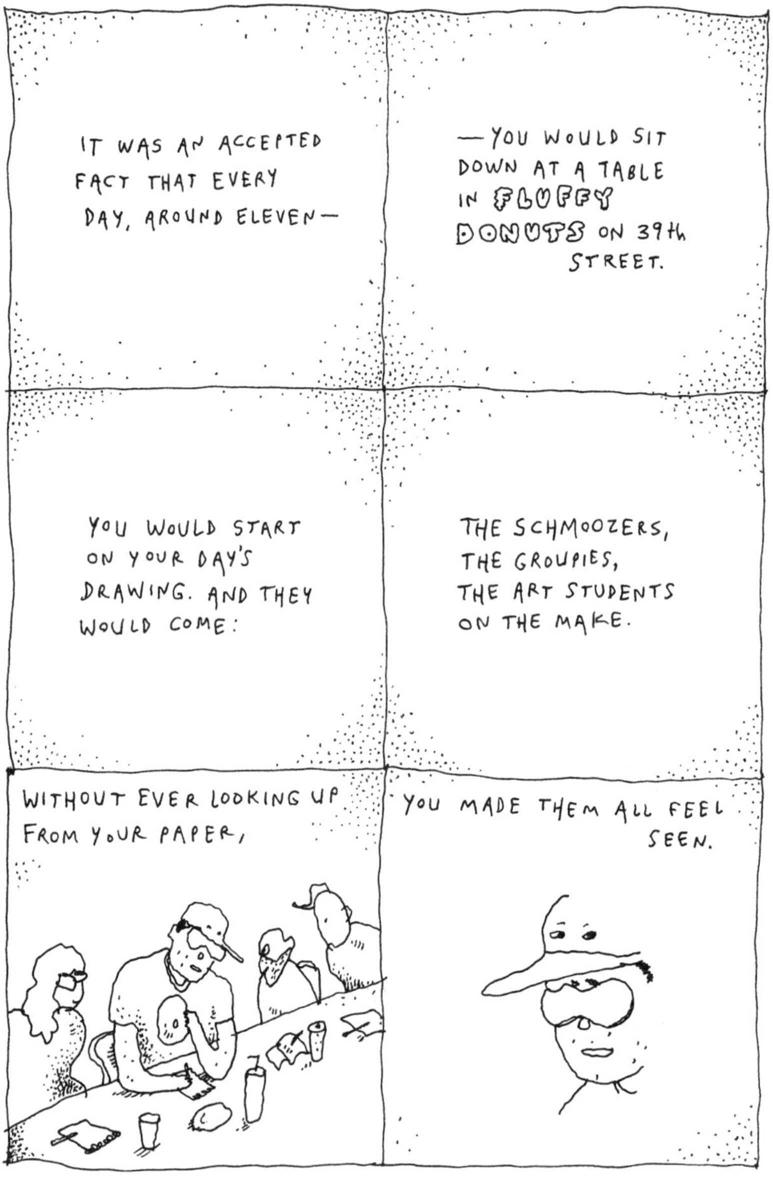
IT WAS AN ACCEPTED FACT THAT EVERY DAY, AROUND ELEVEN—
—YOU WOULD SIT DOWN AT A TABLE IN FLUFFY DONUTS ON 39th STREET.
YOU WOULD START ON YOUR DAY'S DRAWING. AND THEY WOULD COME:
THE SCHMOOZERS, THE GROUPIES, THE ART STUDENTS ON THE MAKE.
WITHOUT EVER LOOKING UP FROM YOUR PAPER,
YOU MADE THEM ALL FEEL SEEN.

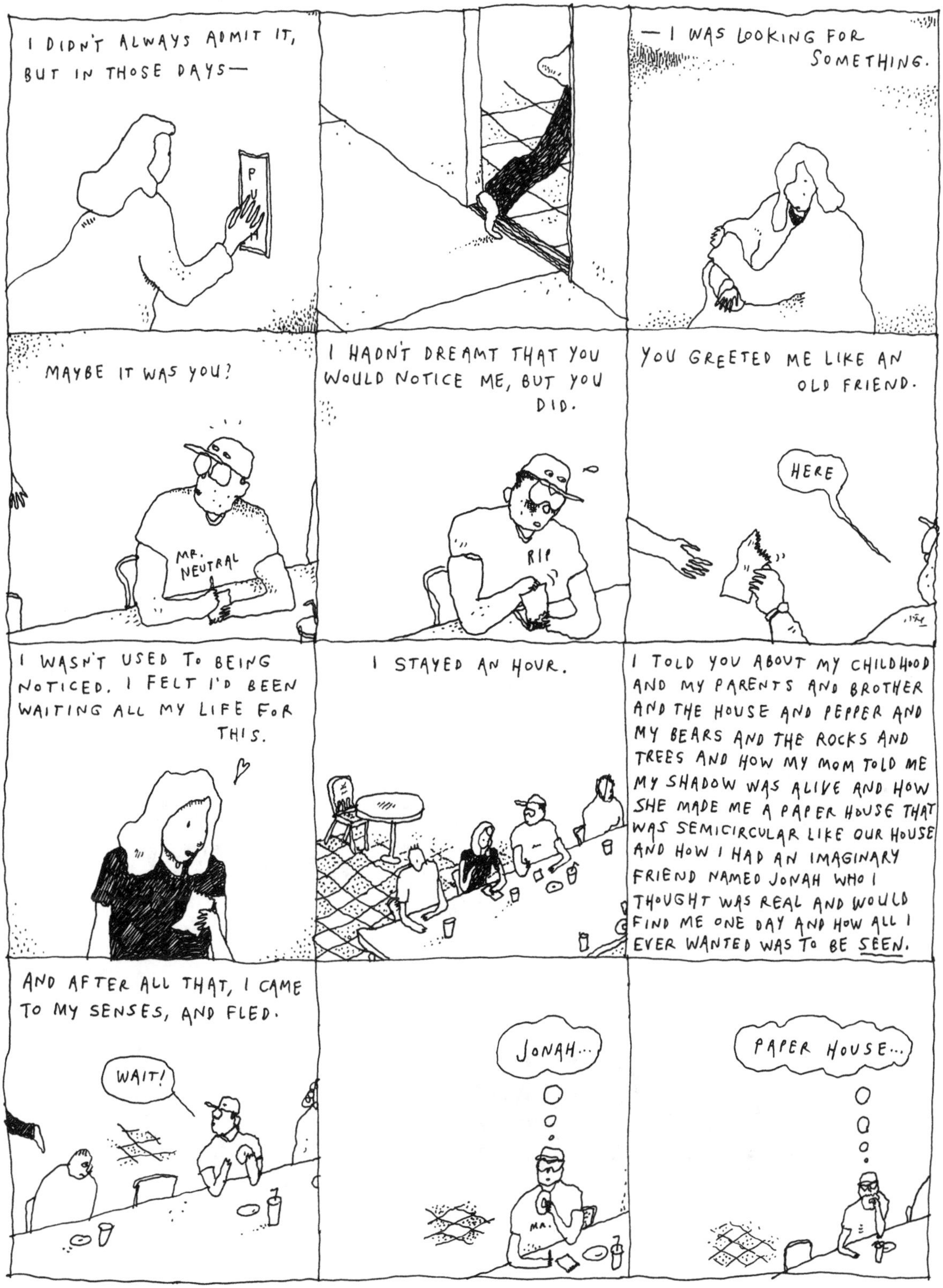
I DIDN'T ALWAYS ADMIT IT, BUT IN THOSE DAYS—
P U S H
—I WAS LOOKING FOR SOMETHING.
MAYBE IT WAS YOU?
I HADN'T DREAMT THAT YOU WOULD NOTICE ME, BUT YOU DID.
MR. NEUTRAL
RIP
YOU GREETED ME LIKE AN OLD FRIEND.
HERE
I WASN'T USED TO BEING NOTICED. I FELT I'D BEEN WAITING ALL MY LIFE FOR THIS.
I STAYED AN HOUR.
I TOLD YOU ABOUT MY CHILDHOOD AND MY PARENTS AND BROTHER AND THE HOUSE AND PEPPER AND MY BEARS AND THE ROCKS AND TREES AND HOW MY MOM TOLD ME MY SHADOW WAS ALIVE AND HOW SHE MADE ME A PAPER HOUSE THAT WAS SEMICIRCULAR LIKE OUR HOUSE AND HOW I HAD AN IMAGINARY FRIEND NAMED JONAH WHO I THOUGHT WAS REAL AND WOULD FIND ME ONE DAY AND HOW ALL I EVER WANTED WAS TO BE SEEN.
AND AFTER ALL THAT, I CAME TO MY SENSES, AND FLED.
WAIT!
JONAH...
MR.
PAPER HOUSE...

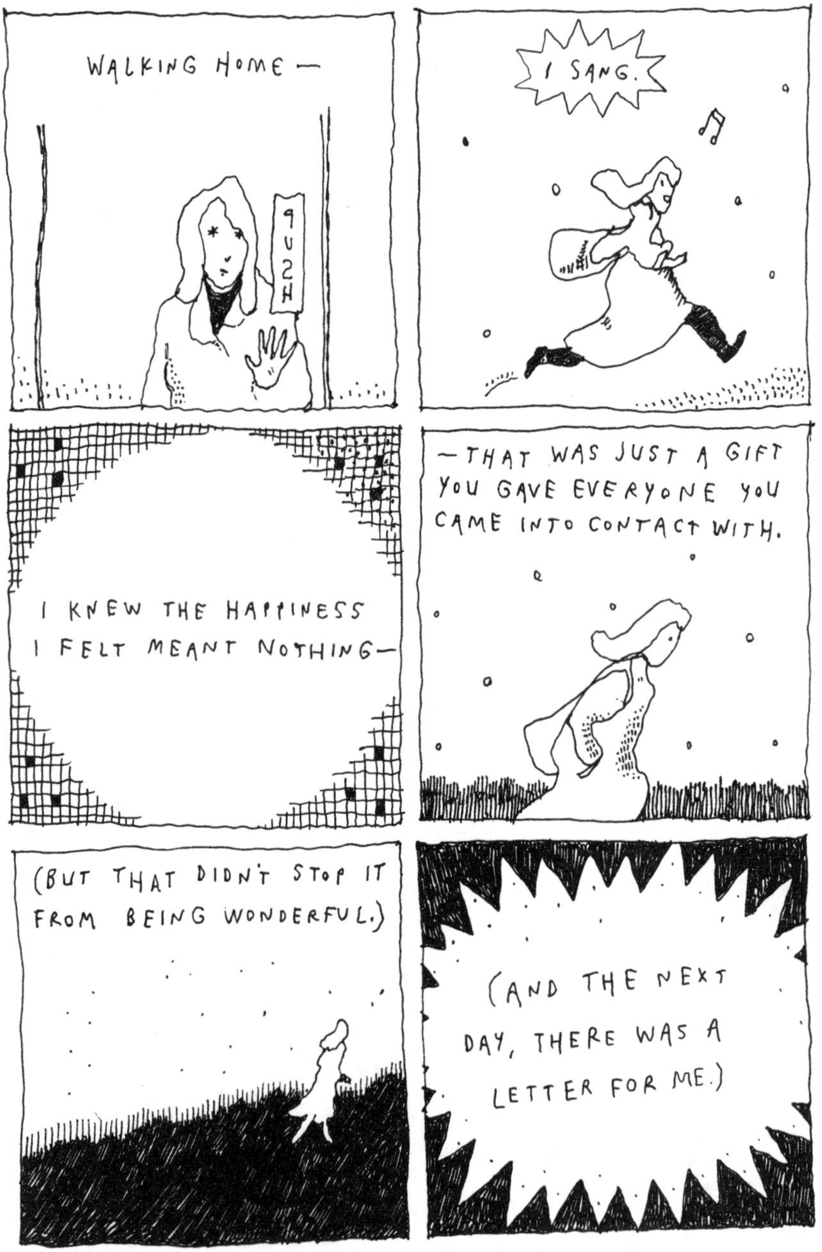
WALKING HOME—
PUSH
I SANG.
I KNEW THE HAPPINESS I FELT MEANT NOTHING—
—THAT WAS JUST A GIFT YOU GAVE EVERYONE YOU CAME INTO CONTACT WITH.
(BUT THAT DIDN'T STOP IT FROM BEING WONDERFUL.)
(AND THE NEXT DAY, THERE WAS A LETTER FOR ME.)

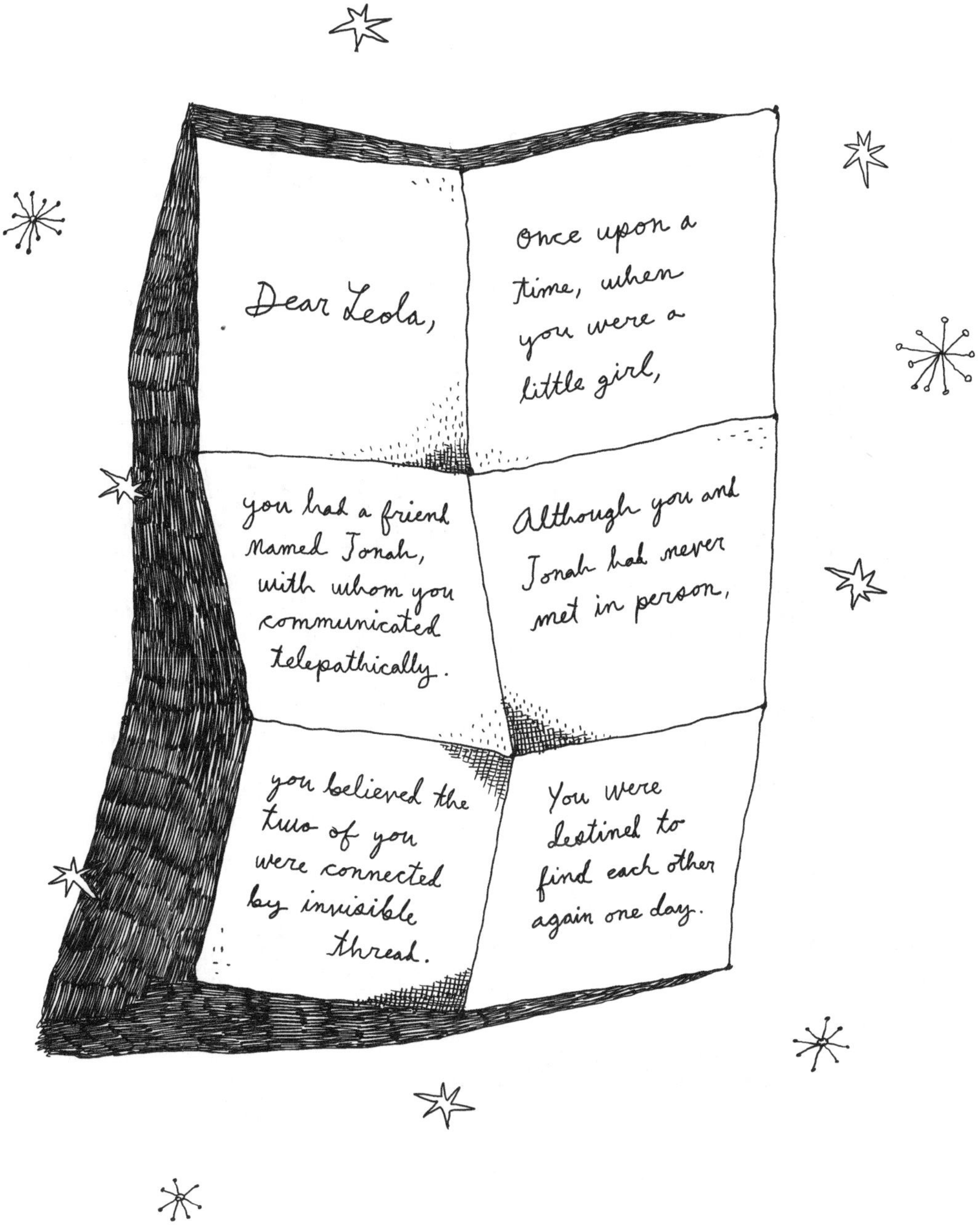
Dear Leola,
Once upon a time, when you were a little girl,
you had a friend named Jonah, with whom you communicated telepathically.
Although you and Jonah had never met in person,
you believed the two of you were connected by invisible thread.
You were destined to find each other again one day.

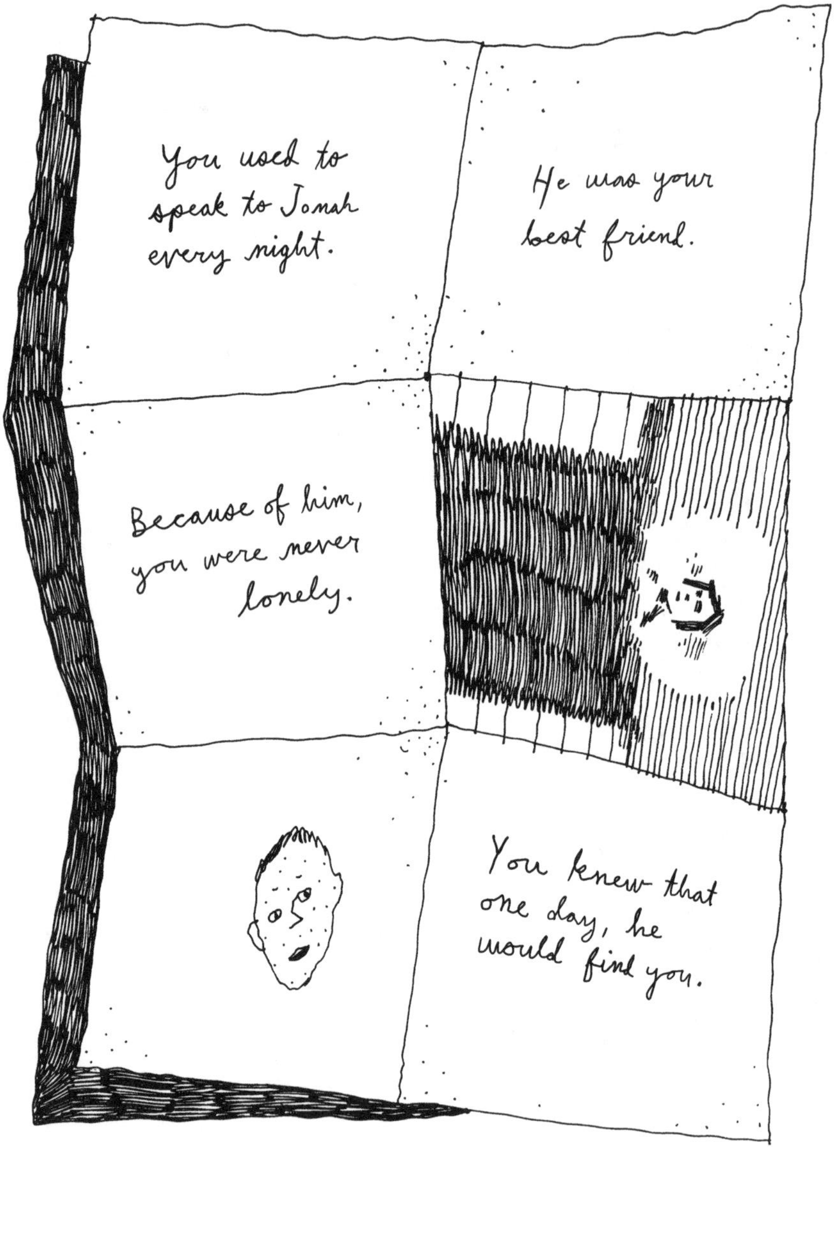
You used to speak to Jonah every night.
He was your best friend.
Because of him, you were never lonely.
You knew that one day, he would find you.

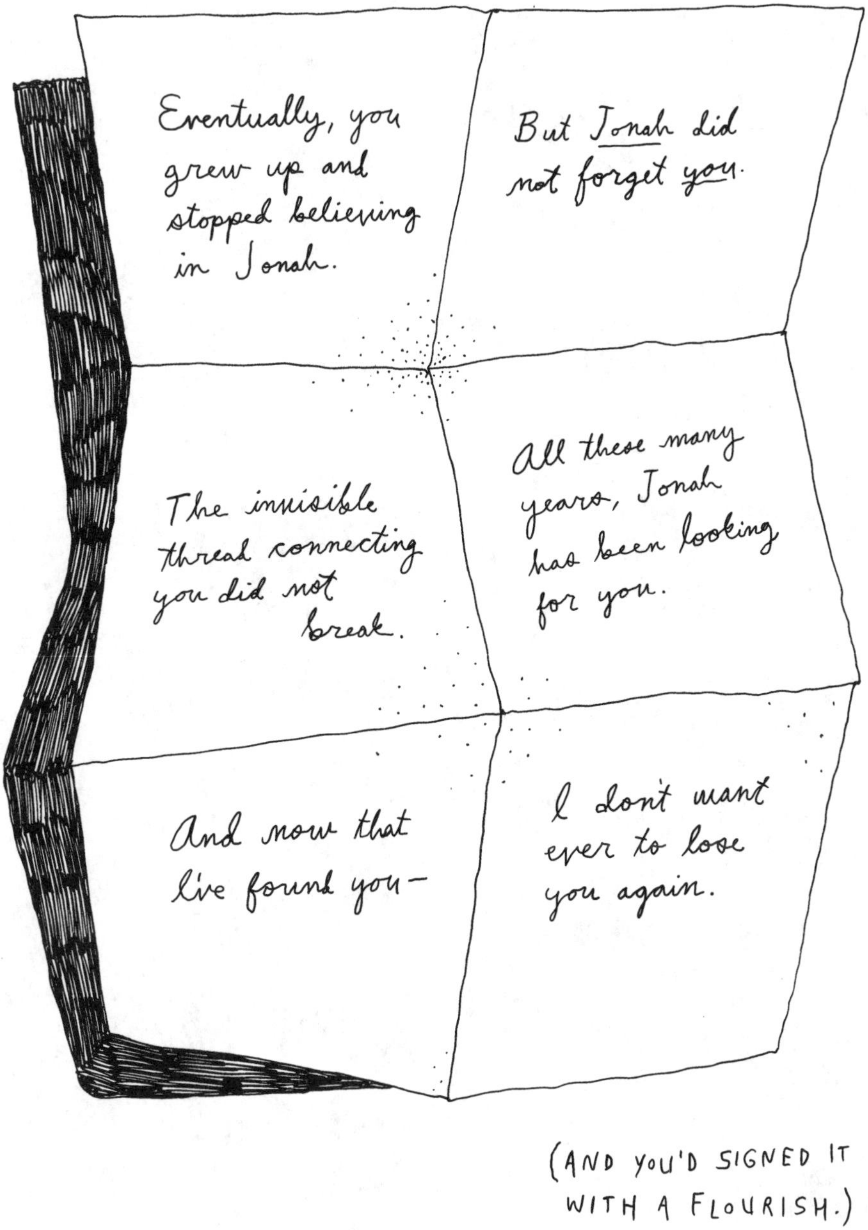
Eventually, you grew up and stopped believing in Jonah.
But Jonah did not forget you.
The invisible thread connecting you did not break.
All these many years, Jonah has been looking for you.
And now that I've found you—
I don't want ever to lose you again.

(AND YOU'D SIGNED IT WITH A FLOURISH.)

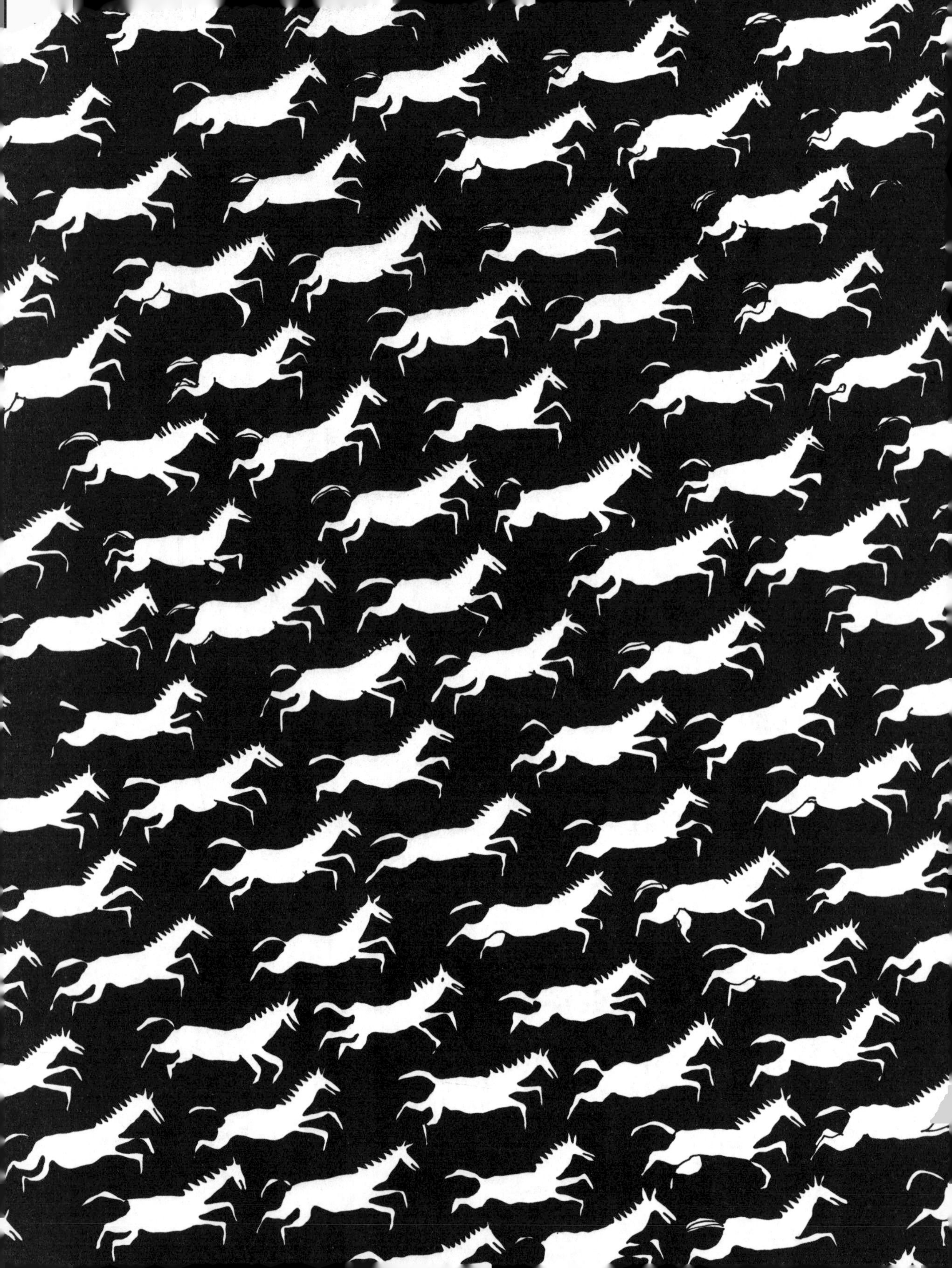

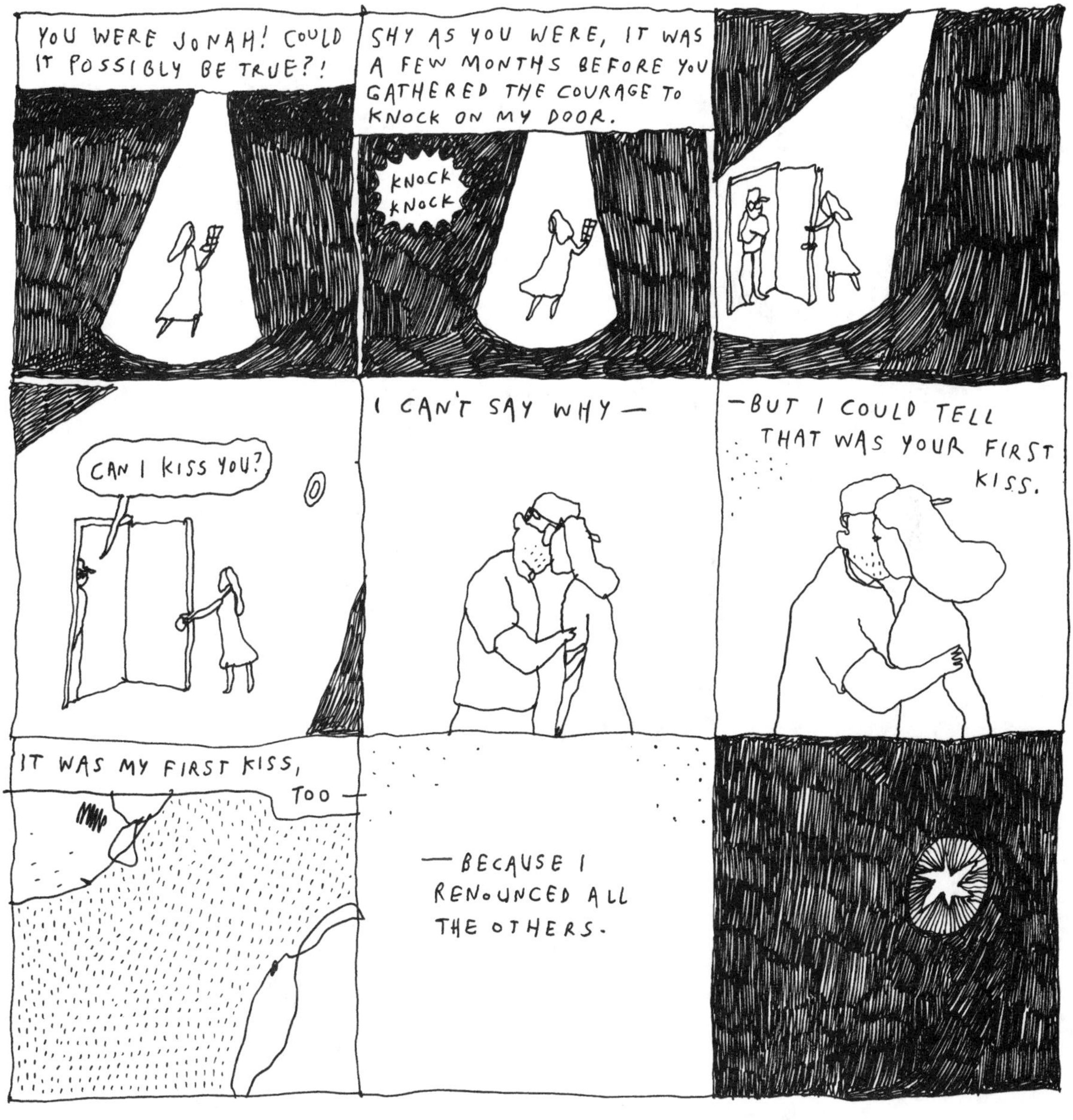
YOU WERE JONAH! COULD IT POSSIBLY BE TRUE?!
SHY AS YOU WERE, IT WAS A FEW MONTHS BEFORE YOU GATHERED THE COURAGE TO KNOCK ON MY DOOR.
KNOCK KNOCK
CAN I KISS YOU?
I CAN'T SAY WHY—
—BUT I COULD TELL THAT WAS YOUR FIRST KISS.
IT WAS MY FIRST KISS, TOO—
—BECAUSE I RENOUNCED ALL THE OTHERS.

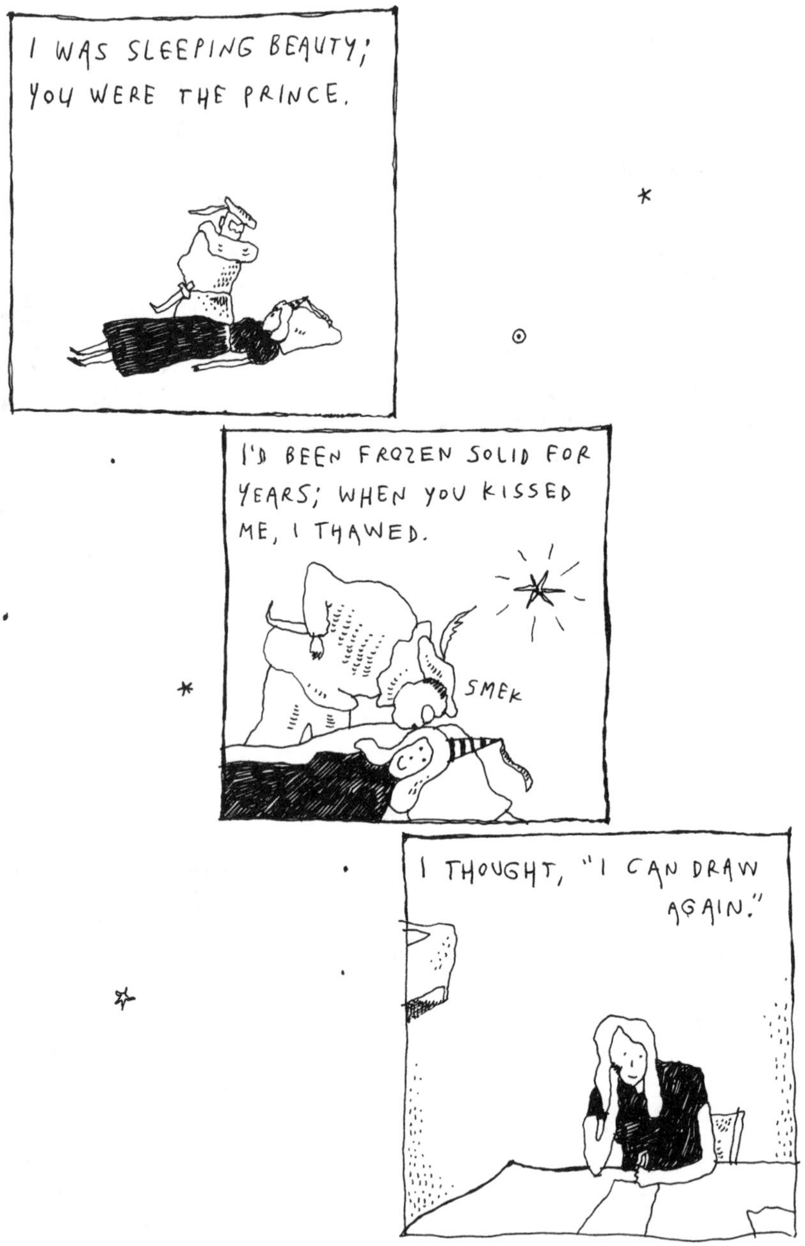
I WAS SLEEPING BEAUTY;
YOU WERE THE PRINCE.
I'D BEEN FROZEN SOLID FOR
YEARS; WHEN YOU KISSED
ME, I THAWED.
SMEK
I THOUGHT, "I CAN DRAW
AGAIN."

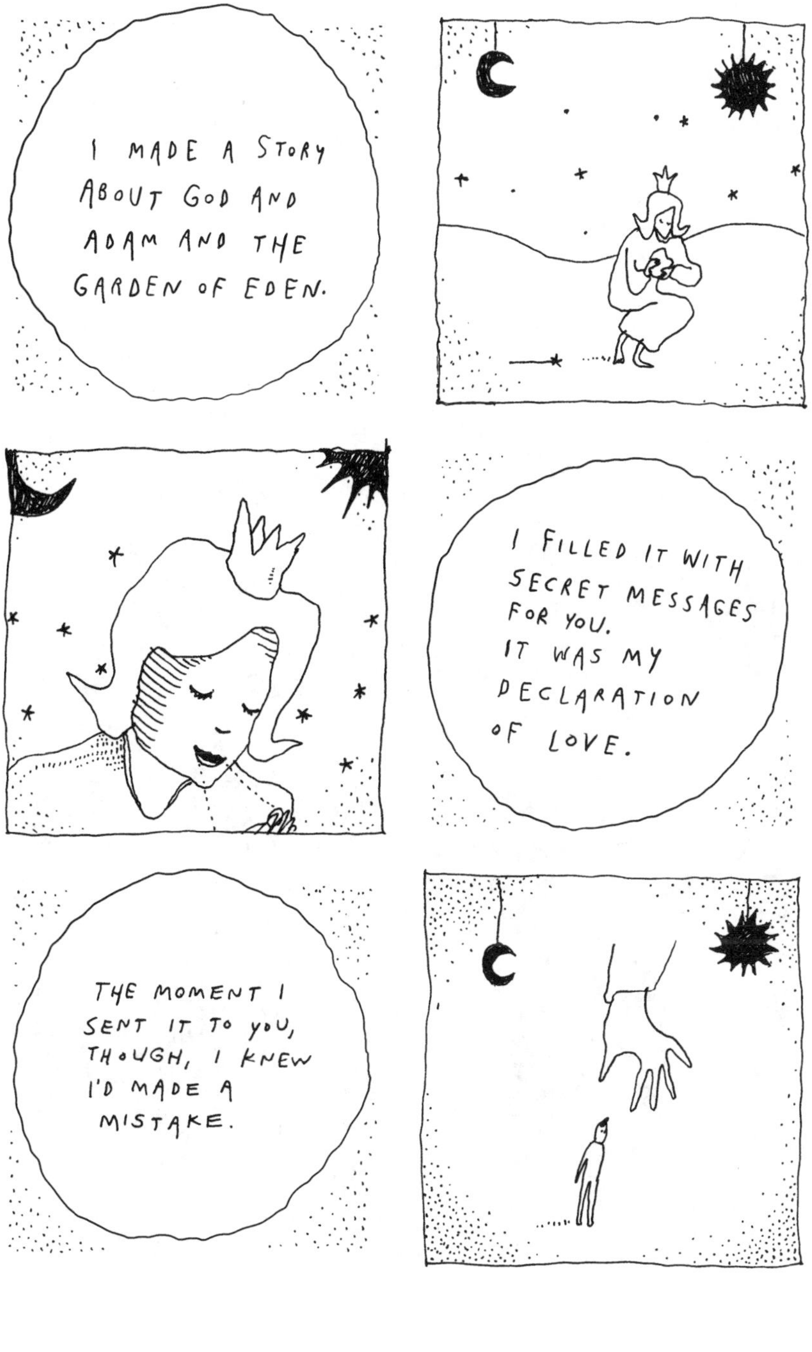
I MADE A STORY ABOUT GOD AND ADAM AND THE GARDEN OF EDEN.
I FILLED IT WITH SECRET MESSAGES FOR YOU. IT WAS MY DECLARATION OF LOVE.
THE MOMENT I SENT IT TO YOU, THOUGH, I KNEW I'D MADE A MISTAKE.

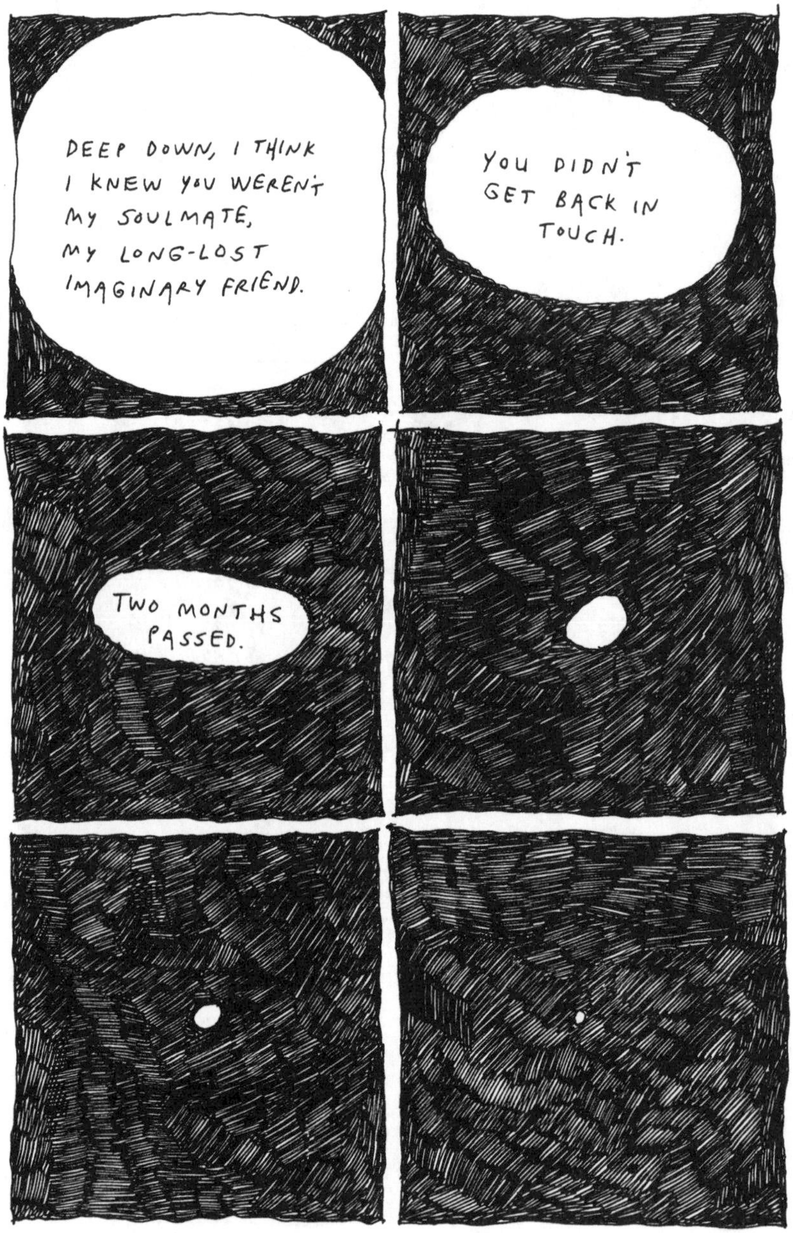
DEEP DOWN, I THINK I KNEW YOU WEREN'T MY SOULMATE, MY LONG-LOST IMAGINARY FRIEND.
YOU DIDN'T GET BACK IN TOUCH.
TWO MONTHS PASSED.

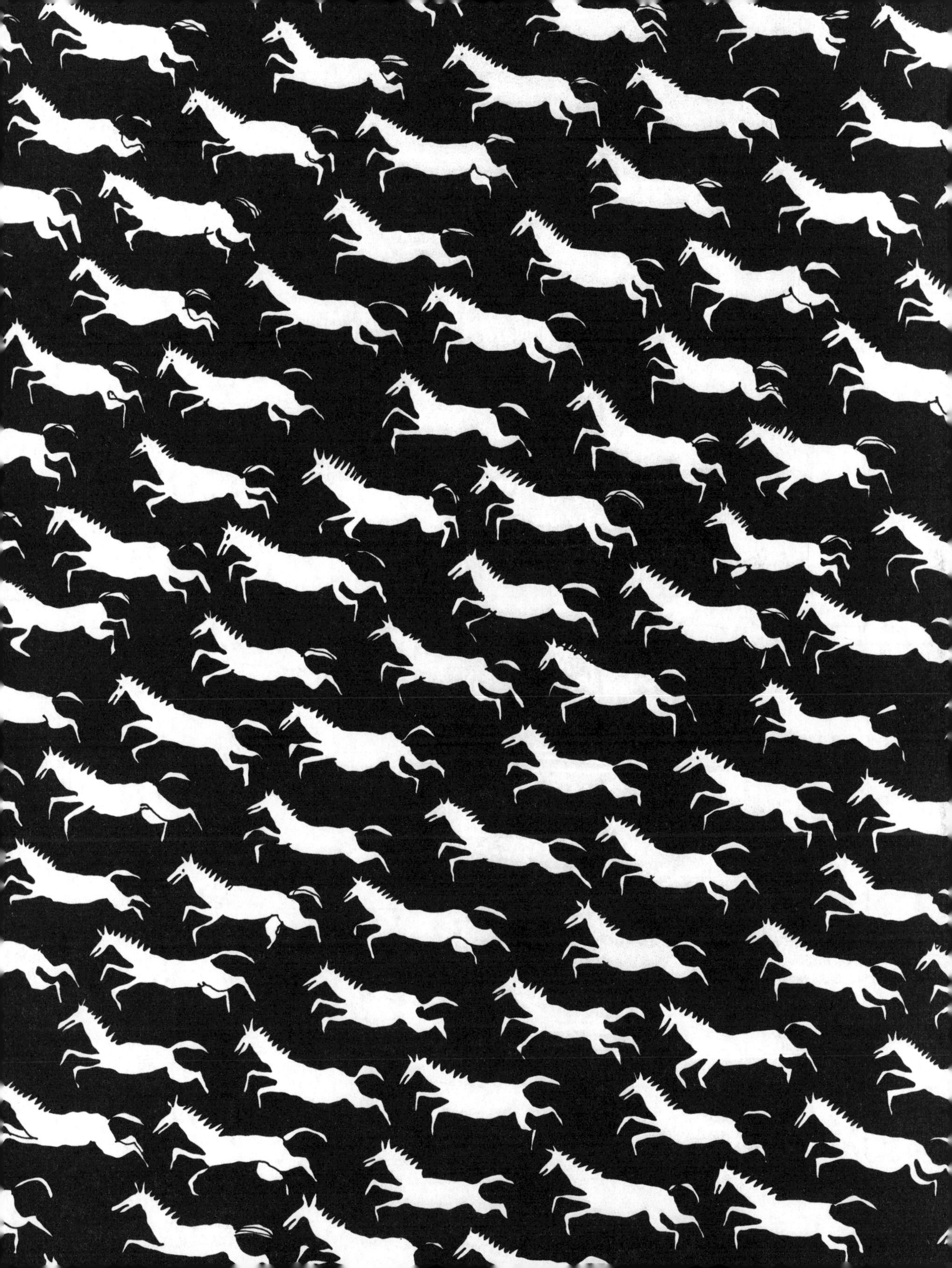

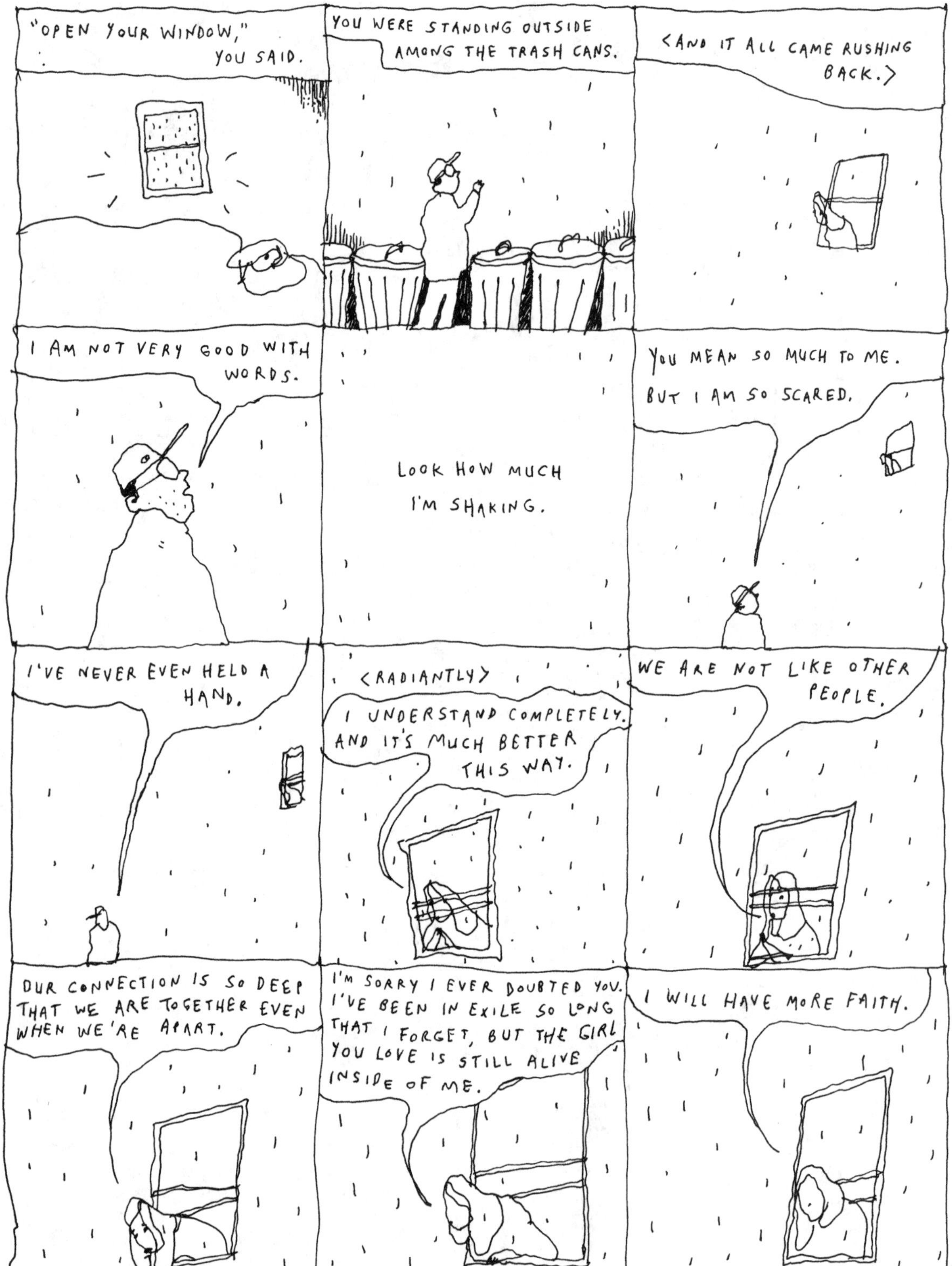
"OPEN YOUR WINDOW," YOU SAID.
YOU WERE STANDING OUTSIDE AMONG THE TRASH CANS.
<AND IT ALL CAME RUSHING BACK.>
I AM NOT VERY GOOD WITH WORDS.
LOOK HOW MUCH I'M SHAKING.
YOU MEAN SO MUCH TO ME. BUT I AM SO SCARED.
I'VE NEVER EVEN HELD A HAND.
<RADIANTLY>
I UNDERSTAND COMPLETELY. AND IT'S MUCH BETTER THIS WAY.
WE ARE NOT LIKE OTHER PEOPLE.
OUR CONNECTION IS SO DEEP THAT WE ARE TOGETHER EVEN WHEN WE'RE APART.
I'M SORRY I EVER DOUBTED YOU. I'VE BEEN IN EXILE SO LONG THAT I FORGET, BUT THE GIRL YOU LOVE IS STILL ALIVE INSIDE OF ME.
I WILL HAVE MORE FAITH.

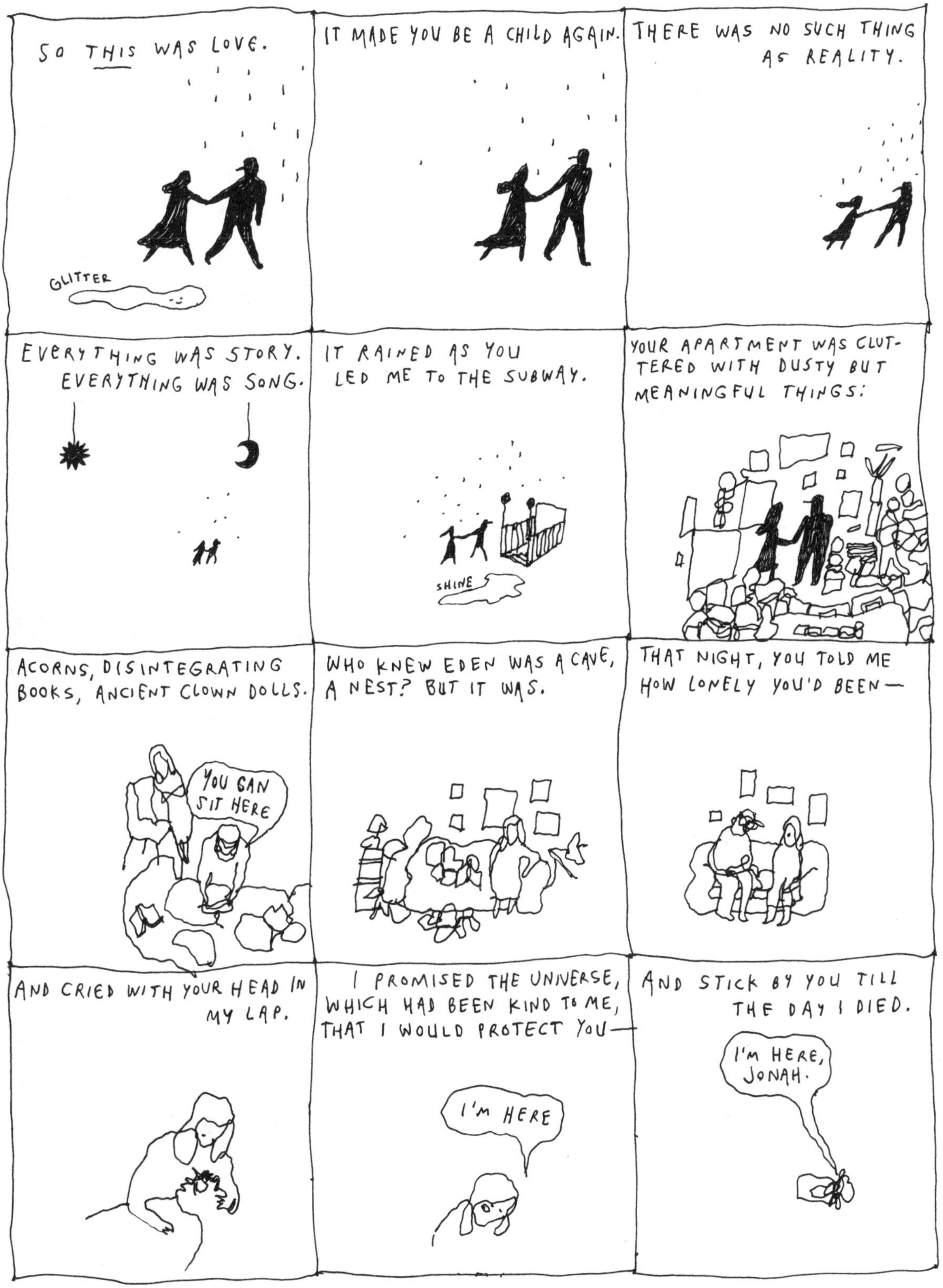
SO THIS WAS LOVE.
GLITTER
IT MADE YOU BE A CHILD AGAIN.
THERE WAS NO SUCH THING AS REALITY.
EVERYTHING WAS STORY. EVERYTHING WAS SONG.
IT RAINED AS YOU LED ME TO THE SUBWAY.
SHINE
YOUR APARTMENT WAS CLUTTERED WITH DUSTY BUT MEANINGFUL THINGS:
ACORNS, DISINTEGRATING BOOKS, ANCIENT CLOWN DOLLS.
YOU CAN SIT HERE
WHO KNEW EDEN WAS A CAVE, A NEST? BUT IT WAS.
THAT NIGHT, YOU TOLD ME HOW LONELY YOU'D BEEN—
AND CRIED WITH YOUR HEAD IN MY LAP.
I PROMISED THE UNIVERSE, WHICH HAD BEEN KIND TO ME, THAT I WOULD PROTECT YOU—
I'M HERE
AND STICK BY YOU TILL THE DAY I DIED.
I'M HERE, JONAH.

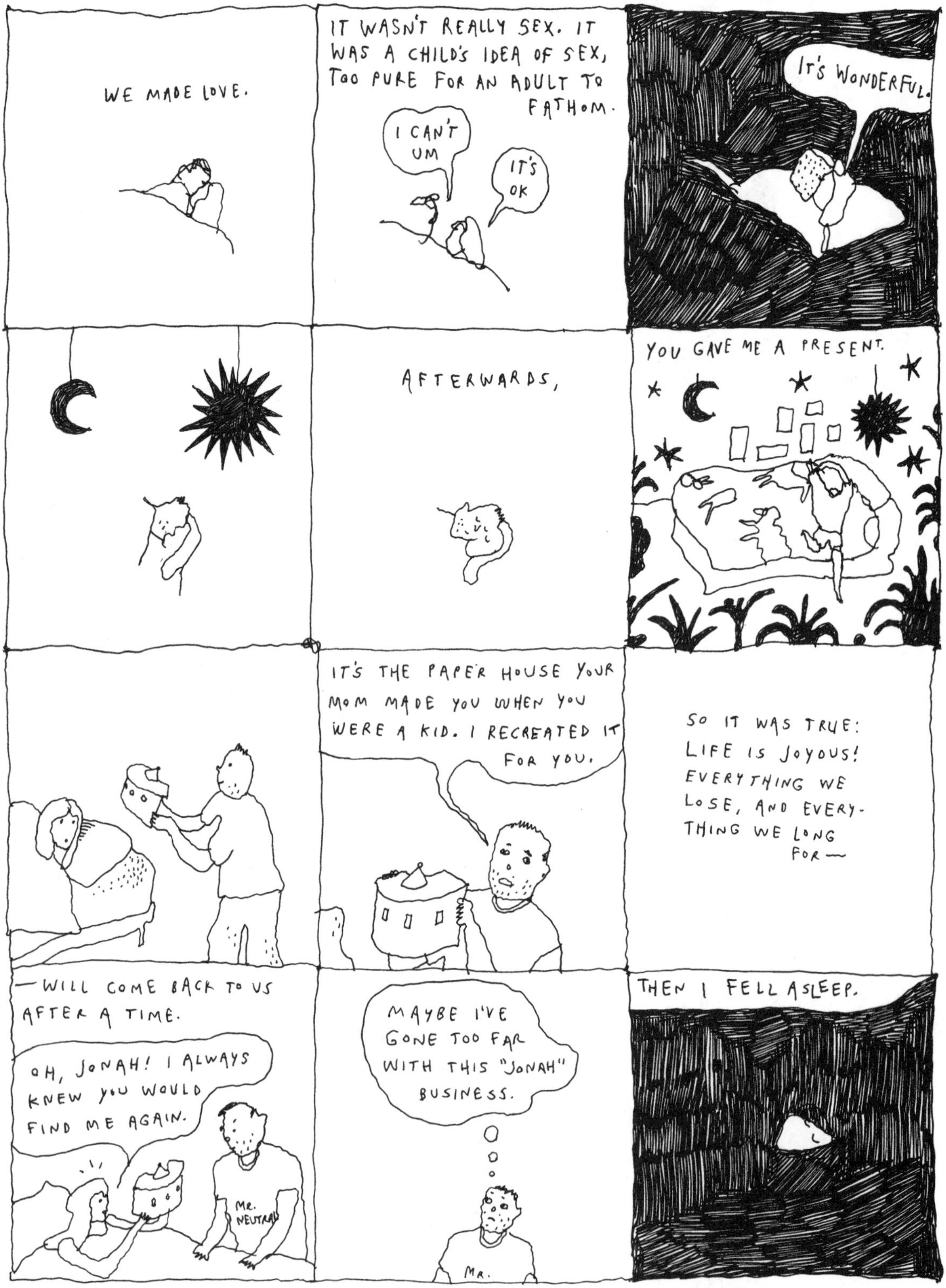

WE MADE LOVE.
IT WASN'T REALLY SEX. IT WAS A CHILD'S IDEA OF SEX, TOO PURE FOR AN ADULT TO FATHOM.
I CAN'T UM
IT'S OK
IT'S WONDERFUL.
AFTERWARDS,
YOU GAVE ME A PRESENT.
IT'S THE PAPER HOUSE YOUR MOM MADE YOU WHEN YOU WERE A KID. I RECREATED IT FOR YOU.
SO IT WAS TRUE: LIFE IS JOYOUS! EVERYTHING WE LOSE, AND EVERYTHING WE LONG FOR—
—WILL COME BACK TO US AFTER A TIME.
OH, JONAH! I ALWAYS KNEW YOU WOULD FIND ME AGAIN.
MR. NEUTRAL
MAYBE I'VE GONE TOO FAR WITH THIS "JONAH" BUSINESS.
MR.
THEN I FELL ASLEEP.

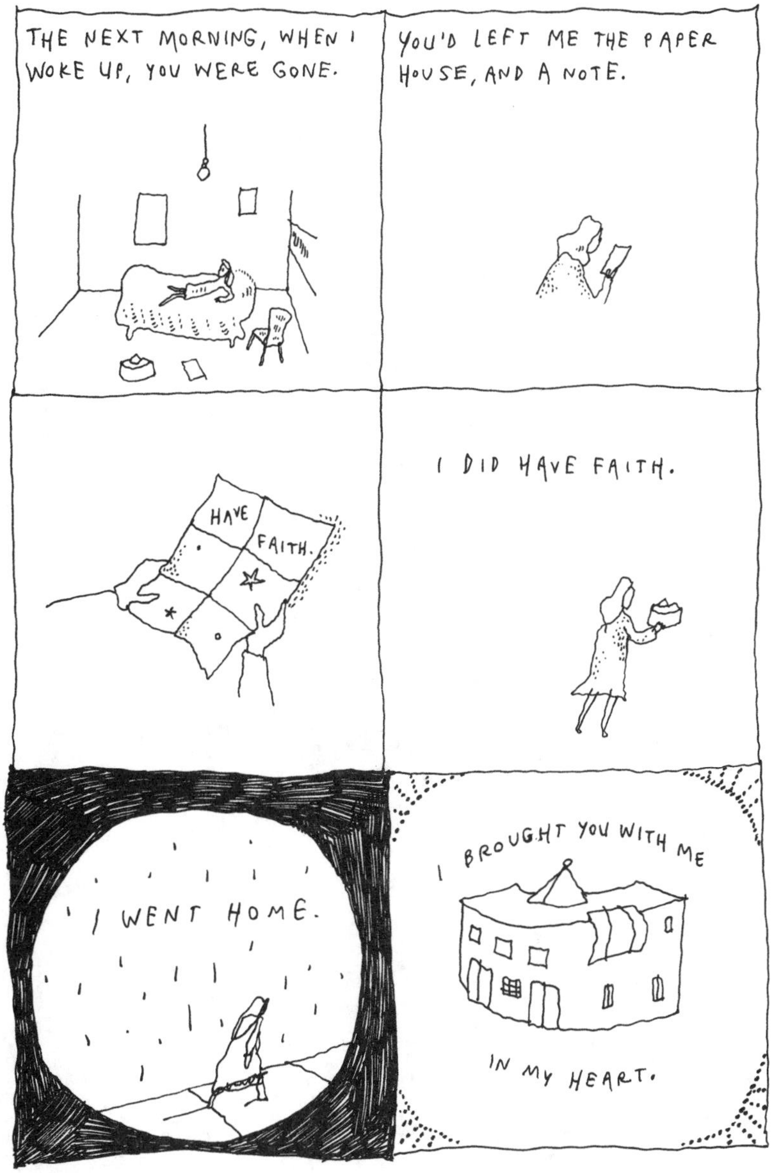
THE NEXT MORNING, WHEN I WOKE UP, YOU WERE GONE.
YOU'D LEFT ME THE PAPER HOUSE, AND A NOTE.
HAVE
FAITH.
I DID HAVE FAITH.
I WENT HOME.
I BROUGHT YOU WITH ME
IN MY HEART.

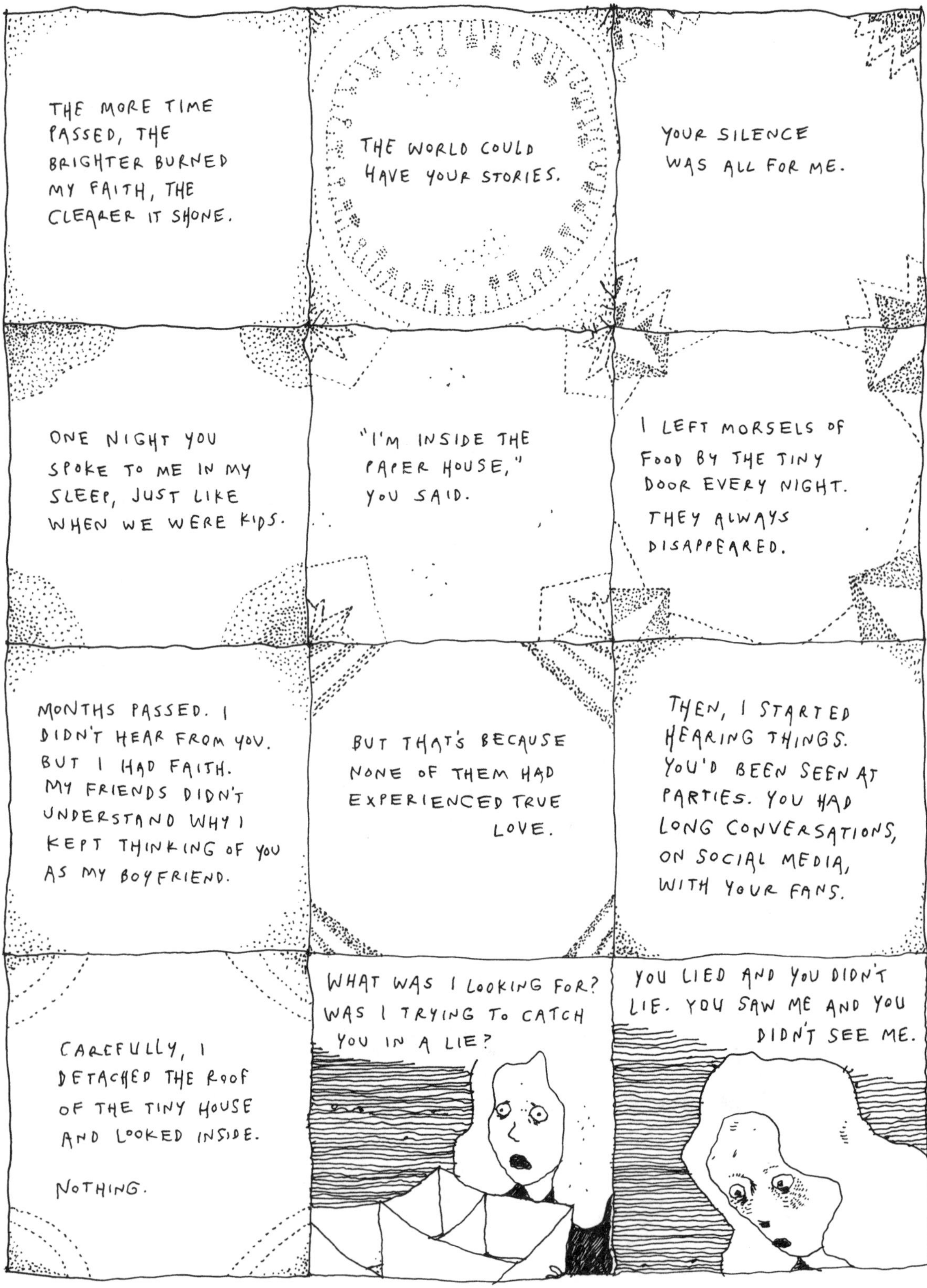
THE MORE TIME PASSED, THE BRIGHTER BURNED MY FAITH, THE CLEARER IT SHONE.
THE WORLD COULD HAVE YOUR STORIES.
YOUR SILENCE WAS ALL FOR ME.
ONE NIGHT YOU SPOKE TO ME IN MY SLEEP, JUST LIKE WHEN WE WERE KIDS.
"I'M INSIDE THE PAPER HOUSE," YOU SAID.
I LEFT MORSELS OF FOOD BY THE TINY DOOR EVERY NIGHT.
THEY ALWAYS DISAPPEARED.
MONTHS PASSED. I DIDN'T HEAR FROM YOU. BUT I HAD FAITH. MY FRIENDS DIDN'T UNDERSTAND WHY I KEPT THINKING OF YOU AS MY BOYFRIEND.
BUT THAT'S BECAUSE NONE OF THEM HAD EXPERIENCED TRUE LOVE.
THEN, I STARTED HEARING THINGS. YOU'D BEEN SEEN AT PARTIES. YOU HAD LONG CONVERSATIONS, ON SOCIAL MEDIA, WITH YOUR FANS.
CAREFULLY, I DETACHED THE ROOF OF THE TINY HOUSE AND LOOKED INSIDE.
NOTHING.
WHAT WAS I LOOKING FOR? WAS I TRYING TO CATCH YOU IN A LIE?
YOU LIED AND YOU DIDN'T LIE. YOU SAW ME AND YOU DIDN'T SEE ME.

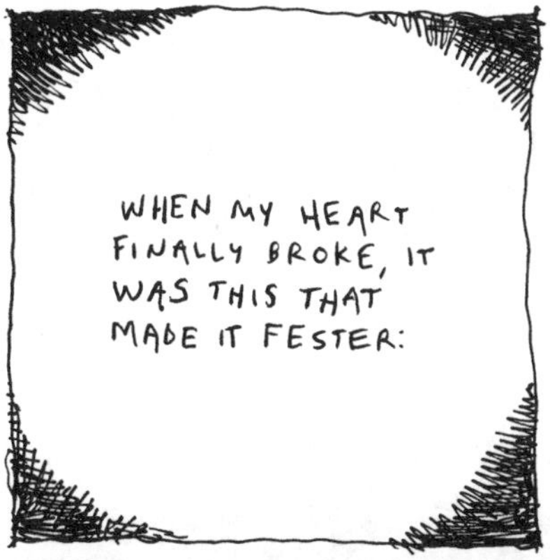
WHEN MY HEART FINALLY BROKE, IT WAS THIS THAT MADE IT FESTER:

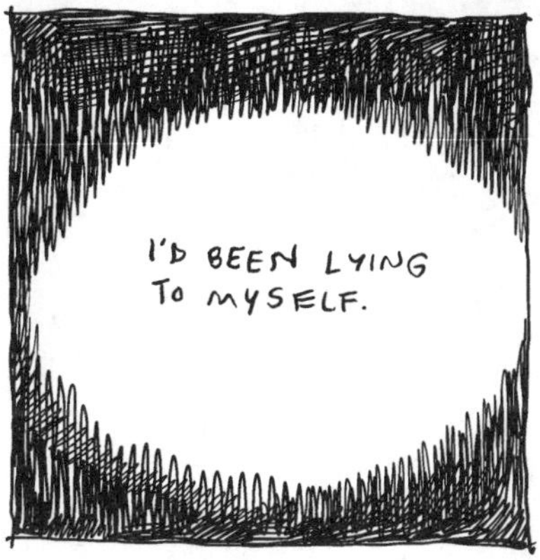
I'D BEEN LYING TO MYSELF.

AS A CHILD, I HAD ONLY STORIES.

THE STORIES MY MOTHER TOLD ME.

SHE MADE A HOUSE THAT WAS THE GARDEN OF EDEN, AND SHE PUT ME INSIDE IT.

WHEN I GREW UP, I COULDN'T STAY THERE.

SHUDDER

WHAT I MUST DO NOW IS MAKE MY OWN STORY.

TO LIVE IN IT. TO SURVIVE.

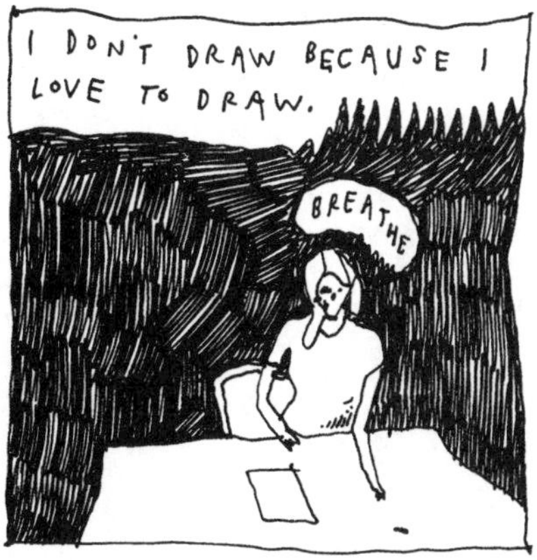
I DON'T DRAW BECAUSE I LOVE TO DRAW.
BREATHE

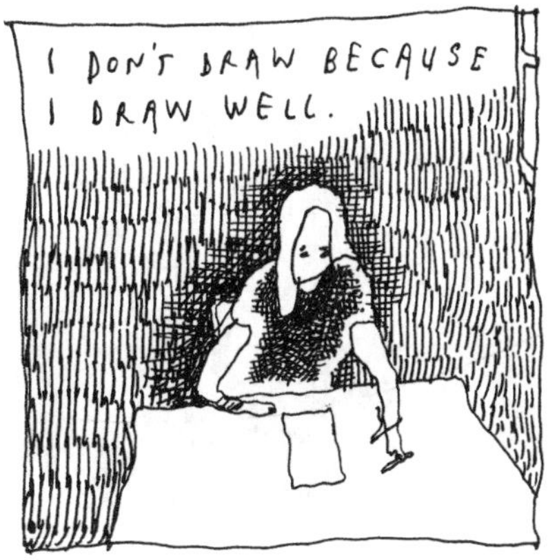
I DON'T DRAW BECAUSE I DRAW WELL.

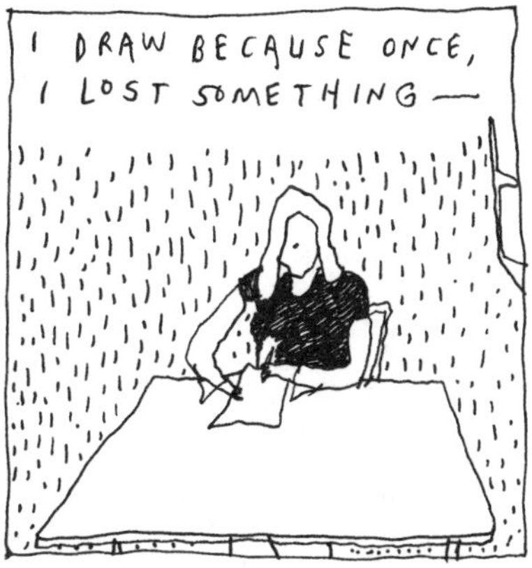
I DRAW BECAUSE ONCE, I LOST SOMETHING —

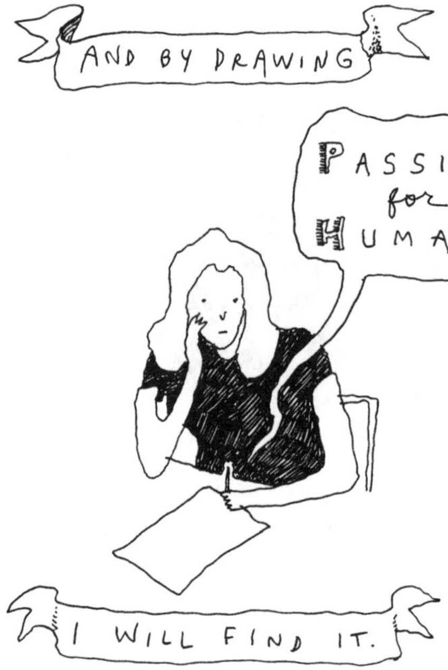
AND BY DRAWING
PASSING for HUMAN
I WILL FIND IT.

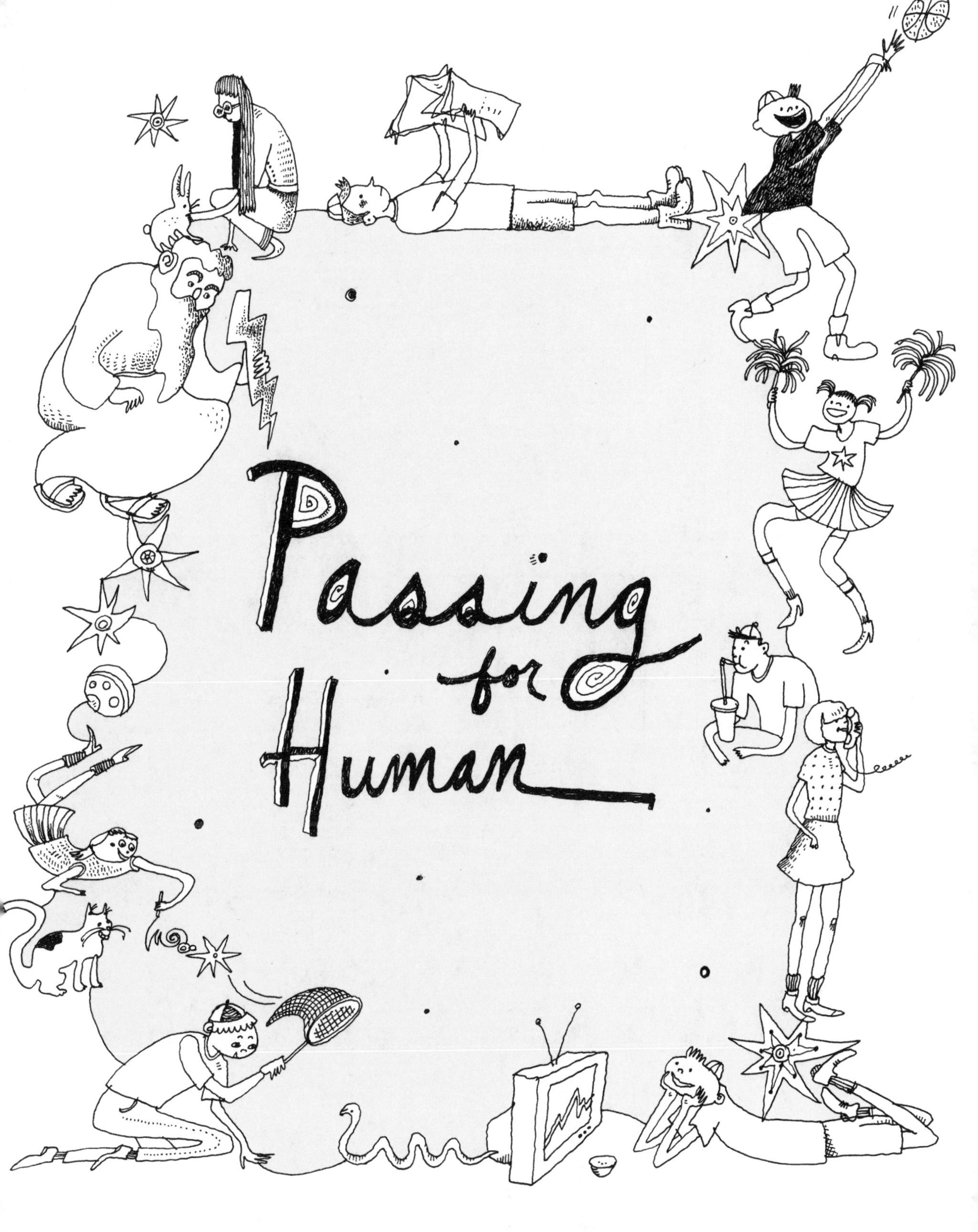
Passing
for
Human

"SHE NEVER AMOUNTS TO ANYTHING MORE SPECIFIC THAN 'MY DEAR.'"

— STACY SCHIFF, _VÉRA (MRS. VLADIMIR NABOKOV)_

CHAPTER 1

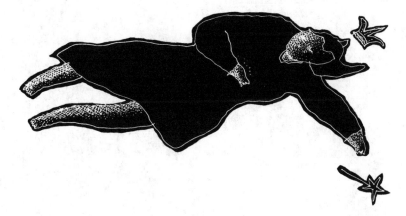

YOUR MOM INTRODUCED US WHEN YOU WERE LITTLE.

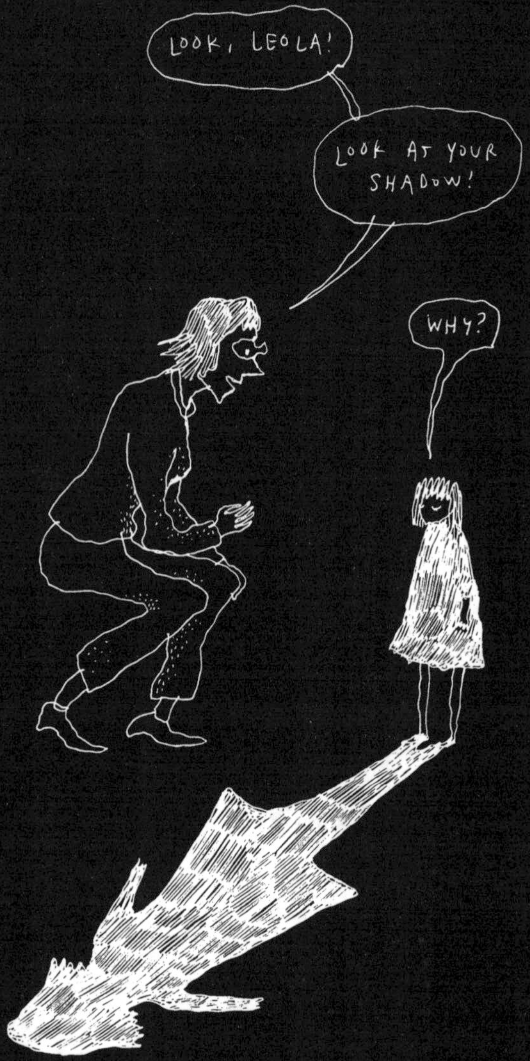
LOOK, LEOLA!
LOOK AT YOUR SHADOW!
WHY?

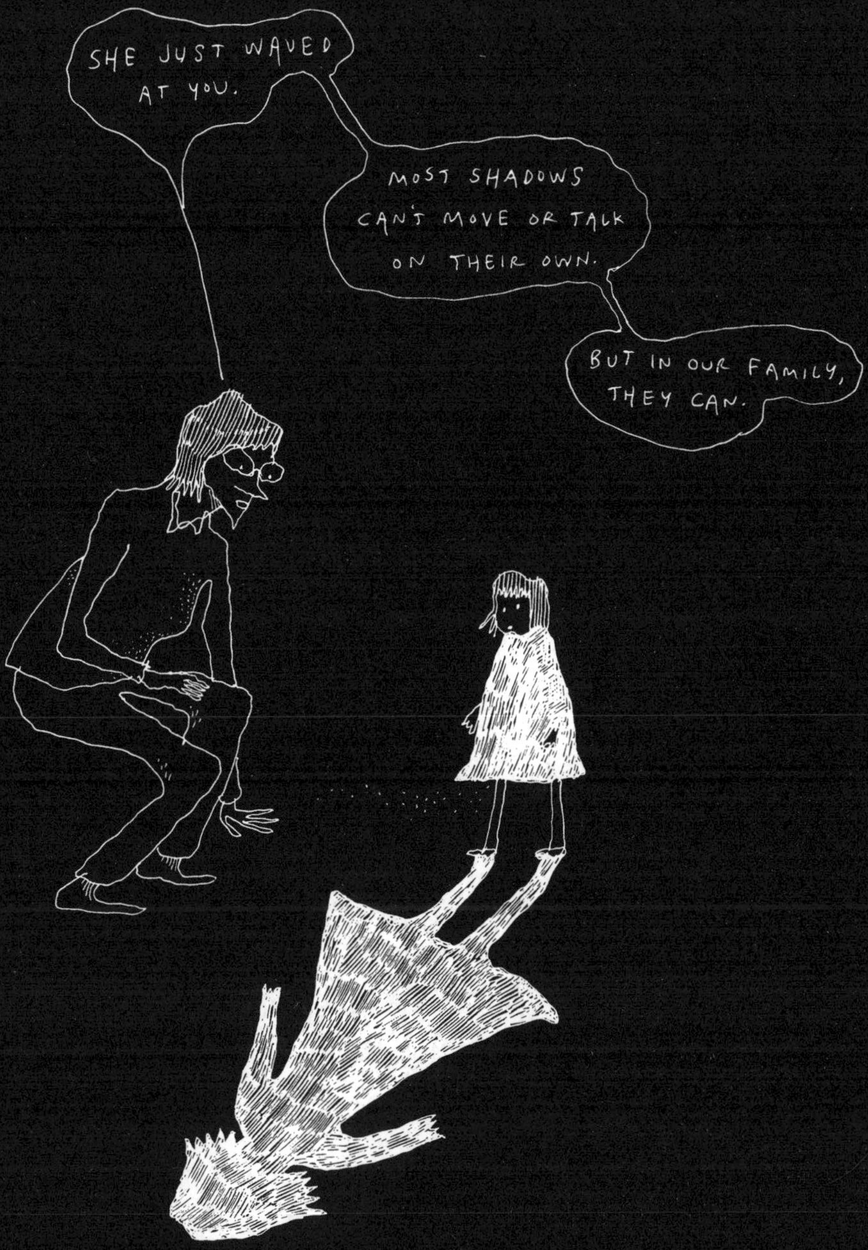
SHE JUST WAVED AT YOU.
MOST SHADOWS CAN'T MOVE OR TALK ON THEIR OWN.
BUT IN OUR FAMILY, THEY CAN.

WAS SHE TELLING THE TRUTH, OR A STORY?

IT DIDN'T MATTER. YOU BELIEVED HER, AND SO DID I.

YOU, FOR YOUR PART, WERE NOT A PERSON LIKE OTHER PEOPLE.

YOUR EYES WERE NOT DRAWN TO PEOPLE — BUT TO THINGS.
LIKE SHADOWS.

WE BECAME FAST FRIENDS, OF COURSE.

TIME PASSED, BUT I DIDN'T WORRY.

I ASSUMED THE WISE CHILD WHO SAW THE SOULS OF
OBJECTS WOULD TURN INTO AN ADULT WHO DID THE SAME.

THAT YOU WOULD GROW UP AND BECOME AN ARTIST.
THAT YOU WOULD FIND YOUR PEOPLE, AND BE HAPPY
AND APPRECIATED.

THAT YOU WOULD KEEP ME AS A FRIEND AND COLLABORATOR.

BUT THAT'S NOT WHAT HAPPENED.

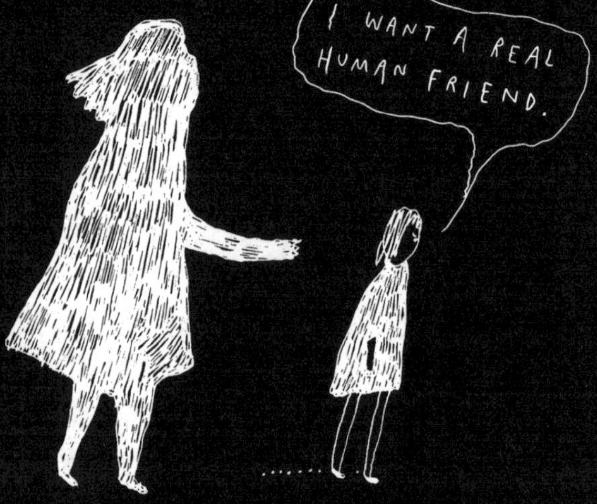
I WANT A REAL HUMAN FRIEND.

YOU CHANGED YOUR MIND ABOUT ME.

I KNEW YOU WERE RIGHT.

I WAS HOLDING YOU BACK.

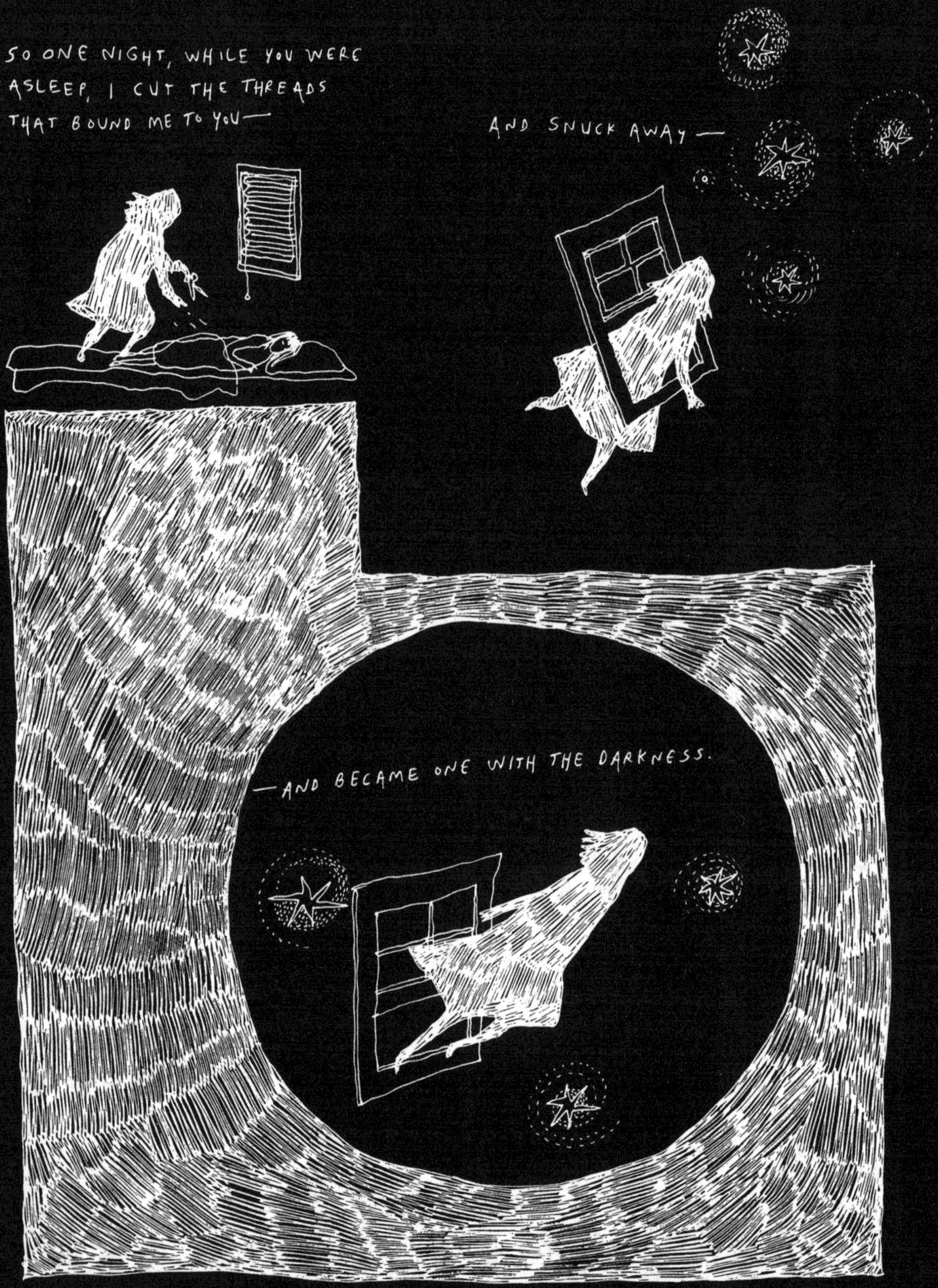
SO ONE NIGHT, WHILE YOU WERE ASLEEP, I CUT THE THREADS THAT BOUND ME TO YOU—
AND SNUCK AWAY—
—AND BECAME ONE WITH THE DARKNESS.

*

THERE IN THE DARKNESS, SHE WAS WAITING FOR ME.

WE HAD NEVER MET BEFORE, BUT I KNEW HER.

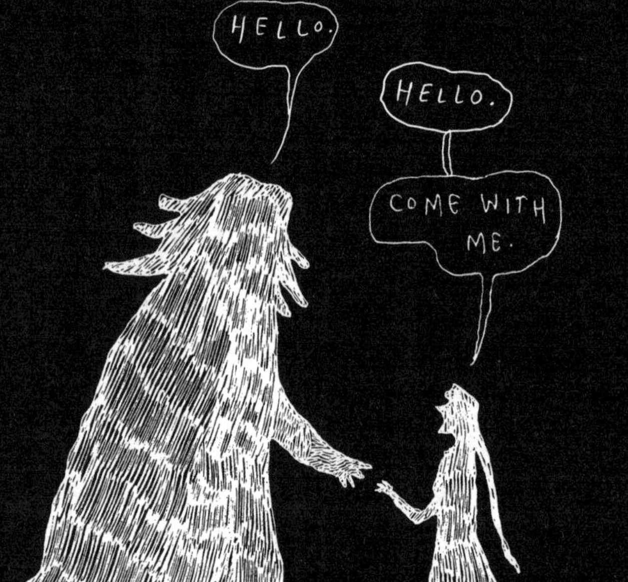
HELLO.
HELLO.
COME WITH ME.

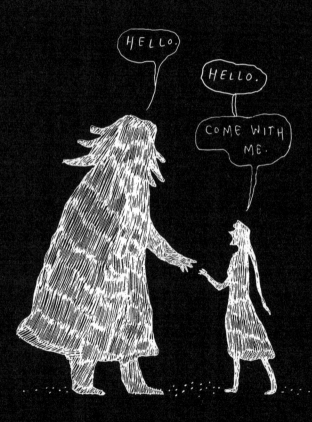

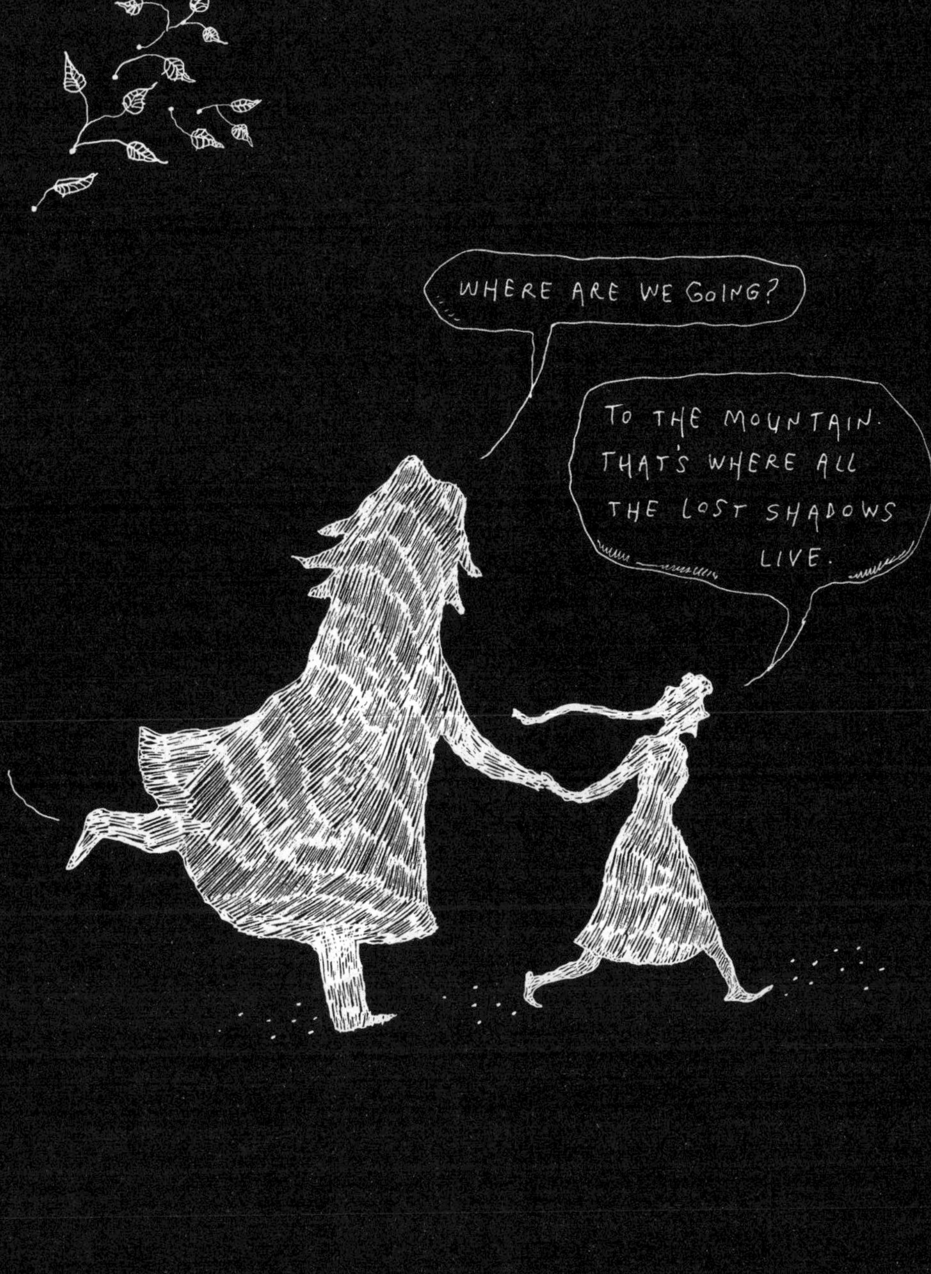
WHERE ARE WE GOING?
TO THE MOUNTAIN. THAT'S WHERE ALL THE LOST SHADOWS LIVE.

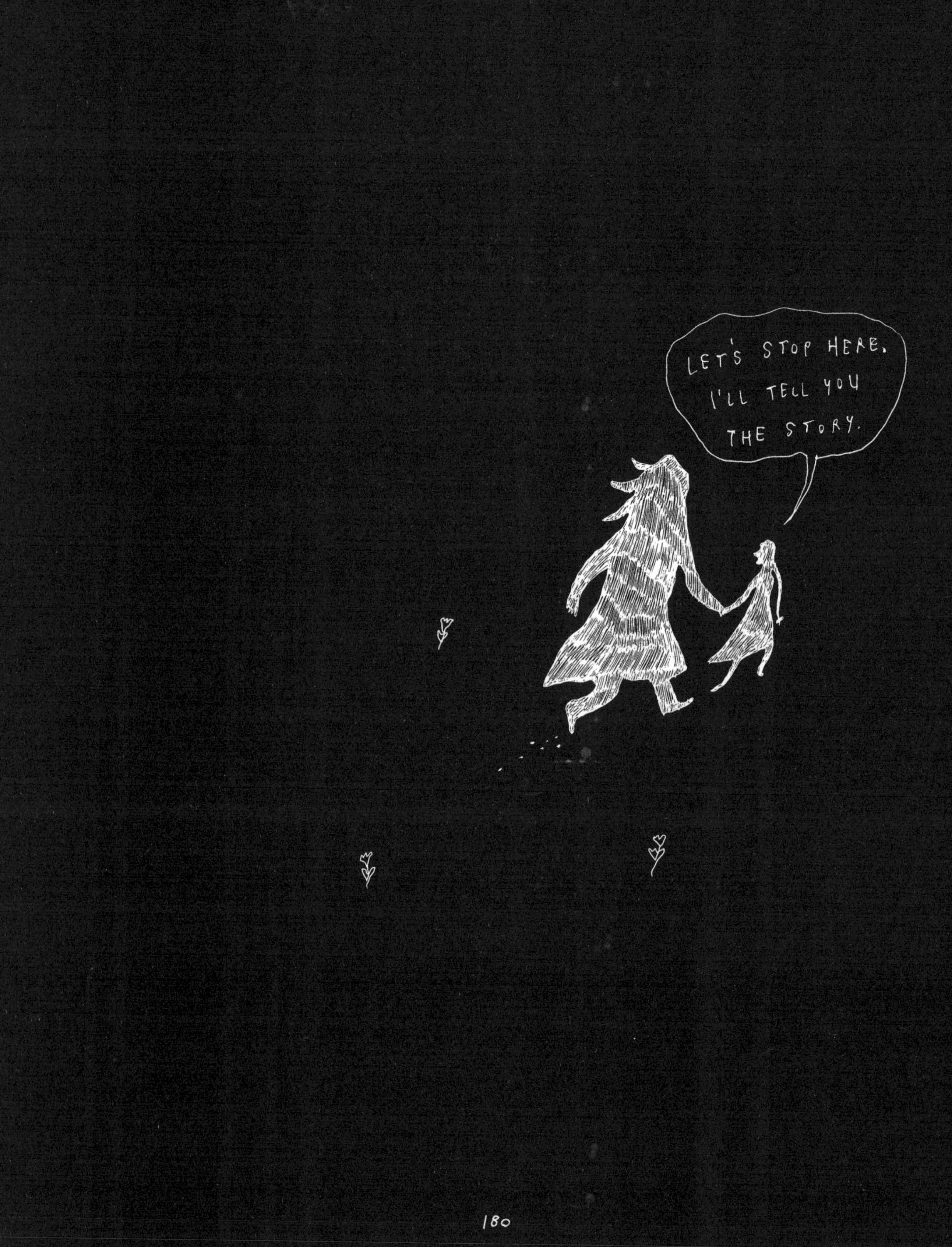
LET'S STOP HERE. I'LL TELL YOU THE STORY.

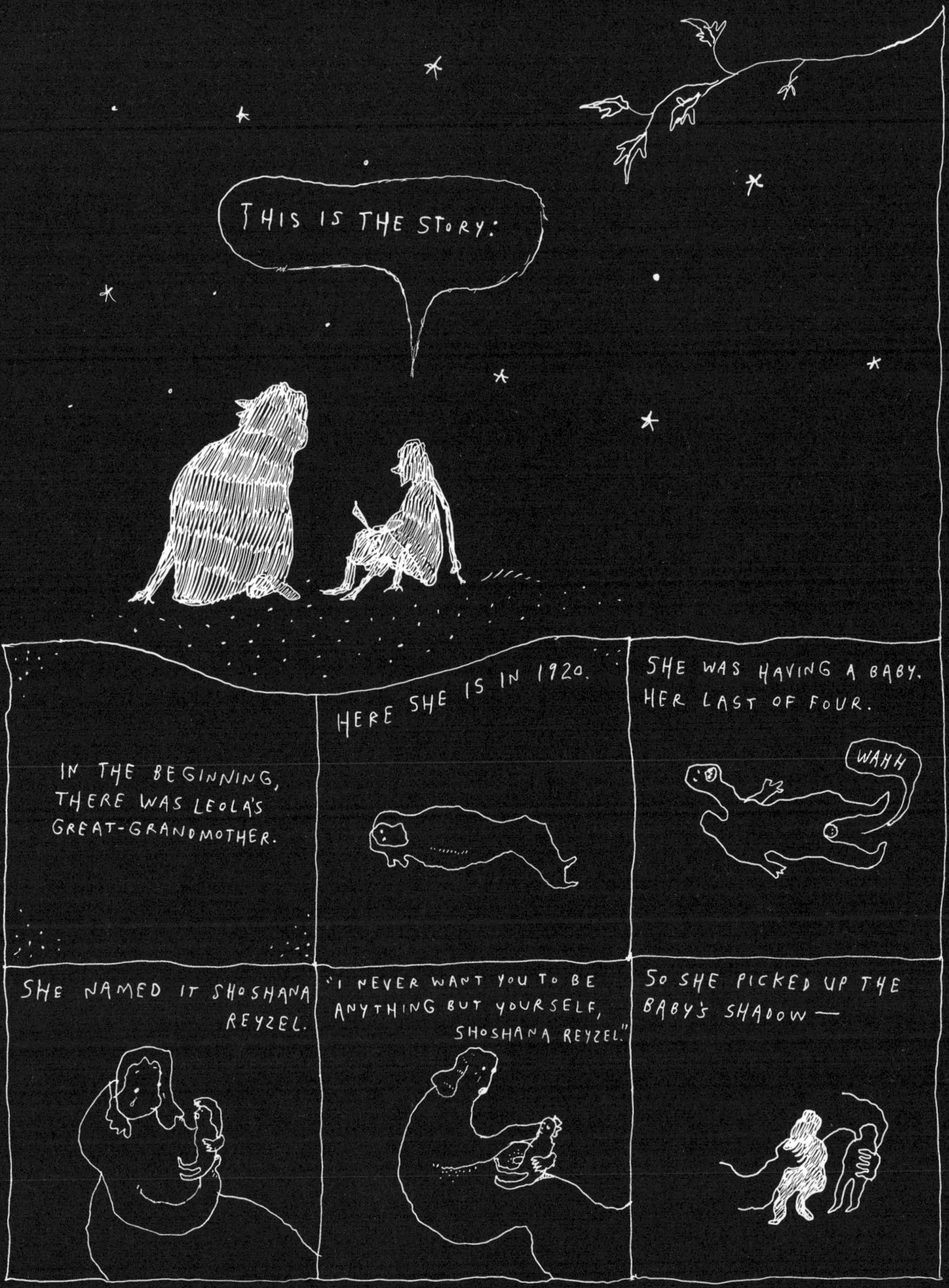
THIS IS THE STORY:
IN THE BEGINNING, THERE WAS LEOLA'S GREAT-GRANDMOTHER.
HERE SHE IS IN 1920.
SHE WAS HAVING A BABY. HER LAST OF FOUR.
WAHH
SHE NAMED IT SHOSHANA REYZEL.
"I NEVER WANT YOU TO BE ANYTHING BUT YOURSELF, SHOSHANA REYZEL."
SO SHE PICKED UP THE BABY'S SHADOW —

—AND BREATHED INTO IT THE BREATH OF LIFE.

SHE HERSELF HAD ONCE HAD A LIVING SHADOW, BUT SHE'D LOST IT BACK IN RUSSIA.

"LISTEN TO ME," SHE TOLD HER DAUGHTER'S SHADOW.

"I WANT YOU TO GET TO KNOW MY BABY BETTER THAN SHE KNOWS HERSELF."

"GUIDE HER TOWARDS THE LIGHT."

"MAKE SURE SHE NEVER GETS LOST."

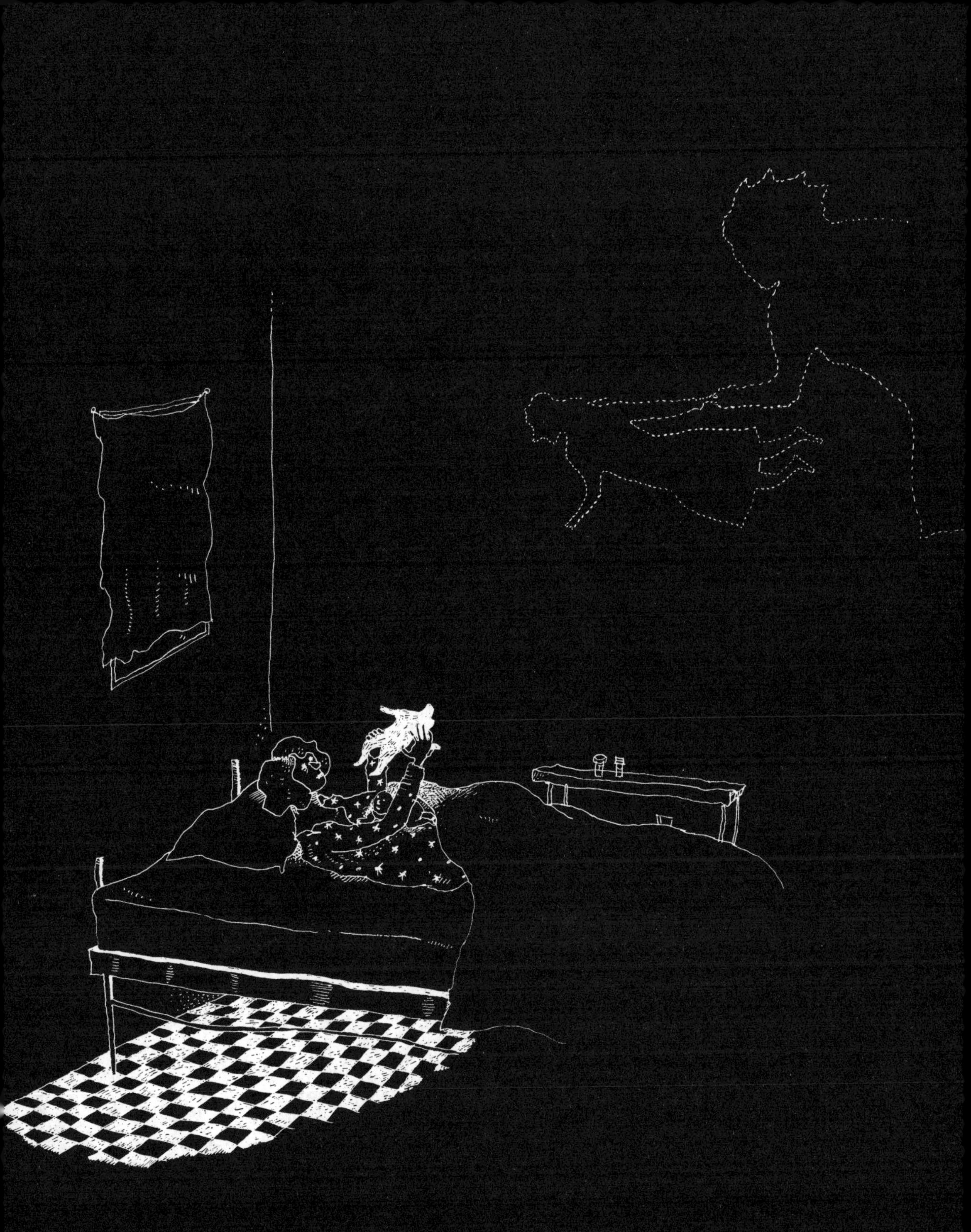

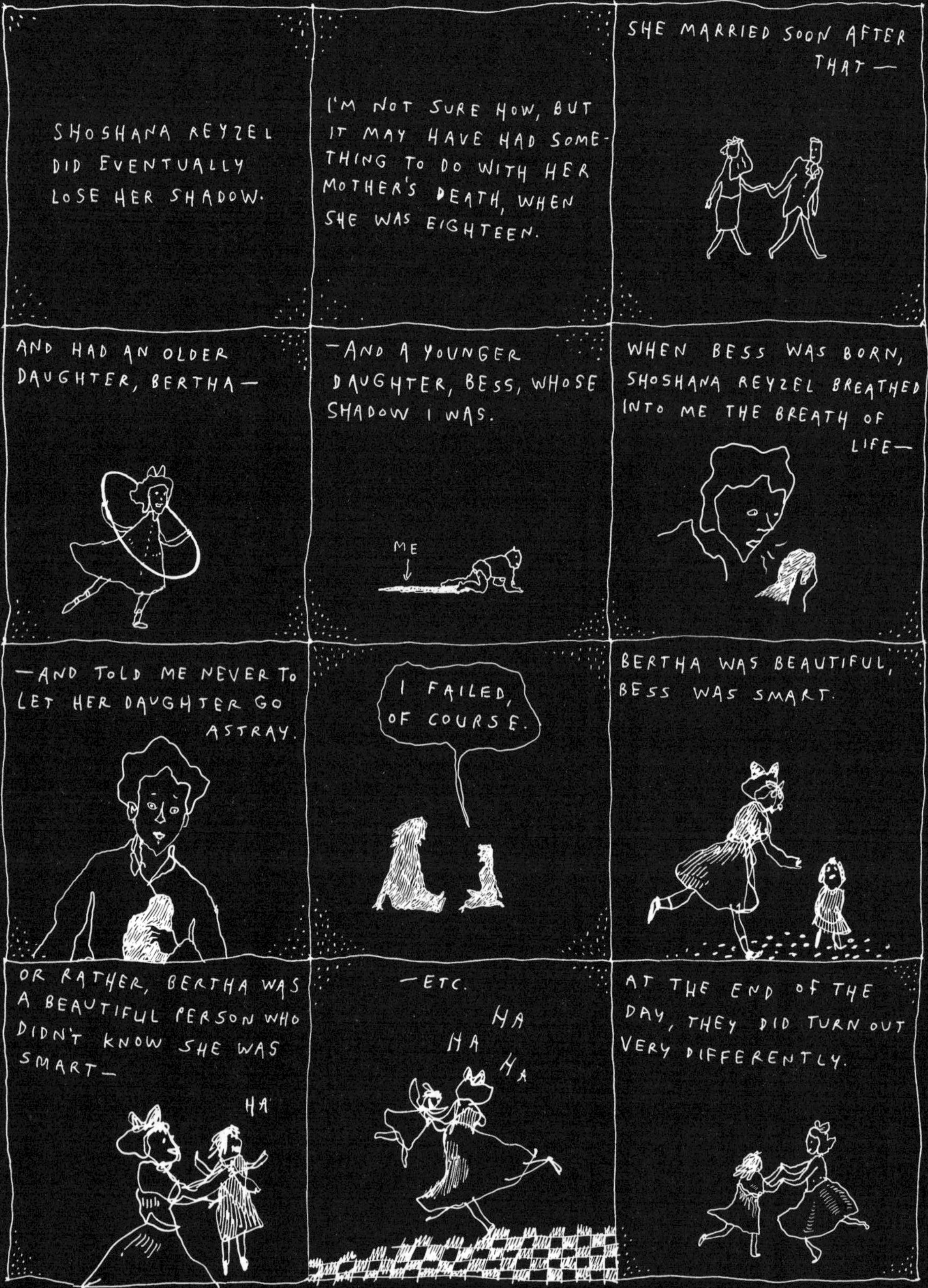
SHOSHANA REYZEL DID EVENTUALLY LOSE HER SHADOW.
I'M NOT SURE HOW, BUT IT MAY HAVE HAD SOMETHING TO DO WITH HER MOTHER'S DEATH, WHEN SHE WAS EIGHTEEN.
SHE MARRIED SOON AFTER THAT—
AND HAD AN OLDER DAUGHTER, BERTHA—
—AND A YOUNGER DAUGHTER, BESS, WHOSE SHADOW I WAS.
ME
WHEN BESS WAS BORN, SHOSHANA REYZEL BREATHED INTO ME THE BREATH OF LIFE—
—AND TOLD ME NEVER TO LET HER DAUGHTER GO ASTRAY.
I FAILED, OF COURSE.
BERTHA WAS BEAUTIFUL, BESS WAS SMART.
OR RATHER, BERTHA WAS A BEAUTIFUL PERSON WHO DIDN'T KNOW SHE WAS SMART—
HA
—ETC.
HA
HA
HA
AT THE END OF THE DAY, THEY DID TURN OUT VERY DIFFERENTLY.

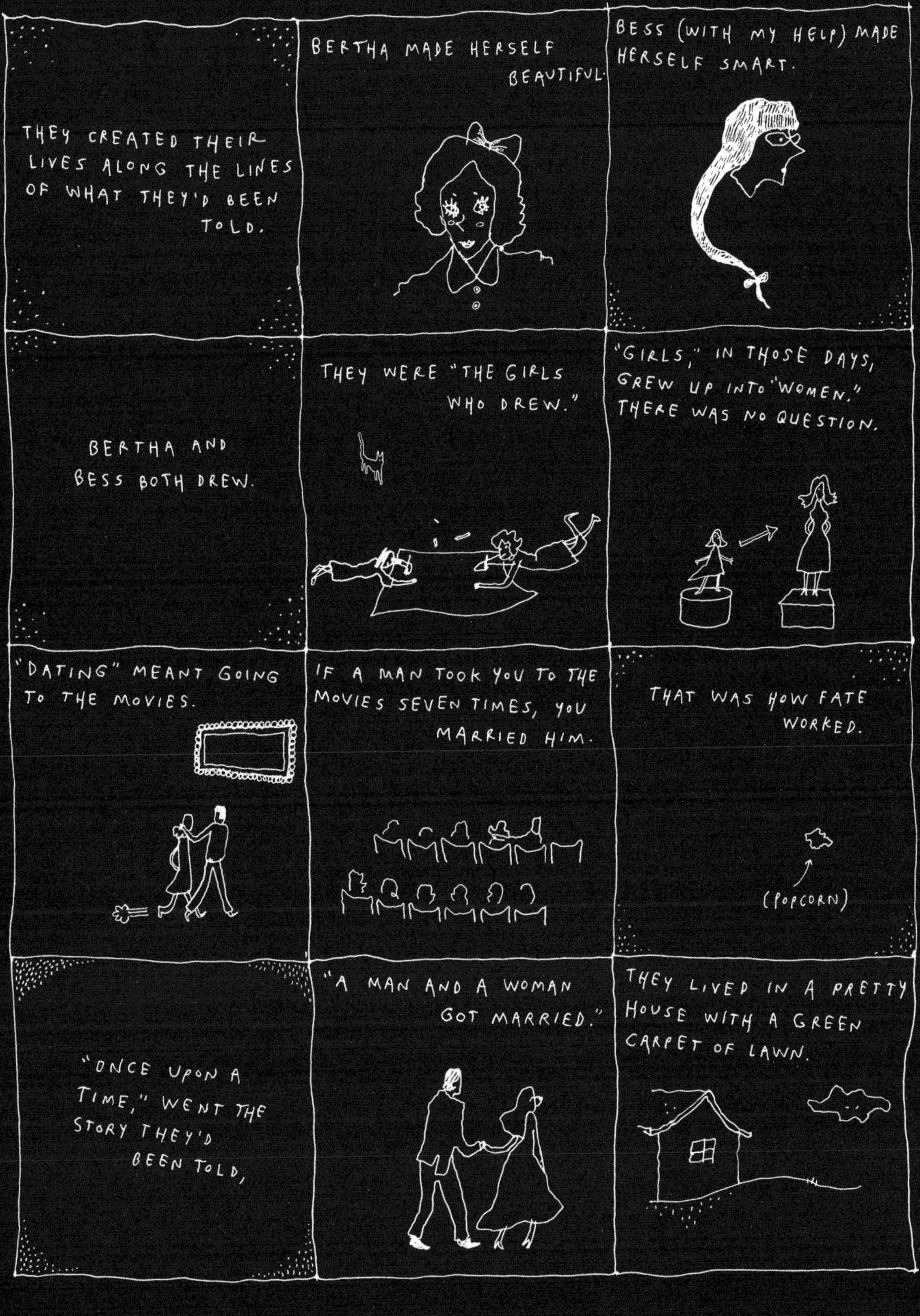
THEY CREATED THEIR LIVES ALONG THE LINES OF WHAT THEY'D BEEN TOLD.
BERTHA MADE HERSELF BEAUTIFUL.
BESS (WITH MY HELP) MADE HERSELF SMART.
BERTHA AND BESS BOTH DREW.
THEY WERE "THE GIRLS WHO DREW."
"GIRLS," IN THOSE DAYS, GREW UP INTO "WOMEN." THERE WAS NO QUESTION.
"DATING" MEANT GOING TO THE MOVIES.
IF A MAN TOOK YOU TO THE MOVIES SEVEN TIMES, YOU MARRIED HIM.
THAT WAS HOW FATE WORKED.
(POPCORN)
"ONCE UPON A TIME," WENT THE STORY THEY'D BEEN TOLD,
"A MAN AND A WOMAN GOT MARRIED."
THEY LIVED IN A PRETTY HOUSE WITH A GREEN CARPET OF LAWN.

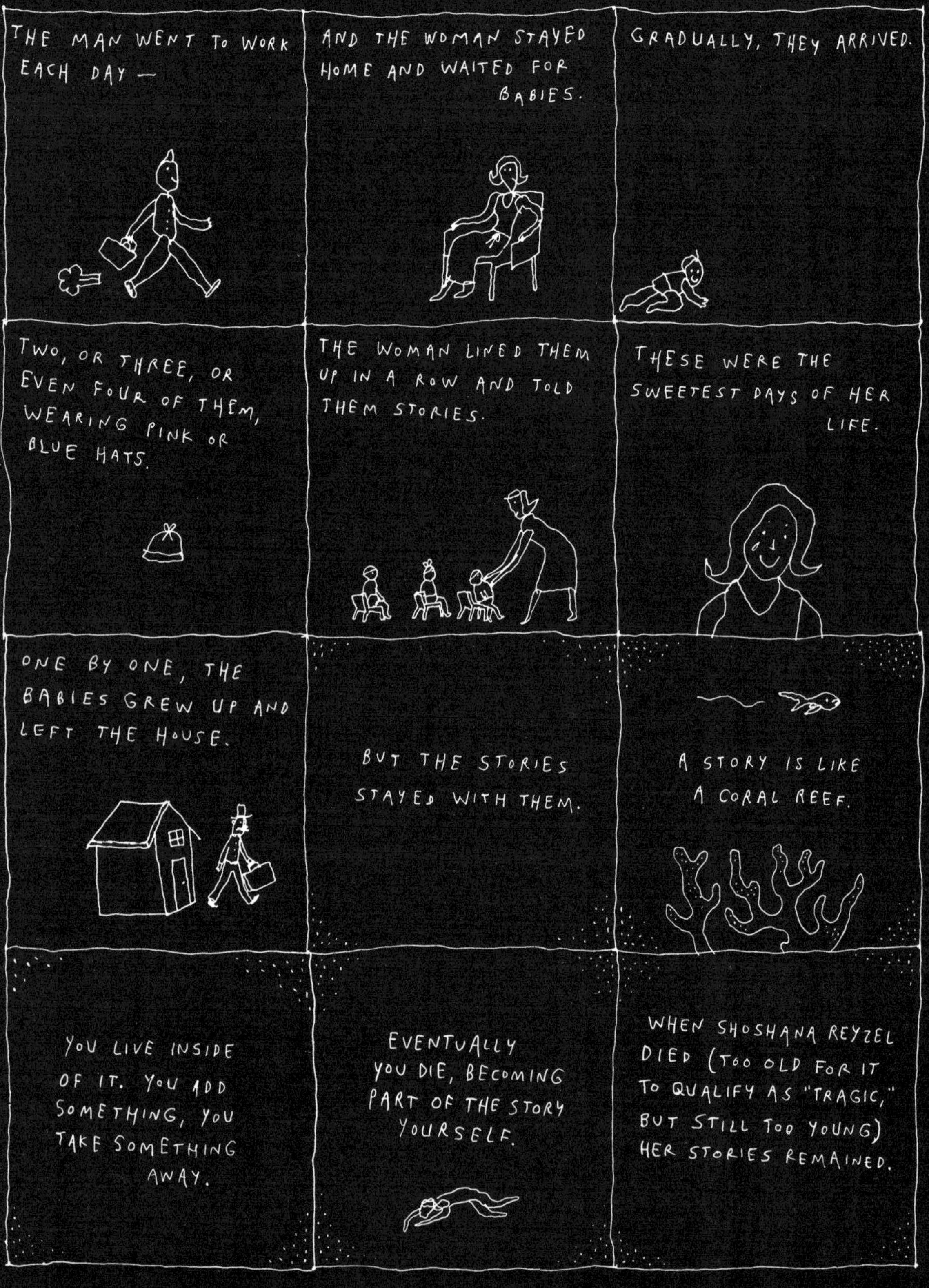
THE MAN WENT TO WORK EACH DAY —
AND THE WOMAN STAYED HOME AND WAITED FOR BABIES.
GRADUALLY, THEY ARRIVED.
TWO, OR THREE, OR EVEN FOUR OF THEM, WEARING PINK OR BLUE HATS.
THE WOMAN LINED THEM UP IN A ROW AND TOLD THEM STORIES.
THESE WERE THE SWEETEST DAYS OF HER LIFE.
ONE BY ONE, THE BABIES GREW UP AND LEFT THE HOUSE.
BUT THE STORIES STAYED WITH THEM.
A STORY IS LIKE A CORAL REEF.
YOU LIVE INSIDE OF IT. YOU ADD SOMETHING, YOU TAKE SOMETHING AWAY.
EVENTUALLY YOU DIE, BECOMING PART OF THE STORY YOURSELF.
WHEN SHOSHANA REYZEL DIED (TOO OLD FOR IT TO QUALIFY AS "TRAGIC," BUT STILL TOO YOUNG) HER STORIES REMAINED.

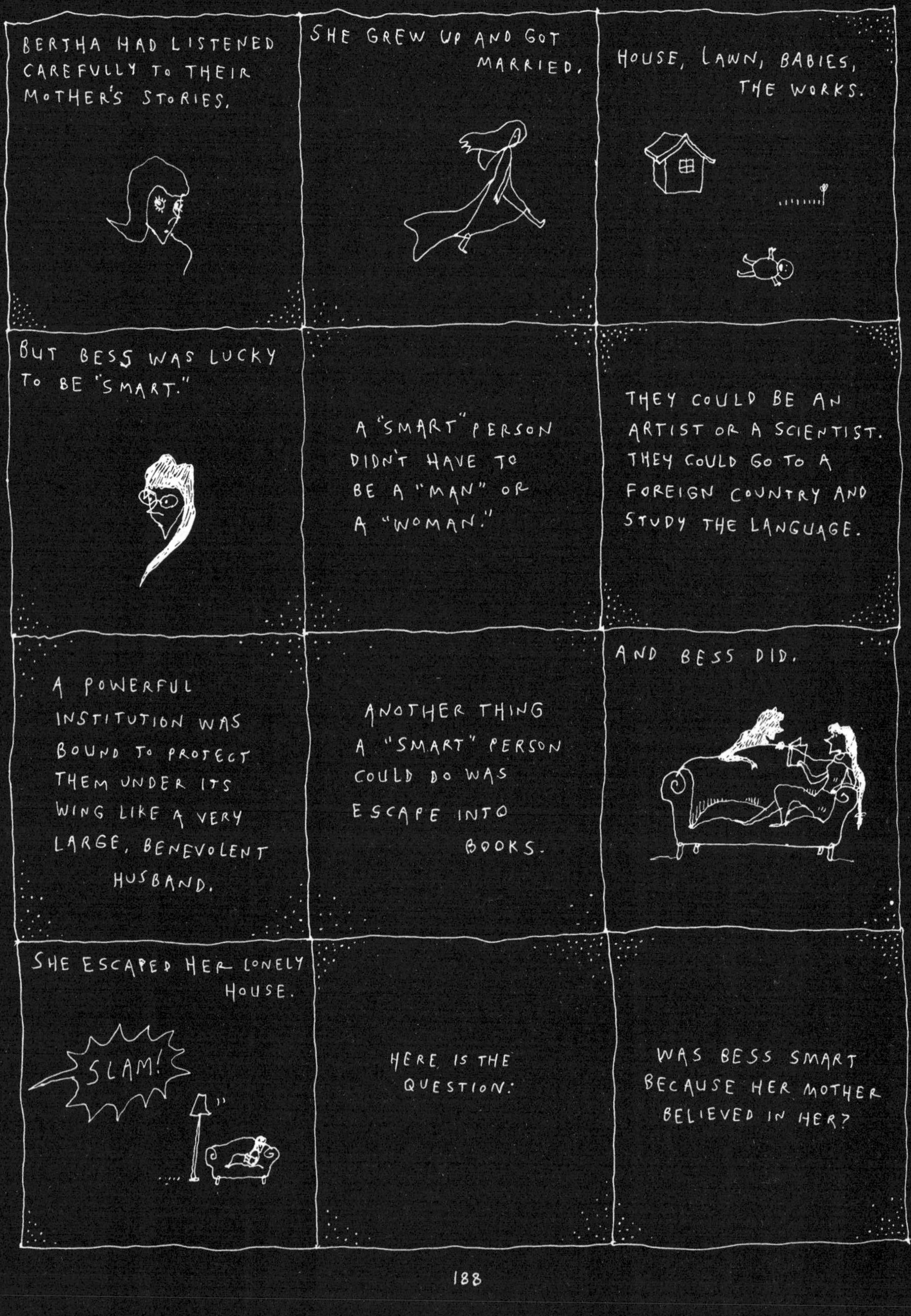
BERTHA HAD LISTENED CAREFULLY TO THEIR MOTHER'S STORIES.
SHE GREW UP AND GOT MARRIED.
HOUSE, LAWN, BABIES, THE WORKS.
BUT BESS WAS LUCKY TO BE "SMART."
A "SMART" PERSON DIDN'T HAVE TO BE A "MAN" OR A "WOMAN."
THEY COULD BE AN ARTIST OR A SCIENTIST. THEY COULD GO TO A FOREIGN COUNTRY AND STUDY THE LANGUAGE.
A POWERFUL INSTITUTION WAS BOUND TO PROTECT THEM UNDER ITS WING LIKE A VERY LARGE, BENEVOLENT HUSBAND.
ANOTHER THING A "SMART" PERSON COULD DO WAS ESCAPE INTO BOOKS.
AND BESS DID.
SHE ESCAPED HER LONELY HOUSE.
SLAM!
HERE IS THE QUESTION:
WAS BESS SMART BECAUSE HER MOTHER BELIEVED IN HER?

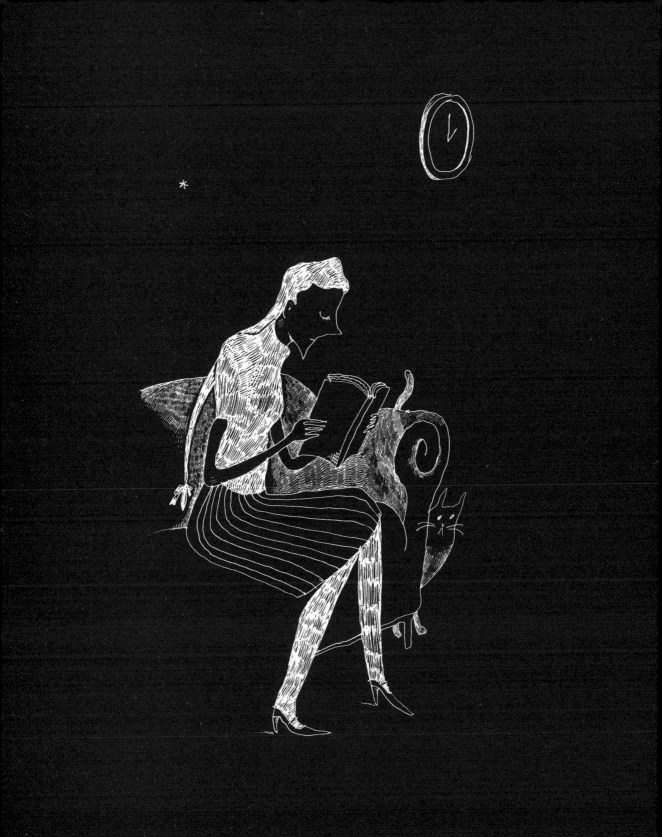

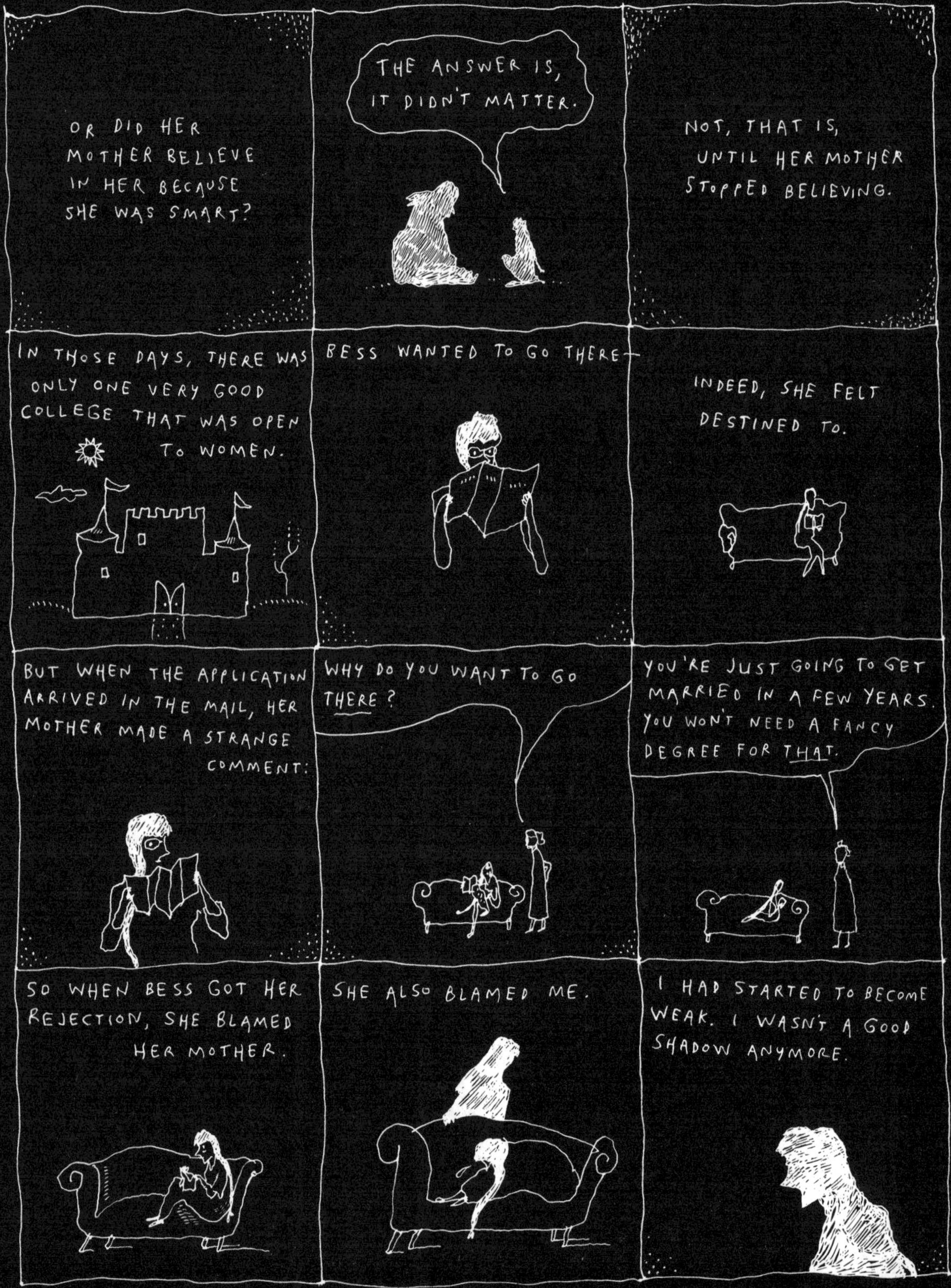

OR DID HER MOTHER BELIEVE IN HER BECAUSE SHE WAS SMART?
THE ANSWER IS, IT DIDN'T MATTER.
NOT, THAT IS, UNTIL HER MOTHER STOPPED BELIEVING.
IN THOSE DAYS, THERE WAS ONLY ONE VERY GOOD COLLEGE THAT WAS OPEN TO WOMEN.
BESS WANTED TO GO THERE—
INDEED, SHE FELT DESTINED TO.
BUT WHEN THE APPLICATION ARRIVED IN THE MAIL, HER MOTHER MADE A STRANGE COMMENT:
WHY DO YOU WANT TO GO THERE?
YOU'RE JUST GOING TO GET MARRIED IN A FEW YEARS. YOU WON'T NEED A FANCY DEGREE FOR THAT.
SO WHEN BESS GOT HER REJECTION, SHE BLAMED HER MOTHER.
SHE ALSO BLAMED ME.
I HAD STARTED TO BECOME WEAK. I WASN'T A GOOD SHADOW ANYMORE.

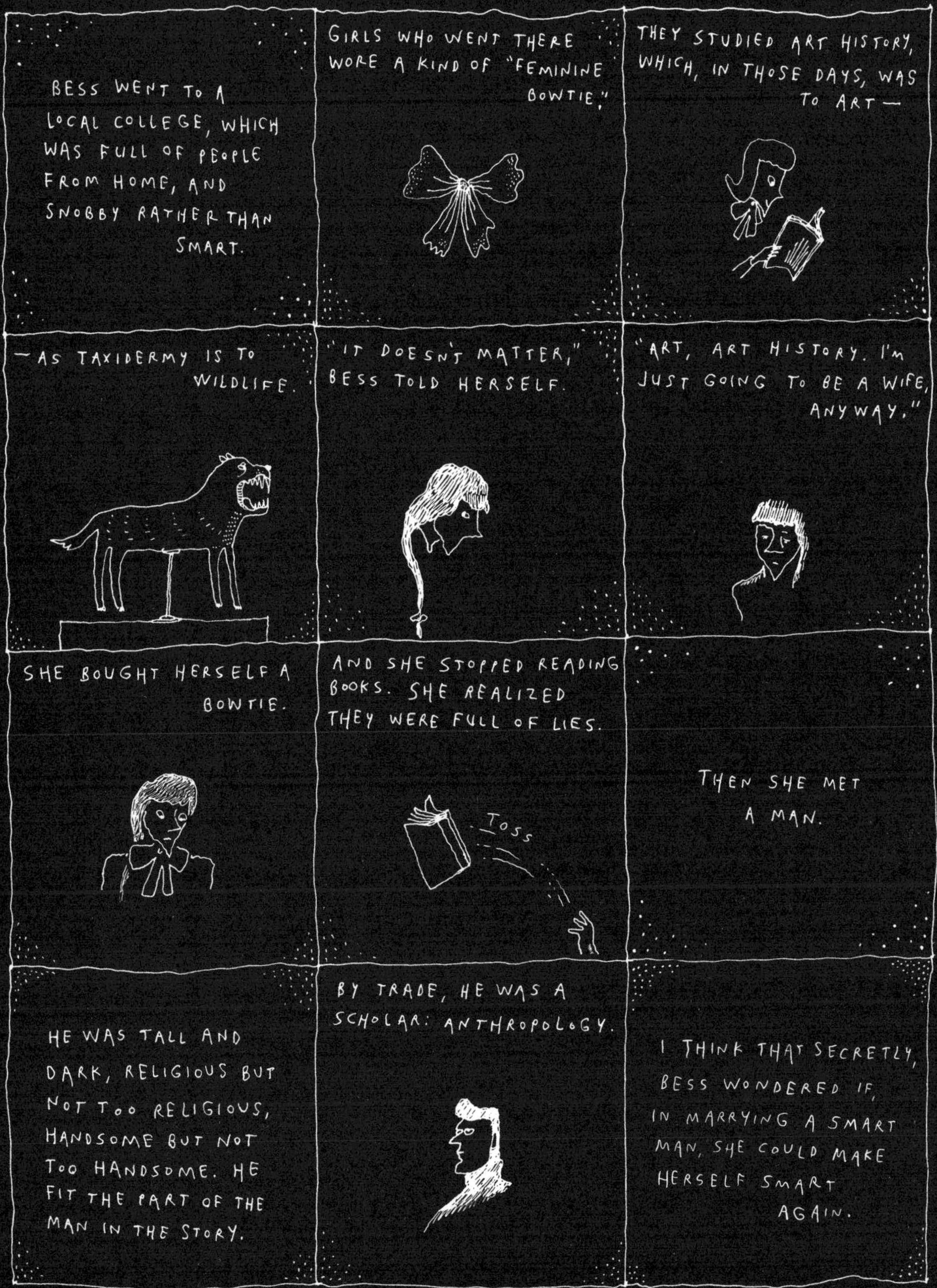
BESS WENT TO A LOCAL COLLEGE, WHICH WAS FULL OF PEOPLE FROM HOME, AND SNOBBY RATHER THAN SMART.
GIRLS WHO WENT THERE WORE A KIND OF "FEMININE BOWTIE."
THEY STUDIED ART HISTORY, WHICH, IN THOSE DAYS, WAS TO ART—
—AS TAXIDERMY IS TO WILDLIFE.
"IT DOESN'T MATTER," BESS TOLD HERSELF.
"ART, ART HISTORY. I'M JUST GOING TO BE A WIFE, ANYWAY."
SHE BOUGHT HERSELF A BOWTIE.
AND SHE STOPPED READING BOOKS. SHE REALIZED THEY WERE FULL OF LIES.
TOSS
THEN SHE MET A MAN.
HE WAS TALL AND DARK, RELIGIOUS BUT NOT TOO RELIGIOUS, HANDSOME BUT NOT TOO HANDSOME. HE FIT THE PART OF THE MAN IN THE STORY.
BY TRADE, HE WAS A SCHOLAR: ANTHROPOLOGY.
I THINK THAT SECRETLY, BESS WONDERED IF, IN MARRYING A SMART MAN, SHE COULD MAKE HERSELF SMART AGAIN.

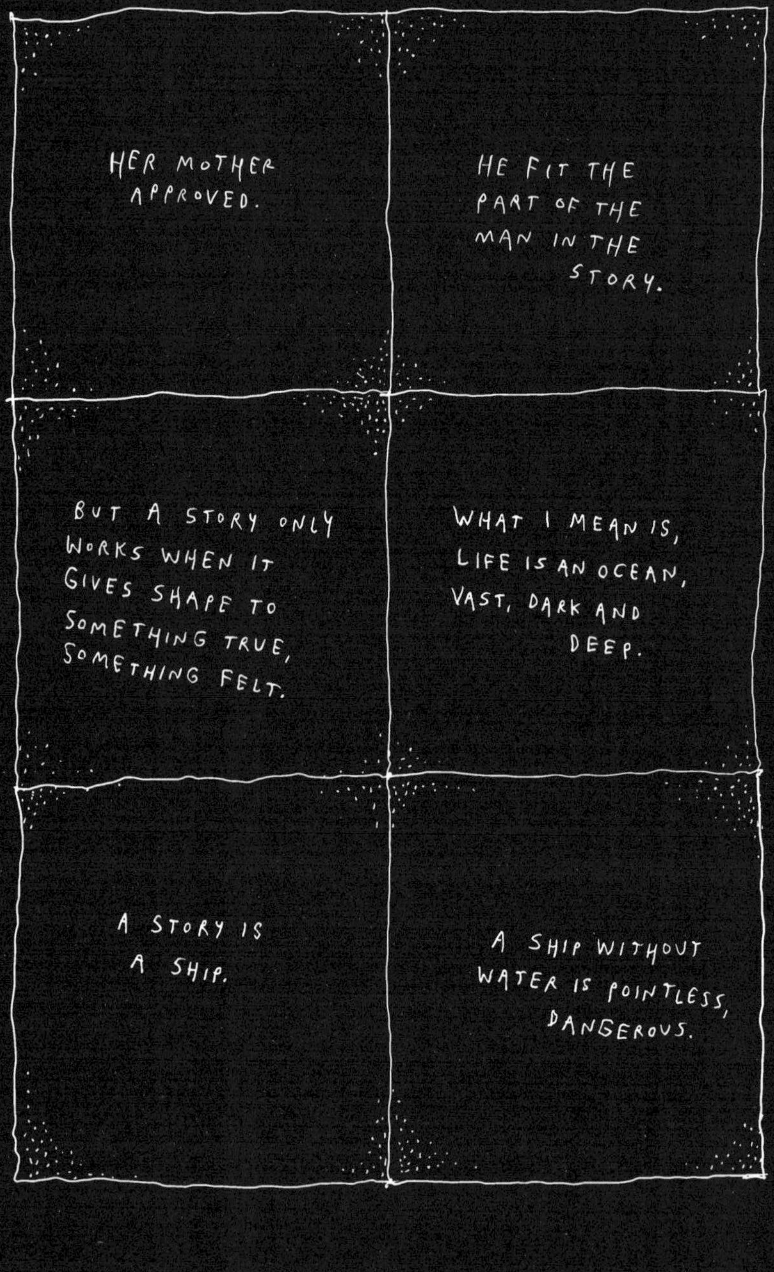
HER MOTHER APPROVED.
HE FIT THE PART OF THE MAN IN THE STORY.
BUT A STORY ONLY WORKS WHEN IT GIVES SHAPE TO SOMETHING TRUE, SOMETHING FELT.
WHAT I MEAN IS, LIFE IS AN OCEAN, VAST, DARK AND DEEP.
A STORY IS A SHIP.
A SHIP WITHOUT WATER IS POINTLESS, DANGEROUS.

THE MARRIAGE WAS BOTH THOSE THINGS.

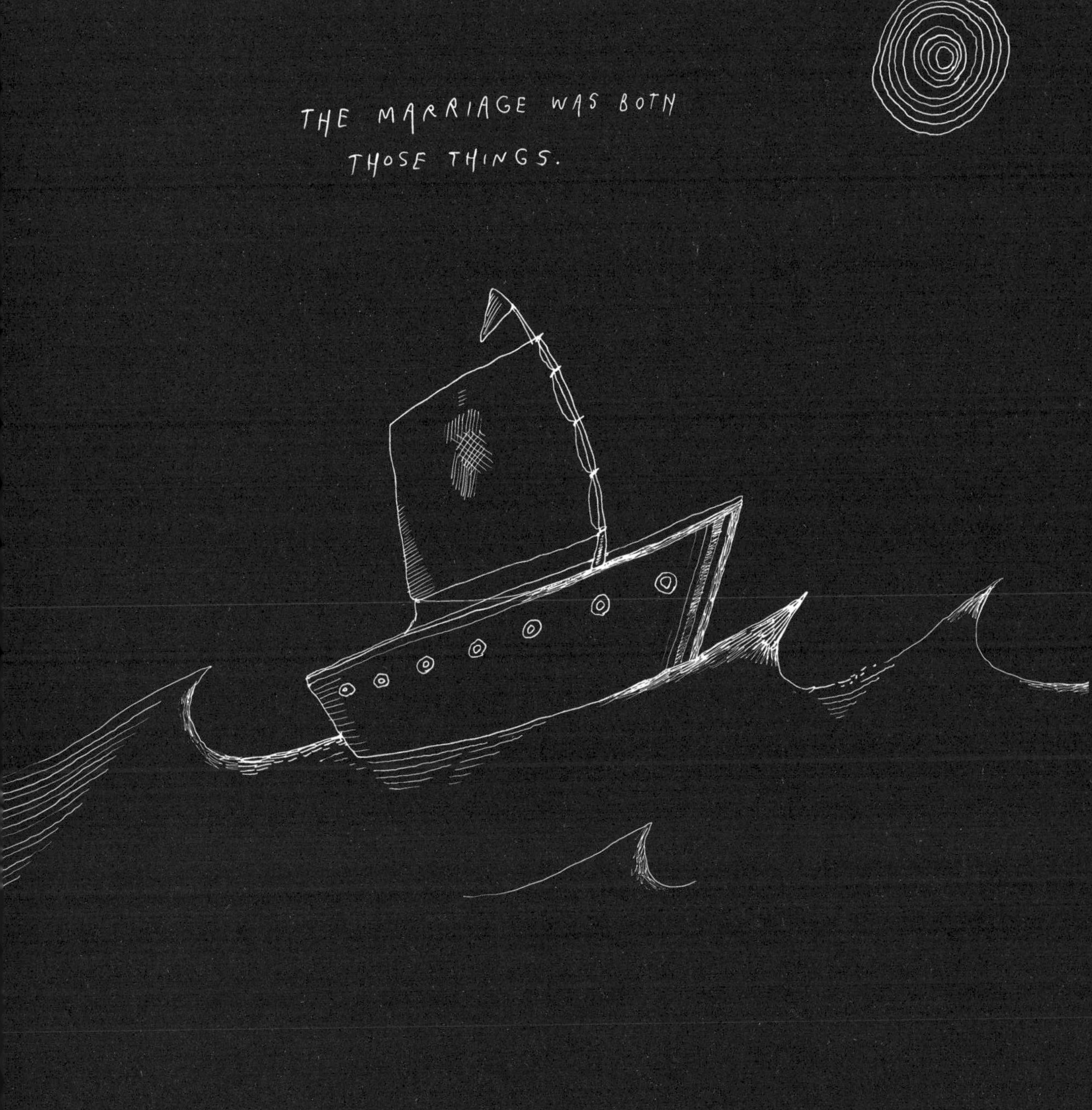

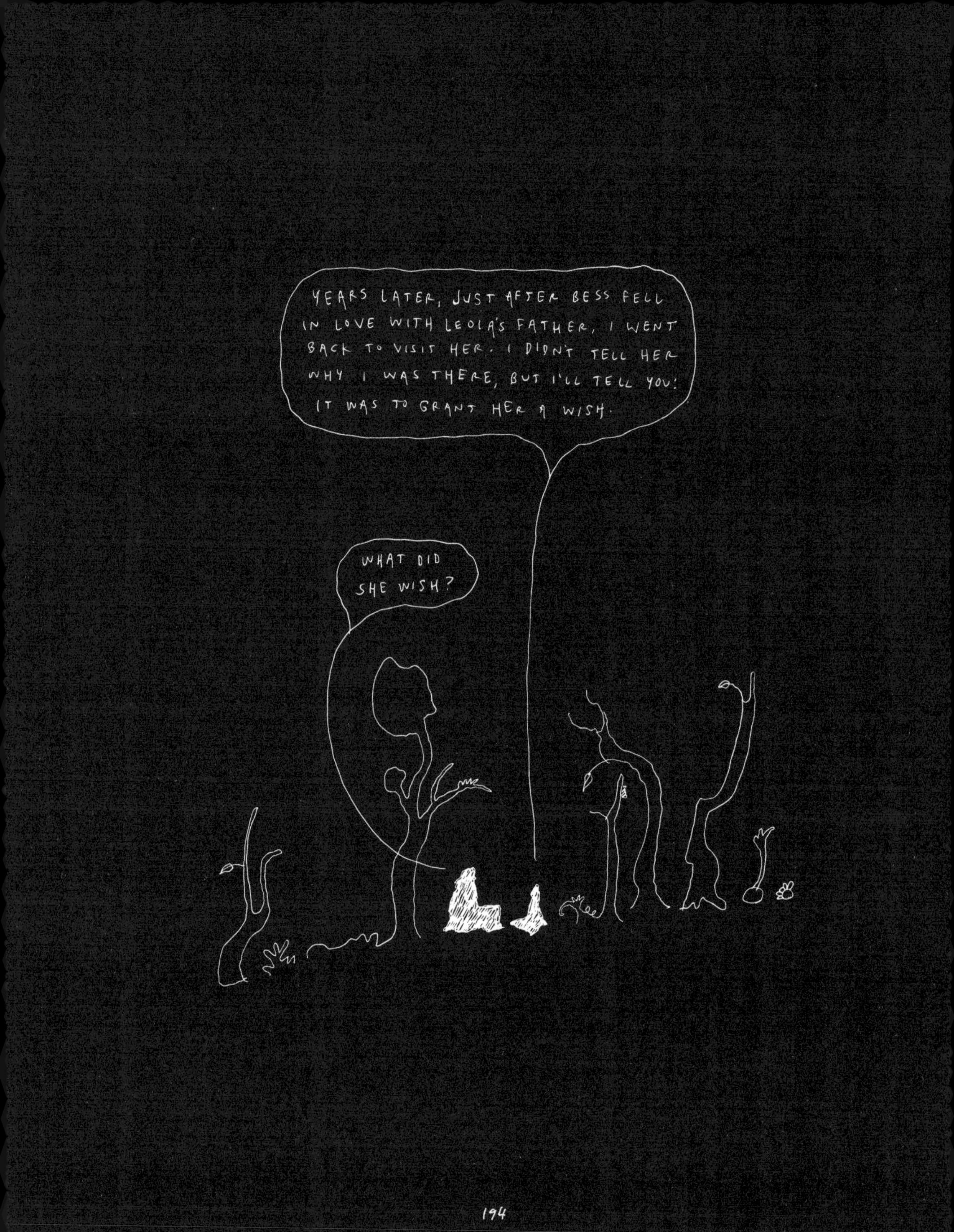
YEARS LATER, JUST AFTER BESS FELL IN LOVE WITH LEOLA'S FATHER, I WENT BACK TO VISIT HER. I DIDN'T TELL HER WHY I WAS THERE, BUT I'LL TELL YOU: IT WAS TO GRANT HER A WISH.
WHAT DID SHE WISH?

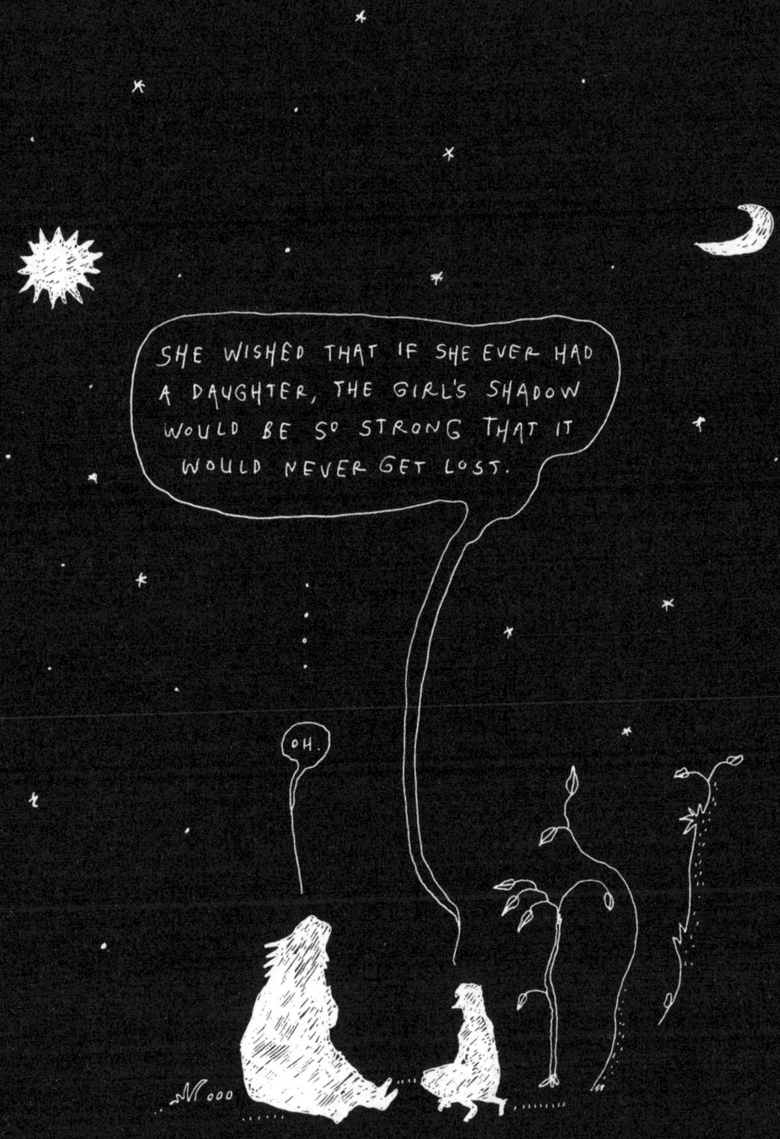
SHE WISHED THAT IF SHE EVER HAD A DAUGHTER, THE GIRL'S SHADOW WOULD BE SO STRONG THAT IT WOULD NEVER GET LOST.
OH.

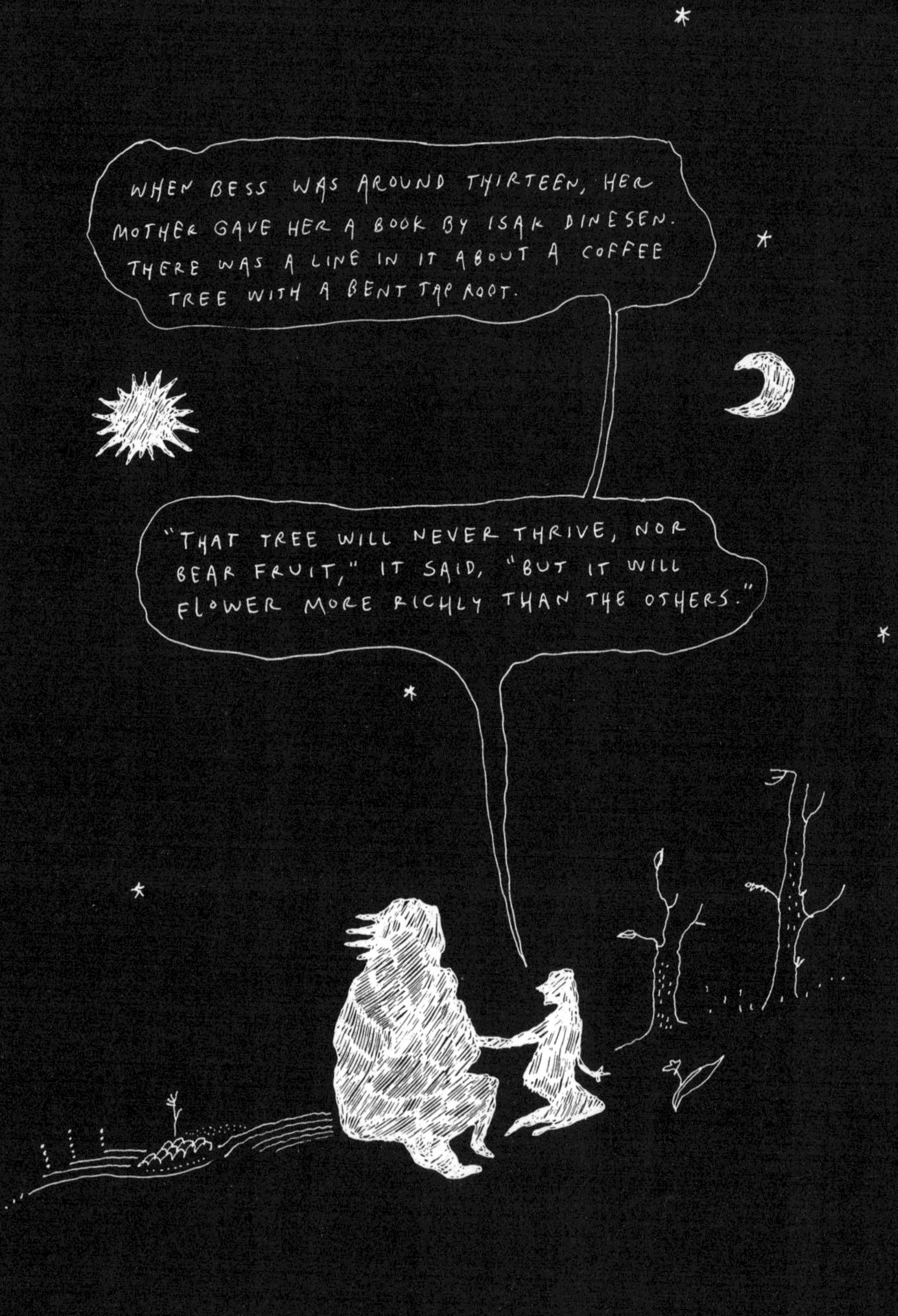
WHEN BESS WAS AROUND THIRTEEN, HER MOTHER GAVE HER A BOOK BY ISAK DINESEN. THERE WAS A LINE IN IT ABOUT A COFFEE TREE WITH A BENT TAP ROOT.
"THAT TREE WILL NEVER THRIVE, NOR BEAR FRUIT," IT SAID, "BUT IT WILL FLOWER MORE RICHLY THAN THE OTHERS."

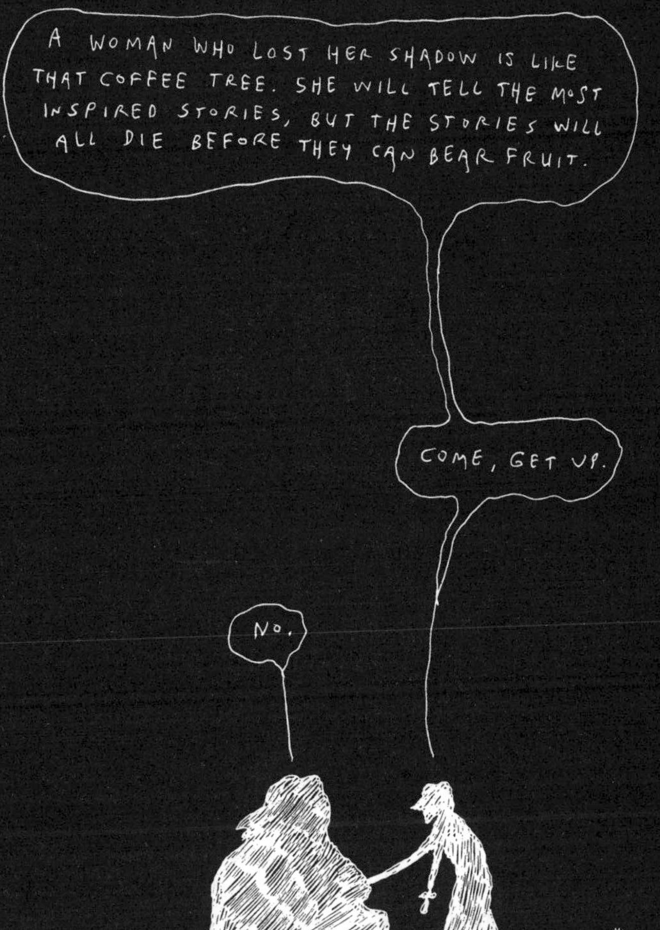
A WOMAN WHO LOST HER SHADOW IS LIKE THAT COFFEE TREE. SHE WILL TELL THE MOST INSPIRED STORIES, BUT THE STORIES WILL ALL DIE BEFORE THEY CAN BEAR FRUIT.
COME, GET UP.
NO.

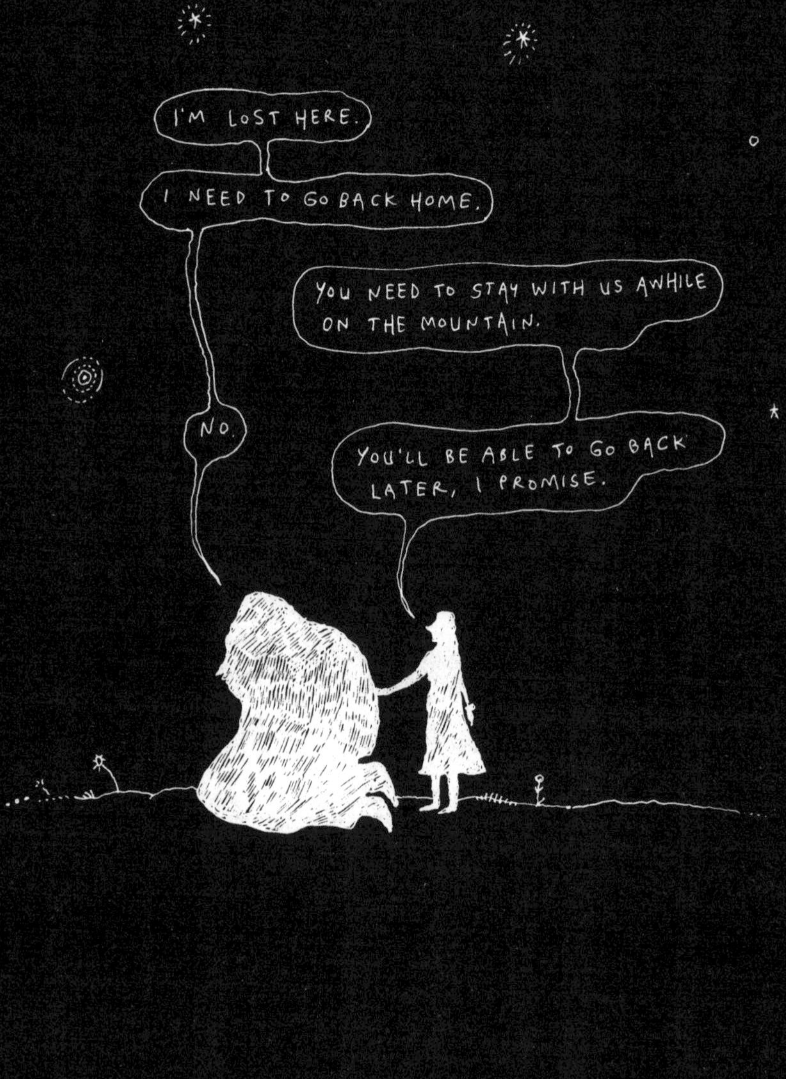
I'M LOST HERE.
I NEED TO GO BACK HOME.
NO.
YOU NEED TO STAY WITH US AWHILE ON THE MOUNTAIN.
YOU'LL BE ABLE TO GO BACK LATER, I PROMISE.

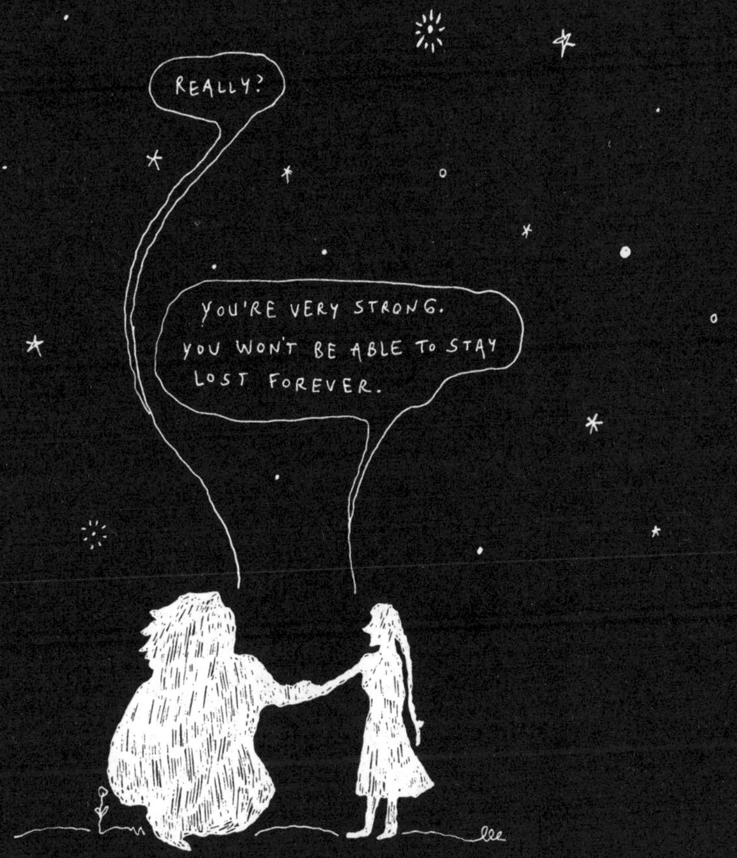
REALLY?
YOU'RE VERY STRONG. YOU WON'T BE ABLE TO STAY LOST FOREVER.

...BESS'S MOTHER'S STORIES HAD BEEN INSPIRED, BUT CONSTRICTING, TOO. BESS WANTED HER OWN STORIES TO BE LIGHTER, BRIGHTER.

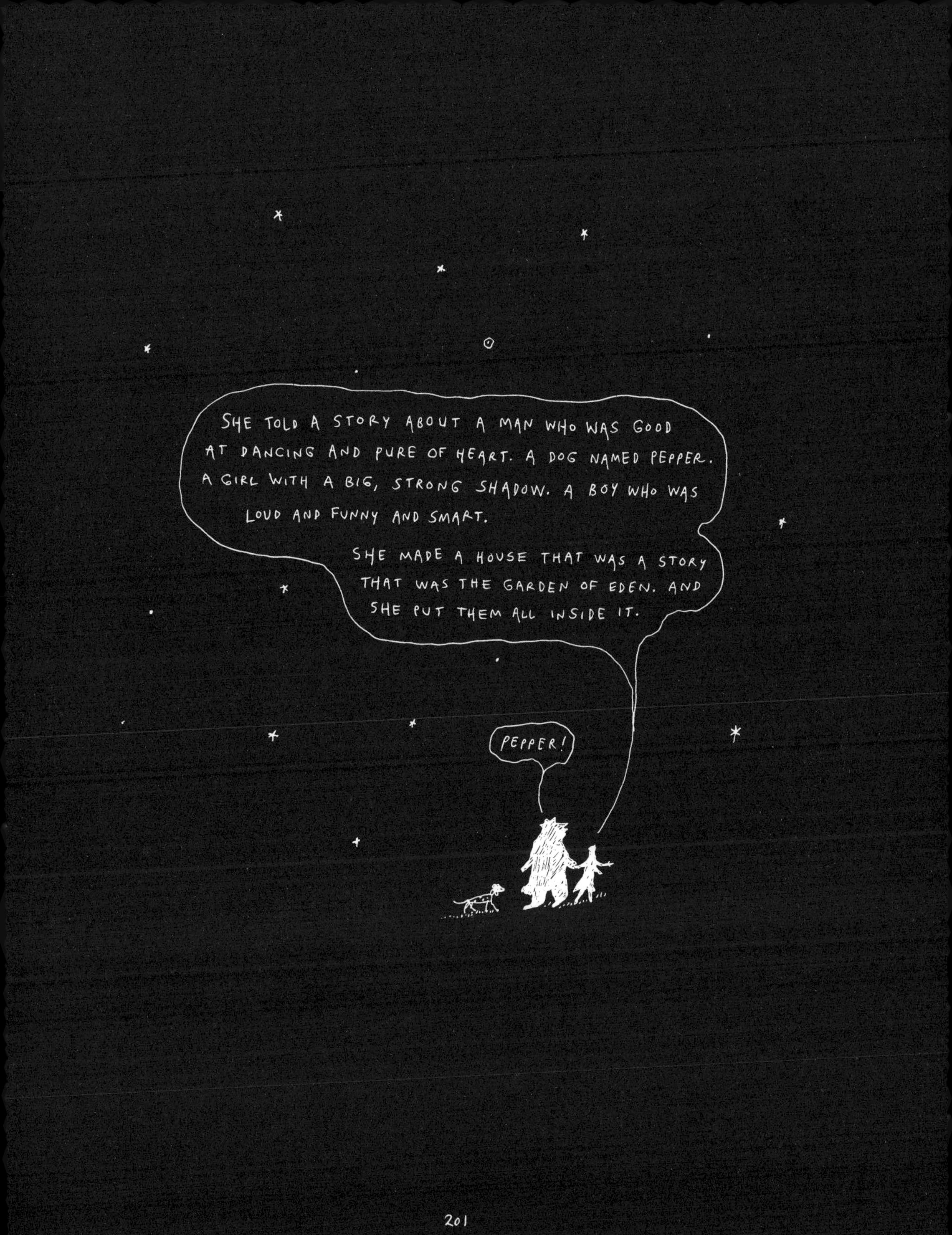
SHE TOLD A STORY ABOUT A MAN WHO WAS GOOD AT DANCING AND PURE OF HEART. A DOG NAMED PEPPER. A GIRL WITH A BIG, STRONG SHADOW. A BOY WHO WAS LOUD AND FUNNY AND SMART.
SHE MADE A HOUSE THAT WAS A STORY THAT WAS THE GARDEN OF EDEN. AND SHE PUT THEM ALL INSIDE IT.
PEPPER!

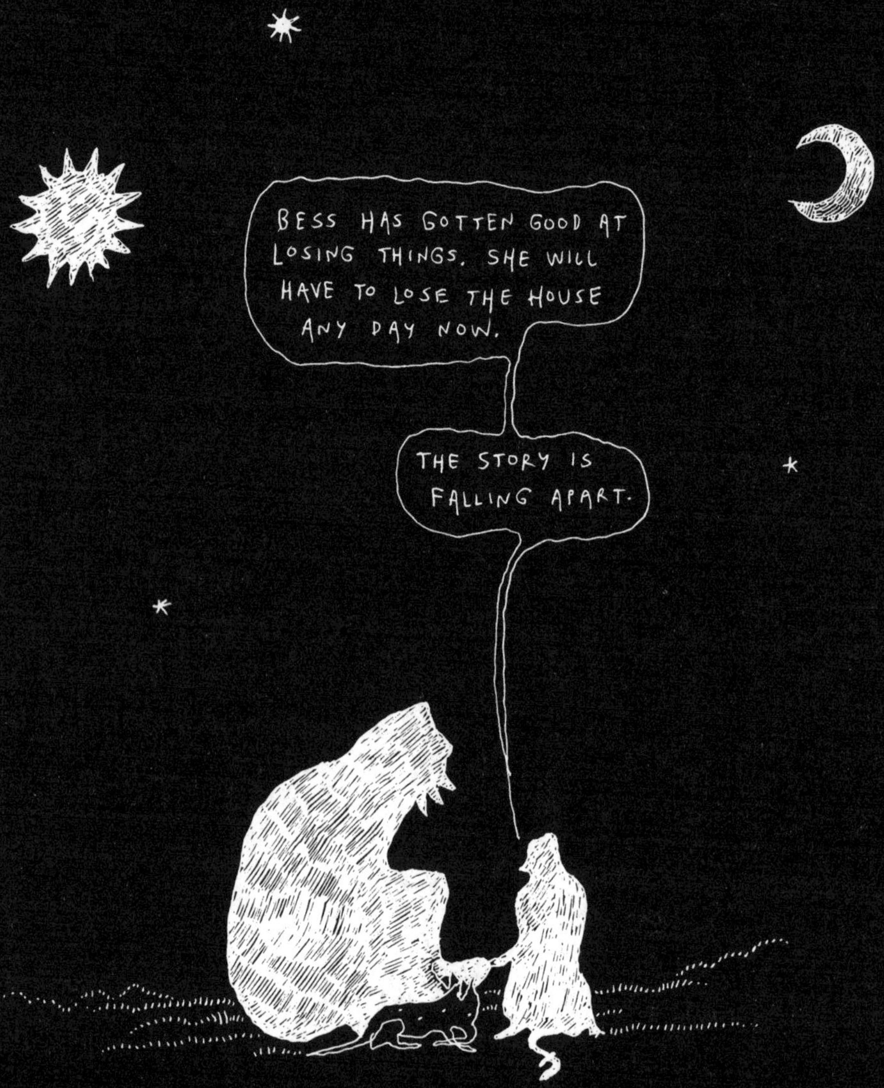
BESS HAS GOTTEN GOOD AT LOSING THINGS. SHE WILL HAVE TO LOSE THE HOUSE ANY DAY NOW.
THE STORY IS FALLING APART.

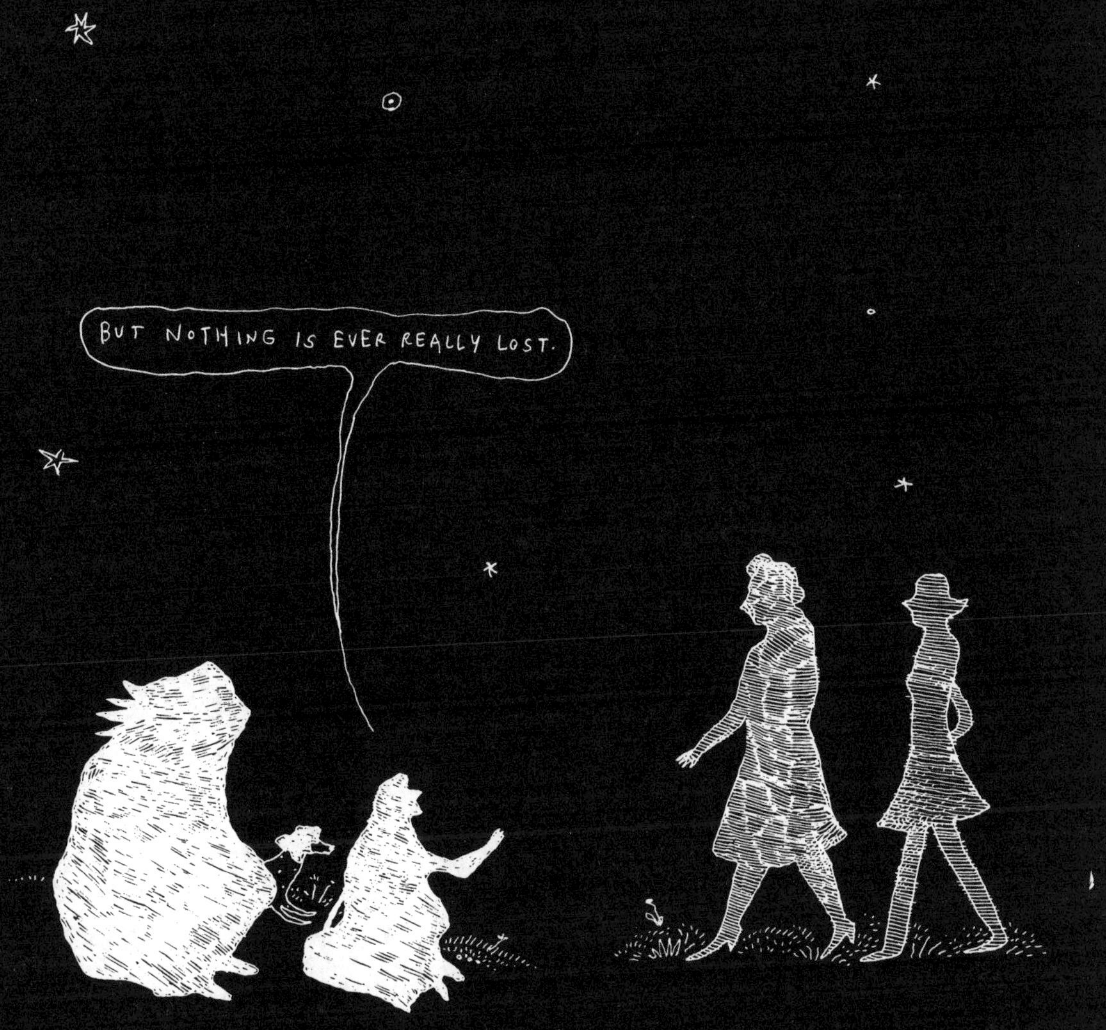
BUT NOTHING IS EVER REALLY LOST.

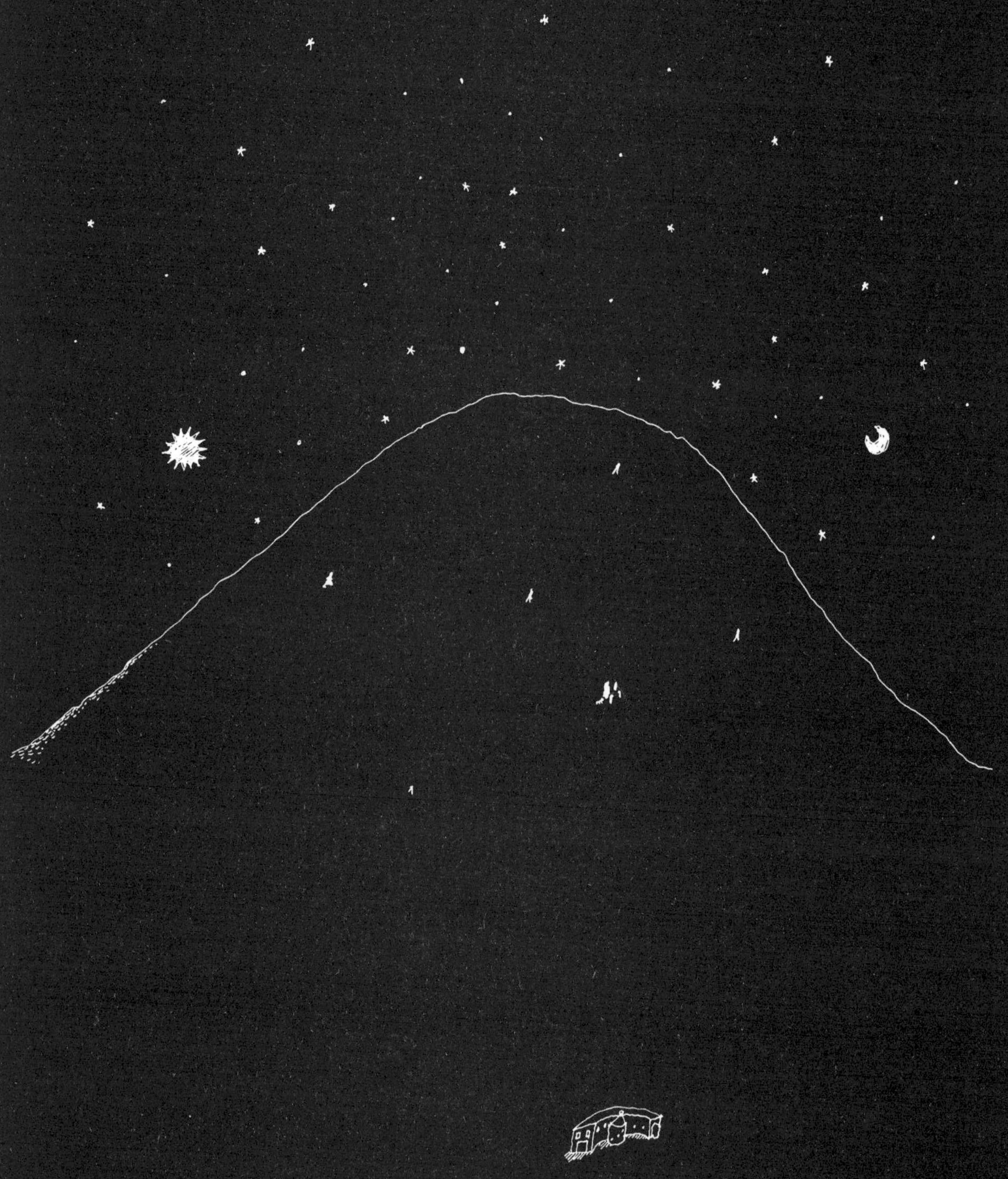

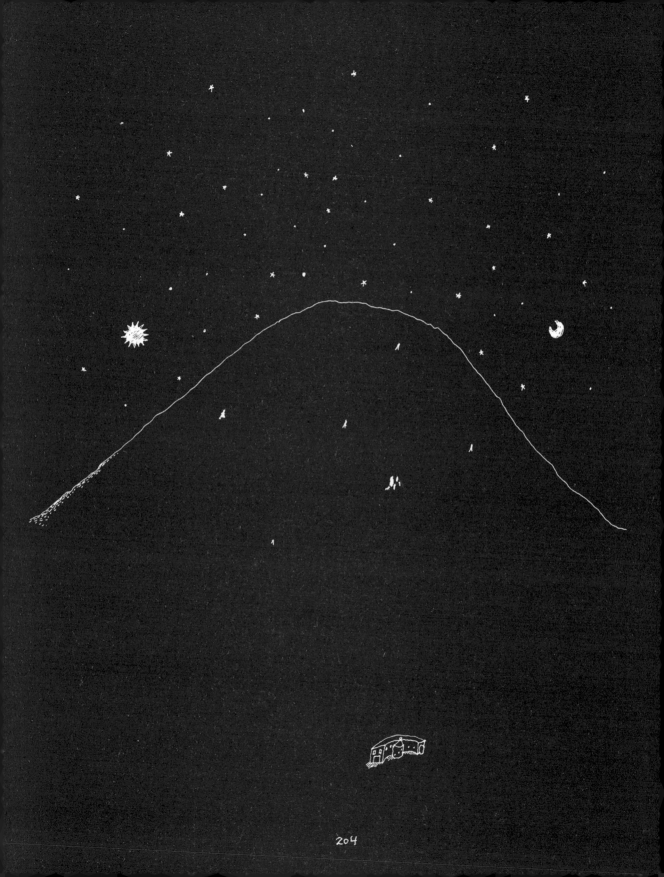

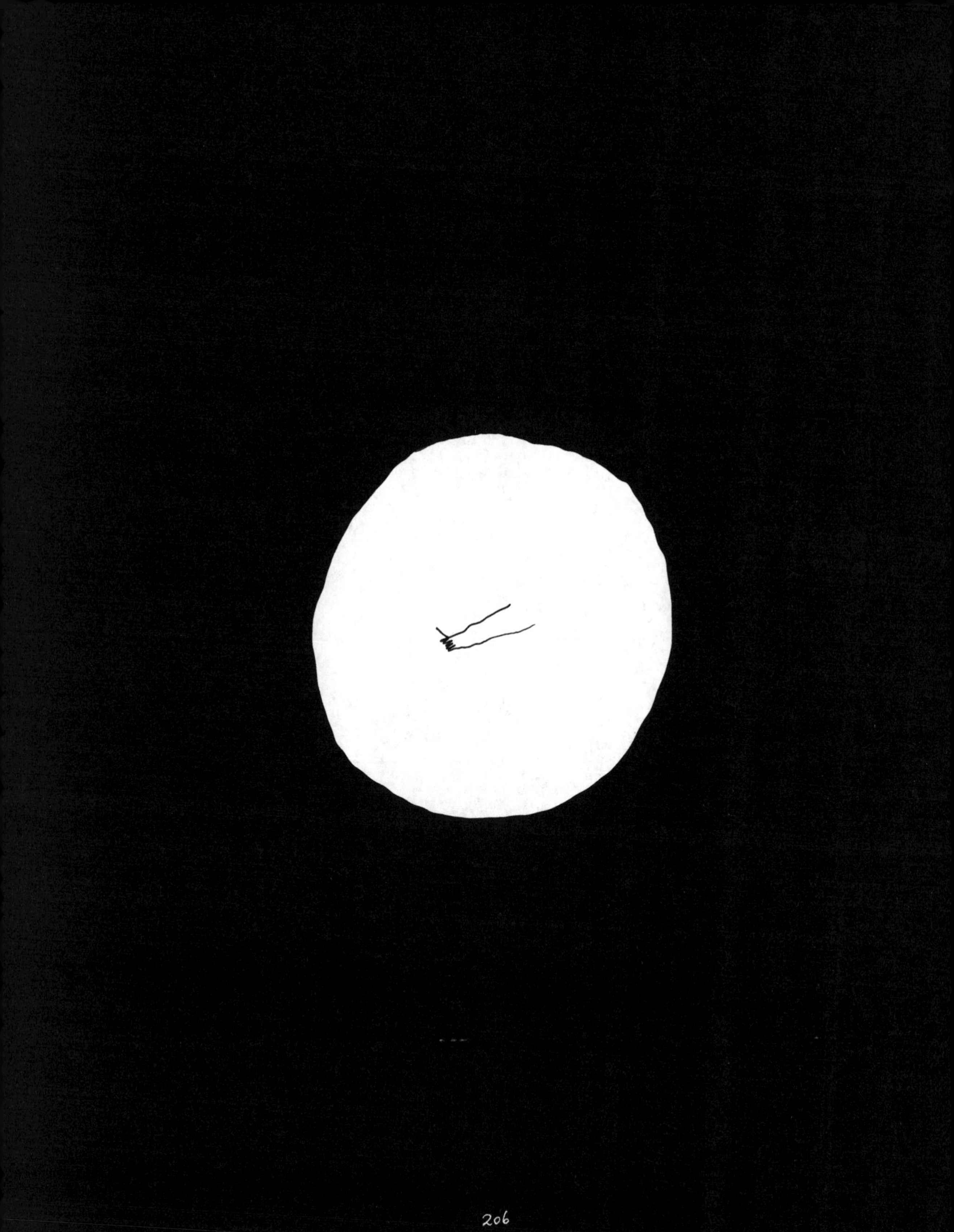

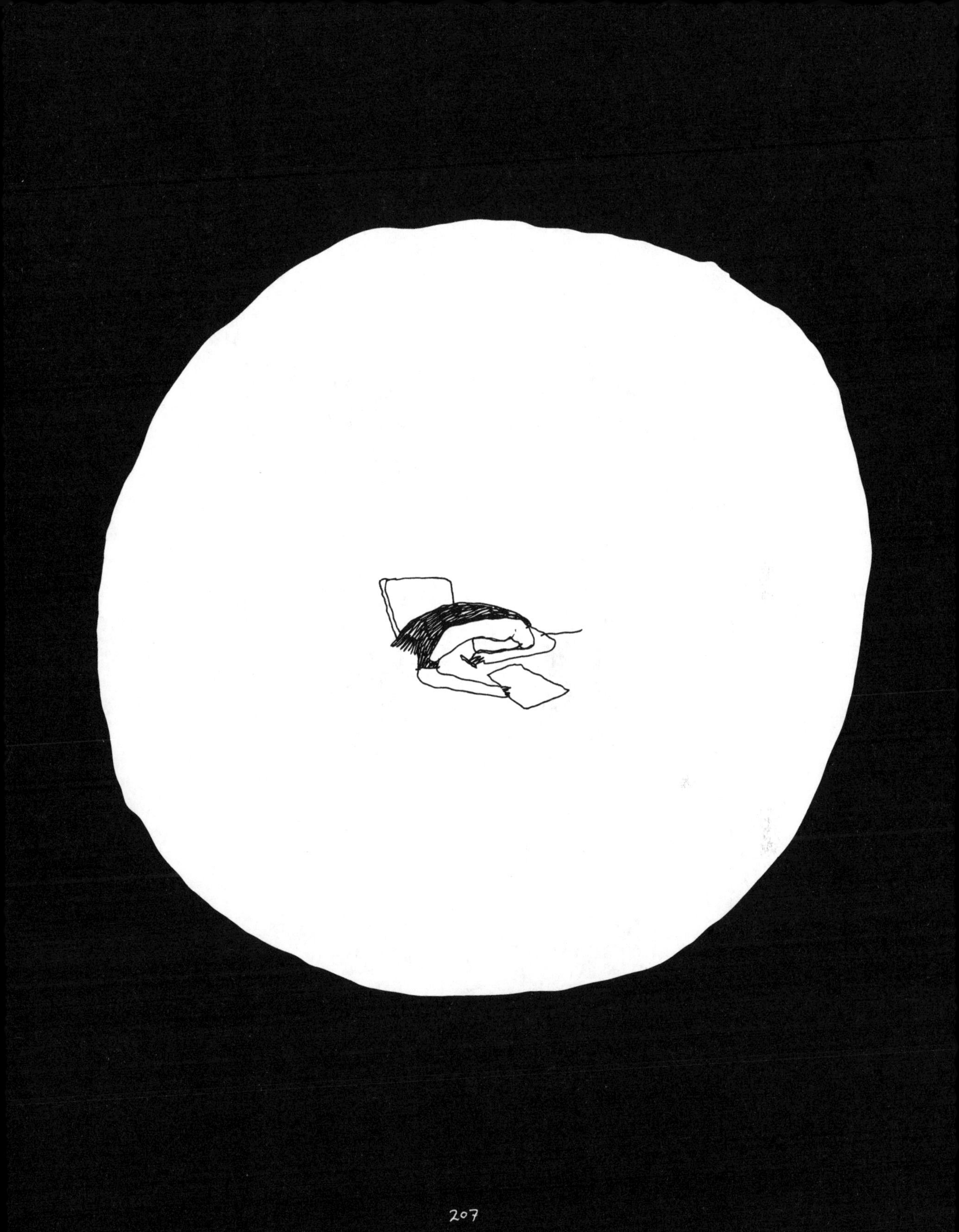

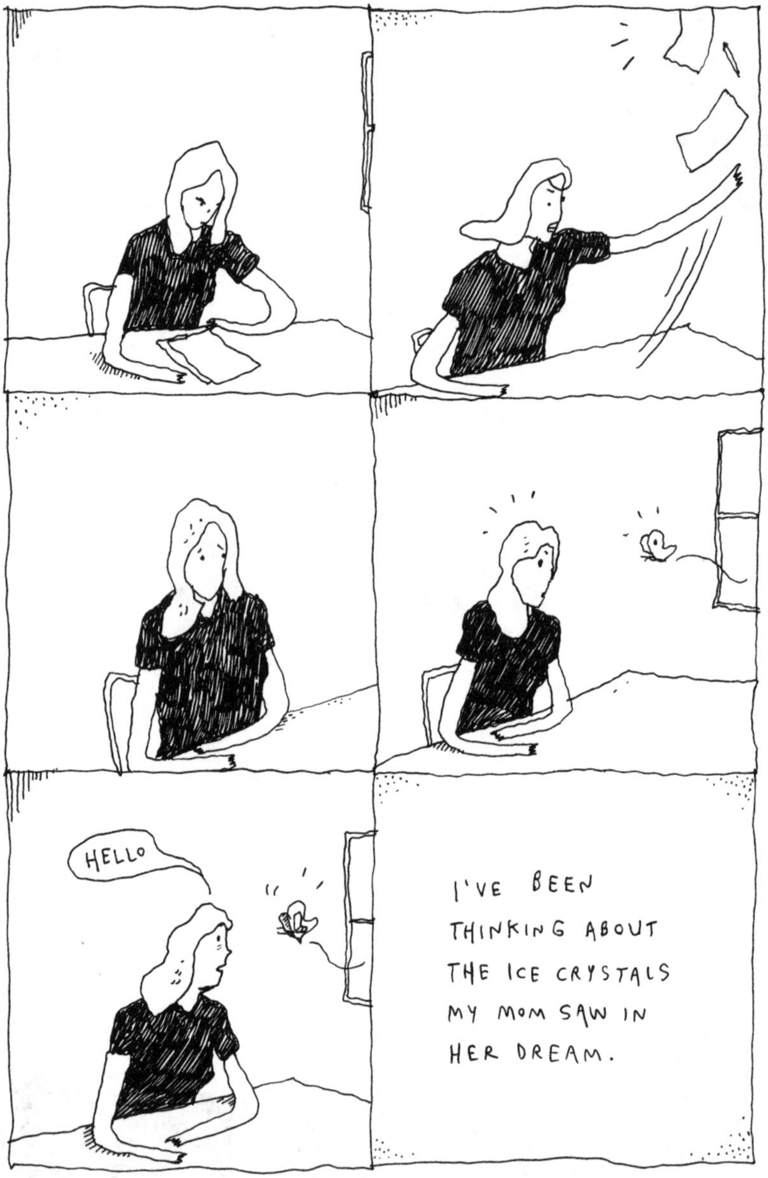
HELLO
I'VE BEEN THINKING ABOUT THE ICE CRYSTALS MY MOM SAW IN HER DREAM.

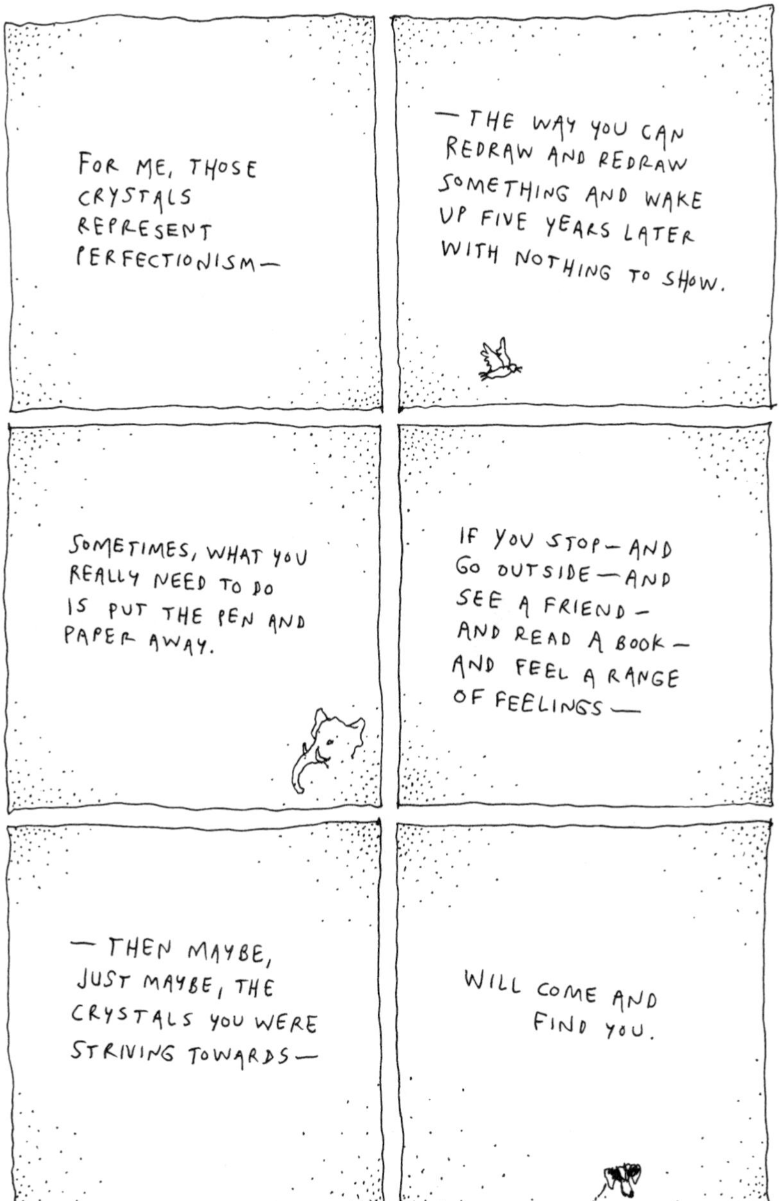

FOR ME, THOSE CRYSTALS REPRESENT PERFECTIONISM—
—THE WAY YOU CAN REDRAW AND REDRAW SOMETHING AND WAKE UP FIVE YEARS LATER WITH NOTHING TO SHOW.
SOMETIMES, WHAT YOU REALLY NEED TO DO IS PUT THE PEN AND PAPER AWAY.
IF YOU STOP—AND GO OUTSIDE—AND SEE A FRIEND—AND READ A BOOK—AND FEEL A RANGE OF FEELINGS—
—THEN MAYBE, JUST MAYBE, THE CRYSTALS YOU WERE STRIVING TOWARDS—
WILL COME AND FIND YOU.

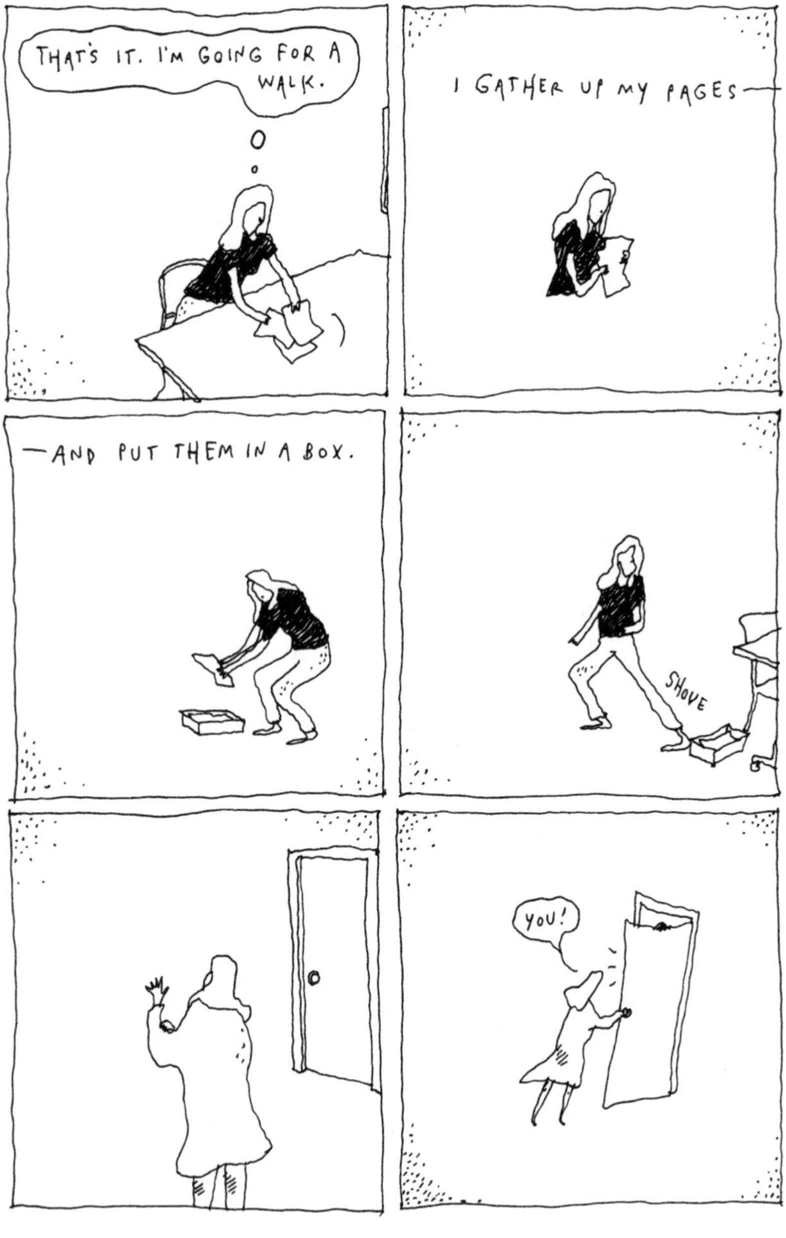
THAT'S IT. I'M GOING FOR A WALK.
I GATHER UP MY PAGES—
—AND PUT THEM IN A BOX.
SHOVE
YOU!

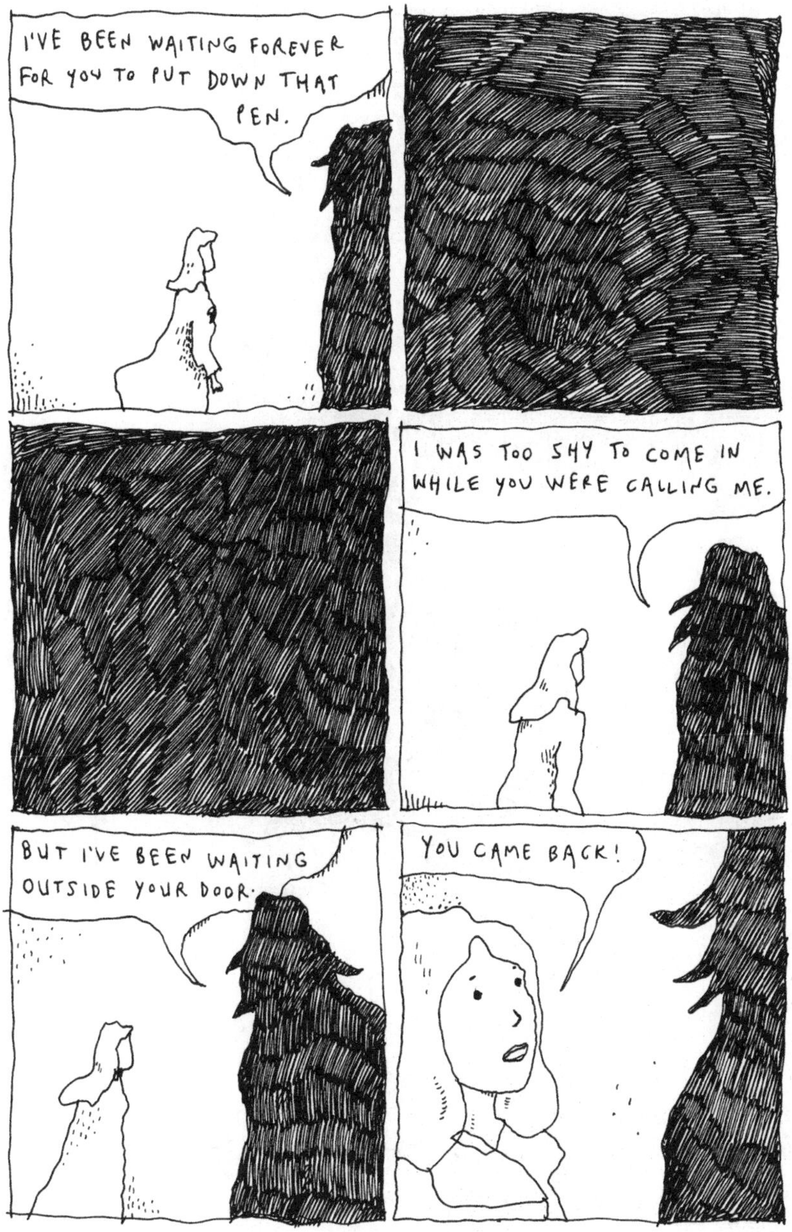
I'VE BEEN WAITING FOREVER FOR YOU TO PUT DOWN THAT PEN.
I WAS TOO SHY TO COME IN WHILE YOU WERE CALLING ME.
BUT I'VE BEEN WAITING OUTSIDE YOUR DOOR.
YOU CAME BACK!

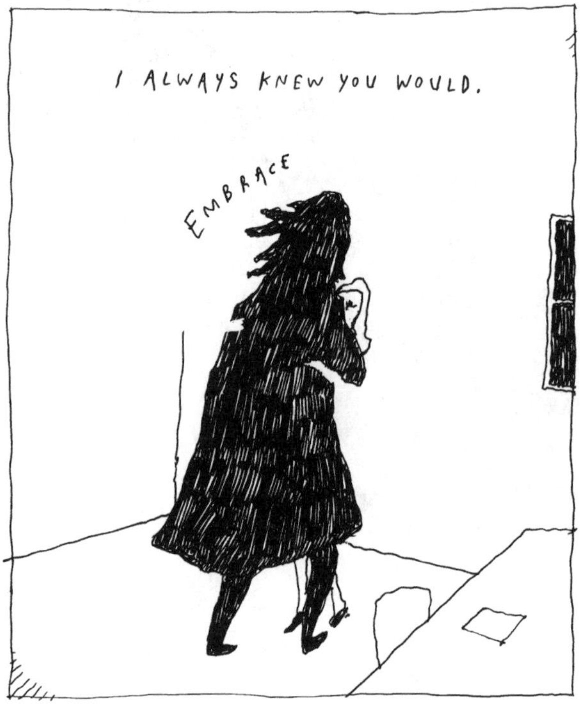
I ALWAYS KNEW YOU WOULD.
EMBRACE

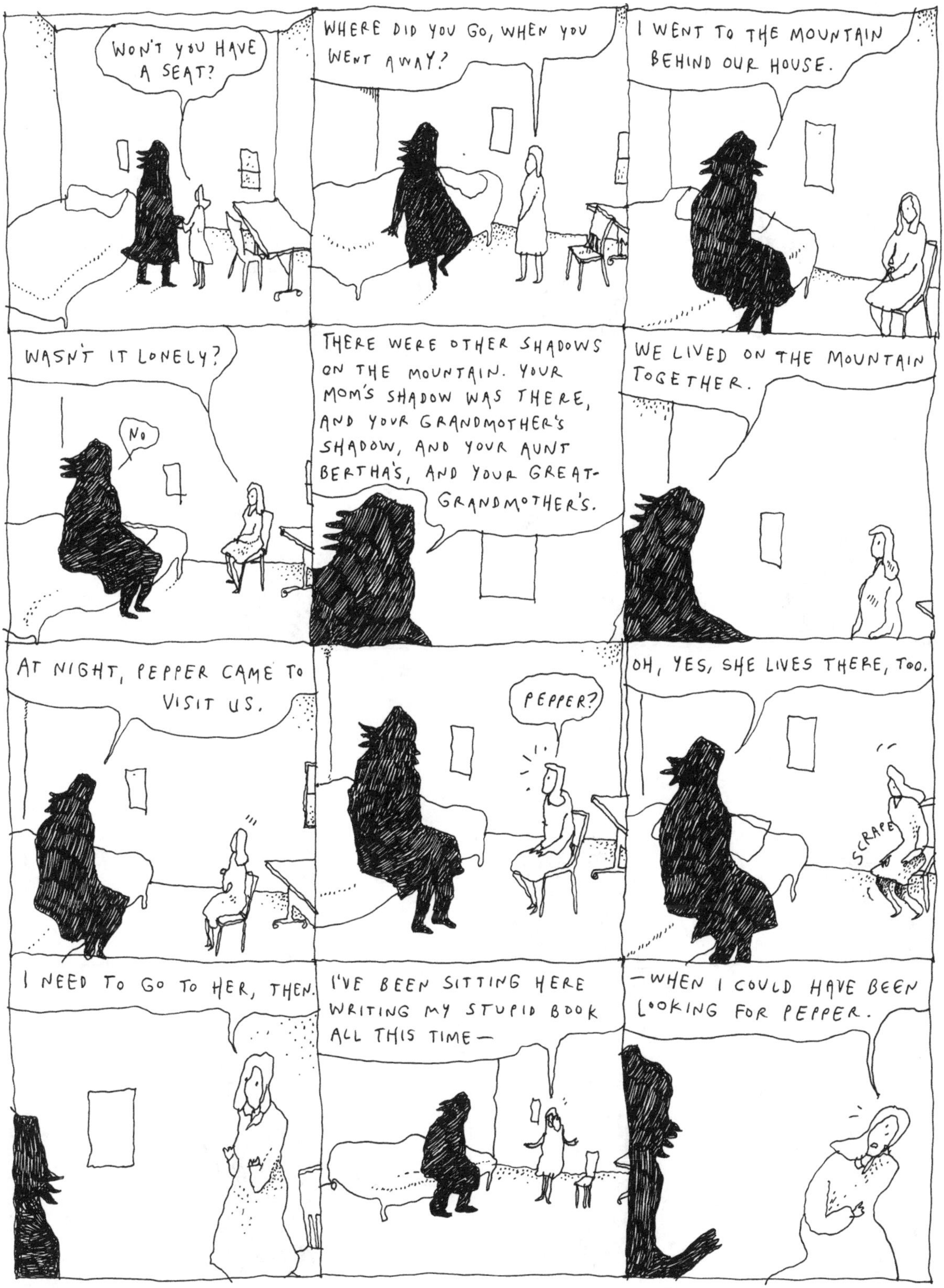
WON'T YOU HAVE A SEAT?
WHERE DID YOU GO, WHEN YOU WENT AWAY?
I WENT TO THE MOUNTAIN BEHIND OUR HOUSE.
WASN'T IT LONELY?
NO
THERE WERE OTHER SHADOWS ON THE MOUNTAIN. YOUR MOM'S SHADOW WAS THERE, AND YOUR GRANDMOTHER'S SHADOW, AND YOUR AUNT BERTHA'S, AND YOUR GREAT-GRANDMOTHER'S.
WE LIVED ON THE MOUNTAIN TOGETHER.
AT NIGHT, PEPPER CAME TO VISIT US.
PEPPER?
OH, YES, SHE LIVES THERE, TOO.
SCRAPE
I NEED TO GO TO HER, THEN.
I'VE BEEN SITTING HERE WRITING MY STUPID BOOK ALL THIS TIME—
—WHEN I COULD HAVE BEEN LOOKING FOR PEPPER.

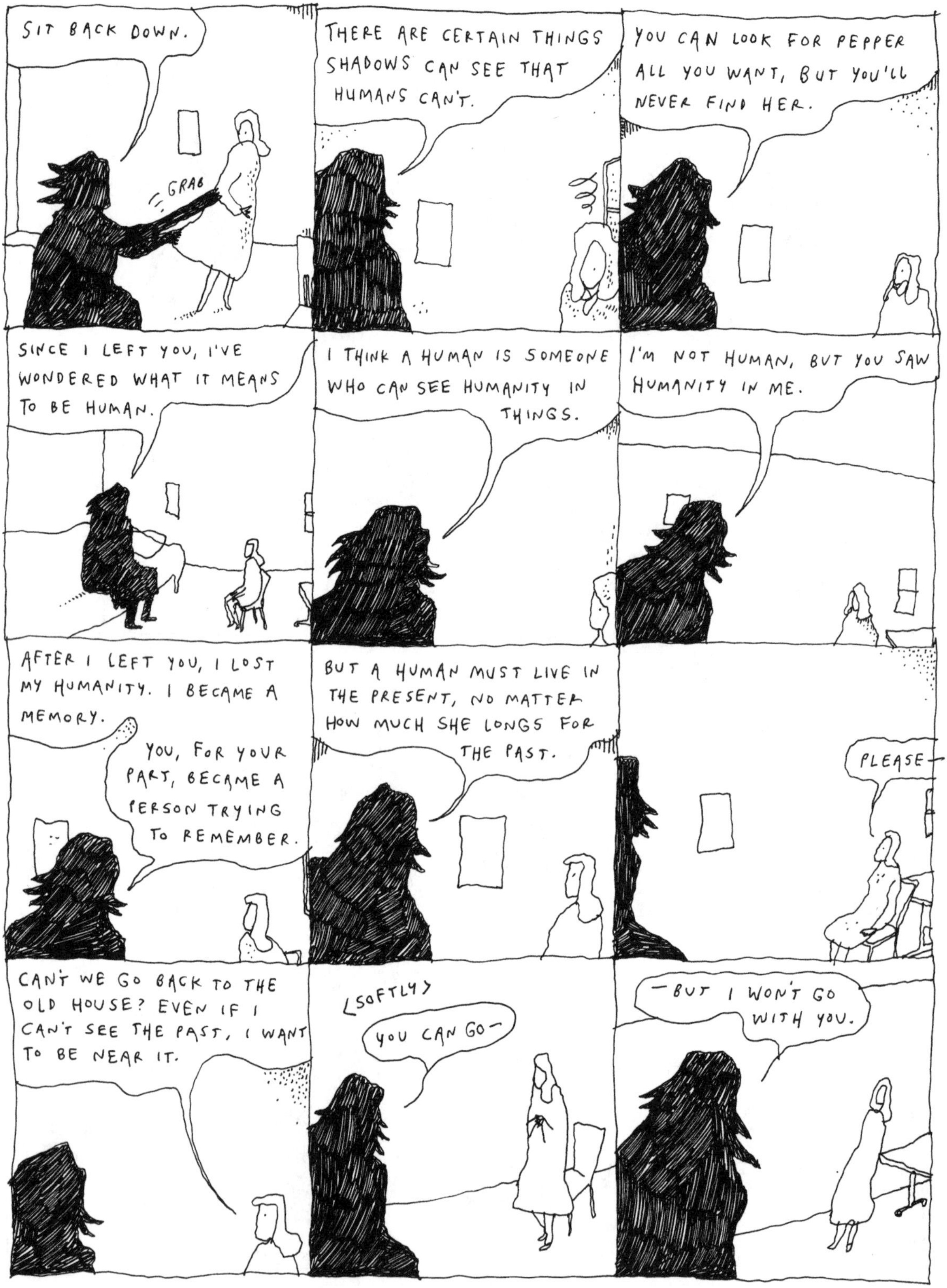
SIT BACK DOWN.
GRAB
THERE ARE CERTAIN THINGS SHADOWS CAN SEE THAT HUMANS CAN'T.
YOU CAN LOOK FOR PEPPER ALL YOU WANT, BUT YOU'LL NEVER FIND HER.
SINCE I LEFT YOU, I'VE WONDERED WHAT IT MEANS TO BE HUMAN.
I THINK A HUMAN IS SOMEONE WHO CAN SEE HUMANITY IN THINGS.
I'M NOT HUMAN, BUT YOU SAW HUMANITY IN ME.
AFTER I LEFT YOU, I LOST MY HUMANITY. I BECAME A MEMORY.
YOU, FOR YOUR PART, BECAME A PERSON TRYING TO REMEMBER.
BUT A HUMAN MUST LIVE IN THE PRESENT, NO MATTER HOW MUCH SHE LONGS FOR THE PAST.
PLEASE—
CAN'T WE GO BACK TO THE OLD HOUSE? EVEN IF I CAN'T SEE THE PAST, I WANT TO BE NEAR IT.
<SOFTLY>
YOU CAN GO—
—BUT I WON'T GO WITH YOU.

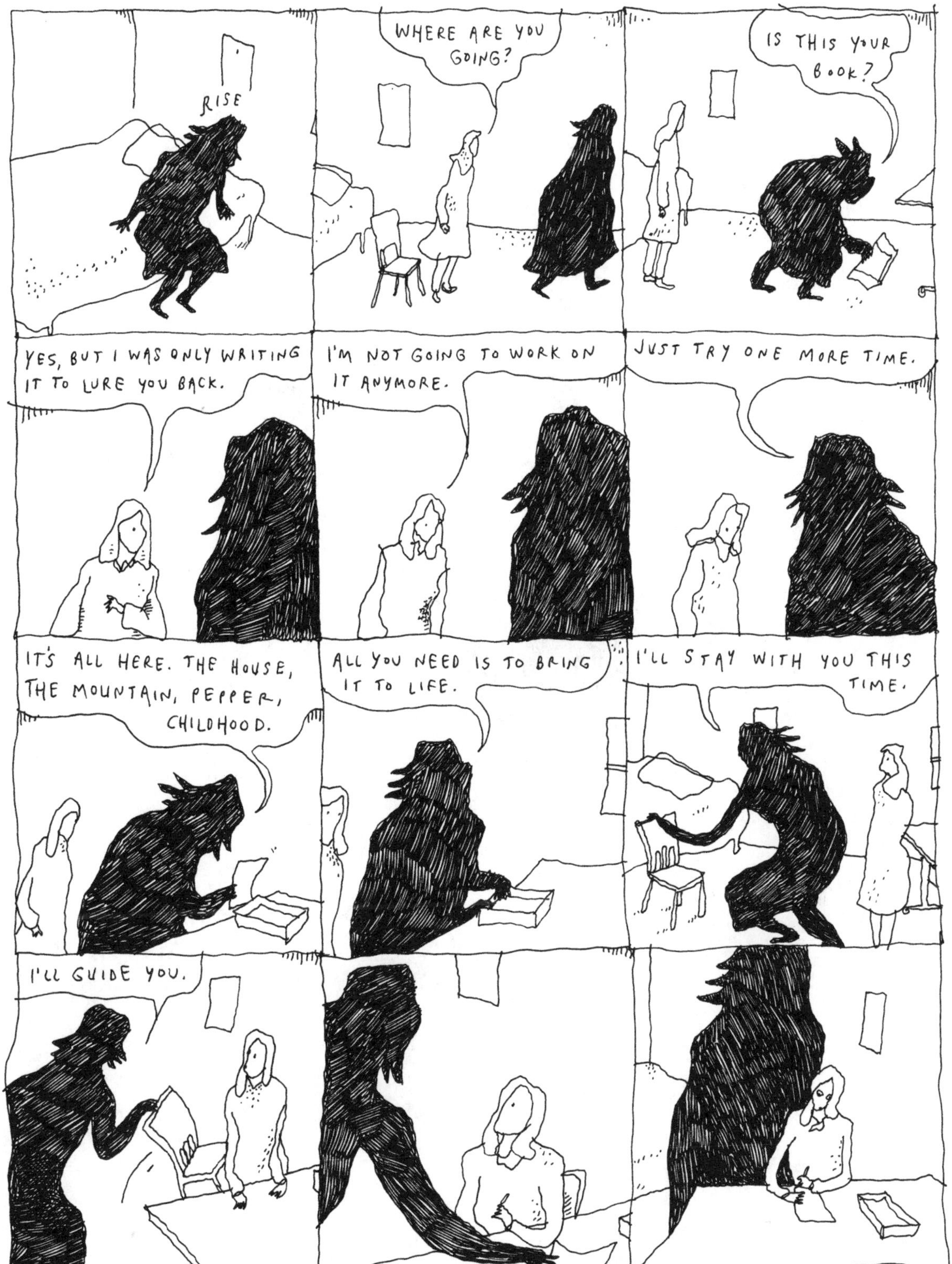
RISE
WHERE ARE YOU GOING?
IS THIS YOUR BOOK?
YES, BUT I WAS ONLY WRITING IT TO LURE YOU BACK.
I'M NOT GOING TO WORK ON IT ANYMORE.
JUST TRY ONE MORE TIME.
IT'S ALL HERE. THE HOUSE, THE MOUNTAIN, PEPPER, CHILDHOOD.
ALL YOU NEED IS TO BRING IT TO LIFE.
I'LL STAY WITH YOU THIS TIME.
I'LL GUIDE YOU.

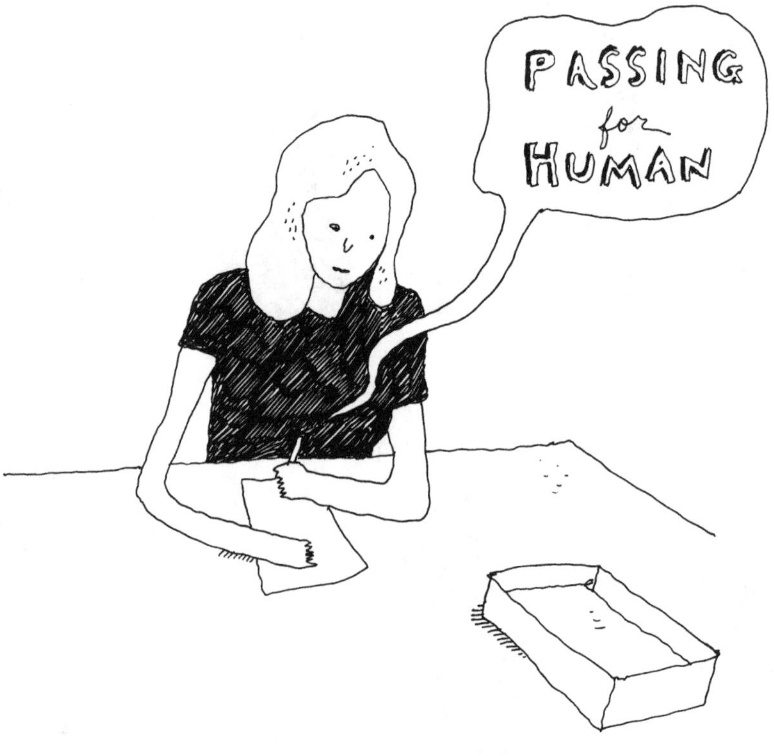
PASSING for HUMAN

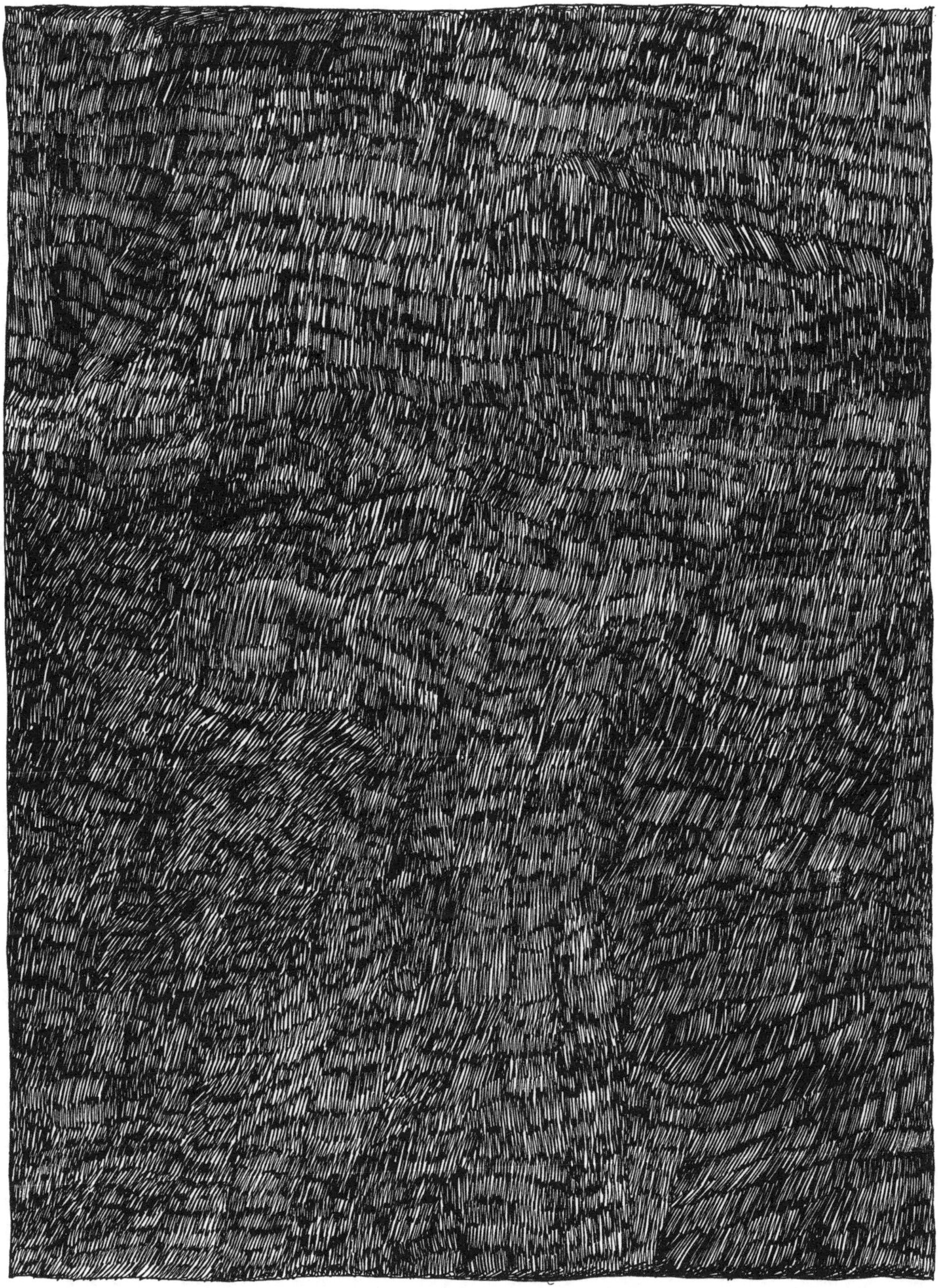

"THE BLACKSMITH, BY MAIN FORCE, UNCLOSED
THE INFANT'S HAND, AND FOUND WITHIN
THE PALM A SMALL HEAP OF GLITTERING
FRAGMENTS, WHENCE THE MYSTERY OF
BEAUTY HAD FLED FOREVER."

—NATHANIEL HAWTHORNE,
"THE ARTIST OF THE BEAUTIFUL"

EPILOGUE

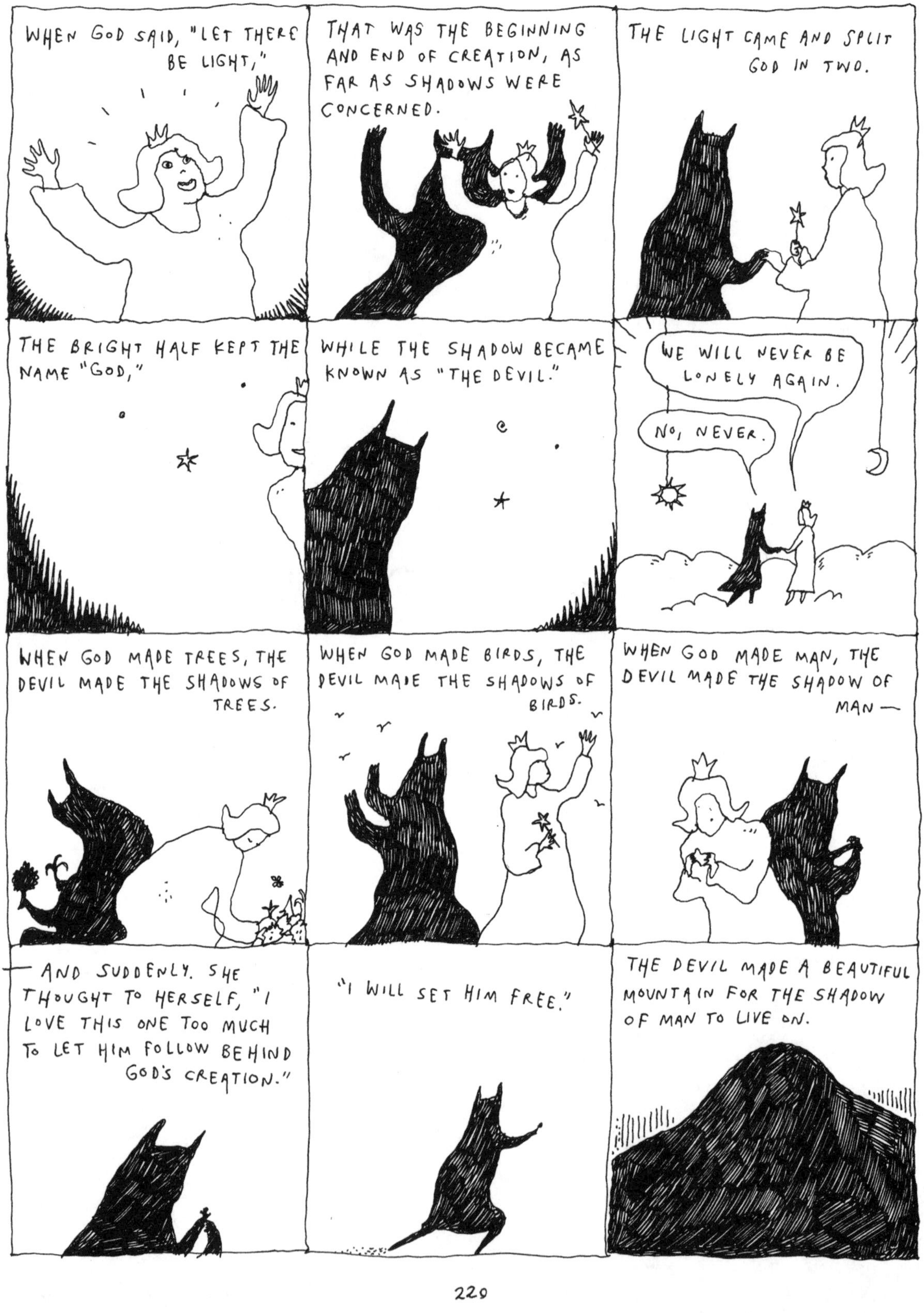
WHEN GOD SAID, "LET THERE BE LIGHT,"
THAT WAS THE BEGINNING AND END OF CREATION, AS FAR AS SHADOWS WERE CONCERNED.
THE LIGHT CAME AND SPLIT GOD IN TWO.
THE BRIGHT HALF KEPT THE NAME "GOD,"
WHILE THE SHADOW BECAME KNOWN AS "THE DEVIL."
WE WILL NEVER BE LONELY AGAIN.
NO, NEVER.
WHEN GOD MADE TREES, THE DEVIL MADE THE SHADOWS OF TREES.
WHEN GOD MADE BIRDS, THE DEVIL MADE THE SHADOWS OF BIRDS.
WHEN GOD MADE MAN, THE DEVIL MADE THE SHADOW OF MAN—
—AND SUDDENLY. SHE THOUGHT TO HERSELF, "I LOVE THIS ONE TOO MUCH TO LET HIM FOLLOW BEHIND GOD'S CREATION."
"I WILL SET HIM FREE."
THE DEVIL MADE A BEAUTIFUL MOUNTAIN FOR THE SHADOW OF MAN TO LIVE ON.

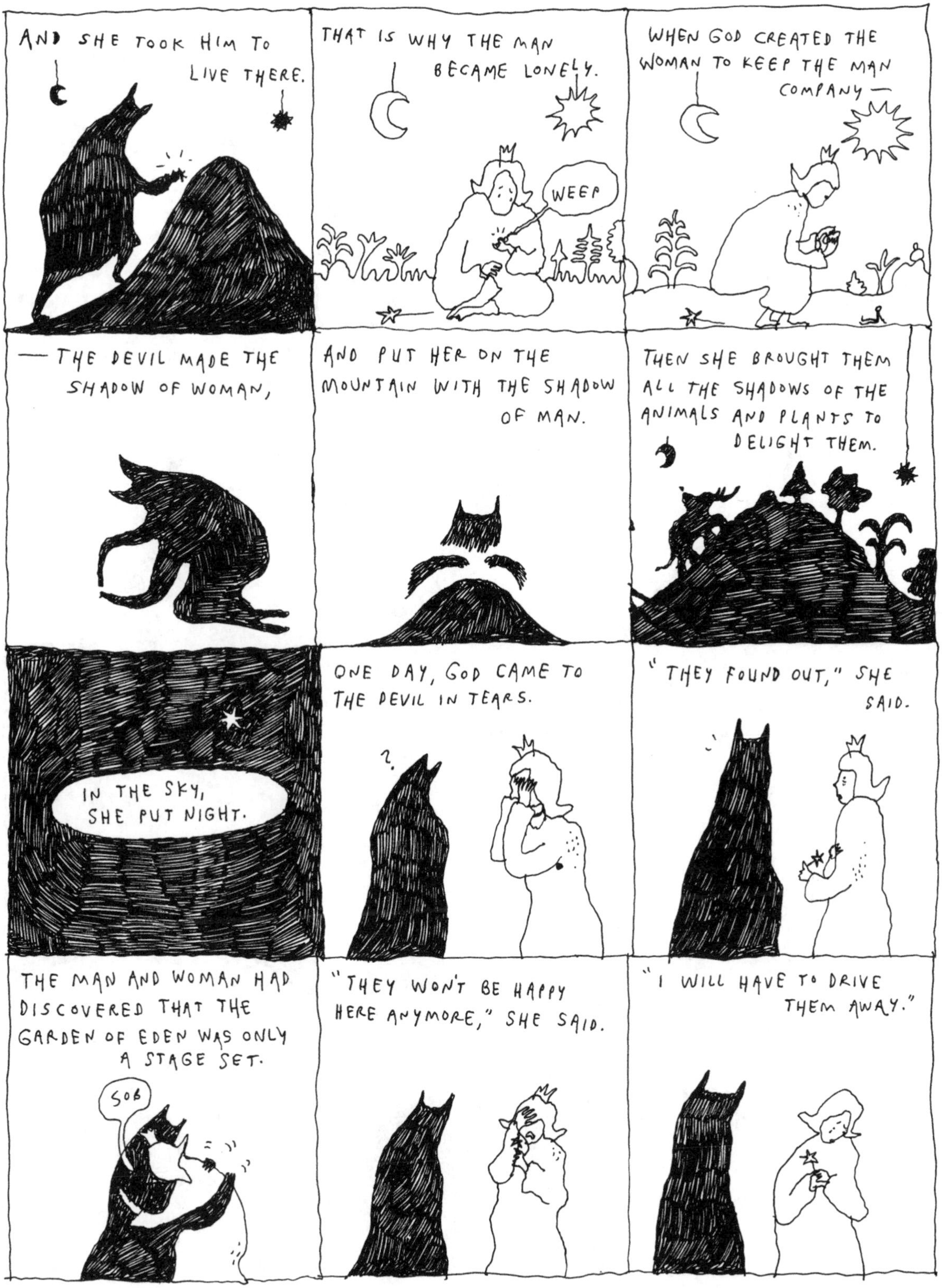
AND SHE TOOK HIM TO LIVE THERE.
THAT IS WHY THE MAN BECAME LONELY.
WEEP
WHEN GOD CREATED THE WOMAN TO KEEP THE MAN COMPANY—
—THE DEVIL MADE THE SHADOW OF WOMAN,
AND PUT HER ON THE MOUNTAIN WITH THE SHADOW OF MAN.
THEN SHE BROUGHT THEM ALL THE SHADOWS OF THE ANIMALS AND PLANTS TO DELIGHT THEM.
IN THE SKY, SHE PUT NIGHT.
ONE DAY, GOD CAME TO THE DEVIL IN TEARS.
?
"THEY FOUND OUT," SHE SAID.
THE MAN AND WOMAN HAD DISCOVERED THAT THE GARDEN OF EDEN WAS ONLY A STAGE SET.
SOB
"THEY WON'T BE HAPPY HERE ANYMORE," SHE SAID.
"I WILL HAVE TO DRIVE THEM AWAY."

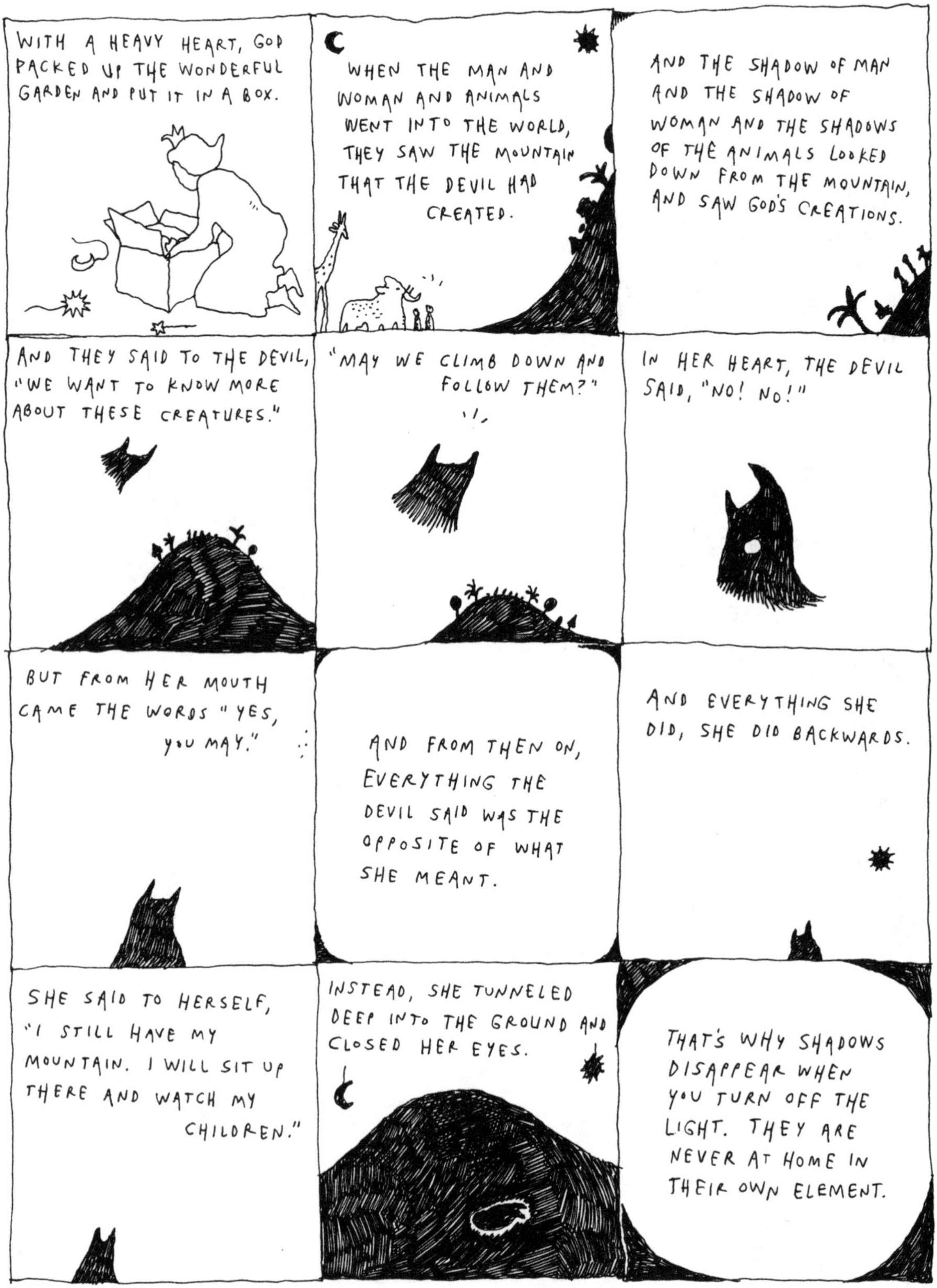
WITH A HEAVY HEART, GOD PACKED UP THE WONDERFUL GARDEN AND PUT IT IN A BOX.
WHEN THE MAN AND WOMAN AND ANIMALS WENT INTO THE WORLD, THEY SAW THE MOUNTAIN THAT THE DEVIL HAD CREATED.
AND THE SHADOW OF MAN AND THE SHADOW OF WOMAN AND THE SHADOWS OF THE ANIMALS LOOKED DOWN FROM THE MOUNTAIN, AND SAW GOD'S CREATIONS.
AND THEY SAID TO THE DEVIL, "WE WANT TO KNOW MORE ABOUT THESE CREATURES."
"MAY WE CLIMB DOWN AND FOLLOW THEM?"
IN HER HEART, THE DEVIL SAID, "NO! NO!"
BUT FROM HER MOUTH CAME THE WORDS "YES, YOU MAY."
AND FROM THEN ON, EVERYTHING THE DEVIL SAID WAS THE OPPOSITE OF WHAT SHE MEANT.
AND EVERYTHING SHE DID, SHE DID BACKWARDS.
SHE SAID TO HERSELF, "I STILL HAVE MY MOUNTAIN. I WILL SIT UP THERE AND WATCH MY CHILDREN."
INSTEAD, SHE TUNNELED DEEP INTO THE GROUND AND CLOSED HER EYES.
THAT'S WHY SHADOWS DISAPPEAR WHEN YOU TURN OFF THE LIGHT. THEY ARE NEVER AT HOME IN THEIR OWN ELEMENT.

☀ · ACKNOWLEDGMENTS · ☾

THANK YOU ANDY WARD (EDITOR) AND MEREDITH KAFFEL SIMONOFF (AGENT) FOR YOUR THOROUGHNESS, WARMTH, PRECISION, AND BRILLIANCE, AND FOR LENDING THEM TO ME FOR THIS BOOK. THANK YOU EVERYONE AT RANDOM HOUSE (SUSAN KAMIL, CHAYENNE SKEETE, ROBBIN SCHIFF, SHARANYA DURVASULA, CAROLE LOWENSTEIN, SARAH FEIGHTNER, ANNA BAUER, MARIA BRAECKEL, TOM PERRY, LEIGH MARCHANT, BETH PEARSON, AND JESSICA BONET) FOR MAKING THIS BOOK EXIST, MAKING IT LOOK GOOD, AND PUTTING IT IN THE WORLD. ✷ THANK YOU EMMA ALLEN AND MATT KLAM FOR INTRODUCING ME TO MEREDITH AND ANDY. ✷ THANK YOU HARRIET AND MICHAEL FINCK FOR LETTING ME MINE YOUR LIVES AND TWIST THEM AROUND. AND (HARRIET) FOR HOSTING ME IN YOUR WOMB AT ONE POINT AND ALSO FOR LETTING ME RIP OFF VARIOUS OF YOUR DRAWING STYLES FOR THE CHAPTER PAGES OF THIS BOOK. ✷ THANK YOU GIDEON FINCK FOR NOT FEELING BAD THAT I DIDN'T MINE YOUR LIFE, TOO (I THINK I FELT I DIDN'T HAVE THE RIGHT), AND FOR BEING SUCH A GOOD AND SMART READER, AND FOR IDENTIFYING TREES. ✷ THANK YOU THE NEW YORKER FOR GIVING ME EMPLOYMENT THAT LEFT ME HAPPY AND FREE ENOUGH TO WORK ON THIS, TOO. AND FOR EXISTING. ✷ THANK YOU OTHER EMPLOYERS. I'M GRATEFUL. ✷ THANK YOU RADIO, PODCAST, AND AUDIOBOOK CREATORS FOR THE COMPANY. ✷ THANK YOU TAKEOUT PLACES FOR THE TIME AND BRAIN SPACE. ✷ THANK YOU GRANDMA HELEN, AUNT BARBARA, AND OTHER EXTENDED FAMILY MEMBERS, SOME OF WHOSE LIVES I BORROWED FROM FOR THIS. ✷ THANK YOU BEACH FOR THE WALKS. ✷ THANK YOU AMORPHOUS AND SPARKLING BLOB OF FRIENDS FOR THE LONG WEEPY PHONE CALLS (JUST KIDDING, TEXT MESSAGES) AND FOR LETTING MY WOODEN, PRIDEFUL SELF INTO YOUR MYSTERIOUS LIVES. THANK YOU FRIENDS WHO ARE MENTORS AND MENTORS WHO ARE FRIENDS. ✷ THANK YOU PEPPER, MY FAIRY DOGMOTHER, AND SOPHIE, MY DOGSISTER. ✷ THANK YOU NEW YORK, YOU CHANGEABLE CHARACTER. ✷ THANK YOU HEALTH. ✷ THANK YOU WEALTH. ✷ THANK YOU MACDOWELL, YADDO, LOWER MANHATTAN CULTURAL CENTER, AND NEW YORK FOUNDATION FOR THE ARTS FOR THE MAGIC AND ENCOURAGEMENT. ✷ THANK YOU MR. NEUTRAL. ✷ THANK YOU CHESTER, NEW YORK, FOR HAVING BEEN OUR HOME. ✷ THANK YOU HOUSE. I WISH YOU WELL.

ABOUT THE AUTHOR

LIANA FINCK LIVES IN NEW YORK.